Saga Six Pack 4

Saga Six Pack 4

By

Peter Christen Asbjørnsen

Abbie Farwell Brown

George Webbe Dasent

Jørgen Engebretsen Moe

Snorri Sturluson

and

Charles W. Whistler

Enhanced Media
2015

Contents

Halfdan the Black by Snorri Sturluson

1. HALFDAN FIGHTS WITH GANDALF AND SIGTRYG.

Halfdan was a year old when his father was killed, and his mother Asa set off immediately with him westwards to Agder, and set herself there in the kingdom which her father Harald had possessed. Halfdan grew up there, and soon became stout and strong; and, by reason of his black hair, was called Halfdan the Black. When he was eighteen years old he took his kingdom in Agder, and went immediately to Vestfold, where he divided that kingdom, as before related, with his brother Olaf. The same autumn he went with an army to Vingulmark against King Gandalf. They had many battles, and sometimes one, sometimes the other gained the victory; but at last they agreed that Halfdan should have half of Vingulmark, as his father Gudrod had had it before. Then King Halfdan proceeded to Raumarike, and subdued it. King Sigtryg, son of King Eystein, who then had his residence in Hedemark, and who had subdued Raumarike before, having heard of this, came out with his army against King Halfdan, and there was great battle, in which King Halfdan was victorious; and just as King Sigtryg and his troops were turning about to fly, an arrow struck him under the left arm, and he fell dead. Halfdan then laid the whole of Raumarike under his power. King Eystein's second son, King Sigtryg's brother, was also called Eystein, and was then king in Hedemark. As soon as Halfdan had returned to Vestfold, King Eystein went out with his army to Raumarike, and laid the whole country in subjection to him.

2. BATTLE BETWEEN HALFDAN AND EYSTEIN.

When King Halfdan heard of these disturbances in Raumarike, he again gathered his army together; and went out against King Eystein. A battle took place between them, and Halfdan gained the victory, and Eystein fled up to Hedemark, pursued by Halfdan. Another battle took place, in which Halfdan was again victorious; and Eystein fled northwards, up into the Dales to the herse Gudbrand. There he was strengthened with new people, and in winter he went towards Hedemark, and met Halfdan the Black upon a large island which lies in the Mjosen lake. There a great battle was fought, and many people on both sides were slain, but Halfdan won the victory. There fell

Guthorm, the son of the herse Gudbrand, who was one of the finest men in the Uplands. Then Eystein fled north up the valley, and sent his relation Halvard Skalk to King Halfdan to beg for peace. On consideration of their relationship, King Halfdan gave King Eystein half of Hedemark, which he and his relations had held before; but kept to himself Thoten, and the district called Land. He likewise appropriated to himself Hadeland, and thus became a mighty king.

3. HALFDAN'S MARRIAGE.

Halfdan the Black got a wife called Ragnhild, a daughter of Harald Gulskeg (Goldbeard), who was a king in Sogn. They had a son, to whom Harald gave his own name; and the boy was brought up in Sogn, by his mother's father, King Harald. Now when this Harald had lived out his days nearly, and was become weak, having no son, he gave his dominions to his daughter's son Harald, and gave him his title of king; and he died soon after. The same winter his daughter Ragnhild died; and the following spring the young Harald fell sick and died at ten years of age. As soon as Halfdan the Black heard of his son's death, he took the road northwards to Sogn with a great force, and was well received. He claimed the heritage and dominion after his son; and no opposition being made, he took the whole kingdom. Earl Atle Mjove (the Slender), who was a friend of King Halfdan, came to him from Gaular; and the king set him over the Sogn district, to judge in the country according to the country's laws, and collect scat upon the king's account. Thereafter King Halfdan proceeded to his kingdom in the Uplands.

4. HALFDAN'S STRIFE WITH GANDALF'S SONS.

In autumn, King Halfdan proceeded to Vingulmark. One night when he was there in guest quarters, it happened that about midnight a man came to him who had been on the watch on horseback, and told him a war force was come near to the house. The king instantly got up, ordered his men to arm themselves, and went out of the house and drew them up in battle order. At the same moment, Gandalf's sons, Hysing and Helsing, made their appearance with a large army. There was a great battle; but Halfdan being overpowered by the numbers of people fled to the forest, leaving many of his men on this spot. His foster-father, Olver Spake (the Wise), fell here. The people now came in swarms to King Halfdan, and he advanced to seek Gandalf's sons. They met at Eid, near Lake Oieren, and fought there. Hysing and Helsing fell, and their brother Hake saved himself by flight. King Halfdan then took possession of the whole of Vingulmark, and Hake fled to Alfheimar.

5. HALFDAN'S MARRIAGE WITH HJORT'S DAUGHTER.

Sigurd Hjort was the name of a king in Ringerike, who was stouter and stronger than any other man, and his equal could not be seen for a handsome appearance. His father was Helge Hvasse (the Sharp); and his mother was Aslaug, a daughter of Sigurd the worm-eyed, who again was a son of Ragnar Lodbrok. It is told of Sigurd that when he was only twelve years old he killed in single combat the berserk Hildebrand, and eleven others of his comrades; and many are the deeds of manhood told of him in a long saga about his feats. Sigurd had two children, one of whom was a daughter, called Ragnhild, then twenty years of age, and an excellent brisk girl. Her brother Guthorm was a youth. It is related in regard to Sigurd's death that he had a custom of riding out quite alone in the uninhabited forest to hunt the wild beasts that are hurtful to man, and he was always very eager at this sport. One day he rode out into the forest as usual, and when he had ridden a long way he came out at a piece of cleared land near to Hadeland. There the berserk Hake came against him with thirty men, and they fought. Sigurd Hjort fell there, after killing twelve of Hake's men; and Hake himself lost one hand, and had three other wounds. Then Hake and his men rode to Sigurd's house, where they took his daughter Ragnhild and her brother Guthorm, and carried them, with much property and valuable articles, home to Hadeland, where Hake had many great farms. He ordered a feast to be prepared, intending to hold his wedding with Ragnhild; but the time passed on account of his wounds, which healed slowly; and the berserk Hake of Hadeland had to keep his bed, on account of his wounds, all the autumn and beginning of winter. Now King Halfdan was in Hedemark at the Yule entertainments when he heard this news; and one morning early, when the king was dressed, he called to him Harek Gand, and told him to go over to Hadeland, and bring him Ragnhild, Sigurd Hjort's daughter. Harek got ready with a hundred men, and made his journey so that they came over the lake to Hake's house in the grey of the morning, and beset all the doors and stairs of the places where the house-servants slept. Then they broke into the sleeping-room where Hake slept, took Ragnhild, with her brother Guthorm, and all the goods that were there, and set fire to the house-servants' place, and burnt all the people in it. Then they covered over a magnificent waggon, placed Ragnhild and Guthorm in it, and drove down upon the ice. Hake got up and went after them a while; but when he came to the ice on the lake, he turned his sword-hilt to the ground and let himself fall upon the point, so that the sword went through him. He was buried under a mound on the banks of the lake. When King Halfdan, who was very quick of sight, saw the party returning over the frozen lake, and with a covered waggon, he knew that their errand was accomplished according to his desire. Thereupon he ordered the tables to be set out, and sent people all round in the neighbourhood to invite plenty of guests; and the same day there was a good feast which was also Halfdan's marriage-feast with Ragnhild, who became a great queen. Ragnhild's mother was Thorny, a daughter of Klakharald king in Jutland, and a sister of Thrye Dannebod who was married to the Danish king, Gorm the Old, who then ruled over the Danish dominions.

6. OF RAGNHILD'S DREAM.

Ragnhild, who was wise and intelligent, dreamt great dreams. She dreamt, for one, that she was standing out in her herb-garden, and she took a thorn out of her shift; but while she was holding the thorn in her hand it grew so that it became a great tree, one end of which struck itself down into the earth, and it became firmly rooted; and the other end of the tree raised itself so high in the air that she could scarcely see over it, and it became also wonderfully thick. The under part of the tree was red with blood, but the stem upwards was beautifully green and the branches white as snow. There were many and great limbs to the tree, some high up, others low down; and so vast were the tree's branches that they seemed to her to cover all Norway, and even much more.

7. OF HALFDAN'S DREAM.

King Halfdan never had dreams, which appeared to him an extraordinary circumstance; and he told it to a man called Thorleif Spake (the Wise), and asked him what his advice was about it. Thorleif said that what he himself did, when he wanted to have any revelation by dream, was to take his sleep in a swine-sty, and then it never failed that he had dreams. The king did so, and the following dream was revealed to him. He thought he had the most beautiful hair, which was all in ringlets; some so long as to fall upon the ground, some reaching to the middle of his legs, some to his knees, some to his loins or the middle of his sides, some to his neck, and some were only as knots springing from his head. These ringlets were of various colours; but one ringlet surpassed all the others in beauty, lustre, and size. This dream he told to Thorleif, who interpreted it thus:—There should be a great posterity from him, and his descendants should rule over countries with great, but not all with equally great, honour; but one of his race should be more celebrated than all the others. It was the opinion of people that this ringlet betokened King Olaf the Saint.

King Halfdan was a wise man, a man of truth and uprightness—who made laws, observed them himself, and obliged others to observe them. And that violence should not come in place of the laws, he himself fixed the number of criminal acts in law, and the compensations, mulcts, or penalties, for each case, according to every one's birth and dignity.

Queen Ragnhild gave birth to a son, and water was poured over him, and the name of Harald given him, and he soon grew stout and remarkably handsome. As he grew up he became very expert at all feats, and showed also a good understanding. He was much beloved by his mother, but less so by his father.

8. HALFDAN'S MEAT VANISHES AT A FEAST.

King Halfdan was at a Yule-feast in Hadeland, where a wonderful thing happened one Yule evening. When the great number of guests assembled were going to sit down to table, all the meat and all the ale disappeared from the table. The king sat alone very confused in mind; all the others set off, each to his home, in consternation. That the king might come to some certainty about what had occasioned this event, he ordered a Fin to be seized who was particularly knowing, and tried to force him to disclose the truth; but however much he tortured the man, he got nothing out of him. The Fin sought help particularly from Harald, the king's son, and Harald begged for mercy for him, but in vain. Then Harald let him escape against the king's will, and accompanied the man himself. On their journey they came to a place where the man's chief had a great feast, and it appears they were well received there. When they had been there until spring, the chief said, "Thy father took it much amiss that in winter I took some provisions from him,— now I will repay it to thee by a joyful piece of news: thy father is dead; and now thou shalt return home, and take possession of the whole kingdom which he had, and with it thou shalt lay the whole kingdom of Norway under thee."

9. HALFDAN S DEATH.

Halfdan the Black was driving from a feast in Hadeland, and it so happened that his road lay over the lake called Rand. It was in spring, and there was a great thaw. They drove across the bight called Rykinsvik, where in winter there had been a pond broken in the ice for cattle to drink at, and where the dung had fallen upon the ice the thaw had eaten it into holes. Now as the king drove over it the ice broke, and King Halfdan and many with him perished. He was then forty years old. He had been one of the most fortunate kings in respect of good seasons. The people thought so much of him, that when his death was known and his body was floated to Ringerike to bury it there, the people of most consequence from Raumarike, Vestfold, and Hedemark came to meet it. All desired to take the body with them to bury it in their own district, and they thought that those who got it would have good crops to expect. At last it was agreed to divide the body into four parts. The head was laid in a mound at Stein in Ringerike, and each of the others took his part home and laid it in a mound; and these have since been called Halfdan's Mounds.

The Saga of Sigurd the Crusader and his brothers *Eystein and Olaf* by Snorri Sturluson

The three brothers became kings in the year A.D. 1103. Olaf died 1115, Eystein 1122 or 1123, Sigurd 1130.

1. BEGINNING OF THE REIGN OF KING MAGNUS'S SONS.

After King Magnus Barefoot's fall, his sons, Eystein, Sigurd, and Olaf, took the kingdom of Norway. Eystein got the northern, and Sigurd the southern part of the country. King Olaf was then four or five years old, and the third part of the country which he had was under the management of his two brothers. King Sigurd was chosen king when he was thirteen or fourteen years old, and Eystein was a year older. King Sigurd left west of the sea the Irish king's daughter. When King Magnus's sons were chosen kings, the men who had followed Skopte Ogmundson returned home. Some had been to Jerusalem, some to Constantinople; and there they had made themselves renowned, and they had many kinds of novelties to talk about. By these extraordinary tidings many men in Norway were incited to the same expedition; and it was also told that the Northmen who liked to go into the military service at Constantinople found many opportunities of getting property. Then these Northmen desired much that one of the two kings, either Eystein or Sigurd, should go as commander of the troop which was preparing for this expedition. The kings agreed to this, and carried on the equipment at their common expense. Many great men, both of the lendermen and bondes, took part in this enterprise; and when all was ready for the journey it was determined that Sigurd should go, and Eystein in the meantime, should rule the kingdom upon their joint account.

2. OF THE EARLS OF ORKNEY.

A year or two after King Magnus Barefoot's fall, Hakon, a son of Earl Paul, came from Orkney. The kings gave him the earldom and government of the Orkney Islands, as the earls before him, his father Paul or his Uncle Erland, had possessed it; and Earl Hakon then sailed back immediately to Orkney.

3. KING SIGURD'S JOURNEY OUT OF THE COUNTRY.

Four years after the fall of King Magnus (A.D. 1107), King Sigurd sailed with his people from Norway. He had then sixty ships. So says Thorarin Stutfeld:—

"A young king just and kind,
People of loyal mind:
Such brave men soon agree,—
To distant lands they sail with glee.
To the distant Holy Land
A brave and pious band,
Magnificent and gay,
In sixty long-ships glide away."

King Sigurd sailed in autumn to England, where Henry, son of William the Bastard, was then king, and Sigurd remained with him all winter. So says Einar Skulason:—

"The king is on the waves!
The storm he boldly braves.
His ocean-steed,
With winged speed,
O'er the white-flashing surges,
To England's coast he urges;
And there he stays the winter o'er:
More gallant king ne'er trod that shore."

4. OF KING SIGURD'S JOURNEY.

In spring King Sigurd and his fleet sailed westward to Valland (A.D. 1108), and in autumn came to Galicia, where he stayed the second winter (A.D. 1109). So says Einar Skulason:—

"Our king, whose land so wide
No kingdom stands beside,
In Jacob's land next winter spent,
On holy things intent;
And I have heard the royal youth

Cut off an earl who swerved from truth.
Our brave king will endure no ill,—
The hawks with him will get their fill."

It went thus:—The earl who ruled over the land made an agreement with King Sigurd, that he should provide King Sigurd and his men a market at which they could purchase victuals all the winter; but this he did not fulfil longer than to about Yule. It began then to be difficult to get food and necessaries, for it is a poor barren land. Then King Sigurd with a great body of men went against a castle which belonged to the earl; and the earl fled from it, having but few people. King Sigurd took there a great deal of victuals and of other booty, which he put on board of his ships, and then made ready and proceeded westward to Spain. It so fell out, as the king was sailing past Spain, that some vikings who were cruising for plunder met him with a fleet of galleys, and King Sigurd attacked them. This was his first battle with heathen men; and he won it, and took eight galleys from them. So says Haldor Skvaldre:—

"Bold vikings, not slow
To the death-fray to go,
Meet our Norse king by chance,
And their galleys advance.
The bold vikings lost
Many a man of their host,
And eight galleys too,
With cargo and crew."

Thereafter King Sigurd sailed against a castle called Sintre and fought another battle. This castle is in Spain, and was occupied by many heathens, who from thence plundered Christian people. King Sigurd took the castle, and killed every man in it, because they refused to be baptized; and he got there an immense booty. So says Haldor Skvaldre:—

"From Spain I have much news to tell
Of what our generous king befell.
And first he routs the viking crew,
At Cintra next the heathens slew;
The men he treated as God's foes,
Who dared the true faith to oppose.
No man he spared who would not take
The Christian faith for Jesus' sake."

5. LISBON TAKEN.

After this King Sigurd sailed with his fleet to Lisbon, which is a great city in Spain, half Christian and half heathen; for there lies the division between Christian Spain and heathen Spain, and all the districts which lie west of the city are occupied by heathens. There King Sigurd had his third battle with the heathens, and gained the victory, and with it a great booty. So says Haldor Skvaldre:—

"The son of kings on Lisbon's plains
A third and bloody battle gains.
He and his Norsemen boldly land,
Running their stout ships on the strand."

Then King Sigurd sailed westwards along heathen Spain, and brought up at a town called Alkasse; and here he had his fourth battle with the heathens, and took the town, and killed so many people that the town was left empty. They got there also immense booty. So says Haldor Skvaldre:—

"A fourth great battle, I am told,
Our Norse king and his people hold
At Alkasse; and here again
The victory fell to our Norsemen."

And also this verse:—

"I heard that through the town he went,
And heathen widows' wild lament
Resounded in the empty halls;
For every townsman flies or falls."

6. BATTLE IN THE ISLAND FORMINTERRA.

King Sigurd then proceeded on his voyage, and came to Norfasund; and in the sound he was met by a large viking force, and the king gave them battle; and this was his fifth engagement with heathens since the time he left Norway. He gained the victory here also. So says Haldor Skvaldre:—

"Ye moistened your dry swords with blood,

As through Norfasund ye stood;
The screaming raven got a feast,
As ye sailed onward to the East."

King Sigurd then sailed eastward along the coast of Serkland, and came to an island there called Forminterra. There a great many heathen Moors had taken up their dwelling in a cave, and had built a strong stone wall before its mouth. They harried the country all round, and carried all their booty to their cave. King Sigurd landed on this island, and went to the cave; but it lay in a precipice, and there was a high winding path to the stone wall, and the precipice above projected over it. The heathens defended the stone wall, and were not afraid of the Northmen's arms; for they could throw stones, or shoot down upon the Northmen under their feet; neither did the Northmen, under such circumstances, dare to mount up. The heathens took their clothes and other valuable things, carried them out upon the wall, spread them out before the Northmen, shouted, and defied them, and upbraided them as cowards. Then Sigurd fell upon this plan. He had two ship's boats, such as we call barks, drawn up the precipice right above the mouth of the cave; and had thick ropes fastened around the stem, stern, and hull of each. In these boats as many men went as could find room, and then the boats were lowered by the ropes down in front of the mouth of the cave; and the men in the boats shot with stones and missiles into the cave, and the heathens were thus driven from the stone wall. Then Sigurd with his troops climbed up the precipice to the foot of the stone wall, which they succeeded in breaking down, so that they came into the cave. Now the heathens fled within the stone wall that was built across the cave; on which the king ordered large trees to be brought to the cave, made a great pile in the mouth of it, and set fire to the wood. When the fire and smoke got the upper hand, some of the heathens lost their lives in it; some fled; some fell by the hands of the Northmen; and part were killed, part burned; and the Northmen made the greatest booty they had got on all their expeditions. So says Halder Skvaldre:—

"Forminterra lay
In the victor's way;
His ships' stems fly
To victory.
The bluemen there
Must fire bear,
And Norsemen's steel
At their hearts feel."

And also thus:—

"'Twas a feat of renown,—
The boat lowered down,
With a boat's crew brave,
In front of the cave;
While up the rock scaling,
And comrades up trailing,
The Norsemen gain,
And the bluemen are slain."

And also Thorarin Stutfeld says:—

"The king's men up the mountain's side
Drag two boats from the ocean's tide;
The two boats lay,
Like hill-wolves grey.
Now o'er the rock in ropes they're swinging
Well manned, and death to bluemen bringing;
They hang before
The robber's door."

7. OF THE BATTLES OF IVIZA AND MINORCA.

Thereafter King Sigurd proceeded on his expedition, and came to an island called Iviza (Ivica), and had there his seventh battle, and gained a victory. So says Haldor Skvaldre:—

"His ships at Ivica now ride,
The king's, whose fame spreads far and wide;
And hear the bearers of the shield
Their arms again in battle wield."

Thereafter King Sigurd came to an island called Manork (Minorca), and held there his eighth battle with heathen men, and gained the victory. So says Haldor Skvaldre:—

"On green Minorca's plains
The eighth battle now he gains:

Again the heathen foe
Falls at the Norse king's blow."

8. DUKE ROGER MADE A KING.

In spring King Sigurd came to Sicily (A.D. 1109), and remained a long time there. There was then a Duke Roger in Sicily, who received the king kindly, and invited him to a feast. King Sigurd came to it with a great retinue, and was splendidly entertained. Every day Duke Roger stood at the company's table, doing service to the king; but the seventh day of the feast, when the people had come to table, and had wiped their hands, King Sigurd took the duke by the hand, led him up to the high-seat, and saluted him with the title of king; and gave the right that there should be always a king over the dominion of Sicily, although before there had only been earls or dukes over that country.

9. OF KING ROGER.

King Roger of Sicily was a very great king. He won and subdued all Apulia, and many large islands besides in the Greek sea; and therefore he was called Roger the Great. His son was William, king of Sicily, who for a long time had great hostility with the emperor of Constantinople. King William had three daughters, but no son. One of his daughters he married to the Emperor Henry, a son of the Emperor Frederik; and their son was Frederik, who for a short time after was emperor of Rome. His second daughter was married to the Duke of Kipr. The third daughter, Margaret, was married to the chief of the corsairs; but the Emperor Henry killed both these brothers-in-law. The daughter of Roger the Great, king of Sicily, was married to the Emperor Manuel of Constantinople; and their son was the Emperor Kirjalax.

10. KING SIGURD'S EXPEDITION TO PALESTINE.

In the summer (A.D. 1110) King Sigurd sailed across the Greek sea to Palestine, and thereupon went up to Jerusalem, where he met Baldwin, king of Palestine. King Baldwin received him particularly well, and rode with him all the way to the river Jordan, and then back to the city of Jerusalem. Einar Skulason speaks thus of it:—

"Good reason has the skald to sing
The generous temper of the king,
Whose sea-cold keel from northern waves
Ploughs the blue sea that green isles laves.
At Acre scarce were we made fast,

In holy ground our anchors cast,
When the king made a joyful morn
To all who toil with him had borne."

And again he made these lines:—

"To Jerusalem he came,
He who loves war's noble game,
(The skald no greater monarch finds
Beneath the heaven's wide hall of winds)
All sin and evil from him flings
In Jordan's wave: for all his sins
(Which all must praise) he pardon wins."

King Sigurd stayed a long time in the land of Jerusalem (Jorsalaland) in autumn, and in the beginning of winter.

11. SIDON TAKEN.

King Baldwin made a magnificent feast for King Sigurd and many of his people, and gave him many holy relics. By the orders of King Baldwin and the patriarch, there was taken a splinter off the holy cross; and on this holy relic both made oath, that this wood was of the holy cross upon which God Himself had been tortured. Then this holy relic was given to King Sigurd; with the condition that he, and twelve other men with him, should swear to promote Christianity with all his power, and erect an archbishop's seat in Norway if he could; and also that the cross should be kept where the holy King Olaf reposed, and that he should introduce tithes, and also pay them himself. After this King Sigurd returned to his ships at Acre; and then King Baldwin prepared to go to Syria, to a heathen town called Saet. On this expedition King Sigurd accompanied him, and after the kings had besieged the town some time it surrendered, and they took possession of it, and of a great treasure of money; and their men found other booty. King Sigurd made a present of his share to King Baldwin. So say Haldor Skvaldre:—

"He who for wolves provides the feast
Seized on the city in the East,
The heathen nest; and honour drew,
And gold to give, from those he slew."

Einar Skulason also tells of it:—

"The Norsemen's king, the skalds relate,
Has ta'en the heathen town of Saet:
The slinging engine with dread noise
Gables and roofs with stones destroys.
The town wall totters too,—it falls;
The Norsemen mount the blackened walls.
He who stains red the raven's bill
Has won,—the town lies at his will."

Thereafter King Sigurd went to his ships and made ready to leave Palestine. They sailed north to the island Cyprus; and King Sigurd stayed there a while, and then went to the Greek country, and came to the land with all his fleet at Engilsnes. Here he lay still for a fortnight, although every day it blew a breeze for going before the wind to the north; but Sigurd would wait a side wind, so that the sails might stretch fore and aft in the ship; for in all his sails there was silk joined in, before and behind in the sail, and neither those before nor those behind the ships could see the slightest appearance of this, if the vessel was before the wind; so they would rather wait a side wind.

12. SIGURD'S EXPEDITION TO CONSTANTINOPLE.

When King Sigurd sailed into Constantinople, he steered near the land. Over all the land there are burghs, castles, country towns, the one upon the other without interval. There from the land one could see into the bights of the sails; and the sails stood so close beside each other, that they seemed to form one enclosure. All the people turned out to see King Sigurd sailing past. The Emperor Kirjalax had also heard of King Sigurd's expedition, and ordered the city port of Constantinople to be opened, which is called the Gold Tower, through which the emperor rides when he has been long absent from Constantinople, or has made a campaign in which he has been victorious. The emperor had precious cloths spread out from the Gold Tower to Laktjarna, which is the name of the emperor's most splendid hall. King Sigurd ordered his men to ride in great state into the city, and not to regard all the new things they might see; and this they did. King Sigurd and his followers rode with this great splendour into Constantinople, and then came to the magnificent hall, where everything was in the grandest style.

King Sigurd remained here some time. The Emperor Kirjalax sent his men to him to ask if he would rather accept from the emperor six lispund of gold, or would have the emperor give the games in his honour which the emperor was used to have played at the Padreim. King Sigurd preferred the games, and the messengers said the spectacle would not cost the emperor less than the money offered. Then the emperor prepared for the games, which were held in the usual way; but this day everything went on better for the king than for the queen; for the queen has always the half part in the games, and their men, therefore, always strive against each other in all games. The Greeks accordingly think that when the king's men win more games at the Padreim than the queen's, the king will gain the victory when he goes into battle. People who have been in Constantinople tell that the Padreim is thus constructed:—A high wall surrounds a flat plain, which may be compared to a round bare Thing-place, with earthen banks all around at the stone wall, on which banks the spectators sit; but the games themselves are in the flat plain. There are many sorts of old events represented concerning the Asas, Volsungs, and Giukungs, in these games; and all the figures are cast in copper, or metal, with so great art that they appear to be living things; and to the people it appears as if they were really present in the games. The games themselves are so artfully and cleverly managed, that people appear to be riding in the air; and at them also are used shot-fire, and all kinds of harp-playing, singing, and music instruments.

13. SIGURD AND THE EMPEROR OF CONSTANTINOPLE.

It is related that King Sigurd one day was to give the emperor a feast, and he ordered his men to provide sumptuously all that was necessary for the entertainment; and when all things were provided which are suitable for an entertainment given by a great personage to persons of high dignity, King Sigurd ordered his men to go to the street in the city where firewood was sold, as they would require a great quantity to prepare the feast. They said the king need not be afraid of wanting firewood, for every day many loads were brought into the town. When it was necessary, however, to have firewood, it was found that it was all sold, which they told the king. He replied, "Go and try if you can get walnuts. They will answer as well as wood for fuel." They went and got as many as they needed. Now came the emperor, and his grandees and court, and sat down to table. All was very splendid; and King Sigurd received the emperor with great state, and entertained him magnificently. When the queen and the emperor found that nothing was wanting, she sent some persons to inquire what they had used for firewood; and they came to a house filled with walnuts, and they came back and told the queen. "Truly," said she, "this is a magnificent king, who spares no expense where his honour is concerned." She had contrived this to try what they would do when they could get no firewood to dress their feast with.

14. KING SIGURD THE CRUSADER'S RETURN HOME.

King Sigurd soon after prepared for his return home. He gave the emperor all his ships; and the valuable figureheads which were on the king's ships were set up in Peter's church, where they have since been to be seen. The emperor gave the king many horses and guides to conduct him through all his dominions. Then King Sigurd left Constantinople; but a great many Northmen remained, and went into the emperor's pay. Then King Sigurd traveled from Bulgaria, and through Hungary, Pannonia. Suabia, and Bavaria, where he met the Roman emperor, Lotharius, who received him in the most friendly way, gave him guides through his dominions, and had markets established for him at which he could purchase all he required. When King Sigurd came to Slesvik in Denmark, Earl Eilif made a sumptuous feast for him; and it was then midsummer. In Heidaby he met the Danish king, Nikolas, who received him in the most friendly way, made a great entertainment for him, accompanied him north to Jutland, and gave him a ship provided with everything needful. From thence the king returned to Norway, and was joyfully welcomed on his return to his kingdom (A.D. 1110). It was the common talk among the people, that none had ever made so honourable a journey from Norway as this of King Sigurd. He was twenty years of age, and had been three years on these travels. His brother Olaf was then twelve years old.

15. EYSTEIN'S DOINGS IN THE MEANTIME.

King Eystein had also effected much in the country that was useful while King Sigurd was on his journey. He established a monastery at Nordnes in Bergen, and endowed it with much property. He also built Michael's church, which is a very splendid stone temple. In the king's house there he also built the Church of the Apostles, and the great hall, which is the most magnificent wooden structure that was ever built in Norway. He also built a church at Agdanes with a parapet; and a harbour, where formerly there had been a barren spot only. In Nidaros he built in the king's street the church of Saint Nikolas, which was particularly ornamented with carved work, and all in wood. He also built a church north in Vagar in Halogaland, and endowed it with property and revenues.

16. OF KING EYSTEIN.

King Eystein sent a verbal message to the most intelligent and powerful of the men of Jamtaland, and invited them to him; received them all as they came with great kindness; accompanied them part of the way home, and gave them presents, and thus enticed them into a friendship with him. Now as many of them became accustomed to visit him and receive gifts from him, and he also sent gifts to some who did not come themselves, he soon gained the favour of all the people who had most influence in the country. Then he spoke to the Jamtaland people, and told them they had done ill in turning away from the kings of Norway, and withdrawing from them their taxes and allegiance. He began by saying how the Jamtaland people had submitted to the reign of Hakon, the foster-son of Athelstane, and had long afterwards been subjected to the kings of Norway, and he represented to them how many useful things they could get from Norway, and how inconvenient it was for them to apply to the Swedish king for what they needed. By these speeches he brought matters so far that the Jamtaland people of their own accord offered to be subject to him, which they said was useful and necessary for them; and thus, on both sides, it was agreed that the Jamtalanders should put their whole country under King Eystein. The first beginning was with the men of consequence, who persuaded the people to take an oath of fidelity to King Eystein; and then they went to King Eystein and confirmed the country to him by oath; and this arrangement has since continued for a long time. King Eystein thus conquered Jamtaland by his wisdom, and not by hostile inroads, as some of his forefathers had done.

17. OF KING EYSTEIN'S PERFECTIONS.

King Eystein was the handsomest man that could be seen. He had blue open eyes; his hair yellow and curling; his stature not tall, but of the middle size. He was wise, intelligent, and acquainted with the laws and history. He had much knowledge of mankind, was quick in counsel, prudent in words, and very eloquent and very generous. He was very merry, yet modest; and was liked and beloved, indeed, by all the people. He was married to Ingebjorg, a daughter of Guthorm, son of Thorer of Steig; and their daughter was Maria, who afterwards married Gudbrand Skafhogson.

18. OF IVAR INGIMUNDSON.

King Eystein had in many ways improved the laws and privileges of the country people, and kept strictly to the laws; and he made himself acquainted with all the laws of Norway, and showed in everything great prudence and understanding. What a valuable man King Eystein was, how full of friendship, and how much he turned his mind to examining and avoiding everything that could be of disadvantage to his friends, may be seen from his friendship to an Iceland man called Ivar Ingimundson. The man was witty, of great family, and also a poet. The king saw that Ivar was out of spirits, and asked him why he was so melancholy. "Before, when thou wast with us, we had much amusement with thy conversation. I know thou art a man of too good an understanding to believe that I would do anything against thee. Tell me then what it is."

He replied, "I cannot tell thee what it is."

Then said the king, "I will try to guess what it is. Are there any men who displease thee?"

To this he replied, "No."

"Dost thou think thou art held in less esteem by me than thou wouldst like to be?"

To this he also replied, "No."

"Hast thou observed anything whatever that has made an impression on thee at which thou art ill pleased?"

He replied, it was not this either.

The king: "Would you like to go to other chiefs or to other men?"

To this he answered, "No."

The king: "It is difficult now to guess. Is there any girl here, or in any other country, to whom thy affections are engaged?"

He said it was so.

The king said, "Do not be melancholy on that account. Go to Iceland when spring sets in, and I shall give thee money, and presents, and with these my letters and seal to the men who have the principal sway there; and I know no man there who will not obey my persuasions or threats."

Ivar replied, "My fate is heavier, sire; for my own brother has the girl."

Then said the king, "Throw it out of thy mind; and I know a counsel against this. After Yule I will travel in guest-quarters. Thou shalt come along with me, and thou will have an opportunity of seeing many beautiful girls; and, provided they are not of the royal stock, I will get thee one of them in marriage."

Ivar replies, "Sire, my fate is still the heavier; for as oft as I see beautiful and excellent girls I only remember the more that girl, and they increase my misery."

The king: "Then I will give thee property to manage, and estates for thy amusement."

He replied, "For that I have no desire."

The king: "Then I will give thee money, that thou mayest travel in other countries."

He said he did not wish this.

Then said the king, "It is difficult for me to seek farther, for I have proposed everything that occurs to me. There is but one thing else; and that is but little compared to what I have offered thee. Come to me every day after the tables are removed, and, if I am not sitting upon important business, I shall talk with thee about the girl in every way that I can think of; and I shall do so at leisure. It sometimes happens that sorrow is lightened by being brought out openly; and thou shalt never go away without some gift."

He replied, "This I will do, sire, and return thanks for this inquiry."

And now they did so constantly; and when the king was not occupied with weightier affairs he talked with him, and his sorrow by degrees wore away, and he was again in good spirits.

19. OF KING SIGURD.

King Sigurd was a stout and strong man, with brown hair; of a manly appearance, but not handsome; well grown; of little speech, and often not friendly, but good to his friends, and faithful; not very eloquent, but moral and polite. King Sigurd was self-willed, and severe in his revenge; strict in observing the law; was generous; and withal an able, powerful king. His brother Olaf was a tall, thin man; handsome in countenance; lively, modest, and popular. When all these brothers, Eystein, Sigurd and Olaf were kings of Norway, they did away with many burthens which the Danes had laid upon the people in the time that Svein Alfifason ruled Norway; and on this account they were much beloved, both by the people and the great men of the country.

20. OF KING SIGURD'S DREAM.

Once King Sigurd fell into low spirits, so that few could get him to converse, and he sat but a short time at the drinking table. This was heavy on his counsellors, friends, and court; and they begged King Eystein to consider how they could discover the cause why the people who came to the king could get no reply to what they laid before him. King Eystein answered them, that it was difficult to speak with the king about this; but at last, on the entreaty of many, he promised to do it. Once, when they were both together, King Eystein brought the matter before his brother, and asked the cause of his melancholy. "It is a great grief, sire, to many to see thee so melancholy; and we would like to know what has occasioned it, or if perchance thou hast heard any news of great weight?"

King Sigurd replies, that it was not so.

"Is it then, brother," says King Eystein, "that you would like to travel out of the country, and augment your dominions as our father did?"

He answered, that it was not that either.

"Is it, then, that any man here in the country has offended?"

To this also the king said "No."

"Then I would like to know if you have dreamt anything that has occasioned this depression of mind?"

The king answered that it was so.

"Tell me, then, brother, thy dream."

King Sigurd said, "I will not tell it, unless thou interpret it as it may turn out; and I shall be quick at perceiving if thy interpretation be right or not."

King Eystein replies, "This is a very difficult matter, sire, on both sides; as I am exposed to thy anger if I cannot interpret it, and to the blame of the public if I can do nothing in the matter; but I will rather fall under your displeasure, even if my interpretation should not be agreeable."

King Sigurd replies, "It appeared to me, in a dream, as if we brothers were all sitting on a bench in front of Christ church in Throndhjem; and it appeared to me as if our relative, King Olaf the Saint, came out of the church adorned with the royal raiment glancing and splendid, and with the most delightful and joyful countenance. He went to our brother King Olaf, took him by the hand, and said cheerfully, to him, 'Come with me, friend.' On which he appeared to stand up and go into the church. Soon after King Olaf the Saint came out of the church, but not so gay and brilliant as before. Now he went to thee, brother, and said to thee that thou shouldst go with him; on which he led thee with him, and ye went into the church. Then I thought, and waited for it, that he would come to me, and meet me; but it was not so. Then I was seized with great sorrow, and great dread and anxiety fell upon me, so that I was altogether without strength; and then I awoke."

King Eystein replies, "Thus I interpret your dream, sire,—That the bench betokens the kingdom we brothers have; and as you thought King Olaf came with so glad a countenance to our brother, King Olaf, he will likely live the shortest time of us brothers, and have all good to expect hereafter; for he is amiable, young in years, and has gone but little into excess, and King Olaf the Saint must help him. But as you thought he came towards me, but not with so much joy, I may possibly live a few years longer, but not become old, and I trust his providence will stand over me; but that he did not come to me with the same splendour and glory as to our brother Olaf, that will be because, in many ways, I have sinned and transgressed his command. If he delayed coming to thee, I think that in no way betokens thy death, but rather a long life; but it may be that some heavy accident may occur to thee, as there was an unaccountable dread overpowering thee; but I foretell that thou will be the oldest of us, and wilt rule the kingdom longest."

Then said Sigurd, "This is well and intelligently interpreted, and it is likely it will be so." And now the king began to be cheerful again.

21. OF KING SIGURD'S MARRIAGE.

King Sigurd married Malmfrid, a daughter of King Harald Valdemarson, eastward in Novgorod. King Harald Valdemarson's mother was Queen Gyda the Old, a daughter of the Swedish king, Inge Steinkelson. Harald Valdemarson's other daughter, sister to Malmfrid, was Ingebjorg, who was married to Canute Lavard, a son of the Danish king, Eirik the Good, and grandson of King Svein Ulfson. Canute's and Ingebjorg's children were, the Danish king, Valdemar, who came to the Danish kingdom after Svein Eirikson; and daughters Margaret, Christina, and Catherine. Margaret was married to Stig Hvitaled; and their daughter was Christina, married to the Swedish king, Karl Sorkvison, and their son was King Sorkver.

22. OF THE CASES BEFORE THE THING.

The king's relative, Sigurd Hranason, came into strife with King Sigurd. He had had the Lapland collectorship on the king's account, because of their relationship and long friendship, and also of the many services Sigurd Hranason had done to the kings; for he was a very distinguished, popular man. But it happened to him, as it often does to others, that persons more wicked and jealous than upright slandered him to King Sigurd, and whispered in the king's ear that he took more of the Laplander's tribute to himself than was proper. They spoke so long about this, that King Sigurd conceived a dislike and anger to him, and sent a message to him. When he appeared before the king, the king carried these feelings with him, and said, "I did not expect that thou shouldst have repaid me for thy great fiefs and other dignities by taking the king's property, and abstracting a greater portion of it than is allowable."

Sigurd Hranason replies, "It is not true that has been told you; for I have only taken such portion as I had your permission to take."

King Sigurd replies, "Thou shalt not slip away with this; but the matter shall be seriously treated before it comes to an end." With that they parted.

Soon after, by the advice of his friends, the king laid an action against Sigurd Hranason at the Thing-meeting in Bergen, and would have him made an outlaw. Now when the business took this turn, and appeared so dangerous, Sigurd Hranason went to King Eystein, and told him what mischief

King Sigurd intended to do him, and entreated his assistance. King Eystein replied, "This is a difficult matter that you propose to me, to speak against my brother; and there is a great difference between defending a cause and pursuing it in law;" and added, that this was a matter which concerned him and Sigurd equally. "But for thy distress, and our relationship, I shall bring in a word for thee."

Soon after Eystein visited King Sigurd, and entreated him to spare the man, reminding him of the relationship between them and Sigurd Hranason, who was married to their aunt, Skialdvor; and said he would pay the penalty for the crime committed against the king, although he could not with truth impute any blame to him in the matter. Besides, he reminded the king of the long friendship with Sigurd Hranason. King Sigurd replied, that it was better government to punish such acts. Then King Eystein replied, "If thou, brother, wilt follow the law, and punish such acts according to the country's privileges, then it would be most correct that Sigurd Hranason produce his witnesses, and that the case be judged at the Thing, but not at a meeting; for the case comes under the law of the land, not under Bjarkey law." Then said Sigurd, "It may possibly be so that the case belongs to it, as thou sayest, King Eystein; and if it be against law what has hitherto been done in this case, then we shall bring it before the Thing." Then the kings parted, and each seemed determined to take his own way. King Sigurd summoned the parties in the case before the Arnarnes Thing, and intended to pursue it there. King Eystein came also to the Thing-place; and when the case was brought forward for judgment, King Eystein went to the Thing before judgment was given upon Sigurd Hranason. Now King Sigurd told the lagmen to pronounce the judgment; but King Eystein replied thus: "I trust there are here men acquainted sufficiently with the laws of Norway, to know that they cannot condemn a lendermen to be outlawed at this Thing." And he then explained how the law was, so that every man clearly understood it. Then said King Sigurd, "Thou art taking up this matter very warmly, King Eystein, and it is likely the case will cost more trouble before it comes to an end than we intended; but nevertheless we shall follow it out. I will have him condemned to be outlawed in his native place." Then said King Eystein, "There are certainly not many things which do not succeed with thee, and especially when there are but few and small folks to oppose one who has carried through such great things." And thus they parted, without anything being concluded in the case. Thereafter King Sigurd called together a Gula Thing, went himself there, and summoned to him many high chiefs. King Eystein came there also with his suite; and many meetings and conferences were held among people of understanding concerning this case, and it was tried and examined before the lagmen. Now King Eystein objected that all the parties summoned in any cases tried here belonged to the Thing-district; but in this case the deed and the parties belonged to Halogaland. The Thing accordingly ended in doing nothing, as King Eystein had thus made it incompetent. The kings parted in great wrath; and King Eystein went north to Throndhjem. King Sigurd, on the other hand, summoned to him all lendermen, and also the house-servants of the lendermen, and named out of every district a number of the bondes from the south parts of the country, so that he had collected a large army about him; and proceeded with all this crowd northwards along the coast to Halogaland, and intended to use all his power to make Sigurd Hranason an outlaw among his own relations. For this purpose he summoned to him the Halogaland and Naumudal people, and appointed a Thing at Hrafnista. King Eystein prepared himself also, and proceeded with many people from the town of Nidaros to the Thing, where he made Sigurd Hranason, by hand-shake before witnesses, deliver over to him the following and defending this case. At this Thing both the kings spoke, each for his own side. Then King Eystein asks the lagmen where that law was made in Norway which gave the bondes the right to judge between the kings of the country, when they had pleas with each other. "I shall bring witnesses to prove that Sigurd has given the case into my hands; and it is with me, not with Sigurd Hranason, that King Sigurd has to do in this case." The lagmen said that disputes between kings must be judged only at the Eyra Thing in Nidaros.

King Eystein said, "So I thought that it should be there, and the cases must be removed there."

Then King Sigurd said, "The more difficulties and inconvenience thou bringest upon me in this matter, the more I will persevere in it." And with that they parted.

Both kings then went south to Nidaros town, where they summoned a Thing from eight districts. King Eystein was in the town with a great many people, but Sigurd was on board his ships. When the Thing was opened, peace and safe conduct was given to all; and when the people were all collected, and the case should be gone into, Bergthor, a son of Svein Bryggjufot, stood up, and gave his evidence that Sigurd Hranason had concealed a part of the Laplanders' taxes.

Then King Eystein stood up and said, "If thy accusation were true, although we do not know what truth there may be in thy testimony, yet this case has already been dismissed from three Things, and a fourth time from a town meeting; and therefore I require that the lagmen acquit Sigurd in this case according to law." And they did so.

Then said King Sigurd, "I see sufficiently, King Eystein, that thou hast carried this case by law-quirks, which I do not understand. But now there remains, King Eystein, a way of determining the case which I am more used to, and which I shall now apply."

He then retired to his ships, had the tents taken down, laid his whole fleet out at the holm, and held a Thing of his people; and told them that early in the morning they should land at Iluvellir, and give battle to King Eystein. But in the evening, as King Sigurd sat at his table in his ship taking his repast, before he was aware of it a man cast himself on the floor of the forehold, and at the king's feet. This was Sigurd Hranason, who begged the king to take what course with regard to him the king himself thought proper. Then came Bishop Magne and Queen Malmfrid, and many other great personages, and entreated forgiveness for Sigurd Hranason; and at their entreaty the king raised him up, took him by the hand, and placed him among his men, and took him along with himself to the south part of the country. In autumn the king gave Sigurd Hranason leave to go north to his farm, gave him an employment, and was always afterward his friend. After this day, however, the brothers were never much together, and there was no cordiality or cheerfulness among them.

23. OF KING OLAF'S DEATH.

King Olaf Magnuson fell into a sickness which ended in his death. He was buried in Christ church in Nidaros, and many were in great grief at his death. After Olaf's death, Eystein and Sigurd ruled the country, the three brothers together having been kings of Norway for twelve years (A.D. 1104-1115); namely, five years after King Sigurd returned home, and seven years before. King Olaf was seventeen years old when he died, and it happened on the 24th of December.

24. MAGNUS THE BLIND; HIS BIRTH.

King Eystein had been about a year in the east part of the country at that time, and King Sigurd was then in the north. King Eystein remained a long time that winter in Sarpsborg. There was once a powerful and rich bonde called Olaf of Dal, who dwelt in Great Dal in Aumord, and had two children,—a son called Hakon Fauk, and a daughter called Borghild, who was a very beautiful girl, and prudent, and well skilled in many things. Olaf and his children were a long time in winter in Sarpsborg, and Borghild conversed very often with King Eystein; so that many reports were spread about their friendship. The following summer King Eystein went north, and King Sigurd came eastward, where he remained all winter, and was long in Konungahella, which town he greatly enlarged and improved. He built there a great castle of turf and stone, dug a great ditch around it, and built a church and several houses within the castle. The holy cross he allowed to remain at Konungahella, and therein did not fulfill the oath he had taken in Palestine; but, on the other hand, he established tithe, and most of the other things to which he had bound himself by oath. The reason of his keeping the cross east at the frontier of the country was, that he thought it would be a protection to all the land; but it proved the greatest misfortune to place this relic within the power of the heathens, as it afterwards turned out.

When Borghild, Olaf's daughter, heard it whispered that people talked ill of her conversations and intimacy with King Eystein, she went to Sarpsborg; and after suitable fasts she carried the iron as proof of her innocence, and cleared herself thereby fully from all offence. When King Sigurd heard this, he rode one day as far as usually was two days' travelling, and came to Dal to Olaf, where he remained all night, made Borghild his concubine, and took her away with him. They had a son, who was called Magnus, and he was sent immediately to Halogaland, to be fostered at Bjarkey by Vidkun Jonson; and he was brought up there. Magnus grew up to be the handsomest man that could be seen, and was very soon stout and strong.

25. COMPARISON BETWEEN THE TWO KINGS.

King Eystein and King Sigurd went both in spring to guest-quarters in the Uplands; and each was entertained in a separate house, and the houses were not very distant from each other. The bondes, however, thought it more convenient that both should be entertained together by turns in each house; and thus they were both at first in the house of King Eystein. But in the evening, when the people began to drink, the ale was not good; so that the guests were very quiet and still. Then said King Eystein, "Why are the people so silent? It is more usual in drinking parties that people are merry, so let us fall upon some jest over our ale that will amuse people; for surely, brother Sigurd, all people are well pleased when we talk cheerfully."

Sigurd replies, bluntly, "Do you talk as much as you please, but give me leave to be silent."

Eystein says, "It is a common custom over the ale-table to compare one person with another, and now let us do so." Then Sigurd was silent.

"I see," says King Eystein, "that I must begin this amusement. Now I will take thee, brother, to compare myself with, and will make it appear so as if we had both equal reputation and property, and that there is no difference in our birth and education."

Then King Sigurd replies, "Do you remember that I was always able to throw you when we wrestled, although you are a year older?"

Then King Eystein replied, "But I remember that you was not so good at the games which require agility."

Sigurd: "Do you remember that I could drag you under water, when we swam together, as often as I pleased?"

Eystein: "But I could swim as far as you, and could dive as well as you; and I could run upon snow-skates so well that nobody could beat me, and you could no more do it than an ox."

Sigurd: "Methinks it is a more useful and suitable accomplishment for a chief to be expert at his bow; and I think you could scarcely draw my bow, even if you took your foot to help."

Eystein: "I am not strong at the bow as you are, but there is less difference between our shooting near; and I can use the skees much better than you, and in former times that was held a great accomplishment."

Sigurd: "It appears to me much better for a chief who is to be the superior of other men, that he is conspicuous in a crowd, and strong and powerful in weapons above other men; easily seen, and easily known, where there are many together."

Eystein: "It is not less a distinction and an ornament that a man is of a handsome appearance, so as to be easily known from others on that account; and this appears to me to suit a chief best, because the best ornament is allied to beauty. I am moreover more knowing in the law than you, and on every subject my words flow more easily than yours."

Sigurd: "It may be that you know more law-quirks, for I have had something else to do; neither will any deny you a smooth tongue. But there are many who say that your words are not to be trusted; that what you promise is little to be regarded; and that you talk just according to what those who are about you say, which is not kingly."

Eystein: "This is because, when people bring their cases before me, I wish first to give every man that satisfaction in his affairs which he desires; but afterwards comes the opposite party, and then there is something to be given or taken away very often, in order to mediate between them, so that both may be satisfied. It often happens, too, that I promise whatever is desired of me, that all may be joyful about me. It would be an easy matter for me to do as you do,—to promise evil to all; and I never hear any complain of your not keeping this promise to them."

Sigurd: "It is the conversation of all that the expedition that I made out of the country was a princely expedition, while you in the meantime sat at home like your father's daughter."

Eystein: "Now you touched the tender spot. I would not have brought up this conversation if I had not known what to reply on this point. I can truly say that I equipt you from home like a sister, before you went upon this expedition."

Sigurd: "You must have heard that on this expedition I was in many a battle in the Saracen's land, and gained the victory in all; and you must have heard of the many valuable articles I acquired, the like of which were never seen before in this country, and I was the most respected wherever the most gallant men were; and, on the other hand, you cannot conceal that you have only a home-bred reputation."

Eystein: "I have heard that you had several battles abroad, but it was more useful for the country what I was doing in the meantime here at home. I built five churches from the foundations, and a harbour out at Agdanes, where it before was impossible to land, and where vessels ply north and south along the coast. I set a warping post and iron ring in the sound of Sinholm, and in Bergen I built a royal hall, while you were killing bluemen for the devil in Serkland. This, I think, was of but little advantage to our kingdom."

King Sigurd said: "On this expedition I went all the way to Jordan and swam across the river. On the edge of the river there is a bush of willows, and there I twisted a knot of willows, and said this knot thou shouldst untie, brother, or take the curse thereto attached."

King Eystein said: "I shall not go and untie the knot which you tied for me; but if I had been inclined to tie a knot for thee, thou wouldst not have been king of Norway at thy return to this country, when with a single ship you came sailing into my fleet."

Thereupon both were silent, and there was anger on both sides. More things passed between the brothers, from which it appeared that each of them would be greater than the other; however, peace was preserved between them as long as they lived.

26. OF KING SIGURD'S SICKNESS.

King Sigurd was at a feast in the Upland, and a bath was made ready for him. When the king came to the bath and the tent was raised over the bathing-tub, the king thought there was a fish in the tub beside him; and a great laughter came upon him, so that he was beside himself, and was out of his mind, and often afterwards these fits returned.

Magnus Barefoot's daughter, Ragnhild, was married by her brothers to Harald Kesia, a son of the Danish king, Eirik the Good; and their sons were Magnus, Olaf, Knut and Harald.

27. OF KING EYSTEIN'S DEATH.

King Eystein built a large ship at Nidaros, which, in size and shape, was like the Long Serpent which King Olaf Trygvason had built. At the stem there was a dragon's head, and at the stern a crooked tail, and both were gilded over. The ship was high-sided; but the fore and aft parts appeared less than they should be. He also made in Nidaros many and large dry-docks of the best material, and well timbered.

Six years after King Olaf's death, it happened that King Eystein, at a feast at Hustadir in Stim, was seized with an illness which soon carried him off. He died the 29th of August, 1123, and his body was carried north to Nidaros, and buried in Christ church; and it is generally said that so many mourners never stood over any man's grave in Norway as over King Eystein's, at least since the time Magnus the Good, Saint Olaf's son, died. Eystein had been twenty years (A.D. 1104-1123) king of Norway; and after his decease his brother, King Sigurd, was the sole king of Norway as long as he lived.

28. BAPTIZING THE PEOPLE OF SMALAND.

The Danish king, Nikolas, a son of Svein Ulfson, married afterwards the Queen Margaret, a daughter of King Inge, who had before been married to King Magnus Barefoot; and their sons were Nikolas and Magnus the Strong. King Nikolas sent a message to King Sigurd the Crusader, and asked him if he would go with him with all his might and help him to the east of the Swedish dominion, Smaland, to baptize the inhabitants; for the people who dwelt there had no regard for Christianity, although some of them had allowed themselves to be baptized. At that time there were many people all around in the Swedish dominions who were heathens, and many were bad Christians; for there were some of the kings who renounced Christianity, and continued heathen sacrifices, as Blotsvein, and afterwards Eirik Arsale, had done. King Sigurd promised to undertake this journey, and the kings appointed their meeting at Eyrarsund. King Sigurd then summoned all people in Norway to a levy, both of men and ships; and when the fleet was assembled he had about 300 ships. King Nikolas came very early to the meeting-place, and stayed there a long time; and the bondes murmured much, and said the Northmen did not intend to come. Thereupon the Danish army dispersed, and the king went away with all his fleet. King Sigurd came there soon afterwards, and was ill pleased; but sailed east to Svimraros, and held a House-thing, at which Sigurd spoke about King Nikolas's breach of faith, and the Northmen, on this account, determined to go marauding in his country. They first plundered a village called Tumathorp, which is not far from Lund; and then sailed east to the merchant-town of Calmar, where they plundered, as well as in Smaland, and imposed on the country a tribute of 1500 cattle for ship provision; and the people of Smaland received Christianity. After this King Sigurd turned about with his fleet, and came back to his kingdom with many valuable articles and great booty, which he had gathered on this expedition; and this levy was called the Calmar levy. This was the summer before the eclipse. This was the only levy King Sigurd carried out as long as he was king.

29. OF THORARIN STUTFELD.

It happened once when King Sigurd was going from the drinking-table to vespers, that his men were very drunk and merry; and many of them sat outside the church singing the evening song, but their singing was very irregular. Then the king said, "Who is that fellow I see standing at the church with a skin jacket on?" They answered, that they did not know. Then the king said:—

"This skin-clad man, in sorry plight,
Puts all our wisdom here to flight."

Then the fellow came forward and said:—

"I thought that here I might be known,
Although my dress is scanty grown.
'Tis poor, but I must be content:
Unless, great king, it's thy intent
To give me better; for I have seen
When I and rags had strangers been."

The king answered, "Come to me to-morrow when I am at the drink-table." The night passed away; and the morning after the Icelander, who was afterwards called Thorarin Stutfetd, went into the drinking-room. A man stood outside of the door of the room with a horn in his hand, and said, "Icelander! the king says that if thou wilt deserve any gift from him thou shalt compose a song before going in, and make it about a man whose name is Hakon Serkson, and who is called Morstrut; and speak about that surname in thy song." The man who spoke to him was called Arne Fioruskeif. Then they went into the room; and when Thorarin came before the king's seat he recited these verses:—

"Throndhjem's warrior-king has said
The skald should be by gifts repaid,
If he before this meeting gave
The king's friend Serk a passing stave.
The generous king has let me know
My stave, to please, must be framed so
That my poor verse extol the fame
Of one called Hakon Lump by name."

Then said the king, "I never said so, and somebody has been making a mock of thee. Hakon himself shall determine what punishment thou shalt have. Go into his suite." Hakon said, "He shall be welcome among us, for I can see where the joke came from;" and he placed the Icelander at his side next to himself, and they were very merry. The day was drawing to a close, and the liquor began to get into their heads, when Hakon said, "Dost thou not think, Icelander, that thou owest me some penalty? and dost thou not see that some trick has been played upon thee?"

Thorarin replies, "It is true, indeed, that I owe thee some compensation."

Hakon says, "Then we shall be quits, if thou wilt make me another stave about Arne."

He said he was ready to do so; and they crossed over to the side of the room where Arne was sitting, and Thorarin gave these verses:—

"Fioruskeif has often spread,
With evil heart and idle head,
The eagle's voidings round the land,
Lampoons and lies, with ready hand.
Yet this landlouper we all know,
In Africa scarce fed a crow,
Of all his arms used in the field,
Those in most use were helm and shield."

Arne sprang up instantly, drew his sword, and was going to fall upon him; but Hakon told him to let it alone and be quiet, and bade him remember that if it came to a quarrel he would come off the worst himself. Thorarin afterwards went up to the king, and said he had composed a poem which he wished the king to hear. The king consented, and the song is known by the name of the Stutfeld poem. The king asked Thorarin what he intended to do. He replied, it was his intention to go to Rome. Then the king gave him much money for his pilgrimage, and told him to visit him on his return, and promised to provide for him.

30. OF SIGURD AND OTTAR BIRTING.

It is told that King Sigurd, one Whitsunday, sat at table with many people, among whom were many of his friends; and when he came to his high-seat, people saw that his countenance was very wild, and as if he had been weeping, so that people were afraid of what might follow. The king rolled his eyes, and looked at those who were seated on the benches. Then he seized the holy book which he had brought with him from abroad, and which was written all over with gilded letters; so that never had such a costly book come to Norway. His queen sat by his side. Then said King Sigurd, "Many are the changes which may take place during a man's lifetime. I had two things which were dear to me above all when I came from abroad, and these were this book and the queen; and now I think the one is only worse and more loathsome than the other, and nothing I have belonging to me that I more detest. The queen does not know herself how hideous she is; for a goat's horn is standing out on her head, and the better I liked her before the worse I like her now." Thereupon he cast the book on the fire which was burning on the hall-floor, and gave the queen a blow with his fist between the eyes. The queen wept; but more at the king's' illness than at the blow, or the affront she had suffered.

Then a man stood up before the king; his name was Ottar Birting; and he was one of the torch-bearers, although a bonde's son, and was on service that day. He was of small stature, but of agreeable appearance; lively, bold, and full of fun; black haired, and of a dark skin. He ran and snatched the book which the king had cast into the fire, held it out, and said, "Different were the days, sire, when you came with great state and splendour to Norway, and with great fame and honour; for then all your friends came to meet you with joy, and were glad at your coming. All as one man would have you for king, and have you in the highest regard and honour. But now days of sorrow are come over us; for on this holy festival many of your friends have come to you, and cannot be cheerful on account of your melancholy and ill health. It is much to be desired that you would be merry with them; and do, good king, take this saving advice, make peace first with the queen, and make her joyful whom you have so highly affronted, with a friendly word; and then all your chiefs, friends, and servants; that is my advice."

Then said King Sigurd, "Dost thou dare to give me advice, thou great lump of a houseman's lad!" And he sprang up, drew his sword, and swung it with both hands as if going to cut him down.

But Ottar stood quiet and upright; did not stir from the spot, nor show the slightest sign of fear; and the king turned round the sword-blade which he had waved over Ottar's head, and gently touched him on the shoulder with it. Then he sat down in silence on his high-seat.

All were silent who were in the hall, for nobody dared to say a word. Now the king looked around him, milder than before, and said, "It is difficult to know what there is in people. Here sat my friends, and lendermen, marshals and shield-bearers, and all the best men in the land; but none did so well against me as this man, who appears to you of little worth compared to any of you, although now he loves me most. I came here like a madman, and would have destroyed my precious property; but he turned aside my deed, and was not afraid of death for it. Then he made an able speech, ordering his words so that they were honourable to me, and not saying a single word about things which could increase my vexation; but even avoiding what might, with truth, have been said. So excellent was his speech, that no man here, however great his understanding, could have spoken better. Then I sprang up in a pretended rage, and made as if I would have cut him down; but he was courageous as if he had nothing to fear; and seeing that, I let go my purpose; for he was altogether innocent. Now ye shall know, my friends, how I intend to reward him; he was before my torchbearer, and shall now be my lenderman; and there shall follow what is still more, that he shall be the most distinguished of my lendermen. Go thou and sit among the lendermen, and be a servant no longer."

Ottar became one of the most celebrated men in Norway for various good and praiseworthy deeds.

31. OF KING SIGURD'S DREAM.

In King Sigurd's latter days he was once at an entertainment at one of his farms; and in the morning when he was dressed he was silent and still, so that his friends were afraid he was not able to govern himself. Now the farm bailiff, who was a man of good sense and courage, brought him into conversation, and asked if he had heard any news of such importance that it disturbed his mirth; or if the entertainment had not satisfied him; or if there was anything else that people could remedy.

King Sigurd said, that none of the things he had mentioned was the cause. "But it is that I think upon the dream I had in the night."

"Sire," replied he, "may it prove a lucky dream! I would gladly hear it."

The king: "I thought that I was in Jadar, and looked out towards the sea; and that I saw something very black moving itself; and when it came near it appeared to be a large tree, of which the branches stretched far above the water, and the roots were down in the sea. Now when the tree came to the shore it broke into pieces, and drove all about the land, both the mainland and the out-islands, rocks and strands; and it appeared to me as if I saw over all Norway along the sea-coast, and saw pieces of that tree, some small and some large, driven into every bight."

Then said the bailiff, "It is likely that you an best interpret this dream yourself; and I would willingly hear your interpretation of it."

Then said the king, "This dream appears to me to denote the arrival in this country of some man who will fix his seat here, and whose posterity will spread itself over the land; but with unequal power, as the dream shows."

32. OF ASLAK HANE.

It so happened once, that King Sigurd sat in a gloomy mood among many worthy men. It was Friday evening, and the kitchen-master asked what meat should be made ready.

The king replies, "What else but flesh-meat?" And so harsh were his words that nobody dared to contradict him, and all were ill at ease. Now when people prepared to go to table, dishes of warm flesh-meat were carried in; but all were silent, and grieved at the king's illness. Before the blessing was pronounced over the meat, a man called Aslak Hane spoke. He had been a long time with King Sigurd on his journey abroad, and was not a man of any great family; and was small of stature, but fiery. When he perceived how it was, and that none dared to accost the king, he asked, "What is it, sire, that is smoking on the dish before you?"

The king replies, "What do you mean, Aslak? what do you think it is?"

Aslak: "I think it is flesh-meat; and I would it were not so."

The king: "But if it be so, Aslak?"

He replied, "It would be vexatious to know that a gallant king, who has gained so much honour in the world, should so forget himself. When you rose up out of Jordan, after bathing in the same waters as God himself, with palm-leaves in your hands, and the cross upon your breast, it was something else you promised, sire, than to eat flesh-meat on a Friday. If a meaner man were to do so, he would merit a heavy punishment. This royal hall is not so beset as it should be, when it falls upon me, a mean man, to challenge such an act."

The king sat silent, and did not partake of the meat; and when the time for eating was drawing to an end, the king ordered the flesh dishes to be removed and other food was brought in, such as it is permitted to use. When the meal-time was almost past, the king began to be cheerful, and to drink.

People advised Aslak to fly, but he said he would not do so. "I do not see how it could help me; and to tell the truth, it is as good to die now that I have got my will, and have prevented the king from committing a sin. It is for him to kill me if he likes."

Towards evening the king called him, and said, "Who set thee on, Aslak Hane, to speak such free words to me in the hearing of so many people?"

"No one, sire, but myself."

The king: "Thou wouldst like, no doubt, to know what thou art to have for such boldness; what thinkest thou it deserves."

He replies, "If it be well rewarded, sire, I shall be glad; but should it be otherwise, then it is your concern."

Then the king said, "Smaller is thy reward than thou hast deserved. I give thee three farms. It has turned out, what could not have been expected, that thou hast prevented me from a great crime,—thou, and not the lendermen, who are indebted to me for so much good." And so it ended.

33. OF A WOMAN BROUGHT TO THE KING.

One Yule eve the king sat in the hall, and the tables were laid out, and the king said, "Get me flesh-meat."

They answered, "Sire, it is not the custom to eat flesh-meat on Yule eve."

The king said, "If it be not the custom I will make it the custom."

They went out, and brought him a dolphin. The king stuck his knife into it, but did not eat of it. Then the king said, "Bring me a girl here into the hall." They brought him a woman whose head-dress went far down her brows. The king took her hand in his hands, looked at her, and said, "An ill looking girl!"

((LACUNA—The rest of this story is missing))

34. HARALD GILLE COMES TO NORWAY.

Halkel Huk, a son of Jon Smiorbalte, who was lenderman in More, made a voyage in the West sea, all the way to the South Hebudes. A man came to him out of Ireland called Gillikrist, and gave himself out for a son of King Magnus Barefoot. His mother came with him, and said his other name was Harald. Halkel received the man, brought him to Norway with him, and went immediately to King Sigurd with Harald and his mother. When they had told their story to the king, he talked over the matter with his principal men, and bade them give their opinions upon it. They were of different opinions, and all left it to the king himself, although there were several who opposed this; and the king followed his own counsel. King Sigurd ordered Harald to be called before him, and told him that he would not deny him the proof, by ordeal, of who his father was; but on condition that if he should prove his descent according to his claim, he should not desire the kingdom in the lifetime of King Sigurd, or of King Magnus: and to this he bound himself by oath. King Sigurd said he must tread over hot iron to prove his birth; but this ordeal was thought by many too severe, as he was to undergo it merely to prove his father, and without getting the kingdom; but Harald agreed to it, and fixed on the trial by iron: and this ordeal was the greatest ever made in Norway; for nine glowing plowshares were laid down, and Harald went over them with bare feet, attended by two bishops.

Three days after the iron trial the ordeal was taken to proof, and the feet were found unburnt. Thereafter King Sigurd acknowledged Harald's relationship; but his son Magnus conceived a great hatred of him, and in this many chiefs followed Magnus. King Sigurd trusted so much to his favour with the whole people of the country, that he desired all men, under oath, to promise to accept Magnus after him as their king; and all the people took this oath.

35. RACE BETWEEN MAGNUS AND HARALD GILLE.

Harald Gille was a tall, slender-grown man, of a long neck and face, black eyes, and dark hair, brisk and quick, and wore generally the Irish dress of short light clothes. The Norse language was difficult for Harald, and he brought out words which many laughed at. Harald sat late drinking one evening. He spoke with another man about different things in the west in Ireland; and among other things, said that there were men in Ireland so swift of foot that no horse could overtake them in running. Magnus, the king's son, heard this, and said, "Now he is lying, as he usually does."

Harald replies, "It is true that there are men in Ireland whom no horse in Norway could overtake." They exchanged some words about this, and both were drunk. Then said Magnus, "Thou shalt make a wager with me, and stake thy head if thou canst not run so fast as I ride upon my horse, and I shall stake my gold ring."

Harald replies, "I did not say that I could run so swiftly; but I said that men are to be found in Ireland who will run as fast; and on that I would wager."

The king's son Magnus replies, "I will not go to Ireland about it; we are wagering here, and not there."

Harald on this went to bed, and would not speak to him more about it. This was in Oslo. The following morning, when the early mass was over, Magnus rode up the street, and sent a message to Harald to come to him. When Harald came he was dressed thus. He had on a shirt and trousers which were bound with ribands under his foot-soles, a short cloak, an Irish hat on his head, and a spear-shaft in his hand. Magnus set up a mark for the race. Harald said, "Thou hast made the course too long;" but Magnus made it at once even much longer, and said it was still too short. There were many spectators. They began the race, and Harald followed always the horse's pace; and when they came to the end of the race course, Magnus said, "Thou hadst hold of the saddle-girth, and the horse dragged thee along." Magnus had his swift runner, the Gautland horse. They began the race again, and Harald ran the whole race-course before the horse. When came to the end Harald asked, "Had I hold of the saddle-girths now?"

Magnus replied, "Thou hadst the start at first."

Then Magnus let his horse breathe a while, and when he was ready he put the spurs to him, and set off in full gallop. Harald stood still, and Magnus looked back, and called, "Set off now."

Then Harald ran quickly past the horse, and came to the end of the course so long before him that he lay down, and got up and saluted Magnus as he came in.

Then they went home to the town. In the meantime King Sigurd had been at high mass, and knew nothing of this until after he had dined that day. Then he said to Magnus angrily, "Thou callest Harald useless; but I think thou art a great fool, and knowest nothing of the customs of foreign people. Dost thou not know that men in other countries exercise themselves in other feats than in filling themselves with ale, and making themselves mad, and so unfit for everything that they scarcely know each other? Give Harald his ring, and do not try to make a fool of him again, as long as I am above ground."

36. OF SIGURD'S SWIMMING.

It happened once that Sigurd was out in his ship, which lay in the harbour; and there lay a merchant ship, which was an Iceland trader, at the side of it. Harald Gille was in the forecastle of the king's ship, and Svein Rimhildson, a son of Knut Sveinson of Jadar, had his berth the next before him. There was also Sigurd Sigurdson, a gallant lenderman, who himself commanded a ship. It was a day of beautiful weather and warm sunshine, and many went out to swim, both from the long-ship and the merchant vessel. An Iceland man, who was among the swimmers, amused himself by drawing those under water who could not swim so well as himself; and at that the spectators laughed. When King Sigurd saw and heard this, he cast off his clothes, sprang into the water, and swam to the Icelander, seized him, and pressed him under the water, and held him there; and as soon as the Icelander came up the king pressed him down again, and thus the one time after the other.

Then said Sigurd Sigurdson, "Shall we let the king kill this man?"

Somebody said, "No one has any wish to interfere."

Sigurd replies, that "If Dag Eilifson were here, we should not be without one who dared."

Then Sigurd sprang overboard, swam to the king, took hold of him, and said, "Sire, do not kill the man. Everybody sees that you are a much better swimmer."

The king replies, "Let me loose, Sigurd: I shall be his death, for he will destroy our people under water."

Sigurd says, "Let us first amuse ourselves; and, Icelander, do thou set off to the land," which he did. The king now got loose from Sigurd, and swam to his ship, and Sigurd went his way: but the king ordered that Sigurd should not presume to come into his presence; this was reported to Sigurd, and so he went up into the country.

37. OF HARALD AND SVEIN RIMHILDSON.

In the evening, when people were going to bed, some of the ship's men were still at their games up in the country. Harald was with those who played on the land, and told his footboy to go out to the ship, make his bed, and wait for him there. The lad did as he was ordered. The king had gone to sleep; and as the boy thought Harald late, he laid himself in Harald's berth. Svein Rimhildson said, "It is a shame for brave men to be brought from their farms at home, and to have here serving boys to sleep beside them." The lad said that Harald had ordered him to come there. Svein Rimhildson said, "We do not so much care for Harald himself lying here, if he do not bring here his slaves and beggars;" and seized a riding-whip, and struck the boy on the head until the blood flowed from him. The boy ran immediately up the country, and told Harald what had happened, who went immediately out to the ship, to the aft part of the forecastle, and with a pole-axe struck Svein so that he received a severe wound on his hands; and then Harald went on shore. Svein ran to the land after him, and, gathering his friends, took Harald prisoner, and they were about hanging him. But while they were busy about this, Sigurd Sigurdson went out to the king's ship and awoke him. When the king opened his eyes and recognised Sigurd, he said. "For this reason thou shalt die, that thou hast intruded into my presence; for thou knowest that I forbade thee:" and with these words the king sprang up.

Sigurd replied, "That is in your power as soon as you please; but other business is more urgent. Go to the land as quickly as possible to help thy brother; for the Rogaland people are going to hang him."

Then said the king, "God give us luck, Sigurd! Call my trumpeter, and let him call the people all to land, and to meet me."

The king sprang on the land, and all who knew him followed him to where the gallows was being erected. The king instantly took Harald to him; and all the people gathered to the king in full armour, as they heard the trumpet. Then the king ordered that Svein and all his comrades should depart from the country as outlaws; but by the intercession of good men the king was prevailed on to let them remain and hold their properties, but no mulct should be paid for Svein's wound.

Then Sigurd Sigurdson asked if the king wished that he should go forth out of the country.

"That will I not," said the king; "for I can never be without thee."

38. OF KING OLAF'S MIRACLE.

There was a young and poor man called Kolbein; and Thora, King Sigurd the Crusader's mother, had ordered his tongue to be cut out of his mouth, and for no other cause than that this young man had taken a piece of meat out of the king-mother's tub which he said the cook had given him, and which the cook had not ventured to serve up to her. The man had long gone about speechless. So says Einar Skulason in Olaf's ballad:—

"The proud rich dame, for little cause,
Had the lad's tongue cut from his jaws:
The helpless man, of speech deprived,
His dreadful sore wound scarce survived.
A few weeks since at Hild was seen,
As well as ever he had been,
The same poor lad—to speech restored
By Olaf's power, whom he adored."

Afterwards the young man came to Nidaros, and watched in the Christ church; but at the second mass for Olaf before matins he fell asleep, and thought he saw King Olaf the Saint coming to him; and that Olaf talked to him, and took hold with his hands of the stump of his tongue and pulled it. Now when he awoke he found himself restored, and joyfully did he thank our Lord and the holy Saint Olaf, who had pitied and helped him; for he had come there speechless, and had gone to the holy shrine, and went away cured, and with his speech clear and distinct.

39. KING OLAF'S MIRACLE WITH A PRISONER.

The heathens took prisoner a young man of Danish family and carried him to Vindland, where he was in fetters along with other prisoners. In the day-time he was alone in irons, without a guard; but at night a peasant's son was beside him in the chain, that he might not escape from them. This poor man never got sleep or rest from vexation and sorrow, and considered in many ways what could help him; for he had a great dread of slavery, and was pining with hunger and torture. He could not again expect to be ransomed by his friends, as they had already restored him twice from heathen lands with their own money; and he well knew that it would be difficult and expensive for them to submit a third time to this burden. It is well with the man who does not undergo so much in the world as this man knew he had suffered. He saw but one way; and that was to get off and escape if he could. He resolved upon this in the night-time, killed the peasant, and cut his foot off after killing him, and set off to the forest with the chain upon his leg. Now when the people knew this, soon after daylight in the morning, they pursued him with two dogs accustomed to trace any one who escaped, and to find him in the forest however carefully he might be concealed. They got him into their hands and beat him, and did him all kinds of mischief; and dragging him home, left barely alive, and showed him no mercy. They tortured him severely; put him in a dark room, in which there lay already sixteen Christian men; and bound him both with iron and other tyings, as fast as they could. Then he began to think that the misery and pain he had endured before were but shadows to his present sufferings. He saw no man before his eyes in this prison who would beg for mercy for him; no one had compassion on his wretchedness, except the Christian men who lay bound with him, who sorrowed with him, and bemoaned his fate together with their own misfortunes and helplessness. One day they advised him to make a vow to the holy King Olaf, to devote himself to some office in his sacred house, if he, by God's compassion and Saint Olaf's prayers could get away from this prison. He gladly agreed to this, and made a vow and prepared himself for the situation they mentioned to him. The night after he thought in his sleep that he saw a man, not tall, standing at his side, who spoke to him thus, "Here, thou wretched man, why dost thou not get up?"

He replied, "Sir, who are you?"

"I am King Olaf, on whom thou hast called."

"Oh, my good lord! gladly would I raise myself; but I lie bound with iron and with chains on my legs, and also the other men who lie here."

Thereupon the king accosts him with the words, "Stand up at once and be not afraid; for thou art loose."

He awoke immediately, and told his comrades what, had appeared to him in his dream. They told him to stand up, and try if it was true. He stood up, and observed that he was loose. Now said his fellow-prisoners, this would help him but little, for the door was locked both on the inside and on the outside. Then an old man who sat there in a deplorable condition put in his word, and told him not to doubt the mercy of the man who had loosened his chains; "For he has wrought this miracle on thee that thou shouldst enjoy his mercy, and hereafter be free, without suffering more misery and torture. Make haste, then, and seek the door; and if thou are able to slip out, thou art saved."

He did so, found the door open, slipped out, and away to the forest. As soon as the Vindland people were aware of this they set loose the dogs, and pursued him in great haste; and the poor man lay hid, and saw well where they were following him. But now the hounds lost the trace when they came nearer, and all the eyes that sought him were struck with a blindness, so that nobody could find him, although he lay before their feet; and they all returned home, vexed that they could not find him. King Olaf did not permit this man's destruction after he had reached the forest, and restored him also to his health and hearing; for they had so long tortured and beaten him that he had become deaf. At last he came on board of a ship, with two other Christian men who had been long afflicted in that country. All of them worked zealously in this vessel, and so had a successful flight. Then he repaired to the holy man's house, strong and fit to bear arms. Now he was vexed at his vow, went from his promise to the holy king, ran away one day, and came in the evening to a bonde who gave him lodging for God's sake. Then in the night he saw three girls coming to him; and handsome and nobly dressed were they. They spoke to him directly, and sharply reprimanded him for having been so bold as to run from the good king who had shown so much compassion to him, first in freeing him from his irons, and then from the prison; and yet he had deserted the mild master into whose service he had entered. Then he awoke full of terror, got up early, and told the housefather his dream. The good man had nothing so earnest in life as to send him-back to the holy place. This miracle was first written down by a man who himself saw the man, and the marks of the chains upon his body.

40. KING SIGURD MARRIES CECILIA.

In the last period of King Sigurd's life, his new and extraordinary resolution was whispered about, that he would be divorced from his queen, and would take Cecilia, who was a great man's daughter, to wife. He ordered accordingly a great feast to be prepared, and intended to hold his wedding with her in Bergen. Now when Bishop Magne heard this, he was very sorry; and one day the bishop goes to the king's hall, and with him a priest called Sigurd, who was afterwards bishop of Bergen. When they came to the king's hall, the bishop sent the king a message that he would like to meet him; and asked the king to come out to him. He did so, and came out with a drawn sword in his hand. He received the bishop kindly and asked him to go in and sit down to table with him.

The bishop replies, "I have other business now. Is it true, sire, what is told me, that thou hast the intention of marrying, and of driving away thy queen, and taking another wife?"

The king said it was true.

Then the bishop changed countenance, and angrily replied, "How can it come into your mind, sire, to do such an act in our bishopric as to betray God's word and law, and the holy church? It surprises me that you treat with such contempt our episcopal office, and your own royal office. I will now do what is my duty; and in the name of God, of the holy King Olaf, of Peter the apostle, and of the other saints, forbid thee this wickedness."

While he thus spoke he stood straight up, as if stretching out his neck to the blow, as if ready if the king chose to let the sword fall; and the priest Sigurd, who afterwards was bishop, has declared that the sky appeared to him no bigger than a calf's skin, so frightful did the appearance of the king present itself to him. The king returned to the hall, however, without saying a word; and the bishop went to his house and home so cheerful and gay that he laughed, and saluted every child on his way, and was playing with his fingers. Then the priest Sigurd asked him the reason, saying, "Why are you so cheerful, sir? Do you not consider that the king may be exasperated against you? and would it not be better to get out of the way?"

Then said the bishop, "It appears to me more likely that he will not act so; and besides, what death could be better, or more desirable, than to leave life for the honour of God? or to die for the holy cause of Christianity and our own office, by preventing that which is not right? I am so cheerful because I have done what I ought to do."

There was much noise in the town about this. The king got ready for a journey, and took with him corn, malt and honey. He went south to Stavanger, and prepared a feast there for his marriage with Cecilia. When a bishop who ruled there heard of this he went to the king, and asked if it were true that he intended to marry in the lifetime of the queen.

The king said it was so.

The bishop answers, "If it be so, sire, you must know how much such a thing is forbidden to inferior persons. Now it appears as if you thought it was allowable for you, because you have great power, and that it is proper for you, although it is against right and propriety; but I do not know how you will do it in our bishopric, dishonouring thereby God's command, the holy Church, and our episcopal authority. But you must bestow a great amount of gifts and estates on this foundation, and thereby pay the mulct due to God and to us for such transgression."

Then said the king, "Take what thou wilt of our possessions. Thou art far more reasonable than Bishop Magne."

Then the king went away, as well pleased with this bishop as ill pleased with him who had laid a prohibition on him. Thereafter the king married the girl, and loved her tenderly.

41. IMPROVEMENT OF KONUNGAHELLA.

King Sigurd improved the town of Konungahella so much, that there was not a greater town in Norway at the time, and he remained there long for the defence of the frontiers. He built a king's house in the castle, and imposed a duty on all the districts in the neighbourhood of the town, as well as on the townspeople, that every person of nine years of age and upwards should bring to the castle five missile stones for weapons, or as many large stakes sharp at one end and five ells long. In the castle the king built a cross-church of timber, and carefully put together, as far as regards the wood and other materials. The cross-church was consecrated in the 24th year of King Sigurd's reign (A.D. 1127). Here the king deposited the piece of the holy cross, and many other holy relics. It was called the castle church; and before the high altar he placed the tables he had got made in the Greek country, which were of copper and silver, all gilt, and beautifully adorned with jewels. Here was also the shrine which the Danish king Eirik Eimune had sent to King Sigurd; and the altar book, written with gold letters, which the patriarch had presented to King Sigurd.

42. KING SIGURD'S DEATH.

Three years after the consecration of the cross-church, when King Sigurd was stopping at Viken, he fell sick (A.D. 1130). He died the night before Mary's-mass (August 15), and was buried in Halvard's church, where he was laid in the stone wall without the choir on the south side. His son Magnus was in the town at the time and took possession of the whole of the king's treasury when King Sigurd died. Sigurd had been king of Norway twenty-seven years (A.D. 1104-1130), and was forty years of age when he died. The time of his reign was good for the country; for there was peace, and crops were good.

King Alfred's Viking by Charles W. Whistler

A Story of the First English Fleet

Preface

The general details and course of events given in this story are, so far as regards the private life and doings of King Alfred, from his life as written by his chaplain, Asser. One or two further incidents of the Athelney period are from the later chroniclers--notably the sign given by St. Cuthberht--as are also the names of the herdsman and the nobles in hiding in the fen.

That Alfred put his first fleet into the charge of "certain Vikings" is well known, though the name of their chief is not given. These Vikings would certainly be Norse, either detached from the following of Rolf Ganger, who wintered in England in 875 A.D. the year before his descent on Normandy; or else independent rovers who, like Rolf, had been driven from Norway by the high-handed methods of Harald Fairhair. Indeed, the time when a Norse contingent was not present with the English forces, from this period till at least that of the battle of Brunanburh in 947 A.D. would probably be an exception.

There are, therefore, good historic grounds for the position given to the hero of the story as leader of the newly-formed fleet. The details of the burning of his supposed father's hall, and of the Orkney period, are from the Sagas.

Much controversy has raged over the sites of Ethandune and the landing place of Hubba at Kynwith Castle, owing probably to the duplication of names in the district where the last campaign took place. The story, therefore, follows the identifications given by the late Bishop Clifford in "The Transactions of the Somerset Archaeological Society" for 1875 and other years, as, both from topographic and strategic points of view, no other coherent identification seems possible.

The earthworks of the Danish position still remain on Edington hill, that looks out from the Polden range over all the country of Alfred's last refuge, and the bones of Hubba's men lie everywhere under the turf where they made their last stand under the old walls and earthworks of Combwich fort; and a lingering tradition yet records the extermination of a Danish force in the neighbourhood. Athelney needs but the cessation of today's drainage to revert in a very few years to what it was in Alfred's time--an island, alder covered, barely rising from fen and mere, and it needs but little imagination to reproduce what Alfred saw when, from the same point where one must needs be standing, he planned the final stroke that his people believed was inspired directly from above.

It would seem evident from Alfred's method with Guthrum that he realized that this king was but one among many leaders, and not directly responsible for the breaking of the solemn peace sworn at Exeter and Wareham. His position as King of East Anglia has gained him an ill reputation in the pages of the later chronicles; but neither Asser nor the Anglo-Saxon Chronicle--our best authorities--blames him as they, for his contemporaries knew him to be but a "host king," with no authority over newcomers or those who did not choose to own allegiance to him.

Save in a few cases, where the original spelling preserves a lost pronunciation, as in the first syllable of "Eadmund," the modern and familiar forms of the names have been used in preference to the constantly-varying forms given by the chroniclers. Bridgwater has no Saxon equivalent, the town being known only as "The Bridge" since the time when the Romans first fortified this one crossing place of the Parret; and the name of the castle before which Hubba fell varies from Cynuit through Kynwith to Kynwich, whose equivalent the Combwich of today is. Guthrum's name is given in many forms, from Gytro to Godramnus. Nor has it been thought worth while to retain the original spelling AElfred, the ae diphthong having been appropriated by us to an entirely new sound; while our own pronunciation of the name slightly broadened as yet in Wessex, is correct enough.

The exact relationship of St. Neot to Alfred, beyond that he was a close kinsman, is very doubtful. He has been identified with a brother, Athelstan of East Anglia, who is known to have retired to Glastonbury; but there is no more than conjecture, and I have been content with "cousinship."

CHAPTER I
The Seeking of Sword Helmbiter

Men call me "King Alfred's Viking," and I think that I may be proud of that name; for surely to be trusted by such a king is honour enough for any man, whether freeman or thrall, noble or churl. Maybe I had rather be called by that name than by that which was mine when I came to England, though it was a good title enough that men gave me, if it meant less than it seemed. For being the son of Vemund, king of Southmereland in Norway, I was hailed as king when first I took command of a ship of my own. Sea king, therefore, was I, Ranald Vemundsson, but my kingdom was but over ship and men, the circle of wide sea round me was nought that I could rule over, if I might seem to conquer the waves by the kingship of good seaman's craft.

One may ask how I came to lose my father's kingdom, which should have been mine, and at last to be content with a simple English earldom; or how it was that a viking could be useful to Alfred, the wise king. So I will tell the first at once, and the rest may be learned from what comes after.

If one speaks to me of Norway, straightway into my mind comes the remembrance of the glare of a burning hall, of the shouts of savage warriors, and of the cries of the womenfolk, among whom I, a ten-year-old boy, was when Harald Fairhair sent the great Jarl Rognvald and his men to make an end of Vemund, my father. For Harald had sworn a great oath to subdue all the lesser kings in the land and rule there alone, like Gorm in Denmark and Eirik in Sweden. So my father's turn came, and as he feasted with his ninety stout courtmen, the jarl landed under cover of the dark and fell on him, surrounding the house and firing it. Then was fierce fighting as my father and his men sallied again and again from the doors and were driven back, until the high roof fell in and there was a sudden silence, and an end.

Then in the silence came my mother's voice from where she stood on the balcony of the living house across the garth. I mind that she neither wept nor shrieked as did the women round her, and her voice was clear and strong over the roaring of the flames. I mind, too, the flash of helms and armour as every man turned to look on her who spoke.

"Coward and nidring art thou, Rognvald, who dared not meet Vemund, my husband, in open field, but must slay him thus. Ill may all things go with thee, till thou knowest what a burning hall is like for thyself. I rede thee to the open hillside ever, rather than come beneath a roof; for as thou hast wrought this night, so shall others do to thee."

Then rose a growl of wrath from Rognvald's men, but the great Jarl bade them cease, and harm none in all the place. So he went down to his ships with no more words and men said that he was ill at ease and little content, for he had lost as many men as he had slain, so stoutly fought my father and our courtmen, and had earned a curse, moreover, which would make his nights uneasy for long enough.

Then as he went my mother bade me look well at him, that in days to come I might know on whom to avenge my father's death. After that she went to her own lands in the south, for she was a jarl's daughter, and very rich.

Not long thereafter Harald Fairhair won all the land, and then began the trouble of ruling it; and men began to leave Norway because of the new laws, which seemed hard on them, though they were good enough.

Now two of Jarl Rognvald's sons had been good friends of my father before these troubles began, and one, Sigurd, had been lord over the Orkney Islands, and had died there. The other, Jarl Einar, fell out with Rognvald, his father, and we heard that he would take to the viking path, and go to the Orkneys, to win back the jarldom that Sigurd's death had left as a prey to masterless men and pirates of all sorts. So my mother took me to him, and asked him for the sake of old friendship to give me a place in his ship; for I was fourteen now, and well able to handle weapons, being strong and tall for my age, as were many of the sons of the old kingly stocks.

So Einar took me, having had no part in his father's doings towards us, and hating them moreover. He promised to do all that he might towards making a good warrior and seaman of me; and he was ever thereafter as a foster father to me, for my own had died in the hall with Vemund. It was his wish to make amends thus, if he could, for the loss his folk had caused me.

Of the next five years I need speak little, for in them I learned the viking's craft well. We won the Orkneys from those who held them, and my first fight was in Einar's ship, against two of the viking's vessels. After that we dwelt in Sigurd's great house in Kirkwall, and made many raids on the Sutherland and Caithness shores. I saw some hard fighting there, for the Scots are no babes at weapon play.

Then when I was nineteen, and a good leader, as they said, the words that my mother spoke to Jarl Rognvald came true, and he died even as he had slain my father.

For Halfdan and Gudrod, Harald Fairhair's sons, deeming that the Jarl stood in their way to power in Norway, burned him in his hall by night, and so my feud was at an end. But the king would in nowise forgive his sons for the slaying of his friend, and outlawed them. Whereon Halfdan came and fell on us in the Orkneys; and that was unlucky for him, for we beat him, and Jarl Einar avenged on him his father's death.

Now through this it came to pass that I saw Norway for the last time, for I went thither in Einar's best ship to learn if Harald meant to make the Orkneys pay for the death of his son--which was likely, for a son is a son even though he be an outlaw.

So I came to my mother's place first of all, and full of joy and pleasant thoughts was I as we sailed into the well-remembered fiord to seek the little town at its head. And when we came there, nought but bitterest sorrow and wrath was ours; for the town was a black heap of ruin, and the few men who were left showed me where the kindly hands of the hill folk had laid my mother, the queen, in a little mound, after the Danish vikings, who had fallen suddenly on the place with fire and sword, had gone. They had grown thus bold because the great jarl was dead, and the king's sons had left the land without defence.

There I swore vengeance for this on every viking of Danish race that I might fall in with; for I was wild with grief and rage, as one might suppose.

I set up a stone over the grave of my mother, graving runes thereon that should tell who she was and also who raised it; for I was skilled in the runic lore, having learned much from one of Einar's older men who had known my father.

Thereafter we cruised among the islands northwards until we learned that Harald was indeed upon us, and then I saw my last of Norway as we headed south again, and the last hilltop sank beneath the sea's rim astern of us. I did not know that so it would be at that time--it is well that one sees not far into things to come--but even now all my home seemed to be with Einar; and that also was not to last long, as things went. How that came about I must tell, for the end was that I came to Alfred the king.

When we came back to Kirkwall, I told the jarl all that I had done and learned; and grieved for me he was when he heard of my mother's death. Many things he said to me at that time which made him dearer to me. Then after a while he spoke of Harald, who, as it seemed, might come at any time.

"We cannot fight Norway," he said, "so we must even flit hence to the mainland and wait until Harald is tired of seeking us. It is in my mind that he seeks not so much for revenge as for payment of scatt from our islands. Now he has a reason for taking it by force. He will seek to fine us, and then make plans by which I shall hold the jarldom from him for yearly dues."

So he straightway called the Thing of all the Orkney folk, who loved him well, and put the matter before them; and they set to work and did his bidding, driving the cattle inland and scattering them, and making the town look as poor as they might.

Then in three days' time we sailed away laughing; for none but poor-looking traders were left, and no man would think that never had the Ork-neys been so rich as in Einar's time. And he bade them make peace with the king when he came, and told them that so all would be well, for Harald would lay no heavy weregild on so poor a place for his son's slaying.

Southward we went to Caithness, and so westward along the Suther-land coast; for we had taken no scatt there for this year, and Einar would use this cruise to do so, seeing that we must put to sea. We were not the first who had laid these shores under rule from the Orkneys, for Jarl Sigurd had conquered them, meeting his death at last in a Sutherland firth, after victory, in a strange way.

He fought with a Scottish chief named Melbrigda of the Tusks, and slew him, and bore back his head to the ships at his saddle bow. Then the great teeth of the chief swung against the jarl's leg and wounded it, and of that he died, and so was laid in a great mound at the head of the firth where his ships lay. After that, the Orkneys were a nest of evil vikings till we came.

So it had happened that, from the time when it was made over him, Jarl Sigurd's mound had been untended, for we ourselves had never been so far south as this firth before. Indeed, it had been so laid waste by Sigurd's men after his death that there was nought to go there for. But at this time we had reason for getting into some quiet, unsought place where we should not be likely to be heard of, for the king had over-many ships and men for us to meet. So after a week's cruising we put into that firth, and anchored in the shelter of its hills.

There is no man of all our following who will forget that day, because of what happened almost as soon as the anchor held. It was very hot that morning, and what breeze had been out in the open sea was kept from us now by the hills, so that for some miles we had rowed the ships up the winding reaches of the firth; and then, as we laid in the oars and the anchorage was reached, there crept from inland a dim haze over the sun, dimming the light, and making all things look strange among the mountains. Then the sounds of the ships seemed to echo loudly over the still water and when all the bustle of anchoring was over, the stillness seemed yet greater, for the men went to their meals, and for a while spoke little.

Einar and I sat on his after deck under the awning, and spoke in low voices, as if afraid to raise our tones.

"There is a thunderstorm about," I said.

"Ay--listen," the jarl answered.

Then I heard among the hills, far up the firth beyond us, a strange sound that seemed to draw nearer, like and yet unlike thunder, roaring and jarring ever closer to us, till it was all around us and beneath us everywhere, and our very hearts seemed to stop beating in wonder.

Then of a sudden the ship was smitten from under the keel with a heavy, soundless blow, and the waters of the firth ebbed and flowed fiercely about us; and then the sound passed on and down the firth swiftly and strangely as it had come, and left us rocking on the troubled waters that plashed and broke along the rocks of the shore, while the still, thick air seemed full of the screams of the terrified eagles and sea birds that had left them.

"Odin defend us!" the jarl said; "what is this?"

I shook my head, looking at him, and wondering if my face was white and scared as his and that of every man whom I could see.

Now we waited breathless for more to come, but all was quiet again. The birds went back to their eyries, and the troubled water was still. Then presently our fears passed enough to let us speak with one another; and then there were voices enough, for every man wished to hear his own again, that courage might return.

Then a man from the Orkneys who had been with Jarl Sigurd came aft to us, and stood at the break of the deck to speak with Einar.

"Jarl," he said, almost under his breath, "it is in my mind that Sigurd, your brother, is wroth because his mound has been untended since we made it."

Then Einar said:

"Was it so ill made that it needs tending?"

"It was well made, jarl; but rain and frost and sun on a new-made mound may have wrought harm to it. Or maybe he thinks that enough honour has not been paid him. He was a great warrior, jarl, and perhaps would have more sacrifice, and a remembrance cup drunk by his own brother at his grave."

Now this man's name was Thord, the same who taught me runes--a good seaman and leader of men, and one who was held to be wise in more matters than most folk. So his word was to be listened to.

"You know more of these matters than I, Thord," Einar answered. "Is it possible that Sigurd could work this?"

"Who knows what a dead chief of might cannot work?" Thord said. "I think it certain that Sigurd is angry for some reason; and little luck shall we have if we do not appease his spirit."

Then the jarl looked troubled, as well he might, for to go near the mound that held an angry ghost was no light matter. It lay far up the firth, Thord said, and the ships could not go so far. But Einar was very brave, and when he had thought for a little while he said:

"Well, then, I will take boat and go to Sigurd's mound and see if he ails aught. Will any man come with me, however?"

I liked not the errand, as may be supposed, but I could not leave my foster father to go alone.

"I will be with you," I said. "Will not Thord come also?"

"Ay," the grim Orkney man answered.

Now all our crew were listening to us, and I looked down the long gangways by chance, and when I did so no man would meet my eye. They feared lest they should be made to go to this haunted place, as it seemed--all but one man, who sat on the mast step swinging his feet. This was Kolgrim the Tall, the captain of the fore deck, a young man and of few words, but a terrible swordsman, and knowing much of sea craft. And when this man saw that I looked at him, he nodded a little and smiled, for he had been a friend of mine since I had first come to Einar.

"Two men to row the boat will be enough, jarl," I said. "Kolgrim yonder will come with us."

"Well," the jarl answered, "maybe four of us are enough. We shall not fright Sigurd with more, and maybe would find it hard to get them to come."

So he called Kolgrim, and he said that he would go with us, and went to get the boat alongside without more words.

Then the jarl and I and Thord armed ourselves--for a warrior should be met by warriors. The men were very silent, whispering among themselves, until the jarl was ready and spoke to them.

"Have no fear for us," he said. "Doubtless my brother needs somewhat, and calls me. I am going to find out what it is and return."

So we pushed off, Thord and Kolgrim rowing. It was strange to look back, as we went, on the ships, for not a soul stirred on board them, as it seemed, so intently were we watched; and the water was like a sheet of steel under them, so that they were doubled.

Presently they were hidden as we rounded a turn in the firth, and we were alone among the hills, and the lonesomeness was very great. There was no dwelling anywhere along the shores, nor in the deep glens that came down to them, each with its noisy burn falling along it. Once I saw deer feeding far up at the head of a valley that opened out, but they and the eagles were the only living things we could see beside the loons that swam and dived silently as we neared them.

The silence and the heat weighed on us, and we went for a mile or more without a word. Then we turned into the last reach of the water, and saw Sigurd's mound beside its edge at the very head of the firth, where the hills came round in a circle that was broken only by the narrow waters and the valley that went beyond them among the mountains. It was a fitting resting place for one who would sleep in loneliness; but I thought that I had rather lie where I could look out on the sea I loved, and see the long ships pass and the white waves break beneath me.

Now all seemed very peaceful here in the hot haze that brooded over the still mountains, and there seemed to be nought to fear. We drew swiftly up to the mound, with the plash of oars only to break the silence, and there was nought amiss that we could see. They had made it on a little flat tongue of land that jutted from the mountain's foot into the deep water, so that on two sides the mound was close to its edge. So we pulled on softly round the tongue of land, being maybe about fifty paces from the mound across the water. And when we saw the other side of Sigurd's resting place, the oars stayed suddenly, and the jarl, who held the tiller, swung the boat away from the shore, and I think I knew then what fear was.

The mound was open. There was a wide, brown scar, as of freshly-moved earth, across its base, reaching from the level to six or eight feet of its height, as though half the grass-grown side had been shorn away by a sword cut; and in the midst of that scar was a doorway, open to the grave's heart, low and stone built. Some of the earth that had fallen lay before it on the water's edge, but the rest was doubtless in the water, for there was but a narrow path between bank and mound.

At that sight we stared, thinking we should surely see the grim form of Sigurd loom gigantic and troll-like across the doorway; and the jarl half rose from his seat beside me, and cried out with a great voice:

"Sigurd--my brother!"

I think he knew not what or why he cried thus, for he sank back into his place and swayed against me, while his cry rang loud among the hills, and the eagles answered it.

And I grasped my sword hilt, as one does in some sudden terror, staring at the open mound; while old Thord muttered spells against I know not what, and Kolgrim looked at me, pale and motionless.

Then came the sharp, mocking cry of a diver, that rang strangely; and at once, without order, Thord dug his oar blade into the water and swung the boat round, and when once Kolgrim's back was towards that he feared, he held water strongly and then the boat was about, and we were flying from the place towards the ships, before we knew what was being done, panic stricken.

But Einar said never a word, and the two rowers slackened their pace only when the bend of the firth hid the mound from our sight.

Then said I, finding that Einar spoke not:

"What are we flying from? there was nought to harm us."

For I began to be ashamed. Thereat Kolgrim stopped rowing, and Thord must needs do likewise, though he said:

"It is ill for us to stay here. The dead jarl is very wroth."

"I saw nought to fray us; the cry we heard was but that of a loon."

But Thord shook his head. The silence of the place had made all things seem strange, with the dull light that was over us, and the great heat among the towering hills.

"The mound was freshly opened," he said. "I saw earth crumbling even yet from the broken side. The blow we felt was that which Sigurd struck when he broke free."

Then at last Einar spoke, and his voice was strange:

"I have left my brother unhonoured, and he is angry. What must be done?"

Now I cannot tell what hardiness took hold of me, but it seemed that I must needs go back and see more of this. I was drawn to do so, as a thing they fear will make some men long to face it and know its worst, not as if they dared so much as when they must.

"I think we should have waited to ask Sigurd that," I said; and Einar looked strangely at me.

"Would you have us return?" he asked.

"Why not?" said I. "If the great jarl has called us as it seems, needs must that we know what he wills."

Then said Thord:

"I helped to lay him in that place, and I mind how he looked at that time. Somewhat we left undone, doubtless. I dare not go back."

Einar looked at the hills, leaning his chin on his hand, and said slowly, when Thord had done:

"That is the first time Thord has said 'I dare not.' Now I would that I had stayed to fight Harald and fall under his sword before. I too must say the same. I have left my brother unhonoured, and I dare not go back."

Pale and drawn the jarl's face was, and I knew he meant what he said. Nevertheless it seemed to me that some one must know what Sigurd willed.

"Jarl Einar," I said, "this is a strange business, and one cannot tell what it means. Now Sigurd was my father's close friend, and I have had nought to do with him. I will go back, therefore, and learn what I can of him. I think he will not harm me, for he has no reason to do so. Moreover if he does, none will learn what he needs."

"I have heard," said Thord, "that a good warrior may ask what he will of a dead hero, so that he shows no fear and is a friend. If his courage fails, however, then he will be surely destroyed."

Then I said:

"I have no cause to fear Sigurd, save that he is a ghost. I do not know if I fear him as such; that is to be seen."

Now Einar laid his hand on mine and spoke gravely:

"I think it is a hero's part to do what you say. If you go back and return in safety, the scalds will sing of you for many a long day. Go, therefore, boldly; this is not a matter from which you should be held back, as it has come into your mind."

Then said Thord:

"It will be well to ask Sigurd for a token whereby we may know that he sends messages by you."

And Einar said on that:

"In Sigurd's hand is his sword Helmbiter. I think he will give that to the man who dares speak to him, for he will know that it goes into brave hands. Ask him for it bravely."

"Put me ashore, therefore, before my courage goes," I said; and they pulled the boat to the bank where I could step on a rock and so to shore. And when I was there, Kolgrim rose up and followed me without a word.

"Bide here for two hours, jarl, and maybe I will return in that time," I said. "Farewell."

So I turned away as they answered me, thinking that Kolgrim held the boat's painter. But he came after me, and I spoke to him:

"Why, Kolgrim, will you come also?"

"You shall not go alone, Ranald the king's son; I will come with you as far as I dare."

"That is well," I answered, and with that wasted no more words, but climbed the hillside a little, and then went steadily towards where the mound was, with Kolgrim close at my shoulder, and the jarl and Thord looking fixedly after us till we were out of sight.

CHAPTER II
The Gifts of Two Heroes

I will not say that my steps did not falter when we came to whence we could see the mound. But it was lonely and still and silent; no shape of warrior waited our coming.

"Almost do I fear to go nearer," said Kolgrim.

"Put fear away, comrade," said I; "we shall fare ill if we turn our backs now."

"Where you go I go," he answered, "though I am afraid."

"The next best thing to not being afraid is to be afraid and not to show it," I said then, comforting myself also with a show of wisdom at least. "Maybe fear is the worst thing we have to face."

So we went on more swiftly, and at last were on the tongue of land on the tip of which the mound stood. Still, since we could not see the open doorway, which was towards the water, the place seemed not so terrible. Yet I thought that by this time we should have seen Sigurd, or maybe heard his voice from the tomb. So now I dared to call softly:

"Jarl Sigurd, here is one, a friend's son, who will learn what you will."

My voice seemed to fill all the ring of mountains with echoes, but there was no answer. All was still again when the last voice came back from the hillsides.

Then I went nearer yet, and passed to the waterside, where I could look slantwise across the doorway. And again I called, and waited for an answer that did not come.

"It seems that I must go even to the door, and maybe into the mound," I said, whispering.

"Not inside," said Kolgrim, taking hold of my arm.

But I had grown bolder with the thought that the hero seemed not angry, and now I had set my heart on winning the sword of which the jarl had told me, and I thought that I dared go even inside the tomb to speak with Sigurd.

"Bide here, and I will go at least to the door," said I.

So I stepped boldly before it, standing on the heap of newly-fallen earth that had slipped from across it. The posts and lintel of the door were of stone slabs such as lay everywhere on the hillsides, and I stood so close that I could touch them. The doorway was not so high that I could see into it without stooping, for it was partly choked with the fallen earth, and I bent to look in. But I could only see for a few feet into the passage, as I looked from light to darkness.

"Ho, Jarl Sigurd! what would you? Why have you opened your door thus?"

Very hollow my voice sounded, and that was all.

"Sigurd of Orkney--Sigurd, son of Rognvald--I am the son of Vemund your friend. Speak to me!"

There was no answer. A bit of earth crumbled from the broken side of the mound and made me start, but I saw nothing. So I stepped away from the door and back to my comrade, who had edged nearer the place, though his face showed that he feared greatly.

"I think that the mound has been rifled," I said. "Sigurd would have us know it and take revenge."

"No man has dared to go near that doorway till you came, Ranald Vemundsson," Kolgrim answered. "Now I fear that he plans to lure you into the mound, and slay you there without light to help you. Go no further, maybe you will be closed up with the ghost."

That was not pleasant to think of, but I had seen nought to make me fear to go in. There was no such unearthly light shining within the mound as I had heard of in many tales of those who sought to speak with dead chiefs.

"Well, I am going in," I said stoutly; "but do you hide here, and make some noise that I may know you are near me. It is the silence that frays me.

"What can I do?" he said. "I know no runes that are of avail. It would be ill to disturb this place with idle sounds."

That seemed right, but I thought I could not bear the silence--silence of the grave. I must know that he was close at hand. Then a thought came to me, and I unfastened the silver-mounted whetstone that hung from my belt and gave it him.

"Whet your sword edge sharply," I said. "That is a sound a hero loves, for it speaks of deeds to be done."

"Ay, that is no idle sound," he said, and drew his sword gladly. The haft of the well-known blade brought the light into his eyes again. I drew my own sword also.

"If you need me, call, and I think I shall not fail you," he whispered. "It shall not be said that I failed you in peril."

"I know it," I answered, putting my hand on his shoulder.

Then I went boldly, and stepped into the passage. The whetstone sang shrill on the sword edge as it kissed the steel behind me, and the sound was good to hear as I went into darkness with my weapon ready.

I half feared that my first step would be my last, but it was made in safety. Very black seemed the low stone-walled passage before me, and I had to stoop as I went on, feeling with my left hand along the wall. The way was so narrow that little light could pass my body, and therefore it seemed to grow darker as I went deeper into the mound's heart.

Five steps I took, and then my outstretched hand was on the post that ended the passage, and beyond that I felt nothing. I had come to the inner doorway, and before me was the place where Sigurd lay. Yet no fiery eyes glared on me, and nothing stirred. The air was heavy with a scent as of peat, and the sound of the whetstone seemed loud as I stood peering into the darkness.

I moved forward, and somewhat rattled under my foot, and I started. Then my fear left me altogether, for I had trodden on dry bones, and shuddered at the first touch of them in that place. I had faced fear, and had overcome it; maybe it was desperation that made me cool then, for it was certain now that I must be slain or else victor over I knew not what.

So I took one pace forward into the chamber, and stood aside from the doorway; and the grey light from the passage came in and filled all the place, so that it fell first on him whom I had come to seek--Jarl Sigurd of Orkney.

And when I saw, a great awe fell upon me, and a sadness, but no terror; and in my heart I would that hereafter I might rest as slept the hero where the hands that had loved him had placed him.

Into the silent place came once more with me the clank of mail and weapons that he had loved, and from without the song of the keen sword edge whispered to him; but these could not wake him. Peacefully he seemed to sleep as I stood by his side, and I thought that I should take back no word of his to the jarl, his brother, whom both he and I loved.

They had brought the great carven chair on which he was wont to sit on his ship's quarterdeck, and thereon had set the jarl, as though he yet lived, and did but sleep as he sat from weariness after fight, with helm and mail upon him. Shield and axe rested on either side of him, ready to hand, against the chair; and behind him, along the wall, were his spears, ashen shafted and rune graven.

His blue, fur-trimmed cloak was round him, and before him was a little table, heavy and carved, whereon were vessels for food, empty now save for dust that showed that they had been full. And across his knees was his sword, golden hilted, with a great yellow cairngorm in the pommel, and with gold-wrought patterns from end to end of the scabbard--such a sword as I had never seen before. His right hand held the hilt, and his left rested on the shield's rim beside him; and so Sigurd slept with his head bowed on his breast, waiting for Ragnaroek and the last great fight of all.

The light seemed to grow stronger as I looked, or my eyes grew used to it, and then I saw that the narrow chamber was full of things, though I minded them afterwards, for now I was as in a dream, noting only the jarl himself. Costly stuffs were on the floor, and mail and helms and more weapons. Gold work there was also, and in one corner lay the dried-up body of a great wolf hound, coiled as in sleep where it had been chained. Another had been tied by the passage doorway, where I had stepped on it; and below a spar that stood across a corner lay a tumbled heap of feathers that had been a falcon.

Many more things there were maybe, but this I saw at last--that the jarl's right foot rested on the skull of a man whose teeth had been long and tusk-like. It was the head of the Scot whose teeth had been his death.

Now the sword drew my eyes, for Einar bade me ask for it, else I think I had gone softly hence without a word, so peaceful seemed the dead. And as I looked again, I saw that the hand holding the hilt was dry and brown and shrunken, so that one might see all the bones through the skin, and at first I was afraid to ask.

At last I said, and my mouth was dry:

"Jarl Einar, your brother, bids me ask for sword Helmbiter, great Sigurd. Let me take it, that he may know how you rest in peace."

But Sigurd stirred not nor spoke; and slowly I put out my hand on the sword to take it very gently, but his grasp was yet firm on it. Then, as I bent to see if it had tightened when I would draw the sword away, I could see beneath the helm the face of the dead, shrunken indeed and brown, but as of one at rest and beyond anger.

Once more then I took the jarl's sword in my right hand, and raised his hand with my left, putting my own weapon by against the wall. And then the hilt slipped from the half-open fingers, and the sword was mine, and my hand held the jarl's. And it seemed to me that he gave it me, and that I must thank him for such a gift. The sword though it was sheathed, was not girt to him, and its golden-studded belt was twisted about it, and it was no imperfect giving.

So I spoke in a low voice:

"Jarl Sigurd, I thank you. If my might is aught, the sword will be used as you would have used it. Surely I will say to Einar that you rest in peace, and we will come here and close your mound again in all honour."

I set back his hand then, and it seemed empty and helpless, not as a warrior's should be. So I ungirt my own weapon--a good plain sword that I had won from a viking in Caithness--and laid it in the place of that he had given me. And as I put the thin fingers on its hilt, almost thinking that they would chose around it, a ring slipped from them into my hand, as if he would give that also, and I kept it therefore.

Then for a minute I stood before Jarl Sigurd, waiting to see if he had any word; but when he spoke not, I lifted the sword and saluted him.

"Skoal to Jarl Sigurd; rest in peace, and farewell."

Then I went forth softly, and came out into sunshine; for the wind was singing round the hilltops, and the dun mist had gone. Then I was ware that the sound of the stone on the sword edge had long ceased, and I looked for Kolgrim.

He was lying on the grass in the place where I had left him, but he was on his face, and the sword and whetstone were flung aside from him. At first I feared that he had been in some way slain because of his terror; but when I came near, I saw that his shoulders heaved as if he wept. Then I stood over him, treading softly.

"Kolgrim," I said.

At that he looked up, and a great light came into his face, and he sprang to his feet and threw his arms round me, weeping, yet with a strong man's weeping that does but come from bitter grief.

"Master," he cried, "O master I thought you lost--and I dared not follow you."

"I have met with no peril," I said, "nor have I been long gone."

"More than two hours, master, have you been in that place--two long hours. See how the sun has sunk since you left me!"

So indeed it seemed, though I knew not that I had been so long. I had stayed still and gazed on that strange sight without stirring for what seemed but a little while. Yet I had thought long thoughts in that time, and I mind every single thing in that dim chamber, even to the markings on the stones that made its walls and roof and floor.

"See," I said, "Jarl Sigurd has given me the sword!"

Kolgrim gazed in wonder. There was no speck of dust on the broad blade as I drew it, and the waving lines of the dwarf-wrought steel and gold-inlaid runes were clear and bright along its middle for half its length. For the mound was very dry, and they had covered all the chamber with peat before piling the earth over it.

"Let us go back to Jarl Einar; he will fear for us," I said, sheathing the sword and girding it to me.

So we went across the meadow, and even as we went a blast of cold wind came from, over the mountains, and with it whirled the black thunder-clouds of the storm that had been gathering all day. We ran to an overhanging rock on the hillside and crept beneath it, while the thunder crashed and the lightning struck from side to side of the firth, and smote the wind-swept water that was white with foam.

"Master," said Kolgrim, "the Jarl Sigurd is wroth; he repents the sword gift."

But I did not think that he had aught to do with this. For, as any hill-bred man could tell, the storm had been brewing in the heat, and was bound to come, and would pass to and fro among the hills till it was worn out.

Nevertheless, when it passed away in pouring rain that swept like a hanging sheet of moving mist down the glens from the half-hidden mountains, and the sun shone out brightly again over the clear-cut purple hillsides and rippling water, I looked at the mound in wonder. For it was closed. We had sought shelter in a place near that whence we saw the mound in coming, and could see the fallen side, though not the doorway, looking across its front. And now the slope of the bank seemed to have been made afresh, as on the day when Sigurd had been closed in, years ago. None could say, save those who had seen it, where the opening into the grave-chamber might be.

Now both the opening and closing of Sigurd's grave mound seem very strange to me. Thord and the scalds will have it that he himself wrought both. As for me, I know not. In after days I told this to Alfred the king when he wondered at my sword, and he said that he thought an earthquake opened and washing rain closed the mound, but that it happened strangely for me. I cannot gainsay his wise words, and I will leave the matter so.

Thereafter Kolgrim and I went back to Einar, who yet waited for us. Glad was he to see us return in safety; but both he and Thord were speechless when they saw the jarl's sword girt to me and the jarl's golden ring on my hand. Neither they nor any one else will believe that I met with no peril; and the tale that the scalds made hereafter of the matter is over wonderful, in spite of all I may say. For they think it but right that I should not be over boastful of my deeds.

But Jarl Einar looked on sword and ring, and said:

"Well have you won these gifts. My brother is in peace in his resting place now. I hold that he called for you."

So we went back to the ships, and there for many days the men stared at Kolgrim and me strangely. They say I was very silent for long, and it is likely enough. Moreover, Einar was wont to say that I seemed five years older from that day forward.

We went no more to the place of the mound, for it seemed to need no care of earthly hands. Nor were any wishing to go to so awesome a place, and we left the firth next day, for the men waxed uneasy there.

But on that day Einar gave me the great ship that we had taken from Halfdan, the king's son, saying that he would add to Sigurd's giving. Also he bade me choose what men I would for her crew, bidding me thank him not at all, for I was his foster son, and a king by birth moreover.

So when I knew that this would please him, I chose Thord for my shipmaster, and Kolgrim for marshal, as we call the one who has charge of the ordering of the crew. And I chose a hundred good men whom I knew well, so that indeed I had the best ship and following in Norway, as I thought. At least there were none better, unless Harald Fairhair might match me.

Now there was one thing that pleased me not at this time, and that was that Kolgrim, my comrade, never called me aught but "master" since I came from Sigurd's presence--which is not the wont of our free Norsemen with any man. Nor would he change it, though I was angry, until I grew used to it in time.

"Call me not 'master,' Kolgrim, my comrade," I said; "it is unfittinq for you."

At last he answered me in such wise that I knew it was of no more use to speak of it.

"Master of mine you are, Ranald the king, since the day when you dared more than I thought man might, while I lay like a beaten hound outside, and dared not go within that place to see what had become of you. Little comradeship was mine to you on that day, and I am minded to make amends if I can. I think I may dare aught against living men for you, though I failed at that mound. I will give life for you, if I may."

I told him that what he had done was well done, and indeed he had had courage to go where none else had dared; for I had ties of friendship that made me bold to meet Jarl Sigurd, and might go therefore where he might not. It was well that he did not come into the presence of the dead.

"Therefore we are comrades, not master and man," I said.

"Nay, but master and man--lord and thrall," he answered.

So I must let him have his way, but he could not make me think of him as aught but a good and brave comrade whom I loved well.

They hailed me as king when I went on board my ship for the first time with my own men, as I have said. Then our best weapon smith asked for gold from the men, and they gave what they had--it was in plenty with us of Einar's following--and made a golden circlet round my helm, that they might see it and follow it in battle.

It was good to wear the crown thus given willingly, but in the end it sent me from north to south, as will be seen. That, however, is a matter with which I will not quarrel, for it sent me to Alfred the king.

We had left the firth two days, cruising slowly northward, when one ship came from the north and met us, not flying from our fleet, but bearing up to join us. And when she was close, there came a hail to tell Einar that she bore a messenger from Harald the king in peace, and presently we hove to while this messenger went on board the Jarl's ship.

Then it seemed that Einar had been right, and that Harald would lay a fine on the islands for Halfdan's slaying, and so give them back to Einar to hold for him. The messenger was Thiodolf, Harald's own scald, and he put the matter very plainly before the jarl, so that he thought well of the offer, but would nevertheless not trust himself in the king's power before all was certain, and confirmed by oath. Whereon Thiodolf said that one must see the king on the Jarl's part, and so I seemed the right man to go, as the jarl's foster son and next in command to him.

"Nevertheless," said Thiodolf, "I would not advise you to sail in Halfdan's ship, for that might wake angry thoughts, and trouble would come especially as Halfdan took her without leave when he was outlawed."

So I took the Jarl's cutter, manning her with enough men of my own crew; and Kolgrim came with me, and we sailed to Kirkwall in company with Thiodolf the scald.

Then when Thiodolf took me into his presence, I saw Harald Fairhair for the first time, as he sat to receive Einar's messenger in the great hall that Sigurd had built and which we had dwelt in. Then I thought that never before could have been one more like a king. Hereafter, when sagamen will sing of a king in some fancied story, they will surely make him like King Harald of Norway. I myself have little skill to say what he was like beyond this--that never had I seen a more handsome man, nor bigger, nor stronger. King-like he was in all ways, and his face was bright and pleasant, though it was plain that it would be terrible if he was angry, or with the light of battle upon it.

The hair, whence he had his name, was golden bright and shining, and beard and eyebrows were of the same colour. But his eyes were neither grey nor blue altogether, most piercing, seeming to look straight into a man's heart, so that none dared lie to him.

I think that it is saying much for King Harald that, though his arms and dress were wonderfully rich and splendid, one cared only to look on his face; and that though many men of worth were on the high place with him, there seemed to be none but he present.

When the scald told the king who I was, and what was my errand, with all ceremony, he looked fixedly at me, so that I was ashamed, and grew red under his gaze. Then he smiled pleasantly, and spoke to me. His voice was as I thought to hear it--clear and steady, and yet deep.

"So, Ranald Vemundsson, you are worthy of your father. It may be that you bear me ill will on his account, but I would have you forget the deeds done that Norway might be one, and the happier therefor."

"Had my father been slain in fair fight, lord king," I said, "no ill will had been thought of. It has not been in my mind that you bade Rognvald slay him as he did. And that Jarl is dead, and the feud is done with therefore. Jarl Einar is my foster father, moreover."

"That is well said," answered Harald. "But I thought Sigurd must have fostered you; he was ever a close friend of Vemund's."

I did not know why the king thought this, though the reason was at my side; so I only said that my mother had given me to Einar's keeping, and the king said no more at that time about it.

After that I gave the Jarl's messages, and the king heard them well enough, though it seemed to Einar that the weregild to be paid was over heavy, and he had bidden me tell Harald that it was so. Therefore the king said that he would give me an answer on the morrow, and I went away into the town well pleased with his kindly way with me.

There was a feast made for me that night, and after it I must sit still and hear the scalds sing of the deeds of Harald the king, which was well enough. But then Thiodolf rose up and sang a great saga about the winning of Sigurd's sword, wherein it seemed that I had fought the dead jarl, and bale fires, and I know not what. He had heard strange tales from Einar's men, if they told him all that he sang.

Some men may be pleased to hear their own deeds sung of, with more added thus; but I was not used to it, and the turning of all eyes to me made me uncomfortable. But Harald had paid no sort of heed to what they sang of him, and so I tried to look at my ease, and gave the scald a bracelet when he ended.

"Overmuch make you of that matter, scald," said I quietly.

He laughed a little, and answered:

"One has to fill in what a warrior will not tell of himself."

Now the men shouted when I gave Thiodolf the bracelet, and Harald looked quickly at me. Then I thought that maybe I had overdone the gift, though Einar had ever told me that a good scald deserved good reward, and Thiodolf was well known as the best in Norway. It was a heavy ring, silver gilt, and of good design, that I took from the same viking whose sword I gave to Sigurd.

"Overpaid am I," the scald said, putting it on his arm.

"You are the first who has ever sung of me," I answered; "and the voice and tune were wonderful, if the saga was too strong for me."

Then Harald smiled again, and praised Thiodolf also, and I thought no more of the matter. The feast was pleasant enough in the hall, full of Harald's best men and chiefs, though it seemed strange to sit as a guest in Einar's house.

Now on the next morning I was to speak with the king about Einar's business, and I went to him unarmed, as was right, save for helm and Sigurd's sword. He was in the jarl's own chamber, and with him were Thiodolf and a young scald named Harek, who sat with things for writing before him, which was what I had never seen before.

We talked for some time, and all went well for peace; but one more message was to go and come between the king and Einar, and so I said I would sail at once.

"Not so much need for haste but that you can bide here for a day or two," Harald said. "I will not have you complain of my hospitality hereafter. And Thiodolf and Harek here want to learn more about Sigurd's sword and its winning."

"If I tell them the truth, I shall spoil their saga, lord king!" I said, laughing.

"Trust the scalds to mind you do not," he answered. "There are times when I have to ask them which of my own doings they are singing about now. But is there no wonder in the tale?"

So I told him just how the matter was. And when he heard of the noise, and the stroke with which the ships were smitten, he said, looking troubled, as I thought:

"Sigurd is stronger now that he is dead than when he lived. We felt that stroke even here."

But when I told how I had seen the dead jarl, his face grew thoughtful, and at last he said:

"So shall I lie some day in a grave mound. It is passing strange to think on. I would that if one comes to my side he may step gently as you, Ranald Vemundsson."

"Else will that comer fare ill," said Thiodolf.

The king glanced up at him, and his face changed, and he said, smiling grimly:

"Maybe. I think none will win my sword from me."

Then he had Kolgrim sent for, and Thord, and they told him truly what they had seen, and how they had fared in the matter.

"You are a truth teller, Kolgrim the Tall," Harald said. "Now if you will leave Einar's service and come and be of my courtmen, I will speak to the jarl and make matters right with him, and it shall be worth your while."

Then my comrade answered plainly:

"I am no jarl's man now, King Harald; I belong to King Ranald here, and I will not leave him."

"So," said Harald, knitting his brows suddenly, "we have two kings in the room, as it seems; and you dare choose another instead of me."

"Not so, King Harald," Kolgrim answered, with all respect; "I chose between the jarl and my king. If there is peace between you and the jarl, I suppose we are all your men."

Now Harald's face was growing black, and I could see that his anger was rising. But he stayed what words he was about to speak, and only said:

"Jarl Einar is well served when he has a king in his train."

Then he rose up and turned to Thiodolf, who was looking anxious.

"Bid King Ranald to the feast tonight. He knows my words to Einar his foster father, and I have no more to say."

So I was dismissed, and was not sorry to be outside the hall.

"Let us get down to the ship," said Thord. "Here is trouble brewing, as I think."

So we went on board, and I wished that we might go. Yet the king had bidden me stay, and I had no reason for what would be discourteous at least, if it did not look like flight. What the trouble was we could hardly understand.

In an hour's time or so I saw Thiodolf and the young scald Harek coming along the wharf and towards our ship, which lay clear of Harald's vessels, and next the harbour mouth. They came over the gang plank, and I welcomed them, but I saw that they had somewhat special to say to me.

They sat down under the after awning with me, and at once Thiodolf said:

"That was an unlucky speech of your comrade's just now. No man dares name himself king in Harald's presence--not even his own sons. It is the one thing that he will not bear."

"So it seemed," said I; "and, in truth, he had enough trouble with under kings not long since. But he knows what a sea king is--no king at all, so to speak. He need not grudge the old title."

"That is not all," Thiodolf said. "It is in his mind that he has to guard yet against risings of men of the old families of the kings, and thinks you are likely to give him trouble. Maybe the portent of the blow that spread from Sigurd's tomb to us has seemed much to him. 'Here,' he says, 'is one who will gather masterless men to him in crowds because he wears Sigurd's sword and ring, and has gained with them the name of a hero. Already he has two of Einar's best men at his heels. Yet I like him well enough, and I have no fault to find with him, save that he puts a gold circle round his helm and is called king--as he would have been but for me. Go to him, therefore, and tell him to keep out of my way. I will not have two kings in Norway.'"

"Well," I said, "that is plain speaking. But I cannot help what the men call me. The king makes overmuch of the business. I am not foolish enough to try to overturn Harald Fairhair."

"Maybe," said Thiodolf, "but those are his words. I rede you get away quickly on the next tide."

"Ay," said Harek. "Harald is mild of mood now, because you made no secret of what men call you. Five years ago you would not have escaped hence at all."

"Then," said I, "I will go. I think you are right. Vemund's son troubles Harald;" and I laughed, and added, "I have to thank you for kindly counsel, scalds, as I think. Farewell. Tide serves at any time now, and I will get my men and be gone."

"That is wise," they answered. "Einar must find some other messenger, if he comes not himself, after you return."

They went, and I called two or three men and sent them into the town for their comrades who were at friends' houses and in the guest house where we were lodged, while Kolgrim made ready for instant sailing.

The next thing that I was ware of was that there was a fight on the wharf end next the town, and men were running to it. Then I heard my own name shouted on one part, and that of Eric, the king's young son, on the other. So I was going to lead down twenty men to quiet the scuffle, when my people had the best of the matter, and broke through the throng, cheering, and came on to me. The rest did not follow them, for they saw that I was coming, and the wharf was clear behind them but for three of their foes who stayed where they had fallen.

Then another man broke away from the crowd, and came running after my folk. It was Harek the scald, with his head broken.

"Here are fine doings," said Kolgrim, as the men swarmed on board. "What is on hand now?"

"It is not done with yet," said a man: "look at yon ship."

Then came Harek, out of breath, and pale.

"Let me on board, King Ranald, or I am a dead man," he cried.

"Come, then!" I answered; and he ran across the plank, and Kolgrim pulled it in after him. All my men were come.

Then I looked at the ship spoken of. Men were swarming into her, and were making ready to sail. But if she meant to stay our going, she was too far up the harbour, and we were already casting off the shore ropes.

"Hold on," said Thord; "here come the other scald and two men."

The crowd that was yet round the fallen men had parted to let Thiodolf pass, and he came quickly. One of the men bore a chest, and the other a bale of somewhat. They gave these over the gunwale to my people, and Thiodolf spoke to me from the wharf.

"These are gifts from Harald to Einar's foster son," he said. "He bids me say that you have done your errand well, and that this is to prove it. Also he says that Ranald, son of Vemund, may need mail to keep his kingship withal, and so he has sent you a suit."

"That is a hard saying," I answered; "is it insult?"

"Nay, but a broad hint only. The gift is most goodly."

"Well," said I, "it is plain that he will warn me from Norway. I will leave you, good friend, to say for me what should be said. Maybe if I sent a message it would go wrongly from my lips."

Thiodolf laughed, and bade me farewell. He paid no heed to Harek, who sat on the deck with his back to him.

Then Kolgrim whistled shrill to his men, and we began to move down to the harbour mouth. I heard a sharp voice hurrying the men in the other ship; but they could not be ready in time to catch us.

When we were well out to sea, I asked Harek what all this was about.

"Your going has spoiled a plan that Eric, the king's son, had made. He wanted your sword, and thought also that to rid himself now of Vemund's son might save him trouble when the crown came to him, as it will. You were to be set on as you came from the feast tonight to the guest quarters, as if in a common broil between your men and his. Then he found you were going, and tried to stay your men, and next to take these gifts from Thiodolf and me, being very angry, even to trying to cut me down. Lucky for me that his sword turned in his hand. But he would have had me slain tonight, certainly, for he says that it was our fault that you are getting away. He fears Thiodolf, however. Now I must take service with you, if you will have me."

It seemed to me that I was making friends with one hand and enemies with the other, and that last rather more quickly than was well. So I laughed, and answered:

"I suppose that if I have a scald of my own, King Harald will blame me for overmuch kingship. However, he is angry enough already, and maybe a good friend will balance that to me. So if you will indeed cast in your lot with me, I am glad!"

So I took his hand, and more than friends have he and I been from that day forward.

Now, when I looked at Harald's strangely-given gifts, I had reason to say that he was open handed. The chest held two mail shirts, one of steel rings, gold ornamented and fastened, and the other of scales on deerskin, both fit for a king. There were two helms also, one to match either byrnie, and a seax that was fit to hang with Sigurd's sword. As for the bale, that held furs of the best, and blue cloth and scarlet. If Harald banished me, it was for no ill will; and it was handsomely done, as though he would fit me out for the viking's path in all honour, that men might not deem me outlawed for wrongdoing. So I have no ill word to say against him. Five years later he would have troubled about me and my kingship not at all; now he must be careful, for his power was not at its full.

As for young Eric, I suppose that he boasted ever after that he had put me to flight; but I do not know that it matters if he did.

So I came back to Durness, where I was to meet with Einar; and peace was made between him and the king, and he thought it well to go and speak with him. Then he and I must part, and that was hard.

"Now must you go your own way, son Ranald, for Harald is too strong for us. Maybe that is best for you, for here shall I bide in peace in Orkney; and that is not a life for a king's son--to sit at a jarl's table in idleness, or fight petty fights for scatt withholden and the like. Better for you the wide seas and the lands where you may make a name, and maybe a kingdom, for yourself. Yet I shall miss you sorely."

So he said, and I knew that he was right. Maybe the spirit of the sword I had won got hold of me, as they say will happen; for I had waxed restless of late, and I had tried to keep it from Einar. Now I hated myself for it, seeing at hand what I had longed for.

So he went north to meet Harald, and of our parting I will not say more. I could not then tell that I should not see him again, and that was well: but I know that when I saw the last flicker of his sails against the sky, I felt more lonely even than at the graveside in Southmere.

Yet I was in no worse case than were many nobly-born men at that time; for whosoever would not bow to Harald and his new laws must leave Norway, and her bravest were seeking new homes everywhere. Some had gone to far-off Iceland, and some to East Anglia; some to the Greek emperor, or Gardariki, and more yet to Ireland. But the greatest viking of all, Rolf, the son of Rognvald, Einar's young brother, had gone to France or England, with a mighty following; for Harald had outlawed him among the first who broke his law by plundering on the Norway coasts. A good law it was, but it was new, and so went against the grain at first. Rolf had sworn to make a new kingdom for himself, and why should not I do the same?

So when I was in the open sea again, with all the world before me, as the long sea-miles passed I grew lighthearted, and many were the thoughts of great deeds to come that filled my mind.

CHAPTER III
Odda, the Ealdorman of Devon

Now I steered eastward from Sutherland, and sailed down the east coasts of Scotland and England; and there is nothing to say about such a cruise, that had nought more wonderful in it than the scaring of the folk when we put in for food. I had made up my mind to go to Ireland for the winter, where, as every Northman knew, there were kingdoms to be won-- having no wish to be Rolf's follower, seeing he was but a jarl's son; and finding that England had no overlord, seeing that even now Alfred of Wessex and Guthrum of East Anglia were fighting for mastery, so that the whole land was racked and torn with strife.

Maybe I thought too much of myself at that time, but I was in no haste to do aught but cruise about and find where I might best make a name. I had but my one ship and crew, and I would not throw them away on some useless business for want of care in choosing.

Now, when we came into the English Channel, a gale began to blow up from the southwest; and we held over to the French shore, and there put into a haven that was sheltered enough. The gale strengthened, and lasted three days; but the people were kindly enough, being of Saxon kin, who had settled there under the headland they call Greynose, since Hengist's times of the winning of England across the water. And when the gale was over, we waited for the sea to go down, and then came a fair wind from the eastward, as we expected. So we got provisions on board, and sailed westward again, taking a long slant over to the English coast, until we sighted the great rock of Portland; and then the wind came off the land, and in the early morning veered to the northwest.

The tide was still with us as the light strengthened; then as the day broke, with the haze of late summer over the land, we found that we were right in the track of a strange fleet that was coming up fast from the westward--great ships and small, in a strange medley and in no sort of order, so that we wondered what they would be.

"Here comes Rolf Ganger back from Valland," said Kolgrim. "He has gathered any vessels he could get together, and is going to land in England."

"We will even head out to sea from across their course," I said. "Maybe they are Danes from Exeter, flying from the Saxons."

So we headed away for the open channel until at least we knew more. The fleet drew up steadily, bringing the tide with them; and presently we fell to wondering at the gathering. For there were some half-dozen ships that were plainly Norse like ourselves, maybe twenty Danish-built longships, and about the same number of heavy trading vessels. There were a few large fishing boats also; but leading the crowd were five great vessels the like of which none of us had ever seen or heard of before. And even as we spoke of them, two of these shook out reefs in their sails, and drew away from the rest across channel, as if to cut us off.

"Ho, men," I said, when I saw that, "get to arms; for here they come to speak with us. Maybe we shall have to fight--and these are no easy nuts to crack!"

Whereat the men laughed; and straightway there was the pleasant hustle and talk of those who donned mail shirt and helm and set the throwing weapons to hand with all good will.

"Let us keep on our course," I said to Kolgrim. "We will see if we cannot weather on these ships, and anyway shall fight them better apart from the rest. It is a fine breeze for a sailing match."

So we held on; and the two great ships to windward of us began to gain on us slowly, which was a thing that had never been done by any ship before. I do not know that even Harald Fairhair had any swifter ship than this that Halfdan had taken in his flight from home. Kolgrim waxed very wroth when it became plain that these could outsail us.

"There is witchcraft about those great hulks," he growled. "They are neither Norse, nor Frisian, nor Danish, but better than all three put together."

"I have sailed in ships, and talked of ships, and dreamed of them moreover, since I could stand alone," said Thord, "but I never so much as thought of the like of these. If they belong to some new kind of viking, there are hard times in store for some of us."

"Faith," said I, "I believe they have swept up and made prizes of all that medley astern of them."

So we held on for half an hour, and all that time they gained steadily on us; and we neared them quickly at last, for we tried to hold across their bows and weather on them. That was no good, for they were as weatherly as we.

Now we could see that their decks were covered with armed men, and it seemed certain that they meant to make prize of us. The leading ship was maybe half a mile ahead of the other, and that a mile from us--all three close-hauled as we strove to gain a weather berth. Then the leading ship put her helm up and stood across our course, and the second followed her.

"We must out oars now if we are to weather on them," said Kolgrim at last.

Then the men shouted; and I looked at the second ship, to which they were pointing. Her great sail was overboard, for the halliards had gone-- chafed through maybe, or snapped with the strain as she paid off quickly. Then a new hope came to me.

"Men," I said, "let us take the other vessel, and then come back on this; they are worth winning."

They cheered. And now the fight seemed to be even--ship to ship at least, if our foe was larger and higher and swifter than ours; for I thought that he would hardly have a crew like mine.

We up helm and stood away on the new course the foe had taken, leaving the crippled ship astern very fast. And now we began to edge up towards the other vessel, meaning to go about under her stern, and so shoot to windward of her on the other tack. But then I thought of a plan which might help us in the fighting. There had seemed little order and much shouting on board the ship we had left when her sail fell, and maybe there was the same want of discipline here.

"Out oars, men! Keep them swinging, but put no weight on them. Let them pull after us and tire themselves. I have a mind to see how our dragon looks on yonder high stem head."

The men laughed grimly, and the oars were run out. One called to me:

"Maybe they beat us in sailing, king; we can teach them somewhat in weapon play."

"See how they get their oars out," said Kolgrim, with a sour grin; "a set of lubbers they are."

One by one, and in no order, the long oars were being got to work. The great ship was half as long again as ours, pulling twenty-eight oars a side to our twenty. But while ours rose and fell as if worked by one man, theirs were pulled anyhow, as one might say.

"Better are they at sailing than rowing," said Thord.

Nevertheless they flew down on us, and that because we only made a show of rowing.

Then we laid on the oars, and came head to wind. The sail rattled down, and was stowed on deck; and silently we waited, arrows on string, for the fight that was now close at hand.

Then the great ship hove up, head to wind, right ahead of us, and a loud hail came from her.

"Who knows what tongue he talks?" I said. "I cannot make him out rightly."

"'Tis West Saxon," said an old warrior from the waist. "He asks who we are and what is our business."

"Tell him therefore, if you can speak in his way," I answered; "and ask the same of him."

So a hail or two went backwards and forwards, and then:

"Says he is Odda, jarl or somewhat of Devon in Wessex, and bids us yield to Alfred the king."

"In truth," said I, "if he had not spoken of yielding, I had had more to say to a king who can build ships like these. Now we will speak with him on his own deck. Tell him he will have to fight us first."

The old warrior sent a mighty curt hail back in answer to Odda's summons; then our war horns blew, and the oars rose and fell, and we were grinding our bows alongside the great ship's quarter before they knew we were there. Alfred's men had yet somewhat to learn of fighting in a sea way, as it seemed, for we were on their deck aft before they had risen from their oar benches. There were but one or two men on the quarter deck, besides the steersman, to oppose us. Odda thought we should lay our ship alongside his towering sides if we fought, as I suppose, for he was amidships.

So we swept the decks from aft forward without any hurt to ourselves: for the Saxons were hampered with the oars, and fell backward over them, and hindered one another. It was strange to hear my men laughing in what seemed most terrible slaughter; for their foes fell before they were smitten, and lay helpless under the oars, while their comrades fell over them.

So we won to the foot of the mast, and then found that there were some on board who were none so helpless: for as we came they swung the great yard athwart ships, and that stayed us; while over the heap of canvas glared those who would make it hard for us to win the ship altogether.

But before we came to stern fighting, I had a word to say; so I called for Odda.

A square built, brown-bearded man with a red, angry face pushed his way to the front of his men, and frowned at me.

"What will you? here am I," he said shortly.

One could understand his words well enough when face to face, for he spoke in the mixed tongue that any Northman understands, the plain words of which all our kin have in common.

"I am no foe of Alfred's," I said; "I do not know, therefore, why I should fight you."

"Are you not for the Danes?" he said.

"I hate them more or less, and I have no traffic with them."

"Well, then, what will you?"

"You bade me yield, and therefore I am here. Now I think it is a matter to be seen whether of us does so."

"It seems that you have slain about half my men," he said. "Nevertheless, I do not give up without fighting for the rest of my ship that you have not won."

"That is well said," I answered.

But the men were laughing, for Kolgrim had stooped, and, reaching under an oar bench, had dragged out a rower by the neck. The man swore and struggled; but Kolgrim hove him up, and lifted him over the yard to Odda's feet.

"They are all like that, Saxon," he said cheerfully. "Maybe there is a head or two broken; 'tis mostly what we call seasickness, however."

Odda looked at the man, who seemed wretched enough, but had no hurt; then he stared at our laughing faces, and his own brow began to clear.

"It comes into my mind," he said, "that maybe you would listen to me if I owned first that you have the best of us, and then asked you to fight for Alfred of Wessex. We need the help of such men as you just now; and if you hate Danes, we have work enough for you."

"One may certainly listen to that," I answered, laughing.

"What say you, men? Shall we cast in our lot with Alfred for a while?"

"We follow you, Ranald the king," Kolgrim answered for all. "If it seems good to you, it is good for us. There will be fighting enough, I trow, if all we have heard is true."

Then said Odda:

"And that before long. There is a Danish fleet in Poole Harbour that is to bring Danes from Wareham to the help of those whom Alfred holds in Exeter. We have to meet this fleet and scatter it."

"Then," said old Thord, "your men must be better handled, for Danes are no new swordsmen or seamen either."

Now the men stood listening to our talk, and this sort of saying was not good for them to hear, if they were to meet the foe soon with a good hope of victory. So Odda said quickly:

"If you will indeed fight for us, you must trust to Alfred to give you fitting reward. I do not know what I might say about that, having thought of no such chance as this. But there is no man who can complain of him."

I had heard that the king was ever open handed, but also that at this time he had little to give. Maybe, however, we might help him to riches again. I had the men to think of, but I will say for myself that I had not thought of asking what reward or pay should be given.

I sheathed my sword, and held out my hand to Odda across the yard that was between us; and he grasped it honestly, while the men on either side cheered.

"Stay here and speak with me," Odda said. "Now we must get back to the fleet."

Then went back to our ship, all but Thord and half a dozen warriors, whom he kept as guard for me, I suppose; and the grappling lines were cast off. Then we made sail again, and headed to rejoin the rest of the Saxon vessels. Odda's crippled ship had repaired her damage at this time, and went with us. But first it was plain that she thought we had taken her consort, for she prepared to fight us, and Odda had to hail her once or twice before she was sure of what had happened. Then her crew cheered also.

Now Odda took me aft, and we sat together on his quarter deck. Thord came also, and leaned on the rail beside us, looking with much disfavour at the crew, who were plainly landsmen at sea for the first time, if they were stout fighting men enough. Maybe there were ten seamen among the hundred and fifty, but these had handled the ship well under canvas, as we knew.

"You have come in good time, King Ranald," Odda said. "You see what state we are in; can you better it for us?"

"Many things I can see that need strengthening," I answered. "But you seem to take me into your counsels over soon, seeing that I have just fallen on you sword in hand."

"Why," said Odda frankly, "it is just your way of speaking to me sword in hand that makes me sure that I can trust you. I cannot deny that you had this ship at your mercy, and that the other would have been yours next; and you knew it, and yet spoke me fair. So it is plain that you mean well by us."

"Ay," said I, "but for your bidding me to yield, there would have been no fighting at all, when I knew to whom the ships belonged."

"You have put a thought in my mind, and I am glad you did board us, seeing there is no harm done," Odda answered. "I will tell you what it is. Send me some of your men to order my people and tell them how to prepare for battle. Here am I sent to sea for the first time, with good warriors enough who are in like case, and a few seamen who can sail the ship and know nought else."

"You have some Norsemen yonder, if I mistake not," I said, looking at the fleet which we were nearing.

"Ay--wandering vikings who care nought for what I say. They were going to Rolf, and the king persuaded them to take this cruise first. If you can make them follow you, there will be another matter for which I shall be more than thankful."

Thereat Thord growled: "They will follow Ranald Vemundsson well enough; have no care about that."

Then said I:

"These are the finest ships I have ever seen. Where did they come from?"

"Alfred, our king, planned them," said Odda, with much pride; "and they were built by our own men, working under Frisian shipwrights, in Plymouth."

"How will you like to command one of these, Thord?" I asked then.

"I like the ship well enough. The crew is bad. And then, whose command is the fleet under?"

"Take the ship, Thord, and lick my crew into shape; and Ranald, your king, shall command the fleet," Odda said plainly.

"Fair and softly," said Thord bluntly. "I can do the two things you ask me; but will your men follow Ranald?"

"Faith," said Odda, "if I say they are to do so, they must."

So in the end I left Thord and my seamen with Odda; but I would not take his place, only saying that I would lead the Norsemen, and that he could follow our plans. I would put more good men into each of his five ships, and they should do what they could. At least they could teach the Saxons how to board a ship, and how to man their own sides against boarders from a foe.

Those Norsemen said they would gladly follow the son of King Vemund and foster son of Einar the jarl; and so we led the strange fleet, and held on eastward with a light breeze all that day, making little way when the tide turned, and held back by the slower vessels. Men in plenty there were, but ill fitted for aught but hand fighting; though I had more Norsemen sent into the larger ships, such as those that had been taken from the Danes and the better trading vessels. One might soon see the difference in the trim and order on board as the vikings got to work and the Saxons overcame their sickness.

Now we might meet the Danes at any time, and I could not tell how matters would go. One thing was certain, however, and that was that they looked for no gathering of ships by Alfred. We should certainly take them by surprise, and I hoped, therefore, that they would be in no trim for fighting.

There was a very swift cutter belonging to the Norsemen, and as night fell I sent her on to keep watch along the shore for the first coming of the Danes, while we shortened sail; for the mouth of Poole Harbour was not far distant, and if we passed that we should be seen, and perhaps it would be guessed that we were not a friendly fleet. Towards evening, too, the wind shifted, and blew more off the shore, and that might bring them out from their haven. Kolgrim, who was weather wise, said that a shift of wind to the southward was coming presently.

When morning came, the high cliffs of Swanage were on our bow, the wind was yet steady from off shore, and beyond the headland lay Poole Harbour, at whose head is Wareham, where the Danes were. It is a great sea inlet with a narrow mouth, and one must have water enough on a rising tide to enter it. Now the ebb was running, and if the Danes came this morning, it would be soon.

They came, as it seemed, for the cutter was flying back to us under sail and oars; and before she reached us, the first Danish ships were clear of the Swanage headlands, making for the offing. Then I got my ships into line abreast, and Thord worked up Odda's five alongside us to seaward; and all the while the Danish sails hove into sight in no sort of order, and seeming so sure that none but friends could be afloat that they paid no heed to us.

Soon there were full a hundred vessels of all sorts off Swanage point, and the cutter brought word that there were but twenty more. Then I ran up my fighting flag, and everywhere along our line rose a great cheering as we hoisted sail and sped down on the foe. It was long since the seas had borne a fleet whence the Saxon war cry rang.

The leading Danes were ahead of us as we gathered way, and their long line straggled right athwart our course. We should strike their midmost ships; and at last they saw what was coming, and heard the din of war horns and men's voices that came down wind to them, and there were confusion and clamour on their decks, and voices seemed to call for order that did not come.

Then one or two longships from among them struck sail and cleared for action, and on these swooped Alfred's great ships. Odda's crashed upon and sank the first she met, and plunged and shook herself free from the wreck, and sought another. And beyond her the same was being wrought; and cheers and cries were strangely mixed where those high bows went forward unfaltering.

Now a ship crowded with men was before me. As we boarded, her crew were yet half armed, and struggling to reach the weapon chests through the press, even while our dragon head was splintering the gunwale; and I leaped on board her, with my men after me and Harek beside me.

Then sword Helmbiter was let loose for the first time since Sigurd wielded her; and though a great and terrible cry came from over the water as one of Alfred's ships sank another Dane, I could look no more, for there was stern fighting before me.

What a sword that was! Hardly could my arm feel the weight of it as it swung in perfect balance, and yet I knew the weight it had as it fell. Helm and mail seemed as nought before the keen edge, and the shields flew in twain as it touched them.

Forward I went, and aft went Harek the scald, and there was soon an end. The Danes went overboard, swimming or sinking, as their fate might be, and only the slain bided before us. The ship was ours, and I looked round to see what should be next. No other ship had come to help our prey.

Then I saw a wonderful sight. Panic terror had fallen on the Danes, and not one ship of all that great fleet was not flying down the wind without thought of fighting. Among them went our vessels, great and small, each doing her work well; and the Saxon shouts were full of victory.

So we must after them, and once more we boarded a longship, and had the victory; and then we were off the haven mouth, and with the flood tide the wind was coming up in gusts from the southeast that seemed to bode angry weather. By that time no two Danish ships were in company, and the tide was setting them out to sea.

"Here is a gale coming," said Kolgrim, looking at the sky and the whitening wave crests. "We had best get our ships into this haven while we can."

It seemed that Thord was of the same mind, for now he was heading homeward, and the other Saxons were putting about and following him. So I got men into the best of the ships we had taken, and waited till Thord in Odda's ship led the way, and so followed into Poole Harbour.

Well it was for us that we had refuge so handy. For by noonday the gale was blowing from the southwest, and two Danish ships were wrecked in trying to gain the harbour--preferring to yield to us rather than face the sea, with a lee shore, rocky and hopeless, waiting for them.

We went into the Poole inlet, which is on the eastern side of the wide waters of the haven, and there found good berths enough. The village was empty, save for a few Saxon fishermen, who hailed us joyfully. And then Odda made for us as good a feast as he might in the best house that was there, bidding every shipmaster to it. Merry enough were all, though we had but ship fare; for the Saxons had great hopes from this victory.

Now Odda made much of what I had done--though it was little enough--saying that I and my men deserved well of Alfred, and that he hoped that we should stay with him for this winter, which would perhaps see the end of the war.

"Why," said I, "things would have been much the same if I had not been here."

"That they would not," he answered. "I should have blundered past this place in the night, and so lost the Danes altogether; or if I had not done that, they would soon have found out what state my men were in. You should have heard old Thord rate them into order; it is in my mind that he even called me--Odda the ealdorman--hard names in his broad Norse tongue. But at least he gave us somewhat more to think of than the sickness that comes of heaving planks that will by no means keep steady for a moment."

He laughed heartily at himself, and then added:

"Good King Alfred thought not at all of that matter. Now I can shift the whole credit of this victory to your shoulders, and then he will not believe that I am the born sea captain that he would have me think myself."

"I will not have that," I said, "for I have not deserved it."

"Ay; but, I pray you, let me put it from myself, else shall I be sent to sea again without any one to look to for advice," he said earnestly, and half laughing at the same time. "I did but take command of this fleet because the king could find no one else at a pinch. Heaven defend me from such a charge again!"

"Now you have only the Exeter Danes to deal with," I said.

"How many men might these ships have held?" he asked.

"Maybe five thousand," I answered.

Thereat his face changed, and he rose up from his seat at the high table, and said that he would go down to see that the ships were safe, for the gale was blowing heavily as the night fell.

So we went outside the house, and called a man, telling him to find one of the Poole fishermen and bring him to speak to us.

"There were twelve thousand Danes in Wareham," he said, "for more have come lately. I thought they would all have been in the ships."

"If that had been possible, not one would have seen the morning's light," I answered, "for their ships are lost in this gale certainly."

Now I will say that I was right. The wrecks strewed the shore of Dorset and Hants next morning; and if any men won to land, there waited for them the fishers and churls, who hated them. No Danish fleet was left in the channel after that gale was spent.

When the fisher came, he told us that as many more Danes were left in Wareham, and that those from Poole had fled thither when they saw what had happened to the fleet.

"Shall you march on Wareham and scatter them, or will they fall on us here?" I asked; for we had no more than two thousand men at most.

"I would that I knew what they thought of this business," he answered; "but I shall not move tonight. It is far by land, and I suppose we could not get the ships up in the dark."

So he posted pickets along the road to Wareham, and we went back to the house for a while. And presently, as it grew dark, a wild thought came into my mind. I would go to Wareham with a guide, and see what I could find out of the Danish plans. Maybe there were fewer men than was thought, or they might be panic-stricken at our coming in this wise; or, again, they might march on us, and if so, we should have to get to sea again, to escape from double our numbers.

Now the more I thought of this, the more I grew bent on going, for I was sure that we must know what was going on. And at last I took Odda aside while Harek sang among the men, and told him what I would do.

At first he was against my running the risk; but I told him that a Norseman might go safely where a Saxon could not among the Danes, and at last I persuaded him. Then I called Kolgrim, and we went out together into the moonlight and the wind, to find the fisherman we had spoken with already and get him to act as guide. I think that Odda did not expect to see either of us again; and when I came to know more of Saxons, I learned that he trusted me most fully, for many thanes would have thought it likely that I went on some treacherous errand.

CHAPTER IV
Jarl Osmund's Daughter

To my mind, no gale seems so wild as one that comes at the time of full moon, when the clouds break up and fly in great masses of black and silver against the deeper sky beyond, while bright light and deepest shadow chase each other across land and sea beneath them. Kolgrim and I stood under the lee of a shed, waiting for the fisher to get his boat afloat, and looked out on bending trees and whitened water, while beyond the harbour we could see the great downs, clear cut and dark, almost as well as by day, so bright it was.

It was low water now, which was good for us, for the winding channels that lead up to Wareham were sheltered under their bare banks. We could hear the thunder of the surf along the rocky coast outside, when the wind ceased its howling for a moment; and at high water the haven had been well nigh too stormy for a small boat. Now we should do best to go by water, for wind was with us; though, unless the gale dropped very quickly, we could not return in her, for there would be a heavy sea and tide against us if we could get away before it turned, while if we were long wind against tide would be worse yet.

The fisherman was eager to help us against the Danes, who had made him work for nought; and so in half an hour we were flying up the haven on the first rise of tide, and the lights of Wareham town grew plainer every moment. From the number of twinkling sparks that flitted here and there, it would seem that many folk were waking, even if some movement were not on hand.

Presently we turned into the channel that bends to the southwest from the more open water, and the town was before us. The fisher took to his oars now, lowering the scrap of sail that had been enough to drive us very swiftly before the gale so far.

Wareham stands on the tongue of land between two rivers' mouths, and the tide was setting us into the northward of these. That was the river one would have to cross in coming to or from Poole, and maybe we should learn as much there as anywhere.

There were three ships on the mud, but even in the moonlight it was plain that they were not seaworthy. There were wide gaps in their bulwarks, which none had tried to mend, and the stem head of one was gone.

"These ships were hurt in the storm of lest week," the fisher said, as we drifted past them; "there was hardly one that came in unhurt. But the Danes were eager to go, and mended them as they could."

Perhaps that was partly the reason why we gained so easy a victory, I thought at the time, and afterwards knew that I was right. They had suffered very much, while we lay across channel in safety.

There loomed before us the timbers of a strong bridge that had been over the north river, when we were fairly in it and under the nearer houses of the town. But now it was broken down, and the gap in its middle was too wide for hasty repair.

"When was this done?" I asked the fisherman.

"Since yesterday," he answered.

Now this seemed to me to indicate that the Danes meant to guard against attack by land from Poole; also that they overrated our numbers, which was probable in any case, seeing that a fleet had fled from before us.

There were wharves on the seaward side of the bridge, but none were beyond; and the houses stood back from the water, so that there was a sort of open green between it and them. There were no people about, but we could hear shouts from the town now and then.

"Let us go ashore and speak with some one," I said; "it is of no use our biding here on the water."

Kolgrim and I were fully armed, and had boat cloaks with us which covered us well, and we thought none would question who we were if we mixed among the men in some inn or other gathering place. So we bade the fisher wait for us, and found the stairs, and went to the wide green along the waterside, and across it to the houses, which were mostly poor enough here.

Many of them stood open, and in one a fire burned on the hearth, but all were empty. So we turned into a street that led seemingly from one bridge to the other across the town. Here men were going hither and thither with torches, and groups were outside some of the houses. To the nearest of these I went, as if I had all right to be in the place.

They were bringing goods out of the house, and loading a cart with them.

"Here is a flitting," said Kolgrim, "and another or two are on hand yonder."

I stayed a man who came past me from out of a house.

"I have fled from Poole," I said. "What is in the wind here? Are we to leave Wareham also?"

"If you come from Poole, you should know that it is time we did so," he answered shortly. "I suppose you saw the whole business."

"So I did," I answered. "What are the orders?"

"Pack up and quit with all haste," said he. "You had better get to work if you have aught to save."

"Shall we go to Exeter, or back to Mercia?" I said.

"Exeter they say; but I know not. Why not go and ask Jarl Osmund himself--or follow the crowd and hinder no one with questions?"

He hurried on; but then some men began to question us about the doings off Swanage, and Kolgrim told them such tales that they shivered, and soon we had a crowd round us listening. Nor did I like to hurry away, for I heard a man say that we were Northmen, by our voices. But there were plenty of our folk among the Danes.

Then came a patrol of horsemen down the street, and they bade the loiterers hurry. I drew Kolgrim into an open doorway, and stood there till they passed, hearing them rate their fellows for delay.

"Wareham will be empty tomorrow," I said. "Now we can go; we have learned enough."

Still I would see more, for there seemed no danger. Every man was thinking of himself. So we went across the town, and as we came near the western bridge the crowd grew very thick.

We heard before long that the army was as great as Odda had thought, and that they were going to Exeter. Already the advance guard had gone forward, but this train of followers would hardly get clear of the town before daylight. They had heard great accounts of our numbers, and I wished we had brought the ships up here at once. There would have been a rout of the Danes.

But the place was strange to me, and to Odda also, so that we could not be blamed.

We got back by the way we came, and then knew that we could in no way take the boat to Poole. The gale was raging at its highest, and thatch was flying from the exposed roofs. It would be dead against us; and the sea was white with foam, even in the haven. So we must go by road, and that was a long way. But we must get back to Odda, for he should be in Wareham before the Danes learned, maybe, that their flight was too hurried.

Now it seemed to me that to leave Wareham was not so safe as to come into it, for no Dane would be going away from the place. However, the bridge was down; and if it had not been done in too great haste, any fugitives from the country would have come in. So that maybe we should meet no one on the road that goes along the shore of the great haven.

The fisherman ferried us over to the opposite shore, and then tied his boat to the staging of the landing place, saying that he was well known and in no danger. He would sleep now, and bring his boat back when the wind fell. So we left him, thanking him for his goodwill.

Grumbling, as men will, we set out on our long walk in the gale. We could not miss the road, for it never left the curves of the shore, and all we had to do was to be heedful of any meetings. There might be outposts even yet, watching against surprise.

However, we saw no man in the first mile, and then were feeling more secure, when we came to a large farmstead which stood a short bowshot back from the road, with a lane of its own leading to the great door. What buildings there were seemed to be behind it, and no man was about; but there was light shining from one of the high windows, as if some one were inside, and plain to be seen in the moonlight were two horses tied by the stone mounting block at the doorway.

"Here is a chance for us, master," said my comrade, coming to a stand in the roadway. "I must try to steal these horses for ourselves. If Danes are in the place, they have doubtless stolen them; and if Saxons, they will get them back."

"There will be no Saxon dwelling so near the Danes," I said. "Maybe the place is full of Danes--some outpost that is careless."

"Careless enough," said Kolgrim. "If they are careless for three minutes more, they have lost their horses."

Then we loosened our swords in their sheaths, and drew our seaxes, and went swiftly up the grassy lane. The wind howled round the house so that none would hear the clank of mail, which we could not altogether prevent. But the horses heard us, and one shifted about and whinnied as if glad to welcome us.

At that we ran and each took the bridle of that next him, and cut the halter that was tied to the rings in the wall, looking to see the doors thrown open at any moment. Then we leaped to the saddles and turned to go. The hoofs made a great noise on the paving stones before the doorway, yet there was no sound from inside the house.

That seemed strange to me, and I sat still, looking back with the horse's head turned towards the main road.

"Stay not, master," Kolgrim said. "'Tis some outpost, and the men have slept over the farmhouse ale. Maybe the stables behind are full of horses. Have a care, master; the door opens!"

He was going; but I waited for a moment, half expecting to see a spear point come first, and my hand was on my sword hilt. But the great heavy door swung slowly, as if the one who opened it had trouble with its weight. So I must needs see who came. Maybe it was some old man or woman whose terror I could quiet in a few words.

Then the red firelight from within shone out on me, and in the doorway, with arms raised to post and door on either hand, stood a tall maiden, white robed, with gold on neck and arm. The moonlight on her seemed weird with the glow of the fire shining through the edges of her hood and sleeves. I could see her face plainly, and it was fair and troubled, but there was no fear in her looks.

"Father, is this you?" she said quietly.

I could make no answer to that, and she looked intently at me; for the moon was beyond me, and both Kolgrim and I would seem black against it, as she came from the light within, while the wind, keen with salt spray, was blowing in her face.

"Who is it?" she said again. "I can scarcely see for moon and wind in my eyes."

"Friends, lady," I said, for that at least was true in a way.

"Where are my horses? Have you seen aught of our thralls, who should have left them?" she asked, looking to whence we had just taken the beasts.

Now I was ashamed to have taken them, for she was so plainly alone and helpless, and I could not understand altogether how it could be so. I was sure that she was Danish, too.

"How is it that you have not fled, lady?" I asked. "Surely you should have gone."

"Ay; but the thralls fled when they heard the news. Has not my father sent you back for me?"

This seemed a terrible plight for the maiden, and I knew not what to say or do. She could not be left in the way of our Saxons if they came on the morrow, and I could not take her to Poole. And so, lest I should terrify her altogether, I made up my mind even as she looked to me for an answer.

"I think your father is kept in Wareham in some way. Does he look for you there?"

"Ay, surely," she answered; but there was a note as of some new fear in her voice. "Has aught befallen him? Have the Saxons come?"

"All is well in Wareham yet," I answered. "Now we will take you to your father. But we are strangers, as you may see."

Then I called to Kolgrim, who was listening open eyed to all this, and backed away from the door a little.

"What is this madness, master?" he whispered hoarsely.

"No madness at all. Ten minutes' ride to Wareham with the maiden, give her to the fisherman to take to her friends, and then ride away--that is all. Then we shall be in Poole long before any look for us, for we are in luck's way."

Kolgrim laughed.

"Strange dangers must I run with you, master; but that is what one might look for with Ranald of the Sword."

Then I got off the horse, which was very strong and seemed quiet, and went to the maiden again.

"It will be best for you to come with us, lady," I said "we will see you safely to Wareham."

The light fell on my arms now, and they were splendid enough, being Harald Fairhair's gift, which I had put on for the fight, seeing that the men loved to see their king go bravely, and being, moreover, nowise loth to do so myself. She seemed to take heart--for she was well nigh weeping now-- when she saw that I was not some wandering soldier of the great host.

"My horses, two of them should be here," she said. "I bade the thralls leave them when they fled."

So she thought not that we had loosed them, and did not know her own in the moonlight. Maybe she had no knowledge as to which of many had been left, and I was glad of that, for so her fear was less.

"You must ride with us," I said, "and I would ask you to come quickly; even now the host is leaving Wareham."

"Ay, is that so? Then my father is busy," she said, and then she faltered a little, and looked at me questioningly. "I cannot go without my nurse, and she is very sick. I think she sleeps now. Men feared her sickness so that we brought her here from the town. But indeed there is nought to fear; there is no fever or aught that another might take from her."

Then I grew fairly anxious, for this was more than I had looked for. I knew that it was likely that she would soon be missed and sought for; yet I could not think of leaving her to that chance, with the bridge broken moreover.

I gave the bridle to Kolgrim then to hold.

"Let me see your nurse," I said gently; "I have some skill in these troubles."

She led me into the house without a word. All the lower story was in one great room, with a hearth and bright fire thereon in the centre. Beyond that was a low bed, to which the maiden went. A very old woman, happed in furs and heavy blankets, lay on it, and it needed but one look to tell me that she needed no care but the last. Past need of flight was she, for she was dead, though so peacefully that her watcher had not known it.

"The sleep is good, is it not?" the maiden said, looking anxiously into my face.

"It is good, lady," I answered, taking off my helm. "It is the best sleep of all--the sleep that heals all things."

The maiden looked once at the quiet face, and once more at me, with wide eyes, and then she knew what I meant, and turned quickly from me and wept silently.

I stood beside her, not daring to speak, and yet longing to be on the road. And so still were we that Kolgrim got off his horse and came to the door and called me, though not loudly.

I stepped back to him.

"Come again in a few minutes and say one word--'Saxons'" I whispered, "then we shall go."

He nodded and drew back. I think the maiden had not heard me move, for she was bent over the bed and what lay thereon. It seemed very long to me before I heard my comrade at the door.

"Saxons, master!" he said loudly.

"Say you so?" I answered, and then I touched the maiden's arm gently.

"Lady, we must go quickly," I said. "The dame is past all help of ours, and none can harm her. Come, I pray you."

She stood up then, still looking away from me, and I drew the covering over the still face she gazed at.

"You must leave her, and I know these Saxons will not wrong the dead," said I gently. "Your father will miss you."

"I am keeping you also in danger," she answered bravely. "I will come."

"Loth to go am I," she said, as she gathered her wrappings to her and made ready very quickly, "for it seems hard. But hard things come to many in time of war."

After that she ceased weeping, and was, as I thought, very brave in this trouble, which was indeed great to her. And when she was clad in outdoor gear, she bent once more over the bed as in farewell, while I turned away to

Kolgrim and made ready the horses. Then she came, and mounted behind me on a skin that I had taken from a chair before the hearth.

Then we were away, and I was very glad. The good horse made nothing of the burden, and we went quickly. Many a time had I ridden double, with the rough grip of some mail-shirted warrior round my waist, as we hurried back to the ships after a foray; but this was the first time I had had charge of a lady, and it was in a strange time and way enough. I do not know if it was in the hurry of flight, or because they had none, but the horses had no saddles such as were for ladies' use.

So I did not speak till we were half a mile from the house, and then came a hill, and we walked, because I feared to discomfort my companion. Then I said:

"Lady, we are strangers, and know not to whom we speak nor to whom we must take you."

There was a touch of surprise in her voice as she answered:

"I am the Lady Thora, Jarl Osmund's daughter."

Then I understood how this was the chief to whom the man I spoke with first had bidden me go for orders. It was plain now that he was up and down among the host ordering all things, and deeming his daughter in safety all the while. He had not had time to learn how his cowardly folk had fled and left their mistress, fearing perhaps the sickness of the old dame as much as the Saxon levies.

Now no more was said till we came to the riverside, where the flood tide was roaring through the broken timbers of the bridge. The fisher slept soundly despite the noise of wind and water, and Kolgrim had some trouble in waking him.

"How goes the flight?" I asked him when he came ashore with the boat's painter in his hand.

"Faith, master, I know not. I have slept well," he said.

Now by this time it seemed to me that I ought to take the lady into a safe place, and I would go myself rather than leave her to the fisherman, who was rough, and hated the Danes heartily, as I knew. Moreover, I had a new plan in my head which pleased me mightily. Then I thought that if I were to meet any man who suspected me, which was not likely, the Lady Thora would be pass enough for me. So I told Kolgrim to bide here for me, and he said at first that he must be with me. However, I made him stay against his will at last, telling him what I thought.

Then the fisher put us across quickly, and went back to the far side to wait my return.

I asked Thora where I must take her to find the jarl.

"To his house, surely," she said.

"I do not know the way from here," I answered; "I fear you must lead me."

"As you will," she said, wondering. "It is across the town certainly."

That was bad for me, perhaps, but I should find that out presently. So we went across the open, and came to the road through the town along which I had been before. It was clearer, though there were yet many people about.

Now when we were in the shadow of the first houses, Thora stopped suddenly and looked hard at me.

"Will you tell me if I am heading you into danger?" she said.

"What danger is possible?" I answered. "There are no Saxons here yet."

"Not one?" she said meaningly. "I may be wrong--it does seem unlikely but I think you do not belong to us. Your speech is not like ours altogether, and your helm is gold encircled, as if you were a king."

"Lady," I said, "why should you think that I am not of your people? Let us go on to the jarl."

"Now I know that you are not. Oh, how shall I thank you for this?"

Then she glanced at my helm again, and drew a sudden little quick breath.

"Is it possible that you are Alfred of Wessex? It were like what they say of him to do as you have done for a friendless maiden."

Then she caught my hand and held it in both of hers, looking half fearfully at me.

"Lady," I said, "I am not King Alfred, nor would I be. Come, let us hasten."

"I will take you no further," she said then. "Now I am sure that you are of the Northmen that were seen with the Saxons. You are not of us, and I shall lose you your life."

Then came the quick trot of horses, and I saw a little troop coming down the street, their arms flashing in the streaks of moonlight between the houses.

"I will see you in good hands, Lady Thora," I answered. "Who are these coming?"

"It is my father," she said, and drew me back deeper into shadow.

After the horsemen and beside them ran men who bore planks and ropes, and it was plain that the jarl had found out his loss, and hastened to bridge the gap and cross the river.

I saw that I could keep up the pretence no longer.

"Let me walk behind you as your servant," I said. "If any heed me, I pray you make what tale you can for me."

"What can I say to you in thanks?" she cried quickly, and letting go my hand which she yet held. "If you are slain, it is my fault. Tell me your name at least."

"Ranald Vemundsson, a Northman of King Alfred's," I said. "Now I am your servant--ever."

Then Thora left my side suddenly, and ran forward to meet the foremost horseman--for they were close to us--calling aloud to Osmund to stay. And he reined up and leaped from his horse with a cry of joy, and took her in his arms for a moment.

I got my cloak around me, pulling the hood over my helm, and stood in the shadow where I was. I saw the jarl lift his daughter into the saddle, and the whole troop turned to go back. The footmen cast down their burdens where each happened to be, and went quickly after them; and I was turning to go my way also, when a man came riding back towards me.

"Ho, comrade," he said, "hasten after us. Mind not the things left in the boat. There is supper ere we go."

I lifted my hand, and he turned his horse and rode away, paying no more heed to me. That was a good tale of things left that Thora had made in case I was seen to be going back to the boat.

Then I waxed light hearted enough, and thought of my other plan. Kolgrim saw me coming, and the boat was ready.

"Have you flint and steel?" I said to the fisher as I got into the boat.

"Ay, master, and tinder moreover, dry in my cap."

"Well, then, take me to those ships we saw. I have a mind to scare these Danes."

It was a heavy pull against the sea to where they lay afloat now, though it was not far. I fired all three in the cabins under the fore deck, so that, as their bows were towards the town, the light would not be seen till I was away.

Then we went swiftly back to Kolgrim, and as I mounted and rode off, the blaze flared up behind us, for the tarred timbers burned fiercely in the wind.

"That will tell Odda that the Danes are flying. And maybe it will save Wareham town from fire, for they will think we are on them. So I have spoiled Jarl Osmund's supper for him."

Then I minded that this would terrify the Lady Thora maybe, and that put me out of conceit with my doings for a moment. But it was plain that she was brave enough, for there were many things to fray her in the whole of this matter, though perhaps it was because Kolgrim stayed beyond the river that she made so sure that I was a man of King Alfred's and no friend to the Danes.

So we rode away, pleased enough with the night's work, and reached Poole in broad daylight, while the gale was slackening. Well pleased was Odda to see me back, and to hear my news.

Then he asked me what I would do next. There seemed to be no more work at sea, and yet he would have me speak with King Alfred and take some reward from him. And I told him that the season grew late, and that I would as soon stay in England for this winter as anywhere.

"What will you do next in the matter of these Danes, however?" was my question.

Then he said:

"I must chase them through the country till they are within the king's reach. He has the rest pent in Exeter, and there will be trouble if they sail out to join these. I must follow them, therefore, end send men to Alfred to warn him. Then he will know what to do. Now I would ask you to take the ships back into the river Exe and join us there."

I would do that willingly, and thought that if the wind held fair after the gale ended, I might be there before he joined the king by land. But I should have to wait for a shift to the eastward before sailing.

So Odda brought his men ashore, and marched on Wareham and thence after the Danes, not meaning to fight unless some advantage showed itself, for they were too many, but to keep them from harming the country. And I waited for wind to take me westward.

Then the strange Norsemen left us. They had gained much booty in the Danish ships, for they carried what had been won from the Saxons, and what plunder should be taken was to be their share in due for their services. They were little loss, for they were masterless vikings who might have given trouble at any time if no plunder was to be had, and I was not sorry to see them sail away to join Rolf Ganger in France.

Now these men would have followed me readily, and so I should have been very powerful at sea, or on any shore where I cared to land. But Odda had made me feel so much that I was one in his counsel, and a friend whom he valued and trusted, that I had made this warfare against the Danes my own quarrel, as it were in his company. Already I had a great liking for him, and the more I heard of Alfred the king, the more I wished to see him. At the least, a man who could build ships like these, having every good point of the best I knew, and better than any ever heard of before, was worth speaking with. I thought I knew somewhat of the shipwright's craft, and one thinks much of the wisdom of the man who is easily one's master in anything wherein one has pride.

Moreover, Alfred's men were wont to speak of him with little fear, but as if longing for his praise. And I thought that wonderful, knowing only Harald Fairhair and the dread of him.

CHAPTER V
Two Meetings in England

It was not long before the shift of wind that I looked for came, and at once I took all the ships round to the river Exe. Odda had left me all the seamen he had, and they were enough for the short, fair passage. We came to the haven in the river, and there heard what news there was, and it was good enough. Odda had sent well-mounted men to reach the king by roads away from the retreating Danes, and he had been ready for them. He drew off his levies from before the walls of the town, and let his enemies pass him; then he and Odda fell on their rear and drove them into Exeter, and there was holding them. It was well done; for though the host sallied from the town to meet the newcomers, they gained nothing but a share in the rout that followed when Odda closed on the rear guard and the king charged the flank.

Now we heard that as soon as we landed. And then I had my first knowledge of the ways of a Saxon levy. For no sooner were the ships berthed than their crews began to leave them, making for their homes.

One or two men I caught in the act of leaving in the early morning, and spoke sharply to them, for it seemed that soon there would be ships enough and not a man to tend them. Whereon they answered:

"We have done what we were called up for, and more also. Now may others take our places. What more would you have? We have won our victory, and the ships are not needed for a while."

So they went, and nothing I could say would stay them. I waxed angry on that, and I thought I might as well sail for Ireland as not. There seemed no chance of doing aught here, where men would throw away what they had won of advantage.

So I went back to my own ship and sat under the after awning, in no good temper. Thord and Kolgrim were yet busy in and about the vessels, making all secure, and setting men to work on what needed repairing. Presently Harek the scald came and sat with me, and I grumbled to my heart's content about this Saxon carelessness and throwing away of good luck.

Many Saxons--men from camp, and freemen of the place, and some thanes--came, as one might expect, to stare at the ships and their prizes. I paid no heed to them as the day went on, only wishing that Odda would come and speak to me about his doings, for I had sent word to him that we were in the river. Sometimes a thane would stay and speak with me from the wharf alongside which my own ship was with one or two others, and they were pleasant enough, though they troubled me with over many thanks, which was Odda's fault. However, I will say this, that if every man made as little of his own doings and as much of those of his friends as did the honest ealdorman, it were well in some ways.

By and by, while we were talking, having got through my grumble, Kolgrim came along the shore with some Saxon noble whom he had met; and this stranger was asking questions about each ship that he passed. I suppose that Kolgrim had answered many such curious folk already; for when he came near and we could hear what he was saying, I was fain to laugh, for, as sailors will, he was telling the landsman strange things.

"What do we pull up the anchor with?" he was saying. "Why, with yonder big rope that goes from masthead to bows." and he pointed to the great mainstay of our ship. "One must have a long purchase, if you know what that is."

"Ah, 'tis wonderful," said the Saxon.

Then he caught my eye, and saw that I was smiling. He paid no heed to me, however, but looked long at the ship that lay astern of ours--one of the captured Danes. Thord had set a gang of shore folk to bend the sail afresh to a new yard, for the old one had been strained in the gale that came before the fight.

"What are those men doing, friend?" he asked Kolgrim directly.

"Bending a sail," answered my comrade listlessly, trusting, as it would seem, to the sea language for puzzlement enough to the landsman.

"So," said the Saxon, quite quietly. "It was in my mind that when a sail was bent to the yard it was bent with the luff to the fore end thereof."

At which words Kolgrim started, in a way, and looked first at the riggers and then back at the Saxon, who moved no muscle of his face, though one might see that his eyes twinkled. And I looked at the riggers also, and saw that the Saxon was right, and that the men had the square-cut sail turned over with the leech forward and the luff aft. The sail was half laced to the yard, and none but a man who knew much of ships would have seen that aught was wrong.

Then Kolgrim's face was so red, and angry, and full of shame all at once, that I had the best laugh at him that had come to me for many a day. And he did not bide with the Saxon any longer, but went on board the ship hastily, and said what he had to say to the riggers. The Saxon stood, and looked after him with a smile breaking over his pleasant face, and I thought that maybe I owed him some amends for my comrade's rough jesting, though indeed he had his revenge.

So I came ashore and spoke to him. He was a slight, brown-haired man of about thirty, bearded and long-haired after the Saxon fashion, and I thought he seemed to be recovering from some wound or sickness that had made him white and thin. He wore his beard long and forked, which may have made him look thinner; but he seemed active and wiry in his movements--one of those men who make up for want of strength by quickness and mastery of their weapons. Soberly dressed enough he was, but the cloth of his short cloak and jerkin was very rich, and he had a gold bracelet and brooch that seemed to mark him as high in rank.

"My comrade has been well caught, thane," I said; "he will be more careful what tales he tells the next comer. But I think he was tired of giving the same answers to the same questions to all who come to see us."

"Likely enough," the Saxon answered, laughing a little. "I asked to see the prizes and the vikings' ships, and he showed me more than I expected."

Then he looked along the line of vessels that he had not yet passed, and added:

"I thought there were more Norse ships with Odda."

I told him how the other vikings had left us with their plunder at Wareham, saying that I thought they could well be spared at that time.

"However," I said, "I did not count on the Saxons leaving their vessels so soon."

"Then I take it that I am speaking with King Ranald, of whom Odda has so much to say," he said, without answering my last words.

"I am Ranald Vemundsson," I said; "but this ship is all my kingdom now. Harald Fairhair has the land that should have been mine. I am but a sea king."

Then he held out his hand, saying that there was much for which every Saxon should thank me, and I passed that by as well as I could, though I was pleased with the hearty grip he gave me.

"So long as Odda is satisfied it is enough," I said. "If I have helped him a little, I have helped a man who is worth it."

"Well," said the thane, "you seem to be pleased with one another. Now I should like to see this ship of yours, of which he has so much to say."

We went over her, and it was plain that this thane knew what he was talking about. I wondered that the king had not set him in command instead of Odda, who frankly said what was true--that he was no sailor. I supposed that this man, however, was not of high rank enough to lead so great a gathering of Saxons, and so I said nothing to him about it.

By and by we sat on the after deck with Harek, and I had ale brought to us, and we talked of ship craft of all sorts. Presently, however, he said:

"What shall you do now--if one may ask?"

"I know not. When I sailed from Wareham, I thought to have seen more sea service with Alfred your king. But now his men are going home, and in a day or two, at this rate, there will be none left to man the ships."

"We can call them up again when need is," he answered.

"They should not go home till the king sends them," I said. "This is not the way in which Harald Fairhair made himself master of Norway. Once his men are called out they know that they must bide with him till he gives them rest and sends them home with rewards. It is his saying that one sets not down the hammer till the nail is driven home, and clinched moreover."

"That is where the Danes are our masters," the Saxon said, very gravely. "Our levies fight and disperse. It was not so in the time of the great battles round Reading that brought us peace, for they never had time to do so. Then we won. Now the harvest wants gathering. Our people know they are needed at home and in the fields."

"They must learn to know that home and fields will be better served by their biding in arms while there is a foe left in the land. What says Alfred the king?" I said.

"Alfred sees this as well as you, or as any one but our freemen," he answered; "but not yet can he make things go as he knows they should. This is the end at which he ever aims, and I think he will teach his people how to fight in time. I know this, that we shall have no peace until he does."

"Your king can build a grand ship, but she is of no use without men in her day by day, till they know every plank of her."

"Ay," said the Saxon; "but that will come in time. It is hard to know how to manage all things."

"Why," I said, "if the care of a ship is a man's business, for that he will care. You cannot expect him to care for farm and ship at once, when the farm is his living, and the ship but a thing that calls him away from it."

"What then?"

"Pay the shipman to mind the sea, that is all. Make his ship his living, and the thing is done."

"It seems to me," the thane said, "that this can be done. I shall tell the king your words."

"As you will," I answered; "they are plain enough. I would say also that Harald our king has about him paid warriors whose living is to serve him, and more who hold lands on condition that they bear arms for him at any time."

Now Harek had listened to all this, and could tell the thane more of Harald's ordering of things than I; so he took up the talk for a time, and presently asked about the war and its beginning.

"Faith," answered the Saxon, with a grim smile, "I cannot tell when the war began, for that was when the first Danes came to the English shores. But if you mean the trouble that is on hand now, it is easily told. Ten years has this host been in England--coming first with Ingvar and Halfden and Hubba, the three sons of Lodbrok. Ingvar has gone away, and Guthrum takes his place. Halfden is in Northumbria, Hubba is in Wales, and Guthrum is king over East Anglia and overlord of Mercia. It is Guthrum against whom we are fighting."

"He is minded to be overlord of all England," said Harek.

"That is to be seen if a Dane shall be so," the Saxon answered, flushing. "We beat them at first, as I have said, and have had peace till last year. Then they came to Wareham from East Anglia. There they were forced to make peace, and they swore on the holy ring to depart from Wessex; and we, on our part, swore peace on the relics of the holy saints. Whereon, before the king, Alfred, was ware of their treachery, they fell on our camp, slew all our horsemen, and marched here. Then we gathered the levies again--ay, I know why you look so impatiently, King Ranald--and came here after them. As for the rest, you have taken your part. Now we have them all inside these walls, and I think we have done."

Then his face grew dark, and he added:

"But I cannot tell. What can one do with oath breakers of this sort?"

Then I said:

"Surely you do not look for the men of one chief to be bound by what another promises?"

He looked wonderingly at me for a moment, and then said:

"How should it be that the oath of their king should not bind the people?"

"Why," said I, "you have spoken of several chiefs. If Guthrum chooses to make peace, that is not Halfden's business, or Hubba's, or that of any chief who likes it not. One is as free as the other."

"What mean you? I say that Guthrum and his chiefs swore by the greatest oath they knew to return to Mercia."

"If they swore by the holy ring, there is no doubt that they who swore would keep the oath. But that does not bind those who were against the peace making. So I suppose that they who held not with the peace made by the rest fell on you, when your levies went home after their wont. One might have known they would do so."

Thereat the thane was silent for a while, and I saw that he was troubled. It seemed to be a new thought to him at this time that the Danish hosts in England were many, and each free to act in the way its own chief thought best, uniting now and then, and again separating. This he must needs have learned sooner or later, but the knowledge came first to him there before Exeter walls.

Presently he said:

"I have believed that all the Danes were as much one under Guthrum their king as are my folk under theirs. I cannot see the end of this war."

"It will end when Alfred the king is strong enough always to have men in the field to face every leader that will fall on him," Harek said. "What King Ranald says is true. It is as if his own father had minded what Harald had sworn in the old days."

"Wherefore Harald brought all Norway under him, that every man should mind what he said," the Saxon answered.

Then came three or four more thanes along the shore, and he rose up and waved his hand to them.

"Here are more butts for Kolgrim," he said, laughing. "Now, King Ranald, I must go to my friends. But I have learned much. I think you must speak with the king before you go, and I will tell him all you have said."

"Maybe we shall meet again," said I, taking his offered hand. "I think I would see Alfred; but he is over wise, from all accounts, to learn aught from me."

"King Alfred says that wisdom comes little by little, and by learning from every one. I belong to the court, and so shall surely meet you if you do come to speak to him."

Then I asked the thane's name.

"Godred men say it is," he answered, laughing; "but that means better counsel than belongs to me."

So he went ashore and joined the thanes, who had gone slowly along the road, and we lost sight of him.

"Yonder goes a pleasant comrade enough," I said to Harek.

"Ay," the scald answered; "but if that is not Alfred the king himself, I am much in error."

"It is not likely. I think he is a bigger man and older, from all accounts," I said carelessly. "Moreover, he would not have put up with Kolgrim's jests as he did."

"One knows not; but I thought he spoke of 'my folk' once. And he seemed to ask more than would a simple thane, and in a different way."

However, it seemed to me that Harek had found a marvel for himself, and I laughed at him for supposing that Alfred the king would come there to speak to any man.

Now towards evening Odda came, and with him many servants and a train of wagons. He would make a feast for us in the best house of the village, by the king's order. Every one of us was called, and all the leading Saxon shipmen, when all was ready, and it was a kingly feast enough.

While they were making it ready, the ealdorman came to me on board the ship, and welcomed me in most friendly wise.

"I have a message for you, King Ranald," he said presently. "Some thanes have been to me from the king, and he bids me ask you to come and speak with him."

"I saw a thane here this morning who was anxious for me to see the king," I said. "A pleasant man enough--one Godred."

"Ay, Godred is pleasant enough," Odda said, smiling, "but he is a terrible man for asking questions."

He laughed again, as if he knew the man well, and was pleased to think of him and his ways.

"None of his questions are foolish, however," I said. "I was pleased with him."

"It is well if you pleased him, for he is a powerful man at court," said Odda.

"I do not know if I pleased him, or if it makes any difference to me what power he has," I said carelessly. "If I want any man to speak for me to the king--which is not likely--I should come to you first."

"Speak for yourself," laughed Odda, "that is the best way with Alfred."

So we planned to go to Exeter with the next morning's light. Odda would bide here for the night, after the feast.

Now after we had finished eating, and the ale and mead and the wine the king had sent in our honour were going round, and the gleemen were singing at times, there came a messenger into the house, and brought me a written message from the king himself, as he said.

"Much good are these scratches to me," said I to Odda. "Can you read them?"

"I can read nought but what is written in a man's face," he said.

So I gave the scroll to Harek, who sat next me, thinking that maybe the scald could read it. He pored over it for a while.

"It is of no use, king," he said. "It is in my mind that I know which is the right way up of the writing, but I am not sure."

So I laughed, and asked aloud if any man present could read. There were a good many thanes and franklins present to feast in our honour.

Then rose up a man, in a long brown hooded habit girt with a cord, from below the salt where he sat among the servants. He had a long beard, but was very bald. His hair grew in a thick ring round his head; which was strange, for he seemed young.

"I am here, ealdorman," he said to Odda; "I will read for King Ranald."

Now all eyes turned to see who spoke, and in a moment Odda rose up hastily and went down the long room till he came to where the man stood. Then I was amazed, for the ealdorman went on one knee before him, and said:

"Good my lord, I knew not that you were here among the crowd. I pray you come to the high seat."

"When will you remember that titles and high places are no longer pleasing to me?" the man said wearily. "I tire of them all. Rise up, Odda, my friend, and let me be."

"I will not rise without your blessing, nevertheless," said the ealdorman.

Whereon the man spoke a few words to him softly and quickly, signing with his hand crosswise over him.

Then I said to those about me, who were watching all this in silence:

"Who is this strange man?"

"It is Neot the holy, King Alfred's cousin," one answered, whispering.

"That is a strange dress for an atheling," I said; but they hushed me.

Now it seemed that Odda tried again to draw this Neot to the high table, but he would not come.

Then I said to old Thord, who sat over against me beyond Odda's empty chair:

"This is foolishness; or will he not honour the king's guests?"

But a thane shook his head at me, whispering behind his hand:

"It is humbleness. He has put his rank from him, and will not be held as being above any man."

Then spoke old Thord:

"Maybe he can put his rank away among men who know him not, and that is a good humbleness in a way. But where all know what his birth is, he has but to be humble and kind in ways and speech, and then men will think more thereof than they will if they see him pretending to be a churl."

Now Thord's voice was rough with long years of speaking against the wash of the waves, and the thunder of wind in sail and rigging, and the roll and creak of oars; and as he said this, every one turned towards him, for a silence had fallen on the crowd of folk who watched Neot the king's cousin and his strife with Odda.

So Neot heard, and his face flushed a little, and he looked hard at Thord and smiled curiously, saying:

"In good truth the old warrior is right, and I am foolish to hide here now I am known. Let me go and sit by him."

Then Odda led him to the upper end of the room, and every one rose as he passed by. I drew myself nearer to the ealdorman's place, and made room for him where only the table was between him and Thord, for that bench was full.

So he put his hand on my shoulder and sat down, looking over to Thord, and saying with a quiet smile:

"Thanks for that word in season, friend."

But the old warrior was somewhat ashamed, and did but shift in his seat uneasily.

"Ay, ay," he growled; "I cannot keep my voice quiet."

Neot laughed, and then turned to me and held out his hand for the king's letter, which I gave him.

He ran his eyes over the writing very quickly, and then said:

"Here is nothing private; shall I read aloud?"

But the thanes fell to talking quickly, and I nodded.

"Alfred the king to his cousin Ranald Vemundsson, greeting. Odda the ealdorman of Devon, and one Godred, have spoken to me of yourself--one telling of help given freely and without question of reward or bargain made, and the other of certain plain words spoken this morning. Now I would fain see you, and since the said Godred seems to doubt if you will come to me, I ask it under my own hand thus. For I have thanks to give both to you and your men, and also would ask you somewhat which it is my hope that you will not refuse me. Therefore, my cousin, I would ask you to come with our ealdorman tomorrow and hear all I would say."

Then Neot said,

"That is all. I think you will not refuse so kindly an invitation. The writing is the king's own, and here is his name at the end."

So he showed it me. The letter was better written than the name, as it seemed to me.

"I will take your word for it," I said, laughing as I looked; "but it is a kindly letter, and I will surely come."

"Ay; he has written to you as to an equal," Odda said.

"That is so. Now I would have the good king know that I am not that; I am but a sea king. Maybe he thinks that I shall be a good ally, and makes more of my power than should be. I told Godred the thane as plainly as I could what I was, this morning."

"Why, then," said Neot, smiling, "Godred has told the king, no doubt."

"I hope he has," I answered, "but I doubt it. Nevertheless it is easy to tell the king myself when I see him."

After that we talked about other matters, and it became plain that this Neot was a wonderfully wise man, and, as I thought, a holy one in truth, as they called him. There is that about such an one that cannot be mistaken.

Harek sang for us, and pleased all, and into his song came, as one might suppose, a good deal about the Asir. And then Neot began to ask me a good deal about the old gods, as he called them. I told him what I knew, which was little enough maybe, and so said that Harek knew all about them, and that he should rather ask him.

He did not care to do that, but asked me plainly if I were a Christian.

"How should I be?" I said. "Odda is the first Christian man I have spoken with, to my knowledge. So, if I were likely to leave my own faith, I have not so much as heard of another."

"So you are no hater of Christians?" he said.

"Surely not. Why should I be? I never thought of the matter."

Then he said:

"Herein you Norsemen are not like the Danes, who hate our faith, and slay our priests because of their hatred."

"More likely because Christian means Saxon to them, or else because you have slain them as heathens. Northmen do not trouble about another nation's faith so long as their own is not interfered with. Why should they? Each country has its own ways in this as in other matters."

Thereat Neot was silent, and asked me no more. Hereafter I learned that hatred of race had made the hatred of religion bitter, until the last seemed to be the greatest hatred of all, adding terror and bitterest cruelty to the struggle for mastery.

Presently, before it was very late, Neot rose up and spoke to Odda, bidding him farewell. Then he came to me, and said:

"Tell the king that we have spoken together, and give him this message if you will that I go to my place in Cornwall, and shall be there for a while."

Then he passed to Thord, and took his hard hand and said:

"Good are words that come from an honest heart. I have learned a lesson tonight where I thought to have learned none."

"I marvel that you needed to learn that," Thord said gruffly.

"So do I, friend," answered Neot; "but one is apt to go too far in a matter which one has at heart, sometimes before one is aware. Then is a word in season welcome."

Then he thanked Harek for his songs, and went, the Saxons bowing as he passed down the long table with Odda.

"That is a wise man and a holy," said Thord.

"Ay, truly," answered the thane who had told me about him. "I mind when he and Alfred the king were the haughtiest and most overbearing of princes. But when Neot found out that his pride and wrath and strength were getting the mastery in his heart, he thrust himself down there to overcome them. So he grows more saintlike every day, and has wrought a wondrous change in the king himself. He is the only man to whom Alfred will listen in reproof."

"That is likely," I said, not knowing aught of the holy bishops who were the king's counsellors; "kings brook little of that sort. But why does he wear yon strange dress?"

"He has taken vows on him, and is a hermit," the thane said; but I did not know what he meant at the time.

It was some Saxon way, I supposed, and cared not to ask more.

So it came to pass that I met one of the two most wonderful men in England, and I was to see the other on the morrow. Yet I had no thought that I should care to stay in the land, for it seemed certain from what Odda told me that peace would be made, and peace was not my business nor that of my men.

So in a way I was sorry that the war was at an end, seeing that we came for fighting and should have none.

Then came a thought to me that made me laugh at myself. I was glad, after all, that we were not going sword foremost into Exeter town, because of the Lady Thora, who was there. I suppose it would not have been reasonable had I not had that much thought for the brave maiden whom I had helped out of danger once.

CHAPTER VI
Alfred the King

Odda the ealdorman and I rode gaily into the king's camp in the bright August morning, with Harek and Kolgrim and Thord beside us, and after us fifty of my men in their best array; which was saying much, for Einar the jarl was generous, and we had spoiled Halfdan, the king's son, moreover. So there was a shouting when we came to the camp, and men ran together to stare at the vikings and their king.

In the midst of the camp, which was strong enough, and looked out on the old city, flew a banner whereon was a golden dragon--the banner of Wessex. And it stood before a great pavilion, which was the court for the time, and where we should find the king waiting for us. There were several other tents joined to this great one, so that into them the king might retire; and there was a wide space, round which walked spearmen as sentries, between it and any other tent.

Some Devon thanes met us, and our men dismounted at the same time as we. Then Odda led us four to the door of the pavilion, and we were ushered in with much ceremony.

Inside the great tent was like a round hall, carpeted, and tapestry-hung in a way I had never seen before. There were many richly-dressed nobles present, and most of these were grouped round a high place over against the door, where I saw at once that the king sat on a throne in all state.

Now, coming from bright sunshine into the cool shadow of the place, I was dazzled at first; but Kolgrim's eyes were quick, and we had hardly crossed the threshold, if I might call it so, when he plucked at my cloak.

"Master," he whispered, "let me bide with the men; this is no place for me."

"Hush," I whispered; "the king is yonder."

"Ay, master--let me go--the king is Godred whom I jested with."

Harek was smiling, and he pulled Kolgrim forward.

"Have no fear," he said; "those who play bowls expect rubs."

Then the king came down from his throne and towards us. He had on gilded armour beneath his long, ermine-trimmed blue cloak, and that pleased me. He had sword and seax, but no helm, though that was on a table by the throne--for he wore a crown.

Then I too saw that Godred, as he called himself, was, as the scald had guessed rightly, the king, and I was a little angry that he had tricked me thus. But he was laughing at Kolgrim as he came, and my anger passed at once. King or thane, here was a pleasant greeting enough.

He held out his hand to Odda first and then to me. The Saxon kissed it, bending one knee, which was doubtless right for him, as owning allegiance thereto. But I shook hands in our own way, saying:

"Skoal to Alfred the king."

Which seemed to please him, for he answered:

"Welcome to King Ranald. I am glad my letter brought you. My counsellor, Godred, feared you might not care to come."

"The letter turned the scale, lord king," I said. "Yet I would have you remember what I said yesterday about my kingship."

"Ay, cousin, I mind it," he answered, laughing. "Also I mind that a king's son is a king's son, whatever else he may be called."

Then he shook hands with Harek, and after that turned to Kolgrim, holding out his hand also to him.

"Concerning sails," he said gravely, "I have many questions to ask you. Is it to the starboard hand that the bolt rope goes, or to the other board?"

"I pray you to forget my foolishness, lord king," cried Kolgrim, growing very red and shame faced.

"That I shall not," the king answered, laughing. "I owe you thanks for such a jest as I have not played on a man for many a long day. Truly I have been more light hearted for my laugh ever since."

"Ay, lord, you had the laugh of me," Kolgrim said, grinning uneasily.

Then the king nodded gaily to him and asked who Thord was.

"This is my master in sea craft," said Odda. "Verily I fear him as I have feared no man since I was at school. But he cured the seasickness of me."

"Maybe I forgot the sickness when I sent landsmen to sea in all haste," said the king. "Nevertheless, Thord, how fought they when blows were going?"

"Well enough, king. And I will say that what I tried to teach them they tried to learn," answered Thord.

"Wherein is hope. You think that I may have good seamen in time, therefore?"

"Ay, lord. It is in the blood of every man of our kin to take to the sea. They are like hen-bred ducklings now, and they do but want a duck to lead them pondwards. Then may hen cackle in vain for them."

The king laughed.

"Faith," he said, "I--the hen--drove Odda into the pond. He is, according to his own account, a poor duckling."

"Let him splash about a little longer, lord king," said Thord.

But Odda spoke with a long face.

"Not so, King Alfred, if you love me. Landsman am I, and chicken-hearted at sea. Keep the gamecock to mind the farmyard; there be more birds than ducks needed."

"Make a song hereof, Harek," said the king. "Here is word play enough for any scald."

Then sang Harek, laughing, and ever ready with verses:

"The gamecock croweth bravely,
And guardeth hawk-scared hen roost;
But when the sea swan swimmeth
Against the shoreward nestings,
There mighty mallard flappeth,
And frayeth him from foray;
Yet shoreward if he winneth,
The gamecock waits to meet him."

"That is in my favour," said Odda. "Mind you the scald's words, I pray you, lord king, and send me to my right place, even with hawk on one side and swan on the other."

So a pleasant laugh went round, and then the king went back to his throne, and spoke words of open thanks to us of the fleet who had gained him such victory. Good words they were, neither too few nor too many, such as would make every man who heard them long to hear the like of himself again.

Now, while he was speaking, men came to the tent door and waited for his words to end; and then one came forward and told a noble, who seemed to be ordering the state which was kept, that Danish lords had come to speak with the king.

It seemed that this was expected, for when he heard it, Alfred bade that they should be brought in.

There were six of them in all, and they were in handsome dresses, but without mail, though not unarmed. The leader of them was Jarl Osmund, whom I had seen for a moment in Wareham street. I thought that his handsome face was careworn, as though peace would be welcome to him. But he and all his comrades carried themselves bravely.

Now there was long converse between the king and these chiefs, and it seemed that peace would be made.

Yet Alfred's face was hard as he spoke to them--not like the bright looks with which he had jested with us just now, or the earnest kingly regard which had gone with his words of thanks.

Presently the Danes said that the whole force would retire into Mercia beyond Thames, harming none by the way, and keeping peace thereafter, if the conditions were honourable.

Then the king flashed out into scorn:

"What honour is to be looked for by oath breakers?"

"We are not oath breakers, King Alfred," Osmund said, looking him in the face.

"Once did the Danes swear to me on their holy ring, which seems to me to be their greatest oath, and they broke the peace so made. What is that but that they are forsworn?"

"We swore nought to you, lord king," Osmund said. "Half of the men with us came newly from across the sea but a week or so since. Guthrum and those who swore are in their own land."

Then the king glanced at me, suddenly, as it would seem, remembering what I had told him of the freedom of the chiefs.

"Ha! now I mind me of a word spoken in time," he said. "It has seemed to me that there was oath breaking; maybe I was wrong. I will take your words that you have not done so. Is that amends enough?"

"It is well said, lord king," Osmund answered gravely.

"But," Alfred went on, "I must have the word of every chief who is in Exeter, and they must speak for every man. Tell me in all truth if there are those who would not make peace with me?"

Then said Osmund:

"Some will not, but they are few."

"What if you make peace and they do not? what shall you do with them?"

"They must go their own way; we have no power over them."

"Has not Guthrum?"

"No more than we. A free Dane cannot be hound, unless he chooses, by another man's word."

Then Alfred said plainly:

"I cannot treat for peace till I have the word of every chief in Exeter. Go your ways and let that be known."

So Osmund bowed, and went out with his fellows. And when he had gone, the king turned to me.

"Have I spoken aright, King Ranald?"

"In the best way possible, lord king," I answered.

"Go after those Danish lords," the king said to one of his thanes, "and bid them to feast with me tonight, for I think that I have said too much to them."

So they were bidden to the king's feast presently, and I suppose they could do nought but come, for it was plain that he meant to honour them. After they had gone back into the town, Alfred spoke with my men, and what he said pleased them well.

Then he went to his resting tent, and I walked with Odda to his quarters, and sat there, waiting for the king to send for me to speak with him, as I expected. But word came that he would wait till he had heard more of the Danish answer to his message before we spoke together of that he had written of to me. So he prayed me to wait in the camp till he had seen the Danes again, and told Odda to find quarters for us.

"So we shall have a good talk together," the ealdorman said. "I am glad you are not going back to the ships yet."

So was I, for all this fresh life that I had not seen before pleased me. Most of all I wished to see more of Alfred and the state in which he lived.

Now, just when I was ready for the feast, and was sitting with Odda, there came a guard to the tent and said that the chief of the Danes was seeking King Ranald.

Then Odda said:

"What wills he? we have no traffic with Danes."

"He would speak with King Ranald," the man said.

Then said I:

"If it is Osmund the jarl, I think I know why he comes.--Let him come in here and speak before you, ealdorman."

"Why, do you know him?"

"I cannot rightly say that I do, but I nearly came to do so."

Then Odda wondered, and answered:

"Forgive me; one grows suspicious about these Danes. I will go hence, and you shall speak with him alone. Maybe he wants your word with the king, because you know the ways of the viking hosts."

"No," said I; "stay here. Whatever it is he has to say cannot be private; nor would I hear anything from him that you might not."

"As you will. Let him come here," Odda said; and the man went out.

Then entered Jarl Osmund, richly dressed for the king's feast, and he looked from one of us to the other as we rose to greet him. Suddenly he smiled grimly.

"I looked to find strangers, and was about to ask for King Ranald. However, Odda the ealdorman and I have met before, as I am certain."

"Faith, we have," said Odda. "Nor am I likely to forget it. It was at Ashdown fight."

"And elsewhere," said the jarl. "But it was ever fair fighting between us."

"Else had you slain me when I was down," said Odda frankly, and with a smile coming into his face.

"The score is even on that count," said Osmund, and with that, with one accord their hands met, and they laughed at each other.

That was good to see, and ever should things be so between brave foes and honest.

Then Osmund looked at me.

"Now have I met with two men whom I have longed to see," he said, "for you must be King Ranald Vemundsson. Two foes I have--if it must be so said--of whom I have nought but good to say."

"So," laughed Odda. "When fought you twain, and which let the other go?"

"We have not fought," the jarl answered. "But I have deeper reason for thanking Ranald than for sparing my own life, or for staying a blow in time out of sheer love of fair play."

Then he took my hand and looked me in the face.

"It was a good deed and noble that you wrought for me but the other day," he said earnestly. "I do not know how to thank you enough. My daughter laid command on me that I should seek you and tell you this; but indeed I needed no bidding when I heard how she escaped."

"I had been nidring had I not helped a lady in need," I said, being in want of better words.

"What is all this?" said Odda; for I had told him nought of the matter, not seeing any reason to do so.

Then Osmund must needs tell him of what Kolgrim and I had done; and the ealdorman laughed at me, though one might see that the affair pleased him.

"This king," he said, "having no kingdom of his own, as he says, goes about helping seasick ealdormen and lonely damsels, whereby he will end with more trouble on his hands than any kingdom would give him."

"I am only one," I said; "Kolgrim and Thord are in this also."

Then Osmund took a heavy gold bracelet from his arm.

"This is for Kolgrim, your comrade," he said, half doubtfully, "if I may give it him in remembrance of a brave deed well done. Will he be too proud to accept it?"

"I may give it him, certainly," I said, taking the gift.

Then Odda would not be behindhand, and he pulled off his own armlet.

"If Kolgrim is to be remembered, Thord will never be forgotten. Give this to him in sheer gratitude for swearing at me in such wise that he overcame the sore sickness that comes of the swaying of the deck that will not cease."

"Give it him yourself, ealdorman," I said. "You know him over well to send it by another. It would not be so good a gift."

"As you will," he answered. "But I fear that viking terribly. Black grows his face, and into his beard he blows, and the hard Norse words grumble like thunder from his lips. Then know I that Odda the ealdorman has been playing the land lubber again, and wonder what is wrong. Nor is it long ere I find out, and I and my luckless crew are flying to mind what orders are howled at us. In good truth, if Alfred ever needs me to hurry in aught, let him send Thord the viking to see that I do so. One may know how I fear him, since I chose rather to risk battle with Jarl Osmund on shore than to bide near him in my own ship any longer."

Then the jarl and I laughed till our sides ached, and Odda joined us when he could not help it, so doleful was his face and solemn were his words when he told his tale. But I knew that he and Thord were the best of friends after those few days in the ship together, and that the rough old viking had given every man of the crew confidence. Nevertheless he was apt to rage somewhat when things went in slovenly wise.

So Odda helped me through with Osmund's thanks, and I was glad. I was glad also that the horns blew for the feast, so that no more could be said about the Wareham doings.

Now I sat close to King Alfred at the feast, and saw much of his ways with men. I thought it plain that he had trouble at times in keeping back the pride and haughtiness which I had heard had been the fault in both Neot and himself, for now and then they showed plainly. Then he made haste to make amends if one was hurt by what he had said in haste. But altogether I thought him even more kingly than the mighty Harald Fairhair in some ways.

Truly he had not the vast strength and stature of Norway's king, but Alfred's was the kingliness of wisdom and statecraft.

Once I said to Odda:

"Can your king fight?"

"Ay, with head as well as with hand," he answered. "His skill in weapon play makes up for lack of weight and strength. He is maybe the best swordsman and spearman in England."

I looked again at him, and I saw that since last I turned my eyes on him he had grown pale, and now his face was drawn, and was whitening under some pain, as it would seem; and I gripped Odda's arm.

"See!" I said, "the king dies! he is poisoned!"

And I was starting up, but the ealdorman held me back.

"I pray you pay no heed," he said urgently. "It is the king's dark hour; he will be well anon."

But nevertheless Alfred swayed in his seat, and two young thanes who stood waiting on him came to either side and helped him up, and together they took him, tottering, into the smaller tent that opened behind the throne; while all the guests were silent, some in fear, like myself, but others looking pityingly only.

Then a tall man in a dress strange to me--a bishop, as I knew presently--rose up, and said to those who knew not what was the matter:

"Doubtless all know that our good king is troubled with a strange illness that falls on him from time to time. This is such a time. Have no fear therefore, for the pain he suffers will pass. He does not will that any should be less merry because of him."

So the feast went on, though the great empty chair seemed to damp the merriment sadly. I asked Odda if this trouble often befell the king.

"Ay, over often," he said, "and one knows not when it will come. No leech knows what it is, and all one can say is that it seems to harm him not at all when it has gone."

I asked no more, but the king did not come back to the feast, as he would at times when things happened thus. It seemed that often the trouble fell on him when feasting, and some have said that it was sent to prevent him becoming over proud, at his own prayer.

Soon the Danes rose up, and would go. Some of the great thanes set them forth with all honour, and the feast ended. There was no long sitting over the wine cup at Alfred's board, though none could complain that he stinted them.

Then the tall bishop who had spoken just now came to me.

"The king will speak with you now, King Ranald, if you will come," he said.

So I went with him, and Odda came also. The king was lying on a couch without his heavy state robes, and when we entered the small tent the attendants left him. He was very pale, but the pain seemed to have gone, and he looked up pleasantly at me.

"My people are used to this, cousin," he said, "but I fear I put you out sorely."

"I thought you poisoned," I said; "but Odda told me not to fear."

"Ay, that has been the thought of others before this," he said. "Have you ever seen the like in any man? I ask every stranger, in hopes that I may hear of relief."

"No, I have not, lord king," I answered; "but I can grave runes that will, as I think, keep away such pain if you bear them on you. Thord, whom you know, taught me them. Maybe it would be better for him to grave them, for runes wrongly written are worse than none, and these are very powerful."

"That is a kindly thought, cousin," Alfred answered; "but I am sure that no runes will avail when the prayers of my people, from holy Neot to the little village children, do not. And I fear that even would they heal me, I must sooner bear the pain than seek to magic spells."

"Nay, but try them, King Alfred," I said; "there is no ill magic in them."

Now he saw that I was in earnest, and put me by very kindly.

"I must ask Sigehelm, our bishop here, who is my best leech next to Neot.

"What say you, father?"

"Even as you have said, my king."

"Maybe, bishop," said I, "you have never tried the might of runes?"

Whereat the good man held up his hands in horror, making no answer, and I laughed a little at him.

"Well, then," said the king, "we will ask Neot, for mostly he seems to say exactly what I do not."

"Neot has gone to Cornwall, and I had forgotten to give you that message from him. He says he will be there for a time," I said, rather ashamed at having let slip the message from my mind.

"So you saw him?" said Alfred.

"I knew he went to the ships yesterday after Godred came back," he added, laughing.

"He read my letter for me, and after that I had a good deal of talk with him," I said.

"Then," said Sigehelm, "you have spoken with the best man in all our land."

Now the king said that he would let the question of the runes, for which he thanked me, stand over thus; and then he asked me to sit down and hear what he would ask me to do for him, if I had no plans already made for myself.

I said that I had nothing so certainly planned but that I and my men would gladly serve him.

"Then," he said, "I would ask you to winter with me, and set my ships in order. There will be work for you and all your men, for you shall give them such command in any ship of mine as you know they are best fitted for. I would ask you to help me carry out that plan of which you spoke to me when I was Godred."

When Odda heard that, he rubbed his hands together, saying:

"Ay, lord king, you have found the right man at last."

"Then in the spring you shall take full command of the fleet we will build and the men we shall raise; and you shall keep the seas for me, if by that time we know that we can work well together."

He looked hard at me, waiting my answer.

"Lord king," I said at last, "this is a great charge, and they say that I am always thought older than I am, being given at least five winters beyond the two-and-twenty that I have seen;" for I thought it likely that the king held that I had seen more than I had.

"I was but twenty when I came to the throne," he answered. "I have no fear for you. More than his best I do not look for from any man; nor do I wonder if a man makes mistakes, having done so many times myself."

Here Sigehelm made some sign to the king, to which he paid no heed at the time, but went on:

"As for your men, I will give them the same pay that Harald of Norway gives to his seamen, each as you may choose to rank them for me. You may know what that is."

"Harek the scald knows," I said. "They will be well pleased, for the pay is good, and places among Harald's courtmen are much sought for."

Then Alfred smiled, and spoke of myself.

"As for King Ranald himself, he will be my guest."

"I am a wandering viking, and I seem to have found great honour," I said. "What I can do I will, in this matter. Yet there is one thing I must say, King Alfred. I would not be where men are jealous of me."

"The only man likely to be so is Odda," the king answered. "You must settle that with him. It is the place that he must have held that you are taking. No man in all England can be jealous of a viking whose business is with ships. But Odda put this into my mind at first, and then Godred found out that he was right."

"Lord king," said I, "had I known who you were at that time, I should have spoken no differently. We Northmen are free in speech as in action."

"So says Odda," replied Alfred, smiling. "He has piteous tales of one Thord, whom you sent to teach him things, and the way in which he was made to learn."

"Nevertheless," said Odda, "I will not have Thord blamed, for it is in my mind that we should have learned in no other way so quickly."

Again the bishop signed to the king, and Alfred became grave.

"Here is one thing that our good Sigehelm minds me of. It seems that you are a heathen."

"Why, no, if that means one who hates Christians," I said. "Certainly I do not do that, having no cause to do so. Those whom I know are yourself, and Neot, and Odda, and one or two more only."

"That is not it," said the king. "What we call a heathen is one who worships the old gods--the Asir."

"Certainly I do that--ill enough."

"Then," said Alfred, while Odda shifted in his seat, seeming anxious as to how I should take this, "it is our rule that before a heathen man can serve with us, he shall at least be ready to learn our faith, and also must be signed with the cross, in token that he hates it not."

"Why should I not learn of your faith?" I said. "Neot asked me of mine. As for the other, I do not know rightly what it means. I see your people sign themselves crosswise, and I cannot tell why, unless it is as we hallow a feast by signing it with Thor's hammer."

"It is more than that," Alfred said, motioning to Sigehelm to say nothing, for he was going to speak. "First you must know what it means, and then say if you will be signed therewith."

Then he said to Sigehelm:

"Here is one who will listen to good words, not already set against them, as some Danes are, by reason of ill report and the lives of bad Christians. Have no fear of telling him what you will."

Now, if I were to serve King Alfred, it seemed to me to be only reasonable that I should know the beliefs of those with whom I had to do. Then I minded me of Neot, and his way of asking about my gods, as if the belief of every man was of interest to him.

"Here is a deep matter to be talked of, King Alfred," I said. "It does not do to speak lightly and carelessly of such things. Nor am I more than your guest as yet, willing to hear what you would have me know. When winter has gone, and you know if I shall be any good to you, then will be question if I enter your service altogether, and by that time I shall know enough. Maybe I shall see Neot again; he and I began to speak of these things."

Then Sigehelm said:

"I think this is right, and Neot can tell you more in a few words than I in many. Yet whatever you ask me I will try to tell you."

"I want to speak with Neot," answered the king, "and we will ride together and seek him when peace is made. I have many things to say to him and ask him. We will go as soon as it is safe."

So ended my talk with King Alfred at that time, and I was well content therewith. So also were my men, for it was certain that every one of them would find some place of command, were it but over a watch, when Alfred's new sea levies were to be trained.

Many noble Saxons I met in the week before peace was made with the Danes in Exeter, for all the best were gathered there. Most of all I liked Ethered, the young ealdorman of Mercia, and Ethelnoth, the Somerset ealdorman, and Heregar, the king's standard bearer, an older warrior, who had seen every battle south of Thames since the long ago day when Eahlstan the bishop taught his flock how to fight for their land against the heathen.

These were very friendly with me, and I should see more of them if I were indeed to ward the Wessex coasts, and for that reason they made the more of me.

Now I saw no more of Osmund the jarl, for Odda knew that the lesser folk would mistrust me if I had any doings with the Danes. Maybe I was sorry not to see the Lady Thora; but if I had seen her, I do not know what I should have said to her, having had no experience of ladies' ways at any time, which would have made me seem foolish perhaps.

CHAPTER VII
The Pixies' Dance

I do not know that there is anything more pleasant after long weeks at sea than to have a good horse under one, and to be riding in the fresh winds of early autumn over new country that is beautiful in sunlight. So when at last every Danish chief had made submission, and the whole host had marched back to what they held as their own land in Mercia, going to Gloucester, as was said, with Odda and Ethered the ealdormen hanging on their rear with a great levy, I rode with King Alfred to find Neot his cousin gaily enough. Thord stayed with the ships, but the scald and Kolgrim were with me, and the king mounted us well. Ethelnoth of Somerset came also, and some forty men of the king's household; and all went armed, for the country we had to cross was of the wildest, though we went by the great road that runs from west to east of England, made even before the Romans came. But it crossed the edge of Dartmoor, the most desolate place in all the land, where outlaws and masterless men found fastnesses whence none could drive them.

One could not wish for a more pleasant companion than Alfred, and the miles went easily. We had both hawks and hounds with us, for there was game in plenty, and the king said that with the ending of the war, and the beginning of new hopes for his fleet, he would cast care aside for a little. So he was joyous and free in speech, and at times he would sing in lightness of heart, and would bid Harek sing also, so that it was pleasant to hear them. Ever does Harek say that no man sings better than Alfred of England.

In late afternoon we came to the wild fringe of Dartmoor, and here the king had a guest house in a little village which he was wont to use on these journeys to see Neot. We should rest there, and so cross the wastes in full daylight. So he went in, maybe fearing his sickness, which was indeed a sore burden to him, though he was wont to make light of it; but Ethelnoth asked me if we should not spend the hours of evening light in coursing a bustard or two, for many were about the moorland close at hand. They would be welcome at the king's table, he said; and I, fresh from the sea and camp, asked for nothing better than a good gallop over the wide-stretching hillsides.

So we took fresh horses from those that were led for us, and rode away. We took hawks--the king had given me a good one when we started, for a Saxon noble ever rides with hawk on wrist--and two leash of greyhounds.

I was for putting my arms aside, but the ealdorman said it was better not to do so, by reason of the moor folk, who were wild enough to fall on a small party at times. It was of little moment, however; for we rode in the lighter buff jerkins instead of heavy mail, and were not going far.

Ethelnoth took two men with him, and my two comrades were with me--Kolgrim leading the hounds in leash beside his horse. We went across the first hillside, and from its top looked northward and westward as far as one could see over the strange grey wastes of the moorland.

Then from the heather almost under our feet rose a great bustard that ran down wind with outstretched wings before us, seeking the lonelier country. Kolgrim whooped, and slipped the leash, and the hounds sprang after it, and we followed cheering. It was good to feel the rush of hillside air in our faces, and the spring and stretch of the horses under us, and to see the long-reached hounds straining after the great bird that might well be able to escape them.

I suppose that Ethelnoth started a second bird. I did not look behind me to see what any man was doing, but followed the chase round the spur of a granite-topped hillside, and forgot him. For when the bustard took wing for a heavy flight, and lit and ran again, and again flew with wings that failed each time more and more, while the strong legs were the stronger for the short rest, and when the good hounds were straining after it, one could not expect me to care for aught but that.

It had been strange if I thought of anything but the sport. I knew there were two horsemen close by, a little wide on either flank, but behind me. So we took the bird after a good chase, and then I knew that we had in some way shaken off the Saxons, and that we three vikings were together. It did not trouble us, for one looks for such partings, and Ethelnoth had his own bounds. So we went on, and found another bustard, and took it.

"Now we must go back," I said; "one must have a thought for the king's horses."

So we turned, and then a heron rose from a boggy stream below us, and that was a quarry not to be let go. I unhooded the falcon and cast her off, and straightway forgot everything but the most wonderful sight that the field and forest can give us--the dizzy upward climbing circles of hawk and heron, who strive to gain the highest place cloudwards, one for attack, the other for safety.

The evening sunlight flashed red from the bright under feathers of the strong wings as the birds swung into it from the shadow of the westward hill, and still they soared, drifting westward with the wind over our heads. Then with a great rushing sound the heron gave up, and fell, stone-like, from the falcon that had won to air above him at last. At once the long wings of his enemy closed halfway, and she swooped after him.

Then back and up, like a sword drawn at need, went the heron's sharp beak; and the falcon saw it, and swerved and shot past her nearly-taken prey. Again the heron began to tower up and up with a harsh croak that seemed like a cry of mockery; then the wondrous swing and sweep of the long, tireless wings of the passage hawk, and the cry of another heron far off, scared by its fellow's note; and again for us a canter over the moorland, eye and hand and knee together wary for both hawk above and good horse below, till the falcon bound to the heron, and both came to the ground, and there was an end in the grey shadow of the Dartmoor tors. Ay, but King Alfred's hawk was a good one!

"Now, where shall we seek Ethelnoth?" I said.

"No good seeking him," said Harek. "We had better make our way back to the village."

We coupled up the greyhounds again and hooded the falcon, and rode leisurely back over our tracks for some way. The sun set about that time into a purple bank of mist beyond the farther hills. One does not note how the miles go when one finds sport such as this, and presently we began to be sure that we had ridden farther than we had thought. We knew, as we thought, the direction from which we had come, and steered, sailor-wise, by the sunset. But we could take no straight course because of the hills, and we were as often off the line as on.

Then crept up the mist from the valleys, and we had nought to steer by, for the wind dropped. Then I said:

"Let the horses take us home; they know better than we."

So we rode on slowly until darkness came, but never saw so much as a light that might guide us. And presently we let the dogs loose, thinking that they would go homewards. But a greyhound is not like a mastiff, and they hung round us, careless, or helpless, in the mists and darkness.

Presently we came to a place where the horses stopped of their own accord. There was a sheer rock on one side, and the hill was steep below us, and a stream brawled somewhere before us.

"Well," I said, "here we stay for the night. It is of no use wandering any longer, and the night is warm."

We thought nothing of this, for any hunter knows that such a chance may befall him in a strange and wild country. So we laughed together and off-saddled and hobbled the horses, and so sat down supperless to wait for morning under the rock. The mist was clammy round us, thinning and then thickening again as the breaths of wind took it; but the moon would rise soon, and then maybe it would go.

We had no means of making a fire, and no cloaks; so sleep came hardly, and we talked long. Then the dogs grew uneasy, and presently wandered away into the fog and darkness. I thought that perhaps they heard some game stirring, and did not wonder at them.

Now I was just sleeping, when I heard the sharp yelp of a dog in pain, and sat up suddenly. Then came a second, and after that the distant sound of voices that rose for a moment and hushed again.

"We must be close to the village after all," I said, for my comrades were listening also; "but why did the hounds yell like that?"

"Some old dame has taken the broomstick to them," said Kolgrim. "They are hungry, and have put their noses into her milk pails."

"It is too late for open doors," I said; "unless they have found our own lodging, where some are waiting for us. But there they would not be beaten."

"Ho!" said Kolgrim, in another minute or so, "yonder is a fire."

The wind had come round the hillside and swept the mist away for a moment, and below us in the valley was a speck of red light that made a wide glow in the denser fog that hung there. One could hardly say how far off it was, for fog of any sort confuses distance; but the brook seemed to run in the direction of the fire, and it was likely that any house stood near its banks.

"Let us follow the brook and see what we can find," I said therefore. "These mists are chill, and I will confess that I am hungry. We cannot lose our way if we keep to the water, and the horses will be safe enough."

Anything was better, as it seemed to us, than trying to think that we slept comfortably here, and so we rose up and went down the banks of the stream at once; and the way proved to be easy enough, if rocky. The bank on this side was higher, and dry therefore, so that we had no bogs to fear. We knew enough of them in the Orkneys and on the Sutherland coast.

The white mist grew very thick, but the firelight glow grew redder as we went on, and at last we came near enough to hear many voices plainly; but presently, when one shouted, we found that the tongue was not known to us.

"Now it is plain whom we have come across," I said. "This is a camp of the Cornish tin traders, of whom the king told us. They are honest folk enough, and will put us on the great road. They must be close to it."

That seemed so likely that we left the brook and began to draw nearer to the fire, the voices growing plainer every moment, though we could see no man as yet.

Now, all of a sudden, every voice was silent, and we stopped, thinking we were heard perhaps; though it did seem strange to me that no dogs were about a camp of traders. I was just about to call out that we were friends, when there began a low, even beating, as of a drum of some sort, and then suddenly a wild howl that sounded like a war cry of maddened men, and after that a measured tramping of feet that went swiftly and in time to a chant, the like of which I had never heard before, and which made me grasp Harek by the arm.

"What, in Odin's name, is this?" r said, whispering.

"Somewhat uncanny," answered the scald. "Let us get back to the horses and leave this place."

Then we turned back, and Kolgrim's foot lit on a stone that rolled from under it, and he fell heavily with a clatter of weapons on the scattered rocks of the stream bank.

There was a howl from the firelight, and the chanting stopped, and voices cried in the uncouth tongue angrily, and there came a pattering of unshod feet round us in the thickness, with a word or two that seemed as if of command, and then silence, but for stealthy footfalls drawing nearer to us. And I liked it not.

We pulled Kolgrim up, and went on upstream, drawing our swords, though I yet thought of nothing but tin merchants whom we had disturbed in some strange play of their own. Doubtless they would take us for outlaws.

Now through the fog, dark against the flickering glow of the fire, and only seen against it, came creeping figures; and I suppose that some dull glitter of steel from helms or sword hilts betrayed us to them, for word was muttered among them, and the rattle of stones shifted by bare feet seemed to be all round us. I thought it time to speak to them.

"We are friends, good people," I said. "We mean no harm, and have but lost our way."

There was a whistle, and in a moment the leaping shadows were on us. Kolgrim went down under a heavy blow on his helm, and lay motionless; and Harek was whirled by a dozen pairs of hands off his feet, and fell heavily with his foes upon him. I slew one, or thought I slew him, and I stood over Kolgrim and kept them back with long sword sweeps, crying to them to hold, for we were friends--King Alfred's guests.

Now they were yelling to one another, and one threw a long-noosed line over me from behind. It fell over my arms, and at once they drew it tight, jerking me off my feet. As I went down, a howling crowd fell on me and took the good sword from me, and bound me hand and foot, having overpowered me by sheer numbers.

Then they looked at Kolgrim, and laughed, and left him. I was sure he was dead then, and I fell into a great dumb rage that seemed like to choke me.

They dragged the scald and me to the fire, and I saw into what hands we had fallen, and I will say that I was fairly afraid. For these were no thrifty Cornish folk, but wild-looking men, black haired and bearded, clad in skins of wolf, and badger, and deer, and sheep, with savage-eyed faces, and rough weapons of rusted iron and bronze and stone. So strange were their looks and terrible in the red light of the great fire, that I cried to Harek:

"These be trolls, scald! Sing the verses that have power to scare them."

Now it says much for Harek's courage that at once he lifted up no trembling voice and sang lustily, roaring verses old as Odin himself, such as no troll can abide within hearing of, so that those who bore him fell back amazed, and stared at him. Then I saw that on the arms and necks of one or two of these weird folk were golden rings flashing, and I saw, too, that our poor greyhounds lay dead near where I was, and I feared the more for ourselves.

But they did not melt away or fly before the spells that Harek hurled at them.

"These be mortal men," he said at last, "else had they fled ere now."

By this time they had left me, helpless as a log, and were standing round us in a sort of ring, talking together of slaying us, as I thought. I mind that the flint-tipped spears seemed cruel weapons. At last one of them said somewhat that pleased the rest, for they broke into a great laugh and clapped their hands.

"Here is a word I can understand," said Harek, "and that is 'pixies.'"

But I was looking to see where our swords were, and I saw a man take them beyond the fire and set them on what seemed a bank, some yards from it. Then they went to the scald and began to loosen his bonds, laughing the while.

"Have a care, Harek," I cried. "Make a rush for the swords beyond the fire so soon as you are free."

"I am likely to be hove into the said fire," said the scald, very coolly. "Howbeit I see the place where they are."

Then he gave a great bound and shout: but the numbers round him were too great, and they had him down again, and yet he struggled. This was sport to these savages, and those who were not wrestling with him leaped and yelled with delight to see it. And I wrestled and tore at my bonds; but they were of rawhide, and I could do nothing.

Then Harek said, breathing heavily:

"No good; their arms are like steel about me."

Then some came and dragged me back a little, and set me up sitting against a great stone, so I could see all that went on. Now I counted fifty men, and there were no women that I could see anywhere. Half of these were making a great ring with joined hands round the fire, and some piled more fuel on it--turf and branches of dwarf oak trees--and others sat round, watching the dozen or so that minded Harek. One sat cross-legged near me, with a great pot covered tightly with skin held between his knees.

Next they set Harek on his feet, and led him to the ring round the fire. Two of the men--and they were among the strongest of all--loosened their hands, and each gripped the scald by the wrist and yelled aloud, and at once the man beat on the great pot's cover drum-wise, and the ring of men whirled away round the fire in the wild dance whose foot beats we had heard as we came. Then those who sat round raised the chant we heard also.

I saw Harek struggle and try to break away; but at that they whirled yet more quickly, and he lost his footing, and fell, and was dragged up; and then he too must dance, or be haled along the ground. My eyes grew dizzy with watching, while the drum and the chant dulled into a humming in my brain.

"This cannot go on for long," I thought.

But then, from among those who sat round and chanted, I saw now one and now another dart to the ring and take the place of a dancer who seemed to tire; and so at last one came and gripped Harek's wrist and swung into the place of his first holder before he knew that any change was coming, and so with the one on the other side of him.

Then it was plain that my comrade must needs fall worn out before long, and I knew what I was looking on at. It was the dance of the pixies, in truth--the dance that ends but with the death of him who has broken in on their revels--and I would that I and Harek had been slain rather with Kolgrim by the stream yonder.

At last the scald fell, and then with a great howl they let him go, flinging him out of the circle like a stone, and he lay in a heap where they tossed him, and was quite still.

Then the dancers raised a shout, and came and sat down, and some brought earthen vessels of drink to refresh them, while they began to turn their eyes to me, whose turn came next.

Whereon a thought came into my mind, and I almost laughed, for a hope seemed to lie in a simple trick enough. That I would try presently.

Now I looked, and hoped to see Harek come to himself; but he did not stir. He lay near the swords, and for the first time now, because of some thinning of the mist, I saw what was on the bank where these had been placed. There was a great stone dolmen, as they call it--a giant house, as it were, made of three flat stones for walls, and a fourth for a roof, so heavy that none know how such are raised nowadays. They might have served for a table, or maybe a stool, for a Jotun. The two side walls came together from the back, so that the doorway was narrow; and a man might stand and keep it against a dozen, for it was ten feet high, and there was room for sword play. One minds all these things when they are of no use to him, and only the wish that they could be used is left. Nevertheless, as I say, I had one little hope.

It was not long before the savage folk were ready for my dance, and they made the ring again, refreshed. The drum was taken up once more, and a dozen men came and unbound me. I also struggled as Harek had struggled, unavailingly. When I was quiet they led me to the circle, and I watched for my plan to work.

When I was within reach of the two who should hold me, I held out my hands to grasp theirs, without waiting for them to seize me. The man on my right took my wrist in a grasp like steel; but the other was tricked, and took my hand naturally enough. Whereat my heart leaped.

"Now will one know what a grip on the mainsheet is like!" I thought; and even as the hand closed there came the yell, and the thud of the earthen drum, and I was whirled away.

Now I kept going, for my great fear was that I should grow dizzy quickly. I was taller than any man in the ring, and once I found out the measure of the chant I went on easily, keeping my eyes on the man ahead of me. That was the one to my right; for they went against the sun, which is an unlucky thing to do at any time.

Once we went round, and I saw the great dolmen and the gleam of sword Helmbiter beneath it. Then it was across the fire, and again I passed it. I could not choose my place, as it seemed, and suddenly with all my force I gripped the hand I held and around the hones of it together, so that no answering grip could come. In a moment the man let go of his fellow with the other hand, and screamed aloud, and cast himself on the ground, staying the dance, so that those after him fell over us. I let go, and swung round and smote my other holder across the face; and he too let go, and I was free, and in the uproar the dancers knew not what had happened. Smiting and kicking, I got clear of them, and saw that the dolmen towered across the fire, and straightway I knew that through the smoke was the only way. I leaped at it, and cleared it fairly, felling a man on the other side as I did so.

Then I had Helmbiter in my hand, and I shouted, and stepped back to the narrow door of the dolmen, and there stood, while the wild men gathered in a ring and howled at me. One ran and brought the long line that had noosed me before, but the stone doorway protected me from that; and one or two hurled spears at me, clumsily enough for me to ward them off.

So we stood and watched each other, and I thought they would make a rush on me. Harek lay within sweep of my sword, and his weapon was nearer them than me, and one of them picked it up and went to plunge it in him.

Then I stepped out and cut that man down, and the rest huddled back a little at my onslaught. Whereon I drew my comrade back to my feet, lest they should bring me out again and noose me.

As I did that, the one who seemed to be the chief leaped at me, club in air; but I was watching for him, and he too fell, and I shouted, to scare back the rest.

There was an answering shout, and Kolgrim, with the Berserker fury on him, was among the wild crowd from out of the darkness, and his great sword was cutting a way to my side.

Then they did not stay for my sword to be upon them also, but they fled yelling and terror stricken, seeming to melt into the mist. In two minutes the firelit circle was quiet and deserted, save for those who had fallen; and my comrade and I stared in each other's faces in the firelight.

"Comrade," I cried in gladness, "I thought you were slain."

"The good helm saved me," he answered; "but I came round in time. What are these whom we have fought?"

I suppose the fury kept him up so far, for now I saw that his face was ashy pale, and his knees shook under him.

"Are you badly hurt?" I asked.

"My head swims yet--that is all. Where is the scald?"

I turned to him and pointed. Kolgrim sat down beside him and bent over him, leaning against the stone of the great dolmen.

"I do not think he is dead, master," he said. "Let us draw him inside this house, and then he will be safe till daylight--unless the trolls come back and we cannot hold this doorway till the sun rises."

"They are men, not trolls," I said, pointing to the slain who lay between us and the fire in a lane where Kolgrim had charged through them, "else had we not slain them thus."

"One knows not what Sigurd's sword will not bite," he said.

"Why, most of that is your doing," I said, laughing a little.

But he looked puzzled, and shook his head.

"I mind leaping among them, but not that I slew any."

Now I thought that he would be the better for food. There had been plenty of both food and drink going among these wild people, whatever they were, and they had not waited to take anything. So I said I would walk round the fire and see what I could find, and went before he could stay me.

I had not far to go either, for there were plentiful remains of a roasted sheep or two set aside with the skins, and alongside them a pot of heather ale; so that we had a good meal, sitting in the door of the dolmen, while the moon rose. But first we tried to make Harek drink of the strong ale. He was beginning to breathe heavily now, and I thought he would come round presently. Whether he had been hurt by the whirling of the dance or by the fall when they cast him aside, I could not tell, and we could do no more for him.

"Sleep, master," said Kolgrim, when we had supped well; "I will watch for a time."

And he would have it so, and I, seeing that he was refreshed, was glad to lie down and sleep inside the dolmen, bidding him wake me in two hours and rest in turn.

But he did not. It was daylight when I woke, and the first ray of the sun came straight into the narrow doorway and woke me. And it waked Harek also. Kolgrim sat yet in the door with his sword across his knees.

"Ho, scald!" I said, "you have had a great sleep."

"Ay, and a bad dream also," he answered, "if dream it was."

For now he saw before us the burnt-out fire, and the slain, and the strangely-trampled circle of the dance.

"No dream, therefore," he said. "Is it true that I was made to dance round yon fire till I was nigh dead?"

"True enough. I danced also in turn," I said.

And then I told him how things had gone after his fall.

"Kolgrim has fought, therefore, a matter of fifty trolls," I said; "which is more than most folk can say for themselves."

Whereat he growled from the doorway:

"Maybe I was too much feared to know what I was doing."

We laughed at him, but he would have it so; and then we ate and drank, and spoke of going to where we had left the horses, being none so sure that we should find them at all.

Now the sun drank up the mists, and they cleared suddenly; and when the last wreaths fled up the hillsides and passed, we saw that the horses yet fed quietly where we had left them, full half a mile away up the steep rise down which the stream came.

And it was strange to see what manner of place this was in daylight, for until the mist lifted we could not tell in the least, and it was confused to us. Now all the hillsides glowed purple with heather in a great cup round us, and we were on a little rise in the midst of them whereon stood the dolmen, and the same hands doubtless that raised it had set up a wide circle of standing stones round about it, such as I have seen in the Orkneys. It was not a place where one would choose to spend the night.

There was no sign of the wild folk anywhere outside the stone circle. They had gone, and there seemed no cover for them anywhere, unless they dwelt in clefts and caves of the bare tors around us. So we feared no longer lest there should be any ambush set for us, and went about to see what they had left.

There were the long line that had noosed me, the earthen drum with its dry skin head, the raw hide thongs we had been bound with, and the food and drink; and that was all save what weapons lay round the slain, and the bodies of the two good greyhounds.

"These are but men, and not trolls as one might well think," I said, looking on those who lay before us.

One whom I had slain had a heavy gold torque round his neck, and twisted gold armlets, being the chief, as I think. Kolgrim took these off and gave them to me, and then he went to the drum and dashed it on a stone and broke it, saying nothing.

"Let us be going," I said. "These folk will come back and see to their dead."

But Kolgrim looked at the drumhead and took it, and then coiled the long line on his arm.

"Trust a sailor for never losing a chance of getting a new bit of rigging," said Harek, laughing; for he seemed none the worse for the things of last night, which indeed began to seem ghostly and dreamlike to us all. "But what good is the bit of skin?"

"Here be strange charms wrought into it," Kolgrim said. "It will make a sword scabbard that will avail somewhat against such like folk if ever we meet them again."

Truly there were marks as of branded signs on the bit of skin, and so he kept it; and I hung the gold trophies in my belt, and Harek took some of the remains of our supper: and so we went to the horses, seeing nothing of the wild men anywhere.

Very glad were the good steeds to see us come, and the falcon, who still sat on the saddle where I had perched her, spread her wings and ruffled her feathers to hear us. I unhooded and fed her; and we washed in the stream, and set out gaily enough, making southward, for so we thought we should strike the great road. And at last, when we saw its white line far off from a steep hillside, I was glad enough.

I cannot tell how we had reached our halting place through the hills in the dark, nor could I find it again directly. It was midday before we reached the road, riding easily; so that, what with the swift gallop of the hunting and the long hours of riding in mist and darkness, we had covered many miles. We saw no house till we were close to the road, and then lit on one made of stones and turf hard by it, where an old woman told us that no party had been by since daylight.

So we turned eastward and rode to meet the king, and did so before long. He had left men at his village to wait for us in case we came back there; but he laughed at us for losing ourselves, though he said he had no fear for sailors adrift in the wilds when Ethelnoth came in without us.

But when, as we rode on, I told him what had befallen us, he listened gravely, and at last said:

"I have heard the like of this before. Men say that the pixies dwell in the moorland, and will dance to death those who disturb them. What think you of those you have seen?"

I said that, having slain them, one could not doubt that they were men, if strange ones.

"That is what I think," he answered. "They are men who would be thought pixies. Maybe they are the pixies. I believe they are the last of the old Welsh folk who have dwelt in these wilds since the coming of the Romans or before. There were the like in the great fens of East Anglia and Mercia when Guthlac the Holy went there, and he thought them devils. None can reach these men or know where they dwell. Maybe they are heathen, and their dance in that stone ring was some unholy rite that you have seen. But you have been very far into the wastes, and I have never seen those stones."

And when he handled the gold rings, he showed me that they were very old; but when he handled the drumhead and looked at the marks thereon, he laughed.

"Here is the magic of an honest franklin's cattle brand. I have seen it on beasts about the hills before now. The pixies have made a raid on the farmer's herds at some time."

Now I think that King Alfred was right, and that we had fallen into the hands of wild Welsh or Cornish moor folk. But one should hear Kolgrim's tale of the matter as he shows his sword sheath that he made of the drumhead; for nothing would persuade him that it was not of more than mortal work.

"Had the good king been in that place with us, he would have told a different tale altogether," he says.

So we went on our journey quietly, and ever as we went and spoke with Alfred, I began to be sure that this pale and troubled king was the most wondrous man that I had ever seen. And now, as I look back and remember, I know that in many ways he was showing me that the faith he held shaped his life to that which seemed best in him to my eyes.

I know this, that had he scoffed at the Asir, I had listened to Neot not at all. But when we came to his place, I was ready, and more than ready, to hear what he had to tell me.

CHAPTER VIII
The Black Twelfth-Night

When we came to the little out of the way village among the Cornish hills near which Neot, the king's cousin, had his dwelling, I thought it strange that any one should be willing to give up the stirring life at court for such a place as this. Here was only one fair-sized house in the place, and that was built not long before by the king for his own use when he came here, which was often. And Neot's own dwelling was but a little stone-walled and turf-roofed hut, apart from all others, on the hillside, and he dwelt there with one companion--another holy man, named Guerir, a Welshman by birth--content with the simple food that the villagers could give him, and spending his days in prayer and thought for the king and people and land that he loved.

But presently, as I came to know more of Neot, it seemed good that some should live thus in quiet while war and unrest were over the country, else had all learning and deeper thought passed away. It is certain from all that I have heard, from the king himself and from others, that without Neot's steady counsel and gathered wisdom Alfred had remained haughty and proud, well-nigh hated by his people, as he had been when first he came to the throne.

At one time he would drive away any who came to him with plaints or tales of wrong and trouble; but Neot spoke to him in such wise that he framed his ways differently. And now I used to wonder to see him stay and listen patiently to some rambling words of trifling want, told by a wayside thrall, to which it seemed below his rank to hearken, and next I would know that it was thus he made his people love him as no other king has been loved maybe. There was no man who could not win hearing from him now.

It is said of him that when Neot showed him the faults in his ways, he asked that some sickness, one that might not make him useless or loathsome to his people, might be sent him to mind him against his pride, and that so he had at first one manner of pain, and now this which I had seen. It may be so, for I know well that so he made it good for him, and he bore it most patiently. Moreover, I have never heard that it troubled him in the times of direst need, though the fear of it was with him always.

Now what Alfred and Neot spoke of at this time I cannot say, except that it was certainly some plan for the good of the land. I and my comrades hunted and hawked day by day until the evening came, and then would sup plainly with the king, and then sit at Neot's door in the warm evening, and talk together till the stars came out.

Many things we spoke of, and Neot told me what I would. I cannot write down those talks, though I mind every word of them. But there was never any talk of the runes I had offered.

Neot spoke mostly, but Alfred put in words now and then that ever seemed to make things plainer; and I mind how Ethelnoth the ealdorman sat silent, listening to questions and answers that maybe he had never needed to put or hear concerning his own faith.

At first I was only asking because the king wished it, then because I grew curious, and because I thought it well to know what a Saxon's faith was if I was to bide among Alfred's folk. Kolgrim listened, saying nought. But presently Harek the scald would ask more than I, and his questions were very deep, and I thought that as days went on he grew thoughtful and silent.

Then one evening the song woke within the scald's breast, and he said to Neot:

"Many and wise words have you spoken, Father Neot. Hear now the song of Odin--the Havamal--and tell me if you have aught to equal it."

"Sing, my son," the good man answered. "Wisdom is from above, and is taught in many ways."

Then Harek sang, and his voice went over the hillsides, echoing wonderfully; while we who heard him were very still, unwilling to lose one word or note of the song. Many verses and sayings of the "Havamal" I knew, but I had not heard it all before. Now it seemed to me that no more wisdom than is therein could be found.

So when Harek ended Neot smiled on him, and said:

"That is a wondrous song, and I could have listened longer. There is little therein that one may not be wiser in remembering."

"There is nought wiser; it is Odin's wisdom," said Harek.

Now the old hermit, Guerir, Neot's friend, sat on the stone bench beside the king, and he said:

"Hear the words of the bards, the wondrous 'triads' of old time."

And he chanted them in a strange melody, unlike aught I had ever heard. And they, the old savings, were wise as the "Havamal" itself. But he stopped ere long, saying:

"The English words will not frame the meaning rightly. I do no justice to the wisdom that is hidden."

Then Neot turned to the king, and said:

"Sing to Harek words from the book of Wisdom that we know. I think you can remember it well."

"I have not rhymed it," the king answered; "but sometimes the song shapes itself when it is needed."

He took Guerir's little harp and tuned it afresh and sang. And in the words were more wisdom than in the Havamal or in the song of the bards, so that I wondered; and Harek was silent, looking out to the sunset with wide eyes.

Not long did the king sing, as it seemed to us; and when he ceased, Harek made no sign.

"Sing now, my cousin, words that are wiser than those; even sing from the songs of David the king."

So said Neot; and Alfred sang again very wondrously, and as with some strange awe of the words he said. Then to me it seemed that beside these the words of Odin were as nought. They became as words of the wisdom of daily life, wrung from the lips of men forced to learn by hardness and defeat and loss; and then the words that Alfred had first sung were as those of one who knew more than Odin, and yet spoke of daily troubles and the wisdom that grows thereout. But now the things that he sang must needs have come from wisdom beyond that of men--wisdom beyond thought of mine. And if so it seemed to me, I know not how the heart of the scald, who was more thoughtful and knew more than I, was stirred.

He rose up when Alfred ceased, and walked away down the hillside slowly, as in a dream, not looking at us; and the kindly Saxons smiled gently, and said nothing to rouse him.

It is in my mind that Harek's eyes were wet, for he had lost somewhat--his belief in things he held dearest and first of all--and had as yet found nothing that should take its place. There is nought harder than that to a man.

When he had passed out of hearing, I said:

"Are there wiser things yet that you may sing?"

"Ay, and that you may learn, my son," answered Neot. "Listen."

Then he spoke words from Holy Writ that I know now--the words that speak of where wisdom may be found. And he said thereafter, and truly, that it was not all.

Then I seemed to fear greatly.

"Not now, my king, not now," I said; "it is enough."

Then those two spoke to me out of their kind hearts. Yet to me the old gods were very dear, and I clung to them. Neither Neot nor the king said aught against them, being very wise, at that time.

Presently Harek came back, and his eyes were shining.

"Tell me more of this learning," he said, casting himself down on the grass at Alfred's feet. "Scald have I been since I could sing, and nought have I heard like this."

"Some day," Neot said; "it is enough now that you should know what you have heard."

So ended that strange song strife on Neot's quiet hillside. The sun set, and the fleecy mists came up from the little river below, and we sat silent till Alfred rose and said farewell, and we went to the guest house in the village.

Now I think that none will wonder that after we had been with Neot for those ten days, we were ready and willing to take on us the "prime signing," as they called it, gladly and honestly. So we were signed with the cross by Neot, and Alfred and Ethelnoth and Guerir were our witnesses.

I know that many scoff at this, because there are heathen who take this on them for gain, that they may trade more openly, or find profit among Christian folk, never meaning or caring to seek further into the faith that lies open, as it were, before them. But it was not so with us, nor with many others. We were free to serve our old gods if we would, but free also to learn the new faith; and to learn more of it for its own sake seemed good to us.

So we went back to Exeter with the king, and Neot came for a few miles with us, on foot as was his wont, parting from us with many good words. And after he was gone the king was cheerful, and spoke with me about the ordering of the fleet we were to build, as though he were certain that I should take command of it in the spring.

And, indeed, after that time there was never any question among us three vikings about it. It seemed to us that if we had lost Norway as a home, we had gained what would make as good a country; and, moreover, Alfred won us to him in such wise that it seemed we could do nought but serve him. There can be few who have such power over men's hearts as he.

Exeter seemed very quiet when we came back; for the Danes were gone, and the king's levies had dispersed, and only the court remained, though that was enough to make all the old city seem very gay to those who had known it only in the quiet of peace.

One man was there whom I had hardly thought to meet again, and that was Osmund the Danish jarl. For he was a hostage in the king's hands, to make more sure that the peace would be kept. I knew there were hostages to be given by the beaten host; but I had not asked who they were, and had been at the ships when they were given up, ten of them in all, and of the best men among the Danes.

Alfred treated his captives very well, giving them good lodgings, and bating them often at his own table, so that I saw much of Osmund. And more than that, I saw much of the Lady Thora, his daughter, who would not leave him. I do not think that there could be more certain manner of beginning a close friendship between a warrior and the lady whom he shall learn to hold first in his heart, than that in which I first met this fair maiden.

Now one will say that straightway I must fall in love with her, but it was not so: first of all, because I had not time, since every day Alfred planned new ships with me and Thord; and next, because I was his guest, and Osmund was his hostage. Maybe I thought not much of that, however, not having the thoughts of a Saxon towards a Dane. But I will say this, that among all the fair ladies of the queen's household there was none of whom I thought at all; while of what Thora would say I thought often, and it pleased me that the Lady Etheldreda, Odda's fair eldest daughter, took pity on the lonely maiden, and made much of her after a time.

Three weeks I was in Exeter, and then the king went eastward through his country to repair what damage had been done. Then I took up my work for him, and got out my ship and sailed westward, putting into every harbour where a ship might be built, and set the shipwrights to work, having with me royal letters to sheriffs and port reeves everywhere that they should do what I ordered them. In each yard I left two or three of my men, that they should oversee all things; because if one Saxon thinks he knows better than his fellow, he will not be ruled by him, whereas no man can dispute what a born viking has to say about ship craft. It seemed that all were glad of our coming, and the work began very cheerfully.

All this took long, but at last I came up the Severn, and so into the river Parret--for the weather would serve me no longer and laid up the ship in a creek there is at Bridgwater, where Heregar, the king's standard bearer, was sheriff. He made me very welcome at his great house near by, at Cannington, and then rode with me to Bristol; and there I set two ships in frame, and so ended all I could do for the winter. King Alfred would have a fleet when the spring came.

Then Heregar and I would go to Chippenham, to spend the time of the Yule feast with King Alfred; and we rode there with Harek and Kolgrim, and were made most welcome. Many friends whom I had made at Exeter were there, and among them, quiet and yet hopeful of release, were the hostages.

That was a wonderful Yule to me; but I will say little of it, for the tale of the most terrible Twelfth Night that England has ever known overshadows it all, though there were things that I learned at that time, sitting in the church with Harek, at the west end, and listening, that are bright to me. But they are things by themselves, and apart from all else.

Now peace was on all the land, and the frost and snow were bright and sharp everywhere; so that men said that it was a hard winter, and complained of the cold which seemed nothing to us Northmen. Maybe there was a foot of snow in deep places, and the ice was six inches thick on the waters; and the Saxons wondered thereat, saying that they minded the like in such and such years before. Then I would tell them tales of the cold north to warm them, but I think they hardly believed me.

The town was full of thanes and their families who had been called to Alfred's Yule keeping, and it was very bright and pleasant among them all, though here and there burnt ruins made gaps between the houses, minding one that the Danes had held the place not so long since.

So they kept high feasting for Yule and the New Year, and the last great feast was for Twelfth Night, and all were bidden for that, and there was much pleasant talk of what revels should be in the evening.

The day broke very bright and fair, with a keen, windless frost that made the snow crisp and pleasant to ride over, hindering one in no way. And there was the sun shining over all in a way that made the cold seem nought to me, so that I had known nothing more pleasant than this English winter, having seen as yet nothing of the wet and cold times that come more often than such as this. Then, too, the clear ringing of the bells from every village near and far was new to me, and I thought I had heard nothing sweeter than the English call to the church for high festival.

So I went to the king, and asked him if I might take with me the Danish jarl for a ride beyond the town; for the hostages were only free inside the walls, and I knew this would please Osmund and Thora well. I said that I would see to his safety and be answerable for him.

"This must be Osmund, I suppose," the king said, smiling. "I have heard how you came to know him and his fair daughter at Wareham. It was well done, though maybe I should blame you for running over-much risk."

"I think I ran little, lord king," I said; "and I could have done no less for the poor maiden."

"Surely; but I meant that to go at all was over dangerous."

"I am ready to do the same again for you, my king," I said. "And after all I was in no danger."

Then said the king, smiling gravely at me:

"Greater often are the dangers one sees not than those which one has to meet. I have my own thoughts of what risk you ran.

"Well, take your fair lady and the jarl also where you will. But the feast is set for two hours after noon, and all must be there."

So I thanked him, and he bade me ask his steward for horses if I would, and I went straight to Osmund from his presence.

"I think it will be a more pleasant ride than our last," said Thora. "Yet that is one that I shall not forget."

Then I tried to say that I hoped she did not regret it either, but I minded me of the loved nurse she had to leave, and was silent in time. Yet I thought that she meant nothing of sorrow in the remembrance as she spoke.

We called out my two comrades, for Osmund liked them well, and rode away northward, that the keen air might be behind us as we returned. That was all the chance that led us that way, and it was well that we were so led, as things turned out.

The white downs and woodlands sparkling with frost were very beautiful as we rode, and we went fast and joyously in the fresh air; but the countryside was almost deserted, for the farmsteads were burned when the Danes broke in on the land last spring, and few were built up as yet. The poor folk were in the town now, for the most part, finding empty houses enough to shelter them, and none left to whom they belonged.

Now we rode for twelve miles or so, and then won to a hilltop which we had set as our turning place. I longed to stand there and look out over all this country, that seemed so fair after the rugged northern lands I had known all my life. But when we were there we saw a farmstead just below us, on the far slope of the gentle hill; and we thought it well to go there and dismount, and maybe find some food for ourselves and the horses before turning back.

So we went on. It was but a couple of furlongs distant, and the buildings lay to the right of the road, up a tree-shaded lane of their own.

We turned into this, and before we had gone ten yards along it I halted suddenly. I had seen somewhat that seemed strange, and unmeet for the lady to set eyes on.

"Bide here, jarl," I said, "and let us go on and see what is here; the place looks deserted."

And I looked meaningly at him, glancing at Thora.

But he had seen what had caught my eye, and he stayed at once, turning back into the main road, and beckoning Harek to come with him and Thora, for some reason of his own.

Then Kolgrim and I went on. What we had seen was a man lying motionless by the farm gate, in a way that was plain enough to me. And when we came near, we knew that the man had been slain. He was a farm thrall, and he had a pitchfork in his hand, the shaft of which was half cut through, as with a sword stroke that he had warded from him, though he had not stayed a second cut, for so he was killed.

"Here is somewhat strangely wrong," I said.

"Outlaws' work," answered Kolgrim; for the wartime had made the masterless folk very bold everywhere, and the farm was lonely enough.

We rode through the swinging gate, and then we saw three horses by the stable yard paling, and with them was an armed man, who saw us as we came round the house, and whistled shrilly. Whereon two others came running from the building, and asked in the Danish tongue what he called for. The first man pointed to us, and all three mounted at once. They were in mail and helm, fully armed.

Now we were not, for we had thought of no meeting such as this, and rode in woollen jerkins and the like, and had only our swords and seaxes, as usual; but for the moment I did not think that we should need either. Outlaws such as I took them for do not make any stand unless forced.

Presently one of the men, having mounted leisurely enough, called to us.

"There is no plunder to be had," he said, "even if you were not too late; our folk cleared out the place over well last time."

Then a fourth man, one who seemed of some rank, rode from beyond the house, passing behind us without paying any heed to us, except that he called to the men to follow him, and so went down the lane towards where Osmund was waiting with Harek.

All this puzzled me, and so I cried to the three men:

"What do you here? Whose men are you?"

At that they looked at one another--they were not more than ten yards from us now--and halted.

"You should know that," one said; and then he put his hand to his sword suddenly, adding in a sharp voice:

"These be Saxons; cut them down."

When hand goes to sword hilt one knows what is coming, and even as the man said his last words I was on them, and Kolgrim was not a pace behind me. The Dane's sword was out first; but I was upon him in time. His horse swerved as mine plunged forward, and I rode him down, horse and man rolling together in the roadway. Then the man to my right cut at me, and I parried the blow and returned it. Then that horse was riderless, and I heard Kolgrim laugh as his man went down with a clatter and howl.

My horse plunged on for a few steps, and then I turned. Kolgrim had one horse by the bridle, and was catching that which had fallen. I caught the other, and so we looked at each other.

"This is your luck, master," said Kolgrim.

"Well," said I, "these are Danes, and I do not think they are wanderers either. Here are forage bags behind the saddles. One would say that they were on the march if this were not mid-winter and time of peace. The horsemen in advance of a host, or the like."

Then Kolgrim said:

"Where has the other man gone? I had forgotten him for the moment."

"Bide here and see if any poor farm folk are yet alive," I said. "I will ride after him."

So I gave the horse I was holding to my comrade, and went back quickly down the lane to where Osmund and the other two were. The man I sought was speaking with the jarl, whose face was white and troubled. Harek was looking red and angry, but on Thora's face was written what I could not understand--as it were some fear of a new terror.

Now it was plain that all three were very glad of my coming; but the stranger looked round for a single glance, and then went on speaking to Osmund.

"Be not a fool, jarl," he said angrily. "Here is your chance; let it not slip."

"I tell you that my word shall not be broken," Osmund replied, very coldly and sternly.

"What say you, girl?" the man said then, turning to Thora. "Short shrift will be the jarl's when Alfred finds that we are on him."

But Thora turned away without a word, and then the Dane spoke to me:

"Here! you are another hostage, I suppose."

"I am not," I answered.

"Well, then, here is Jarl Osmund, if you know him not, and he is one. Tell him that what I say is true, and that Chippenham town will be burned out tonight king and all."

I saw that the Dane, seeing that I was armed, and not clad in the Saxon manner altogether, took me for one of his own people. And from his words it was plain that some of the Danish chiefs had broken away from Guthrum, and were making this unheard-of mid-winter march to surprise Alfred. Most likely they were newcomers into Mercia, and had nought to do with the Exeter host.

"Maybe it is true," I answered; "but I am no Dane."

He laughed loudly.

"Why, then, you are one of Alfred's Norsemen! Now I warn you to get away from Chippenham, for it is unsafe, and there will be no king to pay you tomorrow. I think that you will say with me that it were better for Osmund to come with me to meet the host than to go back to Alfred and be hung before he flies--if he gets news of us in time to do so."

Herein the man was right, for Alfred had warned the chiefs at Exeter that he held the hostages in surety for peace on the part of all and any Danes. But I thought I might learn more, so I said:

"Guthrum thinks little of his friends' lives."

"Guthrum!" the Dane answered sneeringly; "what have we to do with him and his peace making?"

"What then are you Hubba's men?"

"He is in Wales. Think you that we are all tied to the sons of Lodbrok?"

"You might have worse leaders," I said.

And just then Kolgrim came along the lane, leading the three horses, and on them were the armour and weapons of the slain. It was not my comrade's way to leave for other folk aught that was worth having.

At once the Dane knew what had happened, and he swung his horse round and spurred it fiercely, making for flight. Then Harek looked at me and touched his sword hilt, and I nodded. It was well to let no tidings of our knowledge go back to the host. After the Dane therefore went Harek, and I looked at Osmund.

"Jarl," I said, "I am in a strait here. If you go back, your life is in Alfred's hands."

"I know it," he said, smiling faintly. "It is a hard place maybe for us both, but there is only one way. You must get back to the king, and I with you; for you have to answer for me, and my word is passed not to escape."

Then Thora said:

"The king is just, as all men know. How should he slay you for what you cannot help?"

"Ay," he answered, smiling at her, "that is right."

So she was satisfied, knowing nought perhaps of what the place of a hostage is.

So we started back to Chippenham quickly, and after us I heard Harek coming. He had a led horse when he joined us, and I knew that none would take word to the Danish host that the king was warned.

When we came to the hilltop over which we had ridden so blithely an hour ago or less, we looked back, and at first saw nothing. Then over the white brow of a rolling down that shone in the level sunlight came a black speck that grew and lengthened, sliding, as it were, like a snake down the hillside. And that line sparkled like ice in the sunlight from end to end; for it was the Danish host on the march, and in two hours they would be where we stood, and in two more they who were mounted would be in Chippenham streets, where Alfred had not enough men even to guard the gates against such a force as was coming.

Then we rode hard for the lives of all who were in the town, and as I went I thought also that we rode to the death of the brave, honest jarl who was beside me, saying nothing, but never letting his horse falter. Just as bravely rode Thora.

In an hour we were at the gates, and I rode straight to the king's house, and sought him on urgent business.

Ethered of Mercia came out to me.

"What is it, Ranald?" he said. "The Witan is set now."

I told him in few words, and his face changed.

"It seems impossible in frost and snow," he said.

"Ay; but there are proofs," I said, pointing through the great doorway.

There was my party, and Kolgrim was binding a wound on Harek's arm of which I knew nought till that moment, and the led horses and spoils were plain enough to say all.

Then Ethered made haste and took me to the great hall, where Alfred sat with some thirty thanes of his Witan, and many clergy. I knew they were to meet on some business that I had nought to do with. Ethered went to the king without any ceremony, and speaking low told him my message. Whereon the king's face grew white and then red, and he flashed out into terrible wrath:

"Forsworn and treacherous!" he cried, in a thick voice that shook with passion. "The hostages--chain them and bring them here. Their friends shall find somewhat waiting them here that shall make them wish they had kept their oaths!"

Then he said to me:

"Speak out, Ranald, and tell these thanes your news."

I spoke plainly, and they listened with whitening faces and muttered oaths. And when I ceased, one cried, hardly knowing what he said, as I think:

"This outlander rode with Osmund the Dane to bring them on us even now."

"Silence!" Alfred said; and then in a cold voice he asked me:

"Where is this Osmund? I suppose he has fled to his people."

"That he has not, though he could have done so," I answered. "Moreover, the Dane I spoke with said in so many words that this is no host of Guthrum's."

At that Alfred frowned fiercely.

"Whose then? What good is a king if he cannot make his people keep their oaths?"

There was a stir at the door, and the eyes of all turned that way. And when the thanes saw that the hostages were being led in, with Osmund at their head, a great sullen growl of wrath broke from them, and I thought all hope was gone for the lives of those captives.

"Hear you this?" the king said, in a terrible voice, when the noise ceased. "By the deed of your own people your lives are forfeit. They have broken the peace, and even now are marching on us. Your leader, Osmund himself, has seen them."

"It is true," Osmund said. "We are in the king's hands."

Then Alfred turned to the Witan, who were in disorder, and in haste, as one might see, to be gone to their houses and fly.

"You heard the Danish oath taken at Exeter; what is your word on this?"

They answered in one voice:

"Slay them. What else?"

"You hear," said the king to the Danes. "Is not the sentence just?"

"It is what one might look for," Osmund answered, "but I will say this, that this is some new band of Danes, with whom we have nought to do."

"What!" said Alfred coldly; "will you tell me that any Dane in the country did not know that I held hostages for the peace? Go to.

"See to this matter, sheriff."

Then the sheriff of Chippenham came forward, and it seemed to me that it was of no use for me to say aught; yet I would try what I could do, so I spoke loudly, for a talk had risen among the thanes.

"What is this, lord king? Will you slay Osmund the jarl, who has kept his troth, even to coming back to what he knew would be his death? You cannot slay such a man for the oath breaking of others."

Then the king looked long at me, and the sheriff stayed, and at first I expected passionate words; but the king's rage was cold and dreadful now.

"His friends slay him--not I," he answered.

Then of a sudden I minded somewhat, and clear before me stood a test by which I might know certainly if it were good that I should leave the Asir and follow the way of the white Christ.

"King Alfred," I said, "I have heard the bishop tell, in the great church here, of a king who slew the guiltless at Christmastide. There was nought too hard for any to say of that man. Moreover, I have heard strange and sweet words of peace at this time, of forgiveness of enemies and of letting go of vengeance. Are these things nought, or are they indeed those by which you guide yourselves, as Neot says?"

He was silent, gazing fixedly on me; and all the Witan were speechless, listening.

"These men are enemies maybe, but they at least have done nought. Shall you avenge yourself on them for the wrongdoing of others?"

Then the king's face changed, and he looked past me, and in his eyes grew and shone a wondrous light, and slowly he lifted up his hand, and cried, in a great voice that seemed full of joy:

"Hear this, O ye Danes and foes of the Cross. For the love of Christ, and in His name, I bid you go in peace!"

And then, as they stared at him in wonder and awe at his look and words, Alfred said to me:

"Unbind them, my brother, and let them go--nay, see them safely to some strong house; for the poor folk may slay them in their blind anger, even as would I have done."

Then no man hindered me--for it seemed as if a great fear, as of the might of the holy name, had fallen on all--and I went and cut the bonds of the captives. And as I did so, Osmund said in a low voice to me:

"First daughter and then father. We owe our lives to you."

"Nay," I answered, "but to the Christians' faith."

Then I hurried them out before news of what was on hand could get among the townsfolk, and we went quickly to my lodgings; for that was a strong house enough, and could be barred in such wise that even if any tried to attack the place in the flight that would begin directly, it would take too long to break the doors down to be safe with the host at hand.

Then came Heregar, armed and mounted, with a single man behind him, and he called for me.

"Ride out with me, King Ranald, for we must count these Danes, and see that we are not overrating their number. After that we will join the king, who goes to Glastonbury."

So I bade farewell to Osmund and to Thora, who said nought, but looked very wistfully, as if she would say words of thanks but could not; and at that I went quickly, for it seemed hard to leave her, in some way that was not clear to me, amid all the turmoil of the place.

But when we were on the road, Heregar said to me:

"It is in my mind that Osmund, your friend, will fare ill among these Danes. They will hear how he rode back, and will hold that by his means the king escaped."

"What can be done?"

"The man is one of a thousand, as it seems to me. Let us bid him leave the town and get back to Guthrum as he can."

"He can have the Danish horses," I said.

Now before sunset we had seen the Danish force, and our hearts sank. There were full ten thousand men, many of whom were mounted.

Then we rode back, and found the town in such tumult as it is not good to think on. There is nothing more terrible to see than such a flight, and in midwinter.

When we came to my lodging, Heregar went in to find Osmund. I would not see him again, lest Thora should weep. But in a few minutes he came out with the jarl.

"Here is a wise man," said Heregar. "He says that he swore to keep the peace with Alfred, and he will do it. He and the Lady Thora will go with us. There are one or two also of the other hostages who blame him for returning. He cannot stay among the Danes here."

Then I was very glad, and we made haste to have all ready for Thora's comfort on the ride that might be so long. And so we rode out after the king along the road to Glastonbury, and I think that the Danes were in the town half an hour after we left it.

Next we knew that Danes were on the road before us, and that more were hard after us. Some had skirted the town in order to cut off the king, and were pursuing him. So we struck off the road into by-lanes that Heregar knew, resting at lonely houses as we went on. And when we came to Glastonbury at last, the king was not there, nor did any know of his fate.

Then we rode, with the Danes swarming everywhere, through the Sedgemoor wastes to Bridgwater, and found rest at Cannington, Heregar's great house not far off.

CHAPTER IX
The Sign of St. Cuthberht

I suppose that in our flight from Glastonbury to Bridgwater we passed through more dangers than we knew of; for Danes were hard after us, riding even into sight from the town that evening, and next day coming even to the eastern end of the old bridge, and bandying words with the townsfolk who guarded it. Across it they dared not come, for there is a strong earthwork on the little rise from the river, which guards both bridge and town, and in it were my Norsemen with the townsfolk.

So we were in safety for a time; and it seemed likely that we might be so for long if but a few men could be gathered, for here was a stretch of country that was, as it were, a natural fastness. Three hundred years ago the defeated Welsh had turned to bay here while Kenwalch of Wessex and his men could not follow them; and now it seemed likely that here in turn would Wessex stand her ground.

It is a great square-sided patch of rolling, forest-covered country, may-be twelve miles long from north to south, and half as much across. None can enter it from the north, because there is the sea, and a wild coast that is not safe for a landing; on the west the great, steep, fort-crested Quantock Hills keep the border; on the eastern side is the river Parret, and on the north the Tone, which joins it. Except at Bridgwater, at the eastern inland corner, and Taunton, at the western--one at the head of the tidal waters of the Parret, and the other guarding the place where the Quantocks end--there is no crossing the great and wide-stretching fens of Sedgemoor and Stanmoor and the rest that lie on either bank of the rivers. Paths there are that the fenmen know, winding through mere and peat bog and swamp, but no host can win through them; and perhaps those marches are safer borders than even the sea.

If one came from the sea, one must land at Watchet, and then win a path across the Quantocks, and there is the ancient camp of Dowsborough to block the way; or else put into the Parret, and there, at the first landing place, where they say that Joseph of Arimathaea landed, bearing the holy thorn staff in his hand, is the strong hill fort of Combwich, old as the days of that Joseph, or maybe older.

So with walled towns and hill forts the corners of Heregar's land were kept; and with sea and marsh and hill the sides were strong, and we thought to find Alfred the king here before us. But he was not; and next day we rode on to Taunton to seek him there, for that was the strongest fortress in that part of the west. And again he was not to be heard of. Then fear for his life began to creep into our minds, and we came back to Cannington sorely downcast.

Then Heregar spoke to me very kindly of what he thought I could best do, and it was nothing more or less than that I should leave this land, which seemed to have no hope of honour for me now.

"Go rather to Rolf, your countryman," he said. "There is great talk of his doings in Neustria beyond the Channel. It is your kindness only that holds you here, King Ranald, and there wait glory and wealth for you and your men."

So he urged me for a little while, not giving me time to answer him as I would; but when I said nothing he stayed his words, and then I spoke plainly, and it was good to see his face light up as I did so.

"It shall not be said of me that I left King Alfred, who has been my good friend, in time of trouble; rather will I stay here and do what I can to help him out of it. Why, there are ships that I have put in frame for him in the western ports that the Danes will not reach yet, if at all. When spring comes we will man them and make a landing somewhere, and so divide the Danish host at least."

"Now I will say no more," answered the thane, putting his hand on mine. "Speak thus to the king when we find him, and it will do him good, for I think that when he left Chippenham he was well-nigh despairing."

"It is hard to think that of Alfred," I said.

"Ay; but I saw his face as he rode away just before I sought you. Never saw I such a look on a man's face before, and I pray that I may not see it again. It was terrible to look on him, for I think he had lost all hope."

"For the time, maybe," I said; "but I cannot believe that when the first weight of the blow passed he was not himself again."

Presently there came a shift of wind and a quick thaw with driving rain, and floods grew and spread rapidly in the low-lying lands. One good thing can be said of this weather, and that was that because of it the Danes burned neither town nor farmstead, needing all the shelter they could find.

Three days that gale lasted, and then the wind flew round again to the north, with return of the frost in even greater strength than before; and the weather-wise fishers and shepherds said that this betokened long continuance thereof, and so it seemed likely to be.

But through it all we heard no tidings of the king; and in one way that was good, for had he been taken by the Danes, they would have let all men know thereof soon enough. But we feared that he might have been slain by some party who knew not who he was, and that fear hung heavily over us all.

Next we had a messenger from Odda, who was at Exeter, asking for sure word of what had befallen; and the one hope we had yet was gone, for he too knew nothing.

Very sad and silent was Osmund the jarl, though he and Thora were most kindly received as honoured guests by the Lady Alswythe and the household of the thane.

Once I asked him what his plans were, for we were both strangers, and I knew him best.

"Presently," he said, "I shall try to get back to Guthrum. While I am here I will be held as if I were no one--as a harmless ghost who walks the house, neither seeing nor hearing aught. If there were Welsh to be fought, I would fight beside you all, gladly, for Alfred; but as the war is against my own folk, I can do nothing. I will neither fight for them nor fight against them; for King Alfred and you, my friend, gave me life, and it is yours. I think that some day I may be of use to Alfred in helping to bring about a lasting peace."

"If we find him," I said.

"Ay, you will find him. He is hiding now for some wise reason that we shall know. I think it is not known how his plans are feared by our folk. I am sure that of this midwinter march the Danes will say that it is worthy of Alfred himself."

Nevertheless we heard nothing of him, though the thane had men out everywhere trying to gain news. All that they heard was the same tale of dismay from whoever they might meet, and I think that but for a chance we should not have found him until he chose to come forth from his refuge.

Heregar the thane had a strange serving man, the same who had ridden with him and me to meet the Danish forces; and this man was a fenman from Sedgemoor, who knew all the paths through the wastes. Lean and loose-limbed he was, and somewhat wild looking, mostly silent; but where his lord went he went also. They said that he had saved the thane's life more than once in the great battles about Reading, when the Danish host first came.

This man was out daily, seeking news with the rest; and one day, just a week after we had come to Cannington, when the frost had bound everything fast again, he came home and sought his master.

Heregar and I and Osmund sat together silently before the fire, and he looked from one to the other of us outlanders.

"Speak out, Dudda," said Heregar, who knew his ways; "here are none but friends."

"Ay, friends of ours sure enough; but are they the king's?"

"Most truly so. Have you news of him?"

"I have not; but I have heard some fenmen talking."

Then Osmund rose up and went his way silently, as was his wont; and Dudda grinned at us.

"He is a good Dane," he said; "now I can speak. They say there is some great lord hiding in the fens beyond the round hill where Tone and Parret join, that we call the Stane--somewhere by Long Hill, they say. Now I mind that one day when the king rode with you across the Petherton heights, he looked out over all the fens, and called me and asked much of them. And when I told him what he would, he said, 'Here is a place where a man might lie hid from all the world if he chose.' So he laughed, and we rode on."

"I mind it," said Heregar; "but it was many years ago."

"I think he may be there, for our king weighs his words, and does not forget. I held his horse at your door in Chippenham the other day, and he spoke to me by name, and put me in mind of little things for which he had laughed at me in those same old days. He is a good king."

So said Dudda, the rough housecarl; and it is in my mind that the kindly remembrance would have wiped out many a thought of wrong, had there been any. That is a kingly gift to remember all, and no king has ever been great who has not had it; for it binds every man to his prince when he knows that aught he has done is not forgotten, so it be good to recall.

So it came to pass that next day, very early, we rode away, taking Harek and Kolgrim and this man Dudda with us, well armed and mounted and full of hope, across the southward ridge that looks down over the fens of the meeting of Tone and Parret, where they are widest and wildest. No Danes had crossed them yet, and when I saw what they were like I thought that they never could do so.

And as I looked at the long chains of ice-bound meres and pools that ran among dense thickets of alder and wide snow-covered stretches of peat bogs, it seemed that we might search in vain for one who would hide among them. Only the strange round hill on Stanmoor seemed to be a point that might be noted on all the level, though Dudda told us that there were many islets hidden in the wooded parts.

We went to the lower hills and then to the very edge of the fenland, skirting along it, and asking here and there of the cottagers if they knew of any folk in hiding in the islets. But though we heard of poor people in one or two places, none of them knew of any thane; and the day wore on, and hope began to grow dim, save for Dudda's certainty that what he had heard was true.

At last we came to a long spur of high ground that runs out into the fen, about midway between Bridgwater and Taunton; and there is the village they call Lyng, where we most hoped to hear good news. The day was drawing to sunset, and we would hasten; so Heregar went one way and I another, each to distant cottages that we saw. The lane down which I and my two comrades rode seemed to lead fenwards, and it was little more than a track, deep in snow and tree bordered. The cottage we sought was a quarter mile away when we left the thane, and as we drew near it we saw an old woman walking away from it, and from us also. She did not seem to hear us when we called to her; and, indeed, such was the fear of Danes that often folk would fly when they saw us, and the faster because we called, not waiting to find out who we were.

Then from out of the cottage came another old woman, who hobbled into the track and looked after the first, shaking her fist after her, and then following her slowly, looking on the ground. She never glanced our way at all, and our horses made no noise to speak of in the snow.

We drew up to her, and then I saw that she had a hammer in her right hand and a broad-headed nail in her left. I wondered idly what she was about with these things, when she stooped and began to hammer the nail into the iron-hard ground, and I could hear her muttering some words quickly.

I reined up to watch her, puzzled, and said to Harek:

"Here is wizardry; or else what is the old dame about?"

"It is somewhat new to me," the scald said, looking on with much interest; for if he could learn a new spell or charm, he was pleased as if he had found a treasure.

Then I saw that she was driving the nail into a footprint. There were three tracks only along the snow--two going away from the cottage and one returning. That which went and returned was made by this old woman, as one might see from her last steps, which made a fourth track from the door.

"She is hammering the nail into her own footprint," I said, noting this.

Now she sang in a cracked voice, hammering savagely the while; and now and then she shook her fist or hammer, or both, towards where the other old dame had gone out of sight round a bend of the lane.

Then she put her hand to her back and straightened herself with a sort of groan, as old dames will, and slowly turned round and saw us.

Whereat she screamed, and hurled the hammer at Kolgrim, who was laughing at her, cursing us valiantly for Danes and thieves, and nearly hitting him.

"Peace, good mother," I said; "we are not Danes. Here is earnest thereof," and I threw her a sceatta from my pouch.

She clutched it from the ice pool where it fell, and stared at us, muttering yet. Then Harek spoke to her.

"Mother, I have much skill in spells, but I know not what is wrought with hammer and nail and footprint. I would fain learn."

"Little know you of spells if you know not that," she said, having lost all fear of us, as it seemed.

"I am only a northerner," Harek said. "Maybe 'tis a spell against a sprained ankle, which seems likely. I only know one for that."

"Which know you?" she said scornfully; "you are over young to meddle with such like."

"This," said Harek. "It works well if the sprain be bathed with spring-cold water, while one says it twice daily:

"'Baldur and Woden
Went to the woodland;
There Baldur's foal fell,
Wrenching its foot.'

"That is how it begins."

Then the old woman's eyes sparkled.

"Ay; that is good. Learn it me, I pray you. Now I know that you have wizardry, for you name the old gods."

"Tell me first what hammer and nail work in footprint."

"Why, yon old hag has overlooked me," she said savagely. "Now, if one does as I have done, one nails her witchcraft to herself."

"Whose footprint does the nail go into?" Harek asked.

"Why, hers surely. Now this is the spell," and she chanted somewhat in broad Wessex, and save that Baldur's name and Thor's hammer also came into it, I do not know what it all was. I waxed impatient now, for I thought that Heregar might be waiting for us.

But she and Harek exchanged spells, and then I said:

"Now, dame, know you of any thane in hiding hereabouts?"

Thereat she looked sharply at me.

"I know nothing. Here be I, lamed, in the cottage all day."

"There is a close friend of mine in hiding from the Danes somewhere here," I said, doubting, from her manner, if she spoke the truth. "I would take him to a safer place."

"None safer," she answered. "What is his name?"

Then I doubted for a moment; but Harek's quick wit helped me.

"Godred," he said; for the name by which the king had called himself once it was likely that he would use again.

"I know of no thanes," she said, though not at once, so that I was sure she knew somewhat more than she thought safe to tell.

Then she was going, but Harek stayed her.

"Yours is a good spell against the evil eye, mother," he said, "but I can tell you a better."

"What is it?" she said eagerly.

"News for news," he answered carelessly. "Tell us if you know aught of this thane, and I will tell you."

"I said not that there was a thane." she said at once.

"Nay, mother; but you denied it not. Come now; I think what I can tell you will save you trouble."

She thought for a little, weighing somewhat in her mind, as it seemed, and then she chose to add to her store of witchcraft.

"Yonder, then," she said, nodding to the dense alder thickets that hid the river Tone from us, across a stretch of frozen mere or flooded land. "I wot well that he who bides in Denewulf's cottage is a thane, for he wears a gold ring, and wipes his hands in the middle of the towel, and sits all day studying and troubling in his mind in such wise that he is no good to any one--not even turning a loaf that burns on the hearth before his eyes. Ay, they call him Godred."

Then my heart leaped up with gladness, and I turned to seek Heregar; but he was coming, and so I waited. Then the dame clamoured for her reward, which Harek had as nearly forgotten as had I.

"Mother," the scald said gravely, "when I work a spell with hammer and nail, the footprint into which the nail is driven is of her who cast the evil eye on me."

"Why, so it should be."

"Nay, but you drive it into your own," he said.

She looked, and then looked again. Then she stamped a new print alongside the nailed one, and it was true. She had paid no heed to the matter in her fury, and when she knew that she turned pale.

"Man," she cried, "help me out of this. I fear that I have even nailed the evil overlooking fast to myself."

"Ay, so you have," said Harek; "but it is you who know little of spells if you cannot tell what to do. Draw the nail out while saying the spell backwards, and then put it into the right place carefully. Then you will surely draw away also any ill that she has already sent you, and fasten it to her."

"Then I think she will shrivel up," said the old witch, with much content. "You are a great wizard, lord; and I thank you."

"Here is a true saying of a friend of mine," said Heregar, coming up in time to hear this. "But what has come to you, king? have you heard aught?"

Now when the old woman heard the thane name the king, before I could answer she cried out and came and clung to my stirrup, taking my hand and kissing it, and weeping over it till I was ashamed.

"What is this?" I said.

"O my lord the king!" she cried. "I thought that yon sad-faced man in Denewulf's house was our king maybe, so wondrous proud are his ways, and so strange things they hear him speak when he sleeps. But now I am glad, for I have seen the king and kissed his hand, and, lo, the sight of him is good. Ay, but glad will all the countryside be to know that you live."

Then I knew not what to say; but Heregar beckoned to me, saying:

"Come, leave her her joy; it were cruel to spoil it, and maybe she will never know her mistake."

So we rode on, and Heregar called Dudda, asking him if he knew Denewulf's cottage; while in the track stood the witch, blessing her king as eagerly as she had cursed her gossip just now.

"I know not the path, though I have heard of the cottage," Dudda said; "but it will be strange if I cannot find a way to the place."

He took us carefully into the fen for some way until we passed through a thicket and came to the edge of a mere, and there were five men who bore fishing nets and eel spears, which had not been used, as one might suppose, seeing that the ice was nigh a foot thick after the thaw and heavy frost again.

And those two men who came first were Ethelnoth, the Somerset ealdorman, and young Ethered of Mercia. It was strange to see those nobles bearing such burdens; but we knew that we had found the king.

They saw us, and halted; but Heregar waved his hand, and they came on, for they knew him. It would be hard to say which party was the more pleased to meet the other.

"Where is the king?" we asked.

"Come with us, and we will take you to him," Ethered said. "But supperless you must be tonight. We have nought in the house, and nothing can we catch."

Then I was surprised, and said:

"Is it so bad as that here? In our land, when the ice is at its thickest we can take as much fish as we will easily."

"Save us from starvation, Ranald," said Ethered, laughing ruefully, "and we will raise a big stone heap here in your honour."

"Kolgrim will show you," I said; "let me go to the king."

"I am a great ice fisherman," said Harek; "let me go also."

Then Heregar laughed in lightness of heart.

"Ay, wizard, go also. There will be charms of some sort needed before Ethered sees so much as a scale."

Whereon they dismounted, and Kolgrim took his axe from his saddle bow, asking where the river was, while he wondered that such a simple matter as breaking a hole in the ice and dropping a line among the hungry fish, who would swarm to the air, had not been thought of. We had not yet learned that such a winter as this comes but seldom to the west of England, and the thanes knew nothing of our northern ways.

Then Ethelnoth led Heregar and me across twisting and almost unseen paths, safer now because of the frost, though one knew that in some places a step to right or left would plunge him through the crust of hard snow into a bottomless peat bog. The alder thickets grew everywhere round dark, ice-bound pools of peat-stained water, and we could nowhere see more than a few yards before us; and it was hard to say how far we had gone from the upland edge of the swamp when the ground began to rise from the fen, and grew harder among better timber. But for the great frost, one would have needed a boat in many places.

Then we came to a clearing, in which stood a house that was hardly more than a cottage, and round it were huts and cattle sheds. And this was where the king was--the house of Denewulf the herdsman, the king's own thrall. There was a rough-wattled stockade round the place, and quick-set fences within which to pen the cattle and swine outside that, and all around were the thickets. None could have known that such an island was here, for not even the house overtopped the low trees; and though all the higher ground was cleared, there were barely two acres above the watery level--a long, narrow patch of land that lay southeast and northwest, with its southerly end close to the banks of the river Tone. Men call the place Athelney now, since the king and his nobles lay there. It had no name until he came, but I think that it will bear ever hereafter that which it earned thus.

Two shaggy grey sheepdogs came out to meet us, changing their angry bark for welcome when they saw Ethelnoth; and a man came to the door to see what roused them, and he had a hunting spear in his hand. I took him for some thane, as he spoke to us in courtly wise; but he was only Denewulf the herdsman himself.

"How fares the king?" asked Ethelnoth.

"His dark hour came on him after you went," Denewulf answered; "and then the pain passed, and he slept well, and now has just wakened wonderfully cheerful. I have not seen him so bright since he came here; and he is looking eagerly for your return, seeming to expect some news."

"It may be that our coming has been foretold him beforehand," said Heregar. "Our king has warnings given him in his dreams at times."

Then from out of the house Alfred's voice hailed us:

"Surely that is the voice of my standard bearer.

"Come in quickly, Heregar, for all men know that hope comes with you."

We went in; and it was a poor place enough for a king's lodging, though it was warm and neat. Alfred sat over the fire in the middle of the larger room of the two which the house had, and a strew of chips and shreds of feathers and the like was round him; for he was arrow making--an art in which he was skilful, and he had all the care and patience which it needs. When we came in he rose up, shaking the litter from his dress into the fire; and we bent our knees to him and kissed his hand.

"O my king," said Heregar, "why have you thus hidden yourself from us? All the land is mourning for you."

Then Alfred looked sadly at him and wistfully, answering:

"First, because I must hide; lastly, because I would be hidden: but between these two reasons is one of which I repent--because I despaired."

"Nay," said Denewulf, "it was not despair; it was grief and anxiousness and thought and waiting for hope. Never have you spoken of despair, my king."

"But I have felt it," he answered, "and I was wrong. Hope should not leave a man while he has life, and friends like these, and counsellors like yourself. Now have I been rebuked, and hope is given me afresh."

Then he smiled and turned to me.

"Why, Ranald my cousin, this is kindness indeed. I had not thought that you would bide with a lost cause, nor should I have thought of blame for you had you gone from this poor England; you are not bound to her as are her sons."

"My king," I said truly, "there are things that bind more closely even than birth."

I think he was pleased, for he smiled, and shook his head at me as though to say that he could not take my saying to himself, as I meant it. And then, before we could ask him more, he began to think of our needs.

"Here we have been pressed for food, friends, for the last few days, and I fear you must fast with us. The deer have fled from our daily hunting, and the wild fowl have sought open water. Unless our fishers have luck, which seems unlikely, we must do as well as we can on oaten bread."

Then Ethelnoth said:

"There have been no fish caught today, my king."

"Why, then, we will wait till the others return; and meanwhile I will hear all the news, for Ranald and Heregar will have much to tell me."

So we told him all that we knew, and he asked many questions, until darkness fell.

"Why are you here, lord king?" asked Heregar; "my hall is safe."

"Your hall and countryside are safe yet because I am not there," Alfred answered, fixing his bright eyes on the thane. "The Danes are hunting for me, and were I in any known place, thither would they come. Therefore I said that now I choose to bide hidden. Moreover, in this quiet and loneliness there comes to me a plan that I think will work out well; for this afternoon, as I slept, I was bidden to look for a sign that out of hopelessness should come help and victory."

Just then the dogs rose up and whined at the door, as if friends came; and there were cheerful voices outside. The door opened, and in stumbled Ethered, bearing a heavy basket of great fish, which he cast on the floor-- lean green and golden pike, and red-finned roach, in a glittering, flapping heap.

"Here is supper!" he cried joyfully, "and more than supper, for each of us is thus laden. Fish enough for an army could we have taken had we not held our hands. I could not have thought it possible."

Whereat Alfred rose up and stared, crossing himself.

"Deo gratias," he said under his breath, and then said aloud, "Lo, this is the sign of which I spoke even now--that my fishers should return laden with spoil, even for an army, although frost and snow have prevented them from taking fish for many days, and today was less likelihood of their doing so than ever."

"Ranald knew well how this would cheer you, King Alfred," said Ethered, thinking that I had spoken of this as a proof that all was not lost, in some way.

"Ranald said nought; but the sign came from above, thus," the king said gravely. "In my dream the holy Saint Cuthberht stood by my side, and re- proved me sharply for my downheartedness and despair, and for my doubt of help against the heathen; and when he knew that I was sorry, he foretold to me that all would yet be well, and that I should obtain the kingdom once more with even greater honour than I have had--with many more wondrous promises. And then he gave me this sign, as I have told you and, behold, it has come, and my heart is full of thankfulness. Now I know that all will be well with England."

Then said Denewulf, who it was plain took no mean place with the king and thanes:

"Say how this miracle was wrought, I pray you, for it is surely such."

"Hither came King Ranald and his two friends and bade us make holes in the ice and fish through them. So we did, and this is what came thereof," said Ethered.

"Therefore King Ranald and his coming are by the hand of God," said Denewulf. "Therein lies the miracle."

Then I was feared, for all were silent in wonder at the coming to pass of the sign; and it seemed to me that I was most truly under a power stronger than that of the old gods, who never wrought the like of this.

Then came Harek's voice outside, where he hung up fish to freeze against the morrow; and he sang softly some old saga of the fishing for the Midgard snake by Asa Thor. And that grated on me, though I ever waited to hear what song the blithe scald had to fit what was on hand, after his custom. Alfred heard too, and he glanced at me, and I was fain to hang my head.

"Ranald, who brought to pass the sign, shall surely share in its bodings of good," he said, quickly and kindly. "I think that he is highly favoured."

Then in came my comrades, and they bent to the king, and he thanked them; and after that was supper and much cheerfulness. Harek sang, and Alfred, and after them Denewulf. Much I marvelled at the wisdom of this strange man, but I never knew how he gained it. King Alfred was ever wont to say that in him he had found his veriest counsellor against despair in that dark time; and when in after days he took him from the fen and made him a bishop, he filled the place well and wisely, being ever the same humble-minded man that I had known in Athelney.

CHAPTER X
Athelney and Combwich

In the morning King Alfred took us to the southern end of his island, and there told us what his plans were. And as we listened they seemed to us to be wiser than mortal mind could have made, so simple and yet so sure were they, as most great plans will be. It is no wonder that his people hold that he was taught them from above.

He bade us look across the fens to the wooded heights of Selwood Forest, to south and east, and to the bold spur of the Polden Hills beyond the Parret that they call Edington. There was nought but fen and river and marsh between them and us--"impassable by the Danes who prowled there. Only at the place where the two rivers join was a steep, rounded hill, that stood up strangely from the level--the hill that they call the Stane, on Stanmoor; and there were other islands like this on which we stood, unseen among the thickets, or so low that one might not know of them until upon them.

"Now," he said, "sooner or later the Danes will know I am here, where they cannot reach me. Therefore I will keep them watching this place until I can strike them a blow that will end the trouble once for all. They will be sure that we gather men on the Quantock side, whence Heregar can keep them; and so, while they watch for us to attack them thence, we will gather beyond Selwood, calling all the thanes from Hants and Wilts and Dorset and Somerset to meet me on a fixed day, and so fall on them. Now we will build a fort yonder on Stane hill that will make them wonder, and so the plan will begin to work. For I have only told you the main lines thereof; the rest must go as can be planned from day to day."

Then he looked steadfastly at the Selwood heights, and added:

"And if the plan fails, and the battle I look for goes against us, there remain Heregar's places yet. Petherton, Combwich, and Dowsborough are good places, where a king may die in a ring of foes, looking out over the land for which his life is given."

"We shall not fail, my king," said Heregar. "Devon will gather to you across the Quantocks also."

"Ay," he said; "and you will need them with you."

Then said I:

"Hubba is in Wales, and is likely to come here when he hears that his fellows are gathering against us. Then will Devon be needed at Combwich in Parret mouth, or at Watchet."

"That will be Devon's work," the king said. "If Hubba comes before your ships are ready to meet him, he must at least be driven to land elsewhere, or our stronghold is taken behind us."

Now I was so sure that Hubba would come, that this seemed to me to be the weakest part of the king's plan. But Alfred thought little of it.

"My stronghold seems to be on Quantock side; it is rather beyond Selwood, in the hearts of my brave thanes and freemen. Fear not, cousin. Hubba will come, and you and Heregar will meet him; and whether you win or not, my plan holds."

Then I knew that the king saw far beyond what was plain to me, and I was very confident in him. And I am sure that I was the only man who had the least doubt from the beginning.

Now, after all was planned, Heregar and I rode back to his place, and sent word everywhere that the king was safe, though he commanded us to tell no man where he lay as yet. None but thanes were to be in the island with him; and from that time the name we knew it by began, as one by one the athelings crossed the fen paths thereto, and were lost, as it were, in the hiding place.

Then we wrought there at felling timber and hewing, until we had bridged the river and made a causeway through the peat to Stanmoor hill, and then began to make a triple line of earthworks around its summit. No carelessly-built fort was this, for the king said: "If the nobles build badly, there will be excuse for every churl to do the like hereafter. Therefore this must needs be the most handsomely-wrought fort in all Wessex."

There came to us at this fort many faithful workmen, sent from the towns and countryside, until we had a camp there. But every night, after working with us and cheering all with his voice and example, Alfred went back to Athelney with us; and none would seek to disturb him there, so that for long none quite knew, among the lesser folk, where he bided. Presently the queen and athelings came there to him, and were safe.

That time in the fens was not altogether unpleasant, though the life was hard. Ever was Alfred most cheerful, singing and laughing as we wrought, and a word of praise from him was worth more than gold to every man. And then there were the hunting, the fishing, and the snaring of wild fowl, that were always on hand to supply our wants, though now we had plenty of food from the Quantock side. I know this, that many a man who was in Athelney with Alfred was the better therefor all the days of his after life. Men say that there is a steadfast look in the faces of the Athelney thanes, by which they can be well known by those who note the ways of men.

The frost lasted till February went out in rain and south winds. And then the Danes began to gather along the southern hills, watching us. By that time we had made causeways to other islets from the fort, and the best of these was to Othery, a long, flat island that lay to the east, nearer to the Polden Hills and Edington.

So one day the king sent for me as we wrought at the fort, and both he and I were horny handed and clay stained from the work. I came with spade in hand, and he leaned on a pick. Whereat he laughed.

"Faith, brother king, now can I speak in comrade's wise to my churls as you speak to your seamen. Nor do I think that I shall be the worse ruler for that."

Then he took my arm, and pointed to Edington hill.

"For many nights past I have seen watch fires yonder," he said; "and that is a place where I might strike the Danes well. So I would draw them thither in force. Do you feel as if a fight would be cheerful after this spade work?"

Now I could wish for nothing better, and I said so.

"Well, then," he went on, laughing at my eagerness, "go to Ethelnoth, and take twenty men, and do you and he fall on that post from Othery by night; and when you have scattered it, come back into the fen. I would have you lose no men, but I would make the Danes mass together by attack on some one point, and that as soon as may be, before Hubba comes. I do not want to hold their place."

Now that was the first of daily attacks on the Danish posts, at different places along the Selwood and Polden hills, until they thought that we wished to win Edington height, where we began and annoyed them most often. So I will tell how such a raid fared.

Good it was to lay aside pick and spade and take sword Helmbiter again, and don mail and helm; and I made Harek fence with me, lest I should have lost my sword craft through use of the weapons whereby the churl conquers mother earth. But once the good sword was in my hand I forgot all but the warrior's trade.

So Ethelnoth and I and twenty young thanes went in the evening to Othery island, and there found a fenman to guide us, and so went to the foot of Edington hill just as darkness fell. The watch-fire lights, that were our guide, twinkled above us through the trees that were on the hillside; and we made at once for them, sending on the fenman to spy out the post before we were near it. It was very dark, and it rained now and then.

When he came back to where we had halted, he said that there were about twenty tents, pitched in four lines, with a fire between each line; and that the men were mostly under cover, drinking before setting watch, if they set any at all.

So we drew nearer, skirting round into cover of some trees that came up to the tents, for the hilltop was bare for some way. The lighted tents looked very cheerful, and sounds of song and laughter came from them, and now and then a man crossed from one to another, or fed the fires with fresh wood, that hissed and sputtered as he cast it on.

"How shall we attack?" said Ethelnoth.

"Why, run through the camp in silence first and cut the tent lines, and then raise a war shout and come back on them. Then we may slay a few, and the rest will be scared badly enough."

Thereat we both laughed under our breath, for it seemed like a school-boy's prank. Well, after the long toil in the fen, we were like boys just freed from school, though our game was the greatest of all--that of war--the game of Hodur's playground, as we Norse say.

Then I said:

"After we come through for the second time, we must take to this cover, and so get together at some place by the hill foot. There is a shed by a big tree that can be found easily."

So we passed the wood, and our comrades chuckled. It was good sport to see the shadows of the careless Danes on the tent walls, and to know that they dreamed of nothing less than that Saxons were on them. Four rows of tents there were, and there were twenty-two of us; so we told off men to each row, and then made for them at a moment when no man was about-- hacking at the ropes, and laughing to see the tents fall. It was strange to watch the shadows start up and stand motionless, as the first patter of feet came and the first blows fell, and then bustle, helpless and confused, with savage shouts and curses, as the heavy canvas and skins fell in upon them.

Now we were through the camp, and the outcries were loud behind us. Two or three tents did not fall, and from them the men swarmed, half armed and startled, not knowing if this was not some sorry jest at first; and then rang our war cry from the dark, and we were back upon them. We were but two-and-twenty to a hundred, but they knew not what was on hand, while we did; and so we cut through them without meeting with any hurt. Two tents were on fire and blazing high, and blackened men cut and tore their way out of them howling; and I think that more than one Dane was cut down by his comrades in the panic that fell on all.

Yet even as we passed into the cover and went our way back towards the fen, some bolder spirits began to rally, and a horn was blown. But we were gone, leaving six slain and many more wounded among them, while not one of us was scratched.

They did not follow us, and we heard the clamour we had caused going on for some time after we had gained the fen. Presently, too, when we reached Othery, we saw a fire signal lit to call for help, and we were well content. Doubtless those Danes waked under arms all that night through.

After that these attacks were seldom so easy, for the Danes kept good watch enough; but they were ever the same in most ways. Suddenly in the night would come the war cry and the wild rush of desperate men on some Danish outpost, and before they knew what to do we were away and into the fen again. We grew to know every path well before long, and sometimes we would fall on small parties of our foes when they were on the march or raiding the cattle, and cut through them, and get back to our fastness.

Once or twice we were followed in the grey of early morning; but few Danes ever got back from that pursuit. We would cut them off amid the peat bogs, or they would founder therein, and sink under the weight of armour.

Then they tried to force some fenmen they caught to guide them to us at Othery. Once the brave fenman led them to where they dared not move till daylight came, while the blue fen lights flitted round them like ghosts in the dark; and then the fen people swarmed round them, and ended them with arrows and sling stones from a distance. They tried no more night attacks on us after that. But again they came in some force by daylight, and we had a strange fight on a narrow strip of hard land in Sedgemoor, with all advantage on our side. No Danes won back to the Polden Hills.

Then they dared not try the fens any more, and daily we kept their sentries watching, and nightly we fell on outposts, until at last they thought our force grew very great, and began to gather on Edington hill, even as Alfred wished. And this saved many a village and farm and town from plunder, for the fear of Alfred the king began to grow among his foes.

Then the king made his next move; for, now that the way was open, he sent to Odda at Exeter, bidding him move up to Taunton by some northerly road, gathering what Devon men he could on the way. There is hardly a stronger town in Wessex than the great fortress that Ine the king made.

At this time I began to be full of thoughts about my ships. But they could hardly be built as yet; and most of them were in southern havens, whence, even were they ready, one could not bring them round the stormy Land's End in early March. Yet the weather was mild and open, and I began to think that at any time Hubba might bring his Danes across the narrow Severn sea to join his kinsmen at Edington. We heard, too, that Guthrum, the king of East Anglia, was there now, and that he had summoned every warrior who would leave the land he had won to come to him.

Men have blamed Guthrum for treachery in this; but seeing that the peace was broken, and that he must needs fight for the peace at least of his kingdom, I hold that this is not right. At all events, Alfred blamed him not in the time to come. Nevertheless, I suppose that in men's minds he always will be held answerable for what the other chiefs wrought of ill, because he bore the name of king from the first, and ruled East Anglia. No Saxon, who is used to hold his king as over all, will understand how little power a host-king of the north has.

Now all this while my good ship lay at Bridgwater, and with her were fifty of my men, who were well quartered among the townsfolk, and helped to guard the bridge. And, as I have said, two ships were being built there. So one day in the third week in March I rode away with Kolgrim from Athelney, to see how all things were going on there, meaning also to go to Heregar's place for a time, having messages to give him from the king.

Harek was coming with me; but Alfred asked me to spare him for this time.

"I have to learn somewhat from the scald," he said.

"Wizardry, my king?" I asked, laughing, for that was ever a jest at the scald's expense after it was known how we found out that Alfred was at Denewulf's house.

"Nay, but song," he answered. "Now I see not why I should not tell you who put the thought into my mind; but I am going, as you did, to spy out the Danish camp. And I will go as a gleeman, and be welcome enough as a Saxon who has enough love of Danes to learn some northern sagas for them!"

"My king," I cried, "this is too perilous altogether."

He looked quaintly at me.

"Go to, cousin; are you to have all the glory? If you went, why not I? Maybe I too may find a chance of helping some fair maiden on the way back."

Then I prayed him to do nothing rash, for that he was the one hope of England.

"And maybe the one man in England who can do any good by going, therefore," he answered. "And neither you nor I would ask any man to do for us what we durst not do ourselves."

"You will be known, my king," I said.

Whereon he held out his hands, which were hard and horny now with hard work, and he laughed as he did so.

"Look at those," he said, "and at my unkempt hair and beard! Verily I may be like Alfred the king in some ways, but not in these. They will pass me anywhere."

So I could not dissuade him, and ever as I tried to do so he waxed more cheerful, and made sport of me, throwing my own doings in my teeth, and laughing about Thora. So I was fain to get away from his presence, lest I should grow angry at last. And when I was going he said:

"Have no fear, cousin; I will not go unless I am well prepared."

So I went, and next day was back in Athelney, riding hard; for Hubba's ships had been sighted from the Quantocks, and they were heading for the Parret. What I looked for and feared was coming.

Then Alfred sent messengers to Odda, who had come to Taunton two days before this. And he gathered every man from the fen, and we went to Bridgwater, leaving our little force there, and so rode on the way to Combwich, thinking to see the sails of the ships in Bridgwater Bay. But a shift of wind had come, and they were yet over on the Welsh coast, waiting for the tide to enable them to come down on us.

By that time a fire burned on the highest spur of the Quantocks to tell us that Odda was there, and at once another was lit on the Combwich fort to bring him to us, for it seemed certain that here we must fight the first battle of Alfred's great struggle.

"Here you must meet this newcomer and drive him away, if it can be done, or if not, hinder him from coming further; or if that is impossible, do your best. I would have you remember that defeat here is not loss of all hope, for beyond Selwood lies our real gathering. But victory, even if dearly bought, will almost win the day for us."

So Alfred said, and we, who began to see what his great plan was, were cheered.

In the evening Odda came with eight hundred men of Devon. Alfred had two hundred maybe, and my few men and the townsfolk made another two hundred. But Hubba had twenty-three longships, whose crews, if up to fighting strength, would not be less than a hundred in each.

So we watched till the tide fell, when he could not come into the Parret, and then I went back to Heregar's hall. It seemed very bare, for all goods had been sent up to the great refuge camp of Dowsborough, to which all day long the poor folk had been flying, driving with them their sheep and cattle and swine, that they might save what they could. But with Odda had come his daughter, the Lady Etheldreda, who would not leave him; and she and the Lady Alswythe and Thora were yet in the house, and Osmund the jarl sat in the hall, listless and anxious of face. It was an ill time for him; but there were none of us who did not like him well, and feel for him in his helplessness.

"What news?" he said, when he saw me come into the hall.

"Hubba will be here on the next tide--with early morning," I said.

He sighed, and rising up went to the doorway and looked out to the hills.

"I would that I could make these two noble ladies seek refuge yonder," he said; "but one will not leave her father, nor the other her husband."

Then I said:

"At least I think you should take Thora there. This is a difficult place for you."

"I know Hubba," he said, "and if I abide here I may be of use. I need not tell you that you are fighting the best warrior of our time, and that with too small a force."

"Well," I said, "you and I can speak plainly, neither of us being Saxons. We shall be beaten by numbers, and you mean that you will be able to save these ladies by staying?"

"Ay," he said. "And if by any chance Alfred wins, I may be able to ask for mercy for the conquered."

Then came in Thora, and her face was troubled. She had been trying to make Etheldreda go to the hill fort, where all the women and children of the countryside had been sent.

"It is of no use," she said; "they will bide here."

"Well," said Osmund, "then we will stay also. I and our friend have spoken thereof, and it seems well that we do so."

I suppose they had talked of this before, for she made no answer, but sat down wearily enough before the fire; and Osmund and I went out to the courtyard, for we were both restless.

Then Heregar came in on his white horse, and saw Osmund, and called to him, asking of the same business, for he had asked the jarl to speak about it as a friend. So I went in again, and Thora sat by herself yet, looking up to see who came now. I went and stood by her, staring into the fire, and feeling as if I wanted to go out again. Restlessness was in the very air while we waited for the coming fight.

"King Ranald," she said, after a little silence, "I wonder if ever a maiden was in such sad doubt as I. I cannot wish that these dear ladies, who have made a friend of me, should see their folk beaten, and maybe slain; and cannot wish that my own kin should be beaten either. It seems that in either way I must find heavy sorrow."

That was true; but it was certain that her own people were the cause of all the trouble, though I could not say so. I put it this way:

"I think that if your people are driven off there will be peace the sooner, and maybe they will not land when they find us waiting. I know, too, that those who have loved ones in the battle that may be are in a harder case than yours, dear lady."

Then she looked up at me once, and a flush came slowly over her pale face, and she answered nothing. I thought that she felt some shame that a warrior like her father should bide here, without moving hand or foot, when the war horns were blowing. So I said:

"Harder yet would it be if the jarl were in the battle against our friends. Then would the fear of his loss be a terror to you also."

Now came in Osmund, and straightway Thora rose up, turning away from us both, and went from the hall. The jarl looked after her curiously and sadly.

"This is a strange business for the girl," he said.

"She seems almost as troubled because you are not fighting as if you were in danger by doing so," I answered, with that thought still in my mind.

Thereat the jarl stared at me.

"What has put that into your head?" he asked.

I told him what she and I had said, adding that I feared I had seemed to hint somewhat discomforting.

Then said Osmund, looking in my face with a half smile:

"She is glad I am honourably out of this business, and the trouble is not that. There are one or two, maybe, whom she would like to see as safe in the same way."

Then it flashed through my dull mind that perhaps I was one of these, and the thought was pleasant to me.

"Well," I said, "there are the thane, and his young son, the king's page, who is here. They have been very kind to her."

"Also a wandering king who took her out of danger," he said then.

"Ay; I shall be glad if she thinks of me."

There were a little laugh and a rustling behind us, and one said:

"Either you are the least conceited of men or the blindest, King Ranald, or you would know what is amiss."

I turned, and saw the Lady Etheldreda herself, and I bowed to her in much confusion.

"O you men!" she said. "Here you will let the poor girl break her heart in silence, while you fight for glory, or somewhat you think is glory, without a word to say that you care that she shall see what you win. Of course she thinks of you, even night and day. How else should it be, when you have been as a fairy prince to her?"

Then I knew for myself that among all the wild life of Athelney and the troubles of the king the thought of Thora had been pleasant to me; but now I was confused, having the matter brought home to me suddenly, and, as it were, before I was ready to shape all my thoughts towards her. So all that I could say was foolish enough.

"I am a poor sort of fairy prince, lady."

"Ay," she said; "I am as good a fairy godmother, maybe. And perhaps I should have said nothing--at this time. But, Ranald, the maiden weeps for your danger, for, at the very least, she owes you much."

Then I said, humbly as I felt:

"That is more honour to me than I deserve."

"That is for her to say," answered the fair lady, turning to where Osmund had been.

But he was now in the doorway, looking out again to the hills. So she was silent, and I thought of somewhat.

"There is none in this land or in any other--of whom I think as I do of Thora," I said; "but my mind has been full of warfare and trouble with the king. Now, if I may, I will ask for somewhat that I may wear for her sake in the fight, and so she will know that I think of her."

"Now that is well said," answered Etheldreda. "But you must ask it for yourself."

Thereat I thought for a moment, and at last I said that I would not do so.

"If I might, I would ask you to gain this favour for me," I said; "for I think that a parting would be very hard, as things have come about."

"You are a wiser man than I thought you, Ranald," she said; and so she went from me, and I stayed by the fire, thinking thoughts that were sweet and yet troublous, for beyond tomorrow's fight I could not see.

Then the lady came back, and with her she brought a little glove, worn and shapely from the hand that it belonged to.

"She bids me give this to her king and warrior," Etheldreda said. "I did but tell her that you asked a token that she minded you."

"It was well," I answered. "What said she?"

"Nought at once. But her sadness went, and her face changed--ay, but she is beyond any of us in beauty when her eyes light up in that way--and she fetched this, and then said 'Say, if you think that he will care to know it, that this is the glove wherein I rode to Wareham.'"

"Do you care to know it, Ranald?"

"Ay, with all my heart," I said.

And so I put it very carefully under the broad, golden-studded baldric of Sigurd's sword. And it would not stay there, and Etheldreda laughed at me, and took a little golden brooch like a cross that she wore, and pinned it through glove and baldric, making all safe.

"There," she said, "is a token from me also, though it was unasked. Bear yourself well, Ranald, for our eyes are on you. If Hubba comes indeed, we women folk will be in the fort."

Then I said, being at a loss for words enough:

"I would I had the tongue of Harek the scald, that I might thank you for gift and words, my fairy princess."

"I have half a mind to take it back for that fine saying," she answered.

And then she gave me her hand, and I kissed it; and she went from me with her eyes full of tears for all the trouble that was on us, though she had tried bravely to carry it off lightly.

Then I would stay in the house no longer, but went out to the fort, and sat down by the great Dragon banner of Wessex, Heregar's charge, that floated there, and ate and drank with the other chiefs, and waited. But my mind was full of what I had heard, and the war talk went on round me without reaching my ears.

CHAPTER XI
The Winning of The Raven

Now we none of us like much to speak of the fight that came next morning, for it went ill enough. Yet we were outnumbered by twice our force, for some more of the host beyond the fens made Alfred send many of his men back to watch the crossing at Bridgwater.

Hubba brought his ships up on the tide, and when he saw that we were waiting for him, he made as if to go on up the river; and we began to move from our position, thinking that he would go and fall on the town. Then, very suddenly, he turned his ships' bows to the bank at the one place where he saw that the land was high almost to the river's edge; and before we knew that we must be there to stay him, his men were ashore, and had passed the strip of marsh, and were on a long, gentle rise that ends in Cannington hill and the Combwich fort, half a mile away.

We fought well for an hour, and then our men began to give on either wing, for they were, as I would have it remembered, raw levies that Odda had brought with him--valiant men and strong, but with no knowledge of how to fight in line or how to hold together. And when a force like that begins to go, it is ended.

Hard fought we in the centre after that. There were the Athelney thanes, and my fifty men, and Odda's Exeter and Taunton townsfolk, who had fought before; but when the wings broke, Hubba's great force of veterans lapped round us, and we had nought left us but to cut our way out, and make the best retreat we could. My men shouted as they struck, in our Norse way; but a deadly silence fell on the Saxons, and I thought that, as they grew quiet, their blows became ever more stern and fell, until at last even Hubba's vikings gave way before the hard-set faces and steadfast eyes of the west-country spearmen, whom no numbers seemed to daunt, and they drew back from us for a space.

Then we were clear of them, and at once Ethelnoth closed in on the king, taking his horse's rein, and praying him to fly to Bridgwater, where a stand could be made. And at last he persuaded him, and they turned. Then fearing that this might set the example for general flight, I spoke to Odda, and we shouted to the men to stand fast and hold back pursuit; and so a guard of some fifty thanes went with Alfred, and we faced the Danes even yet.

They saw what was done, and roared, and charged on us; and we began to retreat slowly, fighting all the way, up the long slope of land towards the fort. But I saw Heregar's horse rear and fall, and the banner went down, and I thought him slain in that attack.

Presently they let us go. We won ever to better ground, and they had to fight uphill; and then we gained the fort, and there they durst not come.

Then rode towards me a man in silver armour that was dinted and hacked--shieldless, and with a notched sword in his hand. It was Heregar.

"I thought you slain, friend," I said gladly.

"Would that I were! for my charge is lost; they have my banner," he answered.

"That may be won back yet," I said. "But there is no shame to you; we were outnumbered by more than two to one."

"I have borne it through ten battles," he said, and that was all; but he put his face in his hands and groaned.

Now I looked out over the field we had left, and saw the Danes scattering in many ways. Some were going in a long line up the steep hill beyond which the village lay, and over this line swayed and danced the lost banner. There was a crowd of our men from the broken wings gathered there--drawn together by the king as he fled, as I knew afterwards; and I think the Danes bore our banner with them in order to deceive them. I knew that the lane was deep and hollow up which they must go, and there were woods on either side.

Whereat I sprang up.

"Thane," I said, "here is a chance for us to win back the banner, as I think."

He looked up sharply, and I pointed.

"Let us ride at once into the wood, and wait for them to pass us. Then, if we dare, we can surely dash through them."

Kolgrim sat close to me, and our horses were tethered to a spear. He rose up when he heard me speak, saying:

"Here is more madness. But trust to Ranald's luck, thane."

Then in a few more minutes we were riding our hardest towards the wood. I heard Odda shout after us from the entrance to the fort as we went, but we heeded him not.

We edged up to the deep lane through the trees until we were so near that we could almost see into it. The banner was at the head of the column, and there were no mounted men with it. Hubba had brought no horses with him from across the sea.

Then we waited for a long minute, hearing the tramp of the coming men, and their loud talk and laughter as they boasted of their prize. They were going very carelessly.

"If we get it," I whispered to the thane, whose eyes were shining, "ride hard up the hill to our folk who are there."

He nodded and then before us fluttered the folds of his treasure. Instantly he spurred his great white horse, and leaped straight at it into the lane, and after him on either side came Kolgrim and I.

A great howl rose from the startled Danes, and I saw Heregar wheel his horse and tear the banner from the man who held it, cutting down another warrior who tried to catch his bridle. Then Helmbiter was hard at work for a moment, and Kolgrim's axe rattled on a helm or two; and we were away up the lane before the shouting and confusion were over, none of the Danes knowing but that more of us would follow from out the cover.

One or two arrows, shot by men who found their wits sooner than the rest, pattered after us, and we gained the hilltop and the great cheer that went up from our few men who were there made the Danes halt and waver, and at last turn back to the open again.

We stayed on that hilltop for an hour. Then the Danes were coming up in force, and there was no hope in staying, so we got back to the fort before they could cut us off.

Soon after this there was a general movement on the part of our foes, and before evening we were surrounded on all sides by strong posts, and it was plain that we were not to move from the fort.

Now this is not very large, but it is very strong--the hill which has been fortified being some two hundred feet high, and steep sided as a house roof on all sides but the east, where the entrance must needs be. But this again has outworks; and the road into the ramparts from the long slope of Cannington hill to the southward runs slantwise through them, so that the gap it makes in the first line is covered by the second. And both upper and lower rampart go right round the circle of the hilltop, and are very strong, having been made by the British folk, who well understood such matters, and had such fighters as the old Romans and our own forefathers to deal with. Some parts of the works were of piled stones, and the rest of earth, as the ground required.

There is but one way in which that fort could be taken by force, as I think, and that is by attacking on all sides at once, which needs a greater force than would ever be likely to come against it. Moreover, on one side the marshy course of the Combwich stream would hinder any heavy onslaught.

So inside these ramparts were we with some six hundred men, and there we were watched by three times our number. There was a strong post on Cannington hill, between us and Bridgwater; another--and that the main body--between us and the ships, on a little, sharp hill crest across a stony valley two bowshots wide that lay between it and the fort; and so we were well guarded.

At first this seemed of little moment, for we were to stay Hubba before the place; and for a while there was nothing but rejoicing over the return of the banner. Then I found there was no water in the place, and that we had but what food each man happened to carry with him. Presently that want of water became terrible, for our wounded began to cry for it piteously. Maybe it was as well that we had few with us, because the field was left in the hands of the Danes.

Up and down among those few went Etheldreda and Alswythe and Thora, tending them and comforting them, where we had sent them--to the highest point of the hilltop, inside the upper rampart; and I could see the flutter of their dresses now and then from where I watched beside Odda on the lower works. I had spoken to neither since we came here.

Towards dusk I spoke to Odda, and he gave me twenty men; and gathering all the vessels of any sort that would hold water, we climbed over the rampart next the marsh, and stole down to the nearest pool and brought back all we could, using helms and leathern cloaks and the like, for want of buckets. We got back safely that time, and I sent the same men again, thinking that there was no danger, and so not going myself.

They got back, indeed, but with a party of Danes after them; and but for our arrow flights from the earthworks, they would have had to fight, and lose what they brought. After that Hubba knew what we needed, and sent a strong picket to keep us from the marsh.

So the night passed and we had some hopes that a force might come to our help from Bridgwater in the morning, for it was possible that the king would be able to gather men there. It was a slender hope, though, for the host on Polden Hills had to be watched.

All day we waited, and no help came; and with evening the last food had gone. It had rained heavily, however, and the want of water was past for the time. The Danes never moved from their places, waiting to starve us out; and in the last light of evening a small party came across the little valley from the main body, bearing a white flag in token of parley. Hubba bid us yield, and our lives should be spared.

"It is good of Hubba to give us the chance of living a little longer," answered Odda; "but we will wait here a while, so please him."

The Danes threatened us, and mocked, and so went back. We had no more messages from their chief after that.

That night we slept round the standard where it flapped on the hilltop. The men watched, turn by turn, along the lower ramparts; and the Danes were not so near that we could be surprised by them, for there was no cover to hide their coming. Nestled under the northwest rampart was a little hut-- some shepherd's shelter where the three poor ladies were bestowed. Osmund the jarl sat a little apart from us, but all day and night he had been tending the wounded well. Harek who, as befitted a scald, was a good leech, said that the jarl knew almost as much of the craft as he.

Now, in the early morning, when the light was grey, I woke, hearing the rattle of arms and the quiet passing of the word as the men changed guard, and I thought I would go round the ramparts; and then Odda woke also. The rest slept on, for they had taken their turns on watch--Heregar with his arm round the pole of the standard, and his sword beneath his head.

Odda looked at me as we sat up stiffly, and spoke what was in his mind and mine also.

"I have a mind to send Osmund to Hubba, and ask him to let the women go hence. There is nought to eat today."

"There is enough kept for them," I said; for Heregar had seen to that, and none had grudged a share.

"Ay," he answered; "but what are we to do? Are we to be starved like rats here?"

"There are the half-dozen horses," I said.

"And nought to cook them withal. I would that the king would come."

"It is in my mind that he cannot," I answered; "there has been some move of the other host."

Now that was true, for Guthrum's great following had suddenly swept down towards Bridgwater, and that could not be left. They were camped now at the foot of the hill, watching there as Hubba watched us.

Then some one came, stepping lightly, but with clank of mail, towards us; and I glanced round, thinking that some message was brought from the ramparts. Odda turned idly at the same time, and he started up.

"Ah!" he said, under his breath, "what is this?"

A tall maiden, mail clad and bearing a broad-bladed spear, stood beside us; and I thought her one of the Valkyrias--Odin's messengers--come to us, to fight for us in some strife to which she would lead us. I rose too, saluting.

"Skoal to the shield maiden!" I said.

"Skoal to the heroes!" she answered; and then I knew the voice, though, under the helm and in the grey light, the face of the ealdorman's daughter Etheldreda had been strange to me. And Odda knew also.

"What would you in this guise, my daughter?" he cried.

"I think that I have come as Ranald thought--as a Valkyria to lead you to battle," she answered, speaking low, that she might not wake the tired warriors around her. "There is but one thing for us to do, and that is to die sword in hand, rather than to perish for want of food and water here."

I know that this had been in my mind, and most likely in Odda's also; but Alfred might come.

"We wait the king," the ealdorman said.

"No use," she answered. "One may see all the Polden Hills from this place, and tonight there are no fires on Edington height, where we have been wont to see them."

Odda groaned. "My Etheldreda, you are the best captain of us all," he said.

Then suddenly Heregar rose up on his elbow from beside the standard, crying strangely:

"Ay, Father Eahlstan--when the tide is low. Somerset and Dorset side by side. What say you, father--Somerset and Devon? Even so."

The other sleepers stirred, and the lady turned and looked on the thane, but he slept even yet.

"Heregar dreams of the bishop he loved, and of the great fight they fought yonder and won thirty rears ago," she said.

"Worn out is the brave thane," said I. "Strange dreams come to one when that is so."

Then Heregar woke, and saw the maiden, and rose up at her side.

"Dear lady," he asked, "what is this?"

"Ranald thought me a Valkyria, friend; and I come on a Valkyria's errand."

"I had a strange dream but now," Heregar said, as if it dwelt in his mind, so that he hardly heeded what Etheldreda answered him. "I thought that Bishop Eahlstan stood by me as in the old days, and minded me of words that I spoke long ago, words that were taught me by a wise woman, who showed me how to trap the Danes, when the tide left their ships aground, so that they had no retreat. Then he said, 'Even again at this time shall victory be when the tide is low.' And I said that Somerset and Dorset would fail not at this time. Then said he, 'Somerset and Devon.' Then it seemed that he blessed me and passed. Surely I think that he would tell us that victory is before us."

Now the other sleepers woke, and listened wondering. The light was strong, and I looked away towards the Danes between us and the river. Their fires were burning up one by one as they roused also; but I thought there was some bustle down at the shore of the river, where the ships were now afloat on the rising tide.

Then Etheldreda spoke to us in words that were brave and good to hear--words to make a man long to give his life for country and for friends--telling us that, since we must needs die, it was well that we should fall sword in hand, ridding England of her foes man to man, rather than perish in this place for nought.

And when she ended the chiefs were silent, looking on the Danes with eyes that gleamed; and Kolgrim put the thoughts of all into words when he said:

"Once or twice has the Berserker fury come on me when my master has been in peril. Berserker again will you drive me, lady, so that I care not for six foemen against me or sixty."

Then Odda cried:

"What goes on yonder? Do they leave us?" and he shaded his eyes against the rising sun, and pointed. Certainly the Danes were drawing towards the ships in parties of twenty and thirty at a time, but their sentries went on their beats without heeding them. There was no movement, either, among those on the other hill, and the Raven banner that told of Hubba's presence was not borne away.

Now we forgot all but that here was a new hope for us, and we watched for half an hour. Then it was plain that full half the force was drawn off, and that the Danes were crossing the river in the ships. We saw them land on the opposite shore, where the road comes down to the Combwich crossing, that can only be used at lowest tides; and they marched eastward, doubtless in search of cattle and plunder.

Then Heregar's eyes shone, and he said:

"Now has our time come, even as Eahlstan foretold to me. In two hours or three none of that force can return, and we have but half as many again as ourselves left here for us to deal with."

"Let me lead you on them," said Etheldreda.

Then with one voice we prayed her to bide in the fort, and for long she would not be persuaded. But we told her that the men would fight as well under her eye as if they were led by her--if, indeed, her presence did not weaken them, in fear for her safety--and so at last she gave way.

After that there was no more doubt as to what should be done; but Odda went round among the men, and spoke to them in such wise that he stirred their hearts to die bravely hand to hand with the Danes. And I thought that some of us might live to see a great if dearly-bought victory; for it was certain that not one of these Saxons but meant to die before he left the field.

Then Heregar and Osmund went with Etheldreda to the other two ladies, and they bade them take the horses and fly to Dowsborough camp as soon as the fighting drew every Dane to the eastward side of the fort and left the way clear. Osmund would go with them, and so no fear for them was on our minds.

Then we got the soundest of the wounded down to the lower rampart, and drew off the men there towards the gateway, so that the Danes might think our movement was but a changing of guard; then we waited until we saw that the ships on the far bank had taken the ground.

Then we sallied out, and as I went I looked back once. Three women stood alone on the hilltop, and one waved to us. That was the Valkyria, for her mail sparkled in the sun; but I had eyes only for that one whom I thought I should not see again, whose little glove was on my heart.

Now, if we were desperate, Odda was not the man to waste any chance of victory that there might be. We went swiftly up the long slope of Cannington hill, and fell on the post there before they on the main guard could reach them. There was no withstanding the terrible onset of our Saxons; half that force was slain, and the rest were in full flight in a few minutes.

Then we went steadily down the hill to where Hubba himself waited for us. His war horns were blowing, to call in every man who was within hearing; and his men were formed in line four deep at the foot of the spur on which their camp had been.

Now, when I saw this I looked on our men, who were in column again; and it seemed to me that the old Norse plan would be good, for it was certain that on this field we meant to stay.

"Ealdorman," I said, "while there is yet time let us form up in a wedge and go through that line. Then shall we fight back to back, and shall have some advantage. I and my men, who have axes, will go first."

Then my few vikings cried, "Ay, king!" and shouted; whereat Odda laughed grimly.

"Go on, Berserker--axes must needs lead--we will do it."

Then we changed the ranks quickly, and I and Kolgrim and Harek made the point of that wedge. Heregar and the banner were in the midst, and Odda himself was not far behind me, putting his best men along the two foremost faces of the wedge.

"We shall not be foremost long," I said; "we shall be surrounded when once we are through the line."

But as we came on, Hubba closed up his men into a dense, square mass.

"Ho!" said Harek to me; "you are wrong, my king."

Now we were close at hand, and the Danish arrows flew among us, and the javelins fell pretty thickly. I think that a wedge bears this better than any other formation, for it is easy to stop the weapons that reach it.

Our men were silent now, and I was glad, having known already what that meant; but the Danes began to yell their war cries. Then we were within ten paces of them, and I gripped shield and axe and gave the word to charge, and Odda answered it.

Then was such a terrible roar from the Saxons as I had never heard--the roar of desperate men who have their foes before them, more awful than any war shout. And at that even the vikings shrank a little, closing their ranks, and then, with all the weight of the close-ranked wedge behind me, we were among them, and our axes were at work where men were driven on one another before us; and the press thinned and scattered at last, while the Danes howled, and for a moment we three and a few lines behind us stood with no foemen before us, while all down the sides of the wedge the fight raged. Then we halted, and the Danes lapped round us. I do not know that we lost more than two men in this first onset, so heavy was it; but the Danes fell everywhere.

Now began fighting such as I had heard of, but had never seen before. The scalds sing of men who fought as fights a boar at bay in a ring of hounds, unfearing and silent; and so fought we. My axe broke, and I took to sword Helmbiter, and once Kolgrim went Berserker, and howled, and leaped from my side into a throng which fell on us, and drove them back, slaying three outright, and meeting with no hurt.

Our wedge held steady. Men fell, but we closed up; and there grew a barrier of slain before us. I had not seen Hubba since we first closed in, and then he had been a little to the right of where we struck his line, under a golden banner, whereon was a raven broidered, that hung motionless in the still morning air.

Presently the Danish onslaught slackened. Men were getting away from their line to the rear, worn out or wounded, and the hill beyond them was covered with those who had fallen out. They had beaten against our lines as one beats on a wall--hewing out stones, indeed, but without stirring it. They had more hurt than we.

Odda pushed to my side, and said to me:

"What if we advance towards the hill crest?"

"Slowly, then," I said.

He passed the word, and we began to move, and the Danes tried to stay us. Then their attack on the rear face of the wedge slackened and ceased, and they got round before us to fight from the higher ground. At once Odda saw that an attack in line as they wavered thus would do all for us, so he swung his hard Devon levies to right and left on us Norsemen as the centre--maybe there were twenty of us left at that time--and as the wings swung forward with a rolling cheer, the Danes crumbled away before them, and we drove them up the little hill and over the brow, fighting among the half-burnt watch fires and over heaps of plunder, even to where the tall "Raven" drooped from its staff.

Then I saw the mighty Hubba before me; and had I not known it already, one might see defeat written in his face as he looked across to his ships. His men were back now, and stood on the far shore, helpless. Then was a cheer from our left, and he looked there, and I looked also.

Out of the fort came our wounded--every one who could put one foot before another--a strange and ghastly crowd of fifty or sixty men who would yet do what they might for England. And with them was a mixed crowd of thralls and village folk, bearing what arms they could find on the place whence we drove the first Danes, and forks, and bill hooks, and heavy staves.

I do not know if the Danes saw what manner of force came to our help; but I think they did not. Many broke and fled to the ships; but Hubba's face grew hard and desperate, and he cried to his men to stand, and they gathered round him and the Raven banner.

Once again our great wedge formed up, and again charged into the thick of the Danes. Then I faced the great chief, and men fell back from us to see what fight should be. But from beside me came Odda.

"My fight, Ranald," he said, and strode before the Dane.

His sword was gone--the hilt and three inches of blade hung from his wrist--and his shield was notched and gashed. His only weapon was the broad-bladed Saxon spear, ashen shafted, with iron studs along its length below the head. He was a head shorter than the Dane, who was, in truth, the most splendid warrior I had ever seen; and he bore a broad axe, wedge beaten and gold inlaid. There was not much to choose between his shield and Odda's, but I thought the spear the weaker weapon.

"Axe against spear," said Harek; "here is somewhat of which to sing."

Once Odda feinted, lunging at Hubba's face; and the Dane raised his shield a little, but did not move else, nor did his eyelids so much as flinch, and his steady look never left his foe's face. Then, as Odda recovered, the great axe flashed suddenly, and fell harmless as its mark sprang back from its sweep; while like light the spear point went forward over the fallen axe, that recovered too slowly to turn it, and rang true on the round shield that met it.

I had not thought much of spear play until now, for we think little of the weapon.

Again the Saxon lunged, and Hubba hewed at the spear shaft, splintering it a little as the quick-eyed spearman swung it away from the blow. Then the butt was over Odda's left shoulder, and before one could tell that its swing aside had ended, forward flew the point, darting from left to right over Hubba's arm that had not yet recovered from the lost axe blow, and behind the shield's rim. That blow went home, and the mighty Dane reeled and fell.

One moment's silence, and then a howl from the Danes who watched, and they flew on us, bearing us back a pace or two. Odda went down under the rush that was made on him, and I called to my comrades, and stood over him, and beat them back. But Hubba's fall was the end.

Even as I stood there, there came a rash of men from our ranks past me; and I cheered, for I saw Heregar's silver mail driving straight for the Raven standard, at the head of the young thanes who were the shield wall of the Dragon of Wessex. Then, too, closed in the wounded men and the country folk; and the Danes broke and fled towards the ships in disorder. We followed for a little way, and then the thralls ended matters. They say that not one Dane reached the river's bank, beyond which their comrades watched and raged, powerless to help them.

I went back to where Odda had fallen, and at that time there rose a thundering cheer of victory from our wearied line, and helms were cast into the air, and weapons waved in wild joy. That roused one who lay before me, and white and shaking, up rose Odda from among the slain. I went to him, and got my arm round him; and again the men cheered, and little by little the colour came back to his face.

"I thought you slain outright," I said; "are you much hurt?"

"I cannot tell," he said. "I believe I am sound in limb, but my wind is gone. It is ill for a stout man to have mail-clad Danes hurled on him by heavy-handed vikings."

So he said, gasping, but trying to laugh. And, indeed, he was unwounded, save for a cut or two, and he still grasped his red spear in his right hand.

Now I looked on our men, and saw that we might not bide for another fight. Already some whom the wild joy of battle had kept strong in spite of wounds were falling among their comrades, and it seemed to me that wounds were being bound up everywhere.

But there was a token of victory that made these seem as nothing. In the midst of all Heregar stood with the Dragon banner, and by his side his son-in-law, Turkil the thane of Watchet, bore the captured "Raven."

Harek the scald looked at it once, and then went to its heavy folds, and scanned carefully the runes that were thereon.

"Ho, comrades!" he cried joyfully, "here is a winning that will be sung of long after our names are forgotten. This is the magic Raven that was wrought with wizardry and spells by the daughters of Ragnar Lodbrok. Ill will this news fall on Danish ears from end to end of England. This is worth two victories."

"I have seen it many times before," said Heregar; "nor is this the only time that I have tried to win it. But never before have I seen it hanging motionless as it hung today. There seems to be somewhat in the tale they tell of its flapping foreboding victory."

"Ay," said Odda. "Today they despised us, and bore it not forward; therefore it flapped not, seeing that there was no wind where it hung."

The ealdorman called us together then, and pointed to the Danes who were massed beyond the river.

"Now it is time for us to go. We have won a good fight, and some of us are yet alive. It will not be well to lose all by biding here to be slain to the last man now. Shall we go to Bridgwater or to the Quantocks, and so to Taunton?"

Then Heregar said:

"To the hills; for we should be penned in Bridgwater between this force and the other. I think that while we are yonder they will not do much on this side the Parret; and men will ever gather to us."

Then we took our wounded and went back to the fort--four hundred men out of six hundred who sallied out, where we thought that none would return. But how many Danes we left on the field it is hard to say. Some say six hundred, and some more; and it may be so. Their graves are everywhere over the hill where they fell. When the tide rose we were gone; and Hubba's men sought the body of their chief, and raised a mound over it. But they had no mind to stay on our side of the river, and they went to the Polden Hills, and laid the land waste far and wide, even to holy Glastonbury, until they joined Guthrum's force at Edington.

Now one may know in what wise Etheldreda the brave shield maiden met us, as we came back from that hard-won field, with words of praise and thanks. But Thora stood not with her as we passed through the fort gates, where she waited on the rampart with the Lady Alswythe. Nor had she watched the fight at all, being torn with sorrow and fear alike.

I found her presently, while the men made litters whereon to bear our wounded to safety, having cleansed the stains of war from my armour. King Harald's mail had kept me from wound worth notice--though, indeed, I hardly know how it was that I was unhurt thus. Kolgrim would not use his arm for many days, and Harek was gashed in arm and thigh also.

When Osmund heard my tread, he started up from where he sat beside Thora, looking away towards the hills to which we were going, and greeted me warmly.

"It was a good fight, Ranald, and well won," he said.

Then Thora turned slowly, and looked at me fearfully, as if she feared me. I was grieved, and would have gone away; but she drew nearer, and the fear went from her eyes when she saw that I was safe, knowing little of what I had been through. And at last she smiled faintly, saying:

"King Ranald, they say my warrior has fought well."

"It had been strange had I not, Thora," I said.

"I think I should have hated my own kin had you fallen," she said then.

"Ay," said Osmund, "war sees strange chances, and a man's thoughts are pulled in many ways. Many a time have I seen Dane fight with Dane on the old shores; and I can welcome a victor heartily, even if it is my own kin who have been beaten. Presently we Danes will fight for our new homes in England against such a landing from beyond seas as you have met."

There was some scratch on my shield arm that drew Thora's eyes at this time, and as the jarl spoke she came quickly to me, taking some light scarf she had from her dress at the same moment.

"You are hurt," she said; "though it is little. Let me bind it for you."

I suffered her to do so, saying nothing, but smiling at her, while the colour came brightly into her face as she wrought. The jarl smiled also, turning away presently as some new shouting came up from the fort gateway, where men welcomed those who bore back the spoils from the slain.

Then Thora had finished, and I put my arm round her and kissed her once.

"My lady," I said, "it was worth the wound that you should tend it."

And so she looked up at me frankly, and we knew well what had grown up between us since the day when we had ridden together into Wareham streets.

CHAPTER XII
Edington Fight

Now after this we held the great Dowsborough fort on Quantocks for a few days, looking out over the land that should see the greatest deeds of Alfred, the wise king, from Glastonbury in the east to the wide stretches of the great wood, Selwood Forest, beyond the Stanmoor fens; and there, in the clear air, and with plenty of good provender from the smiling Taunton vale behind us, we grew strong again.

The Danes marched on Bridgwater, and the garrison must needs leave the place and retreat to the heights at Petherton, and there hide. I was grieved that my good ship was in Danish hands, but at least I knew that they would not harm her; and such was our faith in Alfred the king, that I believed that I should have her back. Old Thord came up to us when his charge was thus lost.

"Maybe they will finish painting her, and we shall be able to launch her, when we go back, without more trouble," he said. "Two of Hubba's ships, moreover, are worth having."

Then the king rode up to us, and told us that we had done well, and that the great plan yet held. Already he had messengers out throughout all the southern counties, and already men were gathering through the land and filling the towns that the Danes were leaving.

"When I know that the Danes have their eyes fixed on Quantock side again, I shall strike," he said.

So began again the life in Athelney and at Stanmoor fort; but now the Devon men gathered openly on our hills, and every day the Danish force grew also. When the last fight came, there would be an end to either one side or the other, and Guthrum knew it.

Once in that time I rode with Alfred, and saw Neot again; and if it were but for a few hours that we might stay with him, he found time to speak with me, asking if I had learned aught of his faith as yet.

"I have been in Athelney," I answered, "and I saw what might the holy Name has at Chippenham. The old gods have passed from me."

Little have I said of this, for one cannot speak of inmost thoughts; but so it was. Yet I think that, had I been older, the old faith would have died more slowly from my mind. So it was also with Harek the scald, but I think that he was Christian in heart before I had bent my mind to the matter in earnest. Long talks had he with Denewulf, the wise herdsman, while I listened.

So holy Neot rejoiced greatly over us, bidding me seek baptism at once.

"Nay, father," I said; "I fear it, knowing what it is. Let me bide for a time till I am stronger in these deep things."

He tried to persuade me gently, but at last let me be, knowing that I spoke in earnest and with all wish to seek it rightly.

So we left him on the day after we came, and went back to Athelney, and Alfred was very silent all the way.

"What ails you, my king?" I asked him at last, fearing that his pain, which had left him of late altogether, might return.

"I will tell you, cousin," he said. "Plainly has Neot shown me that all these troubles have come from my own pride and self will when first I was king. It is a long chain of happenings, of which you would know nought were I to try to tell you. But so it has been, and I weep therefor in my very heart."

Then said I:

"What is past is past, King Alfred, and best friend. Look on to the days to come, for I think that there shall rise a new and happier England before the winter comes again. There is no man whom I have met in all the hosts in whose heart is not love and best thoughts of you. Old days are forgotten as if they had never been, save that you led and conquered in the great battles beyond the Thames."

He held out his hand to me, and took mine and gripped it, saying no word, and riding on in silence for a mile and more. And after that he was of good cheer again till we came to Exeter, and there I stayed to see how fared my ships, for it was time they were in the water again.

Well had my men and the Saxon wrights wrought at building. If all went like this, King Alfred would have a fleet that could sweep the seas from Dover to Orme's Head, and keep his land from new plunderers at least.

In a week I came back to Athelney, and there was good cheer, and all were in the best of heart, for things went well. Messengers came and went across the winding paths from the southern hills, and Ethered met me laughing, and said:

"The king has robbed you of your glory, Ranald. He has been into the Danish camp--even to the presence of Guthrum himself."

Then I would hear of this from Alfred himself.

"Ay," he said, when he had greeted me and heard that the ships were almost ready, "I have outdone you; for I have played the gleeman as I planned, and have been in the midst of them yonder on Edington hill."

"It was an awesome risk to run, my king," I said.

"Which you taught me yourself, cousin. Howbeit I met no damsel, and I had no companion to return with but him with whom I went--Heregar's young son, my page. Thane is he now by right of unfearing service. Once, when I climbed the hill, I began to fear greatly, and I stayed, and asked the boy if he was afraid to go on. Tell me truly, Ranald, did you fear when you were in Wareham?"

"Truly I feared at first," I answered; "but since I was there when it came on me, I must even go through with the business. So it passed."

"Well, I am glad you confess it," he answered, "for I was minded to turn and run when the first lights of the great camp showed through the trees. Then the boy answered me, 'My king, why should I fear when you are with me?' I was ashamed, and took Harek's harp from him--for he carried it--and went forward boldly, singing the song of Gunnar in the snake pit. And it seemed to me that Harek would have chosen that song as fitting my case; for, putting Danes for snakes, I was in a close place enough. The warriors came out when they heard me; and I was well treated, and listened as I drank. Many things I learned."

Now I cannot believe that Alfred feared at all. He was surely but anxious, and took that feeling for fear. So think all his people.

"It seems that they thought I sang well," he went on; "so they took me to Guthrum. He indeed looked sharply at me once, and maybe twice; but I went on singing Harek's songs, and paid no heed to him. Presently he gave me a great horn of ale from his own table, and this gold bracelet that I wear also, and sent me away. Then I went about the camp and heard the talk. One man asked me if I had seen Alfred, and what he was like. 'Faith,' said I, 'men say I am like him.' Whereat they laughed long at me and at the king also. Then heard I the truth about my own looks for once. I had some trouble in getting away, but at last I seemed to wax hoarse, and so made as if I would go to Bridgwater, and left them, promising to come again. Ay, and I will keep my promise," he said; "but as Harek's heathen songs say, it is the sword's mass that I will sing to them."

Then his eyes glowed, and he was silent, and I wondered at the courage and resource in the slight figure that was before me.

"All goes well, and the plan is good," he went on directly. "They look for some easily-beaten attack from this side of the Parret, and at the first sign thereof will leave Edington height for the level ground below, as they did when Hubba came. Then when they turn, on Edington hill will be our levy suddenly--a levy of which they have not dreamed. And there will be the greatest fight that England has seen yet, and after that there will be a Saxon overlord of England against whom none will dare rise."

"May it be so, my king," I answered.

"It will be so," he said. "Here in this cottage have I had the word that tells me thereof; and you, Ranald, brought the sign that made the word sure to me."

I minded it, and I knew that for all my life my ways were bound to the service of Alfred the king; for my fate was linked with his, as it seemed, from my first coming.

It was not long now before the day came that will never be forgotten; for word was brought in from every quarter that thanes and freemen and churls alike would not be behind when Alfred gave the word, and he sent back to bid them meet him at Ecgbryht's Stone, beyond Selwood, on Whitsunday. There is a great and strong camp there on a rocky hill that looks out far and wide, near the two great roads, British and Roman, that cross in the vale beneath; and to that all were to gather, for there would the Golden Dragon be set up. Men call it White Sheet Castle.

On the day before I rode to Odda, who had already drawn his men to the Petherton ridge above Bridgwater, and told him what the king's word was. Then I went on up the long side of the Quantocks, and spoke in the Maytime woods with Thora, telling her--for she was a warrior's daughter, and was worthy of a warrior's love--that I must be at the king's side. And so she bade me fight bravely, speaking many noble and loving words to me, until I must go. Then I led her back to Osmund in his place among the rough huts within the wide circle of the camp ramparts, that now held but a few poor folk from the Parretside lands.

"King Alfred makes some new move," I said to him, "and it is possible that we may not meet again. I think that what is coming will end all the trouble between Saxon and Dane."

He shook his head.

"Some day it will end," he said, "but not in my time or yours--not until the Danes have grown to know that England is their home, and that they are English by birth and right of time--maybe not till Denmark has ceased to send forth the sons for whom she has no place in her own borders."

Then I answered that perhaps he was right. I did not see into things as far as he, and I was a stranger in the land.

"But this at last will give a strong overlord to England," I said.

"Ay, for the time. So long as a strong king rules, there will be less trouble indeed; but if Alfred's sons are weak, it will begin afresh. England will no longer bear two kings; and while there is a Saxon kingdom alongside a Danish, there cannot be lasting peace."

Then I said:

"What of yourself? Shall you go back to Guthrum when this is over?"

"I cannot tell," he answered. "What my fate is I know not yet. What mean you to do if all goes well for Alfred? Shall you bide in England?"

We had walked apart now, and were looking over all the fair Quantock vale beneath us. I think there is no fairer lookout in all England: land and river and hills and sea, and beyond the sea the blue mountains of the Welsh coast--ever changing and ever beautiful under sun and cloud and flying shadows.

"I have found the fairest land under the northern sun," I said; "and I have found the best king, as I think. I shall bide here. One other thing I have found of which I hardly dare to think, so many are the chances of wartime. Yet, jarl, but for them I should not have met with Thora, though in my heart I believe that I should not have spoken to her yet."

"I would not have had it otherwise," he said, kindly taking my arm. "I have seen what was coming long before Etheldreda spoke. It has been good for Thora that she did so, whatever befalls."

Then we spoke of my promised place with the king, as if his victory were certain. Indeed, I believe that we both had no thought of its being otherwise.

"I do not know, however," said Osmund, "if your taking a Danish wife will be well received. It may be likely that Alfred will wish you to be bound to him by some tie of that nearness which shall be of his making."

I had not thought of that, but it was a thing that was common enough. Harald Fairhair was wont to give a rich wife to some chief whom he would keep at his side.

"If that is so, I shall go hence," I said. "There are things that come before friendship."

"Well," he answered, "we shall see. There is always a place for us both at Rolf's side in his new-won land."

"Yet I should be loth to leave Alfred," I said most truly. "I think that this is the only thing that would make me do so."

"Thora would not stand in your way to honour with him, nor would I," said Osmund.

"Honour with Alfred shall not stand in my way, rather," I answered. "But we speak of chances, as I think."

We said no more, and he bade me farewell.

I went back to Alfred somewhat sad, and yet with many thoughts that were good and full of hope; and soon I had little time to do aught but look on at the way in which the king's plans worked out most wonderfully.

On the eve of the great Whitsunday festival we set out through the fen paths southward to the hills and the first woodlands of Selwood Forest, and when the morning came we were far in its depths, passing eastward towards the place where we were to meet the levy.

Presently we turned aside to a little woodland chapel that had escaped the sight of the Danes, and from a hut beside it came out an old priest, white-bearded and bent with age and scanty fare. At first he feared that the heathen had found him at last; yet he looked bravely at us, catching up the crucifix that hung at his side and clasping it in both his hands as he stood in the open doorway of his church, as if to stay us from it.

Alfred rode forward to him when he saw his fear.

"Father, I am Alfred the king," he said. "Far have I ridden on this holy day. Now I would fain hear mass and have your blessing before we go on."

Thereat the old priest gave thanks openly to the King of kings, who had brought Alfred again into the land, and hastened to make ready. So that was the king's Whitsuntide mass, and we three heathen and our few men must bide outside while the others went into the holy place and returned with bright faces and happy; for this was a service to which we might not be admitted, though all knew that we would be Christians indeed ere long.

So at last we came to the ancient castle, and saw the valley to north and east beneath its height, bright everywhere with sparkling arms that gleamed from lane and field and forest glade, as all Wessex gathered to meet their king.

Then the Golden Dragon that we had lost and won was unfurled; and the war horns blew bravely enough to wake the mighty dead whose mounds were round about us; and soon the hillside was full of men who crowded upwards and filled the camp and ramparts and fosse, so that before sunset Alfred had a host that any king might be proud to call his own. Yet he would call it not Alfred's force, but England's.

Standing on the old ramparts, he spoke to them, while all the great gathering was silent. And the words he said sank into the heart of every man who heard, so that he felt as if on his arm alone it rested to free England, and that his arm could not fail. Not long did the king speak, but when he ended there rose a cheering that was good to hear, for it came from hearts that had been made strong to dare aught that might come.

After that he spoke to the thanes, giving each one his place, and telling them all that he had planned, so that each knew what was looked for from him. It seemed that he had forgotten nothing, and that the day must go as he said he thought it would.

Men slept on their arms that night, without watch fires, lest any prowling Danes should see that somewhat was on hand, although Guthrum had drawn to him every man from out of Wessex, as was said, and as seemed true. I have heard tales from some that in the night the warriors who lie resting in the mounds around their old stronghold came forth and wandered restless along the ramparts, longing to take their part again in the mighty struggle they knew was coming. I saw nothing, but Harek the scald says he saw.

Next day we marched towards our foes. Eighteen miles we went, and then came to the holy place Glastonbury, where the burnt ruins spoke again, as it were, to the warriors of wrong and cruelty to be avenged.

There we were, but eight miles from the foe, and that night we lay in a great meadow they called Iglea, deep down in the folds of the hills, where even so great a host might be hidden for many days if no chance betrayed them. Alfred took a few of us when night came, and climbed the steep tor above Glastonbury town. Thence we could see the long line of fires on Polden Hills that marked where the Danes slept, all unknowing that any host could be gathered in their rear.

In the grey of morning we set our ranks in order. I was with Alfred, with Ethered of Mercia and Ethelnoth, and more nobles whom I knew; and my few men were in the shield wall, among the best warriors of the Saxon levies. None grudged that honour to those who had made the point of the wedge that broke Hubba's ranks and won the Raven banner.

Now, in our Norse land there is ever sacrifice to the Asir when one leads a host to battle, that luck may be on the right side; and now I was to see a more wondrous thing than even that. I knew by this time the meaning of what I saw, and there crept into my heart a wish that I might take full part therein with Alfred, who had taught me.

When all the ranks were ordered, and the deep columns were drawn up on Iglea meadows in three sides of a square, there came a little train of robed monks, at whose head was Bishop Sigehelm of Sherborne, before whom went a tall gilded cross. Careworn and anxious looked the good fathers, for there was not one of them who had not a tale of Danish cruelty and destruction to tell, and more than one had hardly escaped with his life; but now their faces were brighter with new hope as they came into the open side of the armed square and waited for a moment.

Alfred and we stood before them, and the bishop raised his hand. At that we all knelt, with a strange clash and rattle of arms that went round the great host and ceased suddenly, so that the stillness was very great.

Then was only the voice of the bishop, who in a clear tone spoke the words of peace to those who should pass hence in the coming battle, that they might fight bravely, and even rejoice in death.

So he shrived the host, and at the end they said "Amen" in one voice.

Thereafter the bishop prayed to the Lord of hosts--not such a prayer as I had been wont to hear, but more wonderful, and with no boasting therein, nor, as it were, any hate of the foe, but rather the wish that the strife should make for peace, and even blessing to them.

Then he lifted his hand and blessed all the host as they bared their heads, and again the last word rolled deep and strong round the ranks, and that was all; then Alfred cried cheerily to his men, and we began our march that must needs end in battle.

There is a great road that climbs up the slope of the Polden Hills from Glastonbury and then runs along their top to Edington and beyond, and by this way we went, among pleasant woodlands. Guthrum's own place was on the spur of Edington, because thence one looks out on all the land that Alfred held, from the fort at Stane hill to Bridgwater and Combwich and the sea beyond. That was only eight miles from us, and was the point which we would win. Thence to Bridgwater is five miles, and the town was now held in force by the Danes; and where the road leaves the hills to cross the marsh to the bridge and town, two miles away, was a camp that guarded the causeway through the level.

We went quickly as a great host may, and Alfred had so ordered matters that even as we set out from Iglea, Odda and his force were moving in battle array from the Petherton heights on the Quantock side of the town, as if to attack it. That was what Guthrum had looked for since the time we had beaten Hubba, and the only attack which could have seemed possible in any way.

It is likely that he overrated the number which Odda had with him; for those who escaped us at Combwich had not been near enough to see from the far side of the river how small our force was, and would make much of those who had been able to overcome their mightiest chief. Moreover, since that time seven weeks had gone by, and the gathering of Devon might be greater yet. So it was, indeed; but Odda had not a thousand men. Perhaps, too, the Danes feared some sally from the fens; but however it was, they made not the mistake which destroyed Hubba by despising us rashly, for Guthrum drew his whole force together, and left the hills for a march towards the town which he heard was threatened.

So when we came to Edington, Guthrum's hill fort was empty, save for a camp guard to keep the country folk who lurked in wood and fen from pillaging it. These men fled, and we stood on the ridge without striking one blow; and King Alfred turned to us, and cried that surely his plan was working out well.

Then our host lined the ridge, and a mighty Saxon cheer from ten thousand throats went pealing across the valley below us, and they say that shout was heard even in Bridgwater. Guthrum heard it as he rode with his host across the long causeway, and his men heard it and halted, and saw in their rear the blaze of war gear that shone from their own lines, and knew that they were pent in between fens and hills, with an unknown force ready to fall on them.

Whereon a panic very nearly seized them. Hubba's end was fresh in their minds, and it needed all that Guthrum could say to prevent them making for the town. But he minded them of old victories, and bade them not fear to face the despised Saxons once again, and they rallied. But it was noon before he could lead them to attack us, and by that time he learned that Odda had halted above the town, and need not be feared. But by that time also every post of vantage along the hills was in our hands, and if Edington height was to be held by Danes again, it must be won by hard fighting. That is a thing that no Dane shrinks from, and now for Guthrum there was nought else to be done, for he was surrounded, as it were.

No man saw the whole of that fight, for it began at noon, as I have said, when Guthrum turned to find the hillward road blocked behind him. And from that time on it raged from spur to spur and point to point, as step by step the Danes won back to the hillsides. But the crest of the hill they never gained, save where for a time they might set foot and be driven headlong in turn by those who had given way before them at first. And so the fight swept on to the base of Edington hill and along its sides, for there Alfred had held his best men in reserve. Already the Danes had made for themselves some shallow lines of earthworks along the crest, and now these were manned against their own attack.

Men who looked on from afar tell strange tales of the shouts and cries that rang among the quiet Polden hills and woodlands that day for long hours. It was very still, as it chanced, and the noise of battle went far and wide from the place where Saxon and Dane fought their greatest fight for mastery.

Ever rode Alfred with the light of battle on his face, confident and joyous, among his men from post to post. Ever where the tide of battle seemed to set against us his arm brought victory again, until at last Guthrum drew his men together for one final attack that should end the day.

On Edington hillside he massed them, and steadily they came on under shield in a dense column to where, in their own camp, we waited under the Dragon banner. Half our men, the best spearmen of the force, were lying down resting, but along the little ridges of the earthworks the archers stood, each knowing that he fought under the eye of the king he loved.

"This is the end," said Alfred, as the Danes came on. "Be ready, spearmen, when I give the word."

And they lay clutching their weapons, with their eyes fixed on him as he stood on the hilltop, surrounded by his thanes, gazing on the last assault of the Danes, whose archers from the wings were already at work, so that the men of the shield wall closed in around him.

I think that the Danes had no knowledge of what force was hidden by the hill brow. For when they were within half arrow shot, and Alfred gave the word, and the long ranks of spearmen leaped from the ground and closed up for their charge, a waver went along the shielded line, and they almost halted, though it passed, and they came on even more swiftly.

Then Alfred lifted his sword and shouted, and, with that awful roar that I had heard before on the Combwich meadows, over the hill crest and down upon the Danes the spearmen rushed. The lines met with a mighty crash of steel on steel, and while one might count two score they swayed in deadly hand-to-hand strife. Then Guthrum's men gave back one pace, and howled, and won their place again, and again lost it.

Then forward went Alfred and his shield wall, and I was on one side of him and Ethered of Mercia on the other, while after him came Heregar, bearing the banner. The Danes in the centre closed up as they saw us come, and there were shouts in which Guthrum's name was plain to be heard, and I saw him across a four-deep rank of his men.

Straight for him went Alfred, and the Danish line grew thin before us. But as their king went forward our Saxons cheered again and pressed their attack home, and right and left the Danish line fell back and broke. At that a wild shout and charge with levelled spears swept them down the hillside in full rout, and the end had come. His courtmen closed round Guthrum and bore him from before us, and the full tide of pursuit swept him away before we reached him.

Alfred stayed his horse and let the men go on. His face was good to see as he glanced round at the hills to our right; but when it fell on the slain, who lay thickly where the lines had met, he bared his head and looked silently on them for a space, while his lips moved as if he prayed.

Then he said:

"These have given their lives not in vain, for they have helped to bring peace, and have died to set an English king over the English land."

He put on his crown-circled helm again, and as he did so, among the fallen there was a stir and movement, and the wounded rose up on arms and knees and turned on their sides, and raised their hands, waving broken weapons, and crying in a strange, wearied voice that yet had a ring of victory in it:

"Waeshael to Alfred the king!"

For the silence that had fallen, and the lessening shouts of the pursuers, told them that they had won, and they were content.

Thereat Alfred flushed red, and I think that he almost wept, for he turned from us. And then he spoke to the men who yet stood round him, and said:

"Let every man who has any knowledge of care for the wounded, or who has known a wound of his own and the way it was cared for, go among these brave ones and help them."

Nor would he leave the place till he saw men going up and down among the hurt, tending them as well as they could; and he was the more content when he saw Bishop Sigehelm and many other clergy come on the field from the rear, where he had bidden them stay. The bishop had mail under his robes, having been eager to join in the fight, as would Eahlstan, his great forerunner, have certainly joined; but Alfred would not suffer him to do so.

Once more Guthrum tried to rally his men, when the flight bore him to his camp at the hill foot, on the way across the fens to the town. There was a sharp fight there, and Ethelnoth was wounded as he led on his men; and thence the Danes fled to Bridgwater, making no more delay. So close on them were our men that Guthrum's housecarls closed the gates after their king on many of their comrades, who fell under the Saxon spear in sight of safety. Nor did we give them time to drive in the cattle that were gathered from all the countryside to the meadows round the place.

Then came Thord to me and put me in mind of somewhat.

"Now is our work to be done, king. These Danes will take Hubba's ships and be gone down the river next. We must stop them in some way, for the king's plan is to starve them out, as it seems."

We had left the king at that time, for we would not suffer him to join in pursuit, which has its dangers, if men turn desperate and make a stand, as many did, dying like brave warriors that they were. So I rode on quickly with my followers, and came to the river bank below the bridge. The Danes were swarming on the ramparts of the fortress like angry bees, and in the ships, which lay beneath the walls, men were busy, even as Thord had guessed they would be, making ready to sail when tide served. We could not reach them by any means, for every boat had been taken from this side long ago, when the first news of defeat was brought back by flying horsemen.

Then Thord's face glowered under his helm, and he pointed to the ship that was farthest from the bridge, and therefore likely to be the first to start away when the tide was full. It was my own ship, which they had got afloat.

"Thor's hammer smite them!" he growled; "they have launched the old keel without finishing her painting--just as I left her. How are we to stay their going off with her?"

"Is there a chain cable anywhere?" I asked.

"Not one in the place," he said; "and if we did get one across the river, we should have to fight to keep the far end of it."

The tide was rising fast, and I thought we should surely lose every ship, while Guthrum and his chiefs would escape us at the same time. One might line the banks with archers, certainly, but that would not stay the going. Evening was closing in, moreover. By midnight they would be gone, and I was in a difficulty out of which I could not see my way.

Suddenly Thord smote his hands together, and his face grew brighter.

"I have it," he cried. "There is an old vessel that lies in a creek a mile down the river. A great buss she is, and worth nothing; but she will float, and maybe will be afloat now. If we can sink her across the channel in a place that I know, not one of these ships will get away till she is raised."

Then I called every man to me whom I could see, and we went quickly to the place where this buss was, and she was just afloat. Thord knew where her tackle was kept, and he had the oars out--what there were of them at least, for they were old and rotten enough. Then we had to shove her off and get her boat into the water, and the vessel itself floated up on the tide to-wards the narrow place where she might best be sunk to block the channel against ships that came from the town.

We had not gone far when there came a sound at which I started, for it was nothing more or less than the quick beat of oars coming down the river against the tide. Thord and I and eight men of my own crew were in the buss, while I had maybe thirty men ashore who were keeping pace with us along the bank. The rest of my own men were with these, and one shouted that he could see the ship, and that it was our own, crammed with men too.

Now at first it seemed as if the only thing for us to do was to go ashore in the boat as quickly as we could and get away; but Thord cried to me:

"Then will the Danes take our ship to sea, and we have lost her for good. It should not be said of us that we let her go without a blow struck to save her."

"Sink this hulk straightway, then," I said, falling to work, with the axe I had in thy hand, on the lowest strakes. My men leaped to work as well, and in two minutes the seams began to gape, and then was a rush of water from broken planking that sent us over the side and into the boat in hot haste.

Then we pulled for shore, towing the bows of the fast-sinking buss with us till they grounded in the mud, and even as her stern swung with the tide across the channel she lurched and sank.

"We should have bided in her and fought," growled Thord. "Now in five minutes we shall see the bottom ripped out of our own ship by our own deed."

But a foot of the bows and the mast of the buss stood out of the water, and I thought the Danes would see these marks.

Even as we gained the shore our dragon stem swept round the bend that had hidden us, and came on swiftly. Then the Danes saw us, and those on the fore deck shouted, and the oars plashed wildly, and many on the side next to us stopped altogether; and at the same time the steersman saw the stem of the wreck, and, as I think, lost his head between fear of it and the sudden appearance of the foe whom he thought he had escaped. The larboard oars were going yet, and the starboard had almost stopped. He paid no heed to it, and the ship swung over. Then the tide caught her bows, and in a moment she ran hard and fast on our bank, and the men in her fell right and left with the shock.

I had seen what was coming, and so had Thord, and we ran our best to meet her as she struck. The tide was a good one, and she came well on the hard bank, and there was no need to tell my men what to do. Before the Danes knew what had happened we were climbing over the bows on board, and the Danes aft were leaping into the river to get away from us.

Some few tried to fight; but there must have been two hundred men packed along the gangways, and they could do nothing. They threw themselves into the water like the rats that had left the old buss even now, and we slew many, and the good ship was our own again. Some of the Danes got ashore on the far bank, some were met by our Saxons on this side, and but few got back to Bridgwater, for the river had most of them.

Another ship was coming at this time, but those in her heard the shouting and the cries; and it would seem that their hearts failed them, for they went back before we could see more than the tall mast above the banks from our decks.

Then we thought we might rest, for we were wearied out; but Thord would not suffer us to do so till he had got the ship carefully below the wreck, so that she was free. Had we waited for the next tide we could not have done it, as it turned out; for the rise of flood shortened quickly to the neap tides, and a bank of mud grew round the sunken hull, making the channel impassable altogether for the time, and so the last way of escape for Guthrum and his men was barred.

So I thought we had done well, and left Thord and my men to guard the ship and take her back to Combwich, where she would lie safely in the creek, while I rode to Alfred, almost sleeping on my wearied horse as I went.

There were two wrecks in that place in the morning; for they brought down one of Hubba's ships in the dark on the next tide, and she ran on the sunken stem of the buss, and went down almost at once. After that no more attempt was made to fly by water.

Then began a siege that lasted for a fortnight, without anything happening that is worth telling; for the fear of Alfred was on the Danes, and they had not heart so much as to make one sally from the gates.

CHAPTER XIII
The Greatest Victory

Now in a few days it was plain that Alfred held the Danes in the hollow of his hand as it were, and could do what he would with them. At first we looked for messengers from the place, to treat with him for peace; but none came. From the town at times we could hear shoutings and the noise of men who quarrelled, as if there were divided counsels among them that led to blows. They were very short of food also, because all their stores of cattle were left outside the walls, as I have said, so that we fared the better for their plundering while we waited.

At the end of the first week, therefore, Alfred sent a message under flag of truce, and told the chiefs that he was willing to hear what they would say; and next day Guthrum asked that some chiefs might come and speak with him. But Alfred would not trust the Danes enough to send any of his nobles into the town, and bade Guthrum come out to the camp and say what he had to say. But he would not. Then one day, when Alfred held counsel as to what was best to be done to ensure lasting peace, I said that I thought Jarl Osmund might be of use, for he could go between the two camps in safety.

That seemed good to the king, and Heregar and I rode to find him, crossing the tidal ford at Combwich, where we heard from village folk who had returned that the Danish lord bided in Heregar's house beyond the fort.

There I thought I should find Thora, and we went quickly. The place looked very deserted, and when we came to the courtyard gates it seemed more so, for the Maytime had sprinkled the gay-patterned paving of grey and white shore pebbles with blades of grass and weeds that sprang up between them everywhere for want of tendance.

Only the Lady Alswythe and a few of her servants were there now, for the Lady Etheldreda had taken Thora with her to Taunton when she left the hills. It had not been so safe here, though there was little plunder to bring the Danes to the place now. So I need not say that I was grievously disappointed, though in the dismantled hall sat Osmund, listlessly shaping a bow stave, and waiting for what turn of fortune should take him next.

Very glad, as one might think, were both the lady and the jarl for our coming, and we had to tell them all the tale of the working of Alfred's plan, and of the great fight. And when that was heard, we told the jarl of Alfred's wish to treat with Guthrum and the other chiefs through him.

That Osmund would gladly do; indeed, he said that, in hopes of being thus useful, he had stayed so near at hand.

So he and the thane talked long of the matter--for Alfred had sent messages--while I spoke with the lady, of Thora mostly.

It did not seem to me that I had any part in the king's business with the Danes, and so presently I thought that I could do no better than ride to Taunton to see Thora, who I feared might be in trouble or doubt as to my safety.

So I rode there with Kolgrim. At that time the scald was laid up with a wound in the camp, and the king seemed to miss his presence, and to care for his welfare as if he were his brother; but, indeed, he made every man with whom he had to do feel as if his king were his best friend.

There is not much need for me to tell what manner of welcome I had at Taunton from Thora. As for Etheldreda, she would have me tell her everything, and I sat with those two, until night came and rest, talking of all the time past. But of the time to come Thora said nothing, and once or twice when Etheldreda left us and we were alone for a little while, so that I could try to plan out somewhat, she would but turn the talk again.

In the morning I found out how this was. She had gathered from Osmund somewhat of his thoughts about what Alfred's plan for me might be, and was unhappy therefore, not wishing to stand in my way to honour with the king. So she told me when I pressed her a little to speak of what I would do; and when I said that there should be nothing that I would let stand between us, she was the more troubled yet.

So at last I went and found Etheldreda, and prayed her to come and speak with Thora.

"Falling out already?" she said, laughing.

"Not so, but a greater trouble than that," I said, "one that will need your help before it is mended."

"Ay, I suppose you could patch up a quarrel for yourselves," she said. "What is this mighty trouble?"

So she came and sat by Thora, taking her hand and kissing her, and we told her what Osmund's thoughts were.

"There is such enmity between Saxon and Dane," Thora said, "that it is not likely that the king will trust one who will wed one of his foe's daughters."

It was plain that Etheldreda thought the same; but she cheered us both, saying that she would do all that she could to help us, and that Odda would not be behind in the matter. After all, if we were to wait for a while, things might be very different after a little time of peace. And so we were content.

So I went back to Alfred next day, and when he heard where I had been he smiled a little, and said:

"One thing I must tell you, my Norseman, and that is that our thanes who know little of you will be jealous that you should have much dealing with any Dane as yet."

Which made me the more uneasy; for though I might think that the king, at all events, was not displeased with me, others, and the wishes of others, might be too strong for him to go against.

But my affairs are little things compared with what was on hand at this time, and on the same day Alfred spoke to me about somewhat that he would have me do for him.

In the town the Danes were in the greatest straits by this time, for by no means could they get stores of any sort to them, so close was the watch round the place. Osmund had been in and out once or twice, and Guthrum had received him well enough, and it was thought that there would be no long delay now before the siege was at an end by the submission of the Danes to any terms they might gain, and the more so that an assault on the fortress would surely have been successful, ending in the fall of all its defenders.

But Alfred was most willing to be merciful, and he had bidden Osmund tell Guthrum and his chiefs that if he might name twelve hostages for himself the rest should go free, while Guthrum should hold the East Anglian kingdom for him as under-king.

But this was what Alfred would have me do.

"One other thing there is," he said. "If there is to be any brotherhood between us, it must be as between Christians. The ways of persecution must be forgotten and that cannot come to pass until the chiefs at least have accepted the faith."

"It is strange to me, my king," I said, "that Guthrum, who has been in England for ten years, is not Christian by this time."

"Ay, but his hosts are heathen," the king answered. "Now I think I can speak to you as if no longer a heathen at least?"

"As a Christian, my king," I answered.

"Well, then," he said, smiling on me, "go and speak to Guthrum and tell him what I have said. I think that he will listen to you better than if I sent a priest or even Bishop Sigehelm. Warrior may speak to warrior plainly."

Now this was a hard thing for me to do, as it seemed. Maybe it was the hardest thing he could have asked me. But it was in my mind that I could not but go to Guthrum and give the message, else would I seem to deny the faith that I loved. Alfred saw at once that I was troubled in some way, and I believe that he knew well what the seeming doubt was.

"Once you brought a token of good to me," he said. "Now that was all unknowing. Go now and take a message of good to Guthrum openly, and have no fear."

"What shall I say?"

"Mind not that at all," he answered; "what is needed will come to you."

So I said that I would go if Harek might come with me, for his words were ever ready. But Alfred would not suffer that. I must go without help from a scald, taking only my own words; and at last I consented, though indeed my only fear was that I might not succeed by reason of my slowness of speech.

Then I went to Osmund, and told him that I was to go into the town with him next day, for that is how Alfred planned for me; and I told him also what my part in the business was to be. Whereon he surprised me.

"I do not know that your errand is so hopeless as you seem to think," he said. "Guthrum has harmed no Christians in East Anglia since he was king there."

"Well," I answered, "I hope it may be easy, though I doubt it."

I would not say more then, but, being anxious, went and spoke long with Harek. The brave scald's wounds were deep, though he had said little of them. Some say that he saved the life of Ethelnoth at the time when that ealdorman was struck down, and that also is Ethelnoth's story; though the scald says that if so it was by accident, and less worth speaking of than many braver deeds that were wrought and went untold that day.

"Here have I been in England but six months or so, and I have more to sing of than ever I learned with Harald Fairhair," he said one day, as he made songs on his bed while his wounds were healing.

And he spoke the truth. Never was a winter so full of deeds wrought by a king and a valiant people that were worth a scald's remembrance.

Now Osmund had a last message from Alfred that day, and in the morning we went together to the bridge. There Guthrum's own courtmen met us, and they took us into the fortress, beyond which lies the town, so that we saw little of what straits the host might be in by this time. In the fortress itself all seemed in order at least; and there was a guard set at the door of the well-built hut where the Danish king was, as if some state were yet kept up.

There Guthrum welcomed us, and with him were many chiefs, on whose faces was the same care-worn look that Osmund had borne when I saw him at Exeter before Alfred.

"Two messages come to you today," Osmund said; "one by my mouth, and the other by that of King Ranald Vemundsson, who is with me. I think you may hear both, and answer them both favourably."

Guthrum made no reply, but took his seat at the upper end of the one room the hut had; and all the chiefs sat also, leaving us messengers standing.

Then said Osmund:

"I think it right that I should stand in the presence of my king, but the son of King Vemund should not do so in any less presence than that of his overlord."

Thereat Guthrum smiled a little.

"I have heard that Harald of Norway came to blows with his brother kings because they would not stand before him, and that others have left that kingdom because they did not choose to do so. Sit down, King Ranald. Your father's name was well known to all of us in the old days. I am glad to see his son, though maybe I should not say so."

"We would rather that he were on our side," said one of the other chiefs.

Then they set places for both of us, and we waited for Guthrum's word.

"Well," he said, wearily enough, "let us hear what King Alfred says."

"Few are his words," said Osmund:

"'Let Guthrum suffer me to choose any hostages that I will for myself, let him swear to keep the peace hereafter as my under-king beyond Thames, doing homage to me, and he shall go hence with his host in honour.' There is also the message of Ranald to add hereto."

Now I thought that the faces of the chiefs showed that they thought these terms very light; but they said nothing as yet.

Guthrum turned to me.

"Well, King Ranald?"

"Alfred the king bids me say that he would fain treat with you hereafter as a brother altogether. And that can only be if the great trouble between Dane and Saxon is removed--that is, if Guthrum becomes a Christian."

Now I expected some outburst of scorn and wrath on this, but instead of that a silence fell, in which the chiefs looked at one another; and Guthrum gazed at me steadfastly, so that I felt my face growing hot under his eyes, because I knew I must say more, and that of myself and my own wishes most likely.

Then Guthrum said slowly:

"Why has he not sent some priest to say this?"

"Because he thought that a warrior would listen best to a brother warrior," I answered.

"Ay, that is true," said the king. "Are you a Christian, therefore?"

"I am as yet unbaptized," I said. "I have taken the prime signing on me, as have many others; but I shall certainly seek baptism shortly."

"You came here as a heathen, then?"

"As a heathen altogether, except that I had no hatred of Christians," I answered, not quite seeing what the king would know.

"What turned your mind so far from the old gods that you should be a fit messenger on such a matter to us?"

"I have learned from Alfred and Neot," I answered, "and I know that I have found what is true."

Then Guthrum turned to Osmund.

"What say you, jarl? you have been with Alfred also."

"When Ranald is baptized, I shall be so with him," the jarl answered simply.

And that was the first word thereof that I had heard from him.

Then an older chief spoke sharply to us.

"What profit do you look to make thereout--either of you?"

"Certainty of better things both in this life and in that to come," I answered.

"Ay, so they always say," the chief growled; "but what place with Alfred in return?"

"It is likely that I shall gain no place with him," I said. "Jarl Osmund knows that I do not count on that."

"Ay," said Osmund, "I know it. Nor will any man think that I seek honour at Alfred's hands."

Then Guthrum rose up, and spoke gravely and yet very determinedly, as if this was no new matter to him.

"Here, chiefs, are two good and tried warriors who willingly choose Alfred's faith. You and I have heard thereof since we were in England; and many a man have we seen die, since we have been here, because he would not give it up. I mind me of Edmund, the martyred king, whom Ingvar, our great chief, slew, and of Humbert the bishop, and many more lesser folk. Tell me truly how much you have thought of the Asir in these last years?"

But none answered. It was with them as with me: the Asir were not of England.

"One thing," said Guthrum, "has gone against our taking up the English faith--we have thought the words of peace have made men cowardly. Now we know that is not so. Here is one who withstood Hubba, and round the walls watch Christian men who have beaten us sturdily."

Then he stayed his words for a little, and his voice sank, and he looked round and added:

"Moreover, the words of the new faith are good. I will accept King Alfred's brotherhood altogether."

Then one or two more of the younger chiefs spoke, and said that they would do so also; but again the elder warrior spoke fiercely.

"Is this forced on us as part of the peace making?"

"It is not," I answered. "It is, as I have said, the wish for brotherhood altogether."

Then said Guthrum:

"That is enough. I do not think that we need be ashamed to be conquered altogether by King Alfred."

"One more word," said the old chief. "Are we to have no hostages?"

"There can be no exchange of hostages," said Osmund.

"Things are all on the side of the Saxon," he growled.

"Ay, they are, in more ways than that," said Guthrum. "We have no power to say a word. It is in my mind that we could not have looked for such mildness at the king's hands. For there is no denying that we are at his mercy.

"What say you, as a stranger, Ranald?"

"I have known the ways of Harald of Norway," I answered. "I think that he would not have left a man of this host alive."

Whereon the old warrior laughed shortly, and was silent while Guthrum bade us go back to Alfred and thank the king for his word, saying that an answer should be given as soon as the word of the host had been taken in open Thing.

So Alfred won Guthrum to the faith, and greatly did he rejoice when he heard what the Danish king had said. I think he was more glad yet when he knew that Osmund would become Christian also, and he urged us both to be baptized at once.

"Let us be so with Guthrum," I asked.

"That will be fitting," he answered, "for I think you have won him over."

But I hold that Guthrum and more of his chiefs had been won by the deaths of those martyrs of whom he spoke long before the choice was set before him. One cannot tell how this was wrought in the mind of the Danes altogether by the hand of God. Some will ever say, no doubt, that they took the Cross on them by necessity; but I know that it was not so. Nor have their lives since that time given any reason for the thought.

Then Alfred asked the name of that old warrior who withstood us, and Osmund told him.

"I will have that chief as a hostage," the king said, "for I think that he is worth taming."

"I think that King Alfred's hostages are not in any way to be pitied," Osmund said.

"Save that they are kept from home and friends, I would have them as happy as may be," the king answered; "but I would have none presume on what mercy came to you, Jarl Osmund, for the sake of the Christmastide message."

"I think that none will do so," Osmund said. "There is full knowledge among my kin that you showed mercy when justice was about to be done, and well they know that your kindness was not weakness. It is likely that the mercy shown here also will do more for peace than would even destruction of your enemies."

So it seemed at last, for on the fourteenth day of the siege the Danes accepted the king's terms with one consent. And more than that, Guthrum and thirty of his chiefs asked that they might be baptized; which was a wonder to all of our host.

Now I have said nothing about the life in the great camp before Bridgwater, for it had nothing of much note to me, though it was pleasant enough. I think there was some jealousy of me among the younger thanes at one time; but it passed because I would not notice it, and also because I took no sort of authority on me, being only the king's guest and warrior as yet. But I did find a few young thanes of Odda's following who knew somewhat of the sea, and I was wont to talk with them often of the ships and the like, until I knew they would be glad to take to the viking's path with me in the king's ships, bringing their men with them. And often Alfred spoke with me of the matter, until I was sure that he would have me stay.

It was but a few days after the peace had been made when Alfred went to a great house he had at Aller, which lies right amidst the marshes south of Athelney. We had saved that house and the church by our constant annoyance of the Danes, with many another house and village along the fen to which they dared not come for fear of us at last. Guthrum was to come to him there, and I think that he chose the place because there at least was nought to bring thoughts of defeat to the Danes, and there they could be treated as guests, apart from the great camp and fortress. Great were the preparations there for the high festival that should be when Alfred himself should take Guthrum to the font.

Then came Neot on foot, with Guerir his fellow hermit, from Cornwall, to be present; and Harek and I rejoiced as much as the king that he had come.

"I think I must answer for you two at the font," he said.

"For Kolgrim also, I pray you, Father Neot," said I; "for he will be baptized with us."

"Ay, for honest Kolgrim also," he answered; "but what of old Thord, my reprover?"

"He will have nought to do with the new faith," I said. "But at least he does not blame us for leaving the old gods. He says he is too old to learn what we younger men think good."

"I will seek him and speak with him again," Neot said. "I think I owe him somewhat."

Then we thanked the holy man for the honour that he was showing us; but he put thanks aside, saying that we were his sons in the truth, and that the honour was his rather.

Now in the seven weeks that we waited for Guthrum at Aller, while the priests whom Alfred sent taught him and his chiefs what they should know rightly before baptism, Osmund and I were wont to go to Taunton, across the well-known fens, and bide for days at a time in Odda's house there, and we told Thora for what we waited.

She had come to England, when she was quite a child, with the first women who came into East Anglia, and already she knew much of Christianity from the Anglian thralls who had tended her. And when she had heard more of late from Etheldreda and Alswythe, she had longed to be of the same faith as these friends of hers, and now rejoiced openly.

"Ranald," she said, "I had not dared to speak of this to my father, but I was wont to fear the old gods terribly. They have no place for a maiden in their wild heaven. There are many more Danish ladies who long for this change, even as I have longed. Yet I still fear the wrath of Odin for you and my father."

"The old gods are nought--they have no power at all," I said, bravely enough; though even yet I had a little fear in thus defying them, as it seemed.

"Then I will dread them no more," she answered. "Nor do I think that you need fear them."

So I comforted her, and bade her ask more of Etheldreda, who would gladly teach her; and the matter passed by in gladness, as a trouble put away, for she and I were at one in this. I will say that I had half feared that she whom I loved would have been angry with me.

Now on that night Osmund and I and Harek would ride to Heregar's house over the shoulder of the Quantocks, with some message we had to take to him from Alfred; and we went without any attendants, for the twelve miles or so would have no risk to any one, and the summer evening was long and bright.

Yet we were later in starting away than we should have been, and so when we were among the wilder folds of the hills, where the bare summits rise from wooded slopes and combes, we were overtaken by a heavy thunderstorm that came up swiftly from the west behind us, darkening the last sunset light with black clouds through which the lightning flickered ceaselessly.

We rode on steadily, looking for some place of shelter; but it grew very dark, and the narrow track was rough, and full of loose stones that made the going slow. Presently the clouds settled down on the hill crest and wrapped us round, and the storm broke afresh on us, with thunder that came even as the darkness was changed to blue brightness with the lightning flashes that played around us almost unceasing. There was no rain yet and no wind, and the heat grew with the storm.

Soon the nearness of the flashes scared our horses, and we had to dismount and lead them, and in the darkness we lost the little track among the heavy heather. And then there seemed to me to be a new sound rising among the thunder, and I called to Harek, bidding him hearken.

It came from seaward, and swelled up louder and louder and nearer, until it passed over our heads--the yelp and bay of Odin's wild hounds, and the trample and scream of his horses and their dead riders. A great fear fell on me, so that the cold sweat stood on my forehead, while the hunt seemed everywhere above us for a moment, and then passed inland among the thunder that hardly drowned its noises.

Then Osmund the jarl cried out:

"That was Odin's hunt. I have heard it before, and ill came thereof. He hunts us who forsake him."

And out of the darkness Harek answered, without one shake in his brave voice:

"Odin's hunt in truth it was, and the ill comes to Odin, who must leave this land before the might of the Cross. We who bear the sign of might he cannot touch."

Then I remembered myself, and the fear passed from me, and I was ashamed. I had no doubt now that there was need for Odin's wrath, seeing that he was surely defeated. And Osmund was silent also, thinking doubtless the same things; for he had taken on him the prime signing long ago, and had forgotten it maybe.

Then we went on, and the storm grew wilder. Harek sang now, but what the words were I cannot tell. I think they were some that he had learned from Alfred.

Now we began to go down the southern slope of the highest neck of the hill, as it seemed, though we could not rightly say where we were, and in a little silence that came between the thunderclaps I heard the rattle of hoofs as of another rider coming after us, going faster than we dared.

"Here is one who knows the hill well," I said; "maybe he will guide us."

And then the lightning showed the horseman close to us. He reined up, and cried in a great voice:

"Ho, strangers! are you wandering here?"

"Ay; we are lost till the storm passes. Can you guide us to shelter before the rain comes?" I said.

"Whence come you?" he asked.

"We are Alfred's men from Taunton--going to the thane's house at Cannington."

"Ay, is that so? Then I will guide you. Follow," he said, and he rode on.

One could see him plainly when the lightning came, and it showed a tall man, grey bearded, and clad in a long hooded horseman's cloak, under which gleamed golden-shining mail. Well mounted on a great horse he was also, and its sides were white with foam on the dark skin, as though he had ridden hard.

We mounted and went after him, with the lightning playing round us and glancing from the mail of our leader as his arm threw the cloak back over his shoulder from time to time. He led us along the hill crest northward, crossing the places where the fire beacons had been; and we wondered whither he was taking us, for shelter here was none. And now the storm grew wilder, with the wind and chill of coming rain.

Then he turned downhill, riding fast until we came to a place where rocks lay loose and scattered everywhere, and our horses stumbled among them. There he reined up suddenly, holding up his hand, and shouting through the uproar of wind and thunder:

"Hold, for your lives! Hearken!"

We stayed motionless, listening, and again we heard the cry and clang of Odin's hunt, coming now from inland over us, and I made the sign of the Cross on my breast, in fear thereof.

"Ho for Odin's hunt!" the strange man cried, in his mighty voice. "Hear it, Alfred's men, for you shall join it and ride the wind with him if you defy him."

"We fear him not," said Harek; "he has no power over us."

"Has he not?" the man roared, facing full upon us; and as he did so the lightning glared on him, and I saw that his drawn sword was aloft, and that from its point glowed a blue flame, and that blue flames also seemed to start from his horse's ears. One-eyed the man was also, and he glowered on us under shaggy eyebrows.

Harek saw also, and he raised his hand towards the man and signed the holy sign, crying:

"Speak! who are you?"

Thereat the man gave a hoarse roar as of rage, and his horse reared, trampling wildly on the loose rocks, and, lo, he was gone from before our eyes as if he had never been, while the thunder crashed above us and below us everywhere!

"Odin! the Cross has conquered!" Harek cried again, in a voice that was full of triumph; and the blood rushed wildly through me at the thought of what I had seen.

Then Harek's horse shifted, and his hoof struck a great stone that rolled as if going far down the hill, and then stopped, and maybe after one could count five came a crash and rattle underneath us that died away far down somewhere in the bowels of the hill. And at that Osmund shouted suddenly:

"Back to the hill; we are on the brink of the old mine shaft! Back, and stay not!"

Nor did we wait, but we won back to the higher ground before we drew rein.

"We have met with Odin himself," Osmund said when we stopped and the thunder let him speak.

"Ay, and have driven him hellwards by the might of the holy sign," said Harek. "Nearly had he lured us to death, unbaptized as we are, in that place."

"Come," said Osmund; "I know where we are now. We are well-nigh under the great fort, and there is a farm near at hand."

We found that soon and the rain came, and the storm spent its fury and passed as we sat under cover in the stables waiting. Then came the moonlight and calm, and the sweetness of rain-soaked earth and flowers refreshed, and we went on our way wondering, and came to the thane's with the first daylight. And I thought that our faces were pale and marked with the terror of the things through which we had gone, and maybe also with a new light of victory.

CHAPTER XIV
King Alfred's Will

When we came back to Aller, the first thing that I did was to tell Neot of our meeting with Odin while his wild hunt went on through the tempest, telling him how that I had feared unwisely, and also of Harek's brave withstanding of the danger.

"It is said that our forefathers met Odin in like wise in the days of the first christening of our race," he said. "I do not know what to make thereof, seeing that I hold Odin as nought; but I think this, that in some way Satan tried to destroy you before you were baptized. Wherefore, whether Odin or mortal man drew you to that place, I have no doubt what power saved you."

But Sigehelm thought that we had met with Satan himself in the shape of the old god, and so also thought Guerir the hermit, who told strange tales of like appearings among the Welsh hills where he was born.

As for Alfred the king, he marvelled, and said even as Neot. But he added this:

"I know the mine shaft well, and it is in my mind that some day Odin's bones will be found at the bottom thereof. Nevertheless there is more than mortal in what has happened to you by way of trial."

Now came the time when Guthrum and his thirty comrades should seek the king, and I have no words to tell of that time when in the peaceful church we heathen stood white-robed and unarmed altogether at the font, while Sigehelm, with a wonderful gathering of priests, enlisted us as warriors of the Cross. It was, as all men think, the most mighty victory that Alfred had ever gained.

At that time he chose Guthrum as his own son in the faith, and named him Athelstan, as the first and most noble stone of the new building up of the church among the Danes. Neot would not have our names changed, for he said we had wronged the faith in them not at all. Odda stood for Osmund, as Neot for us.

After that was joyous feasting, and the loosing of the chrism bands at Alfred's royal town of Wedmore, whither we went in bright procession through the long summer day. Four days we bided there, till we knew that the great Danish host was on its march homewards, and then Guthrum and his comrades must join it. But before he went he accepted from Alfred the gifts that an under-king should take from his overlord, and they were most splendid. All men knew by those tokens given and taken that Alfred was king indeed, and that Guthrum did but hold place by his sufferance. Those two parted in wondrous friendship with the new bond of the faith woven round them, and the host passed from Wessex and was gone.

Yet, as ever, many a long year must pass by before the track of the Danes should be blotted out from the fair land they had laid waste. Everywhere was work to hand on burnt hall and homestead, ruined church, and wasted monastery. There was nought that men grieved over more than the burning of King Ine's church at Glastonbury, for that had been the pride of all the land. Once, after the Chippenham flight, the monks had dared to go out in sad procession to meet the fierce raiders at the long dike that bars the way to Avalon, and for that time they had won safety for the place--maybe by the loss of their treasures given as ransom, or, as some say, by the power of fearless and unarmed men; for there were men in the Danish host whose minds were noble, and might well be touched thereby. But Hubba's men could not be withheld after they had lost their mighty leader, and the place must feel their fury of revenge.

Now after the host was gone we went back to Taunton, and there Alfred called together his Witan, that he might set all things in order with their help; and at that time, before the levies were dismissed, he bade me seek out such men as would take to the ships as his paid seamen. Therein I had no hard task, for from the ruined coast towns came seafarers, homeless and lonely, asking nought better than to find a place in the king's fleet, and first of all were the Parret-mouth men and my fisher of Wareham. Presently, with one consent, the Witan made me leader of the king's Wessex sea levies, offering me the rank and fee of an English ealdorman, with power to demand help in the king's name from all sea-coast sheriffs and port reeves in whatever was needed for the ships, being answerable to the throne only for what I should do. And that I accepted willingly for love of Alfred, who was my friend, and for the sake of comradeship with those valiant men who had fought beside me when Hubba fell, and at Edington.

Then must I set myself to my new charge, having nought to do with all the inland work that was before the king; and when the next day's business was over, I went to tell him of this wish of mine, and of some other matters that were on my mind whereof one may easily guess.

Alfred sat in his private chamber in the great house that King Ine built, and on the table before him were a great ink horn and other writing gear, and beside him sat on a low stool his chaplain, reading to him out of a great book while the king wrote. The rough horn cage wherein was a candle, that he had planned in wind-swept Athelney, stood close at hand, against the time of dusk that was near. Ever was Alfred planning things like this, even in his greatest troubles; and therein he was wise, for it is not good to keep the mind full of heavy things alone. Moreover, as we wondered at his skilful devices in these little things, we took heart from his cheerful pleasure in them.

When the chamberlain brought me in, the great book was put aside, and the pen set down, and the king looked up at me with his bright smile.

"Welcome, my ship thane," he said. "Come and sit here beside me. I have somewhat to read to you."

So I sat down wondering, and he turned back to some place in his writing, and took the little knife that lay by him--for he had lost his jewelled book staff in Athelney--and running its point along the words, read to me from the writings of some old Roman what he had been busy putting into good Saxon:

"Now when the Roman folk would make a fleet hastily, and had no rowers, nor time to train them rightly, they built stages like to the oar benches of a ship in a certain lake, and so taught the men the swing and catch of the long oars."

"Will not that plan serve us, Ranald?" he said.

"Ay, lord," I answered, laughing. "In good truth, if a man can learn to keep time, and swing rightly, and back water, and the like, on such a staging, it is somewhat. But it will be hard work pulling against dead water from a stage that moves not. Nor will there be the roll and plunge of waves that must be met."

"Nor the sore sickness whereof Odda speaks," Alfred said, with his eyes twinkling. "But I think that if the Romans found the plan good, it will be so for us."

So we talked of this for a while, and I will say now that in after days we tried it, and the plan worked well enough, at least in the saving of time. Alfred's book learning was ever used for the good of his people, and this was but one way in which he found ready counsel for them.

This was pleasant talk enough, and neither I nor the king grew weary thereof, but the good monk slept at last, and presently the darkness fell, and Alfred dismissed him.

One came and lit the torches on the wall, and still we spoke of my work, until at last Alfred said:

"So you must be busy, and I am glad. When will you set out, and where will you go first?"

Now what I wanted to ask him was where Osmund the jarl had gone. He had ridden to Taunton from Aller, that he might be present at Thora's christening, and that their chrism loosing might be held at the same time; and I had looked to find both here, but they were gone. Nor had they left any word for me, and I was troubled about that. So I was about to tell the king what was in my mind concerning Thora first of all, and my heart began to beat strangely. But he waited not for me to answer him.

"Stay," he said, smiling a little. "Before you go I must have a hostage from my wild viking, lest he be, as it were, let loose on the high seas where I cannot reach him."

Then he laughed, at my puzzled face, I suppose, and I saw that he had some jest that pleased him.

"What hostage can I give, lord king?" I said. "Shall I leave Harek and his harp with you?"

"Harek would charm our ears, and would escape," Alfred answered. "Nay, but I must give you house and lands for a home, and therein you shall leave a fair wife, whose loneliness will bring you ashore now and then."

I thought there was more to come, and I liked not this at all, for it went too closely with my fears of what might be. So I bowed, and answered nothing as yet, while he looked laughingly at me.

"Why," he cried, "half my thanes would have gone wild with joy if I had promised them either half of what I have said I would give to you. Are you so fond of the longships and the restless waves that you will not be bound to the shore?"

"Nay, my king," I said; "but I cannot yet rightly understand all that you mean for me."

"Well, it means that I must find you a rich wife, as I think I can. What say you to that fair lady of Exeter town and Taunton--Odda's daughter, Etheldreda?"

"My king," I answered, somewhat over-gladly maybe, "Ethelnoth of Somerset, my good comrade, might have some grudge against me if I cast favouring eyes in that direction. Let this bide for a little while, I pray you, King Alfred. Yet I would not have you think me ungrateful, for indeed I know well what kindness is in your thought for me."

"Nay, but I have it in my mind that you were fond of going to Taunton not so long since, and one might well think that a maiden's hair drew you. Well, if Ethelnoth has outdone you there, I am sorry for your sake, not his. Cheer up, nevertheless. There are more maidens and well dowered in our broad Wessex coasts, and I am minded to see how far you will obey your new overlord."

"This is great kindness, King Alfred," I answered; "but we Northmen are apt to keep some matters wherein to prove our freedom. I pray you not to press this on me."

"Faith," he said, as if to himself, "this viking might be in love already, so wrathful grows he--

"Now, Ranald, it is true that I have set my mind on your wedding a maiden who is rich, and dowered with a coast town, and a good harbour, moreover, where you might keep all your ships under your own eye. I would not have you disappoint me so soon."

Then I said plainly,

"King Alfred, I am loth to do so. But from the very first day that I set foot in England there has been one maiden whose ways have seemed to be bound up with my own, and I can wed none but her. If it does not seem good to you that I should do so now, let me wait till times have grown easier between Saxon and Dane. I think that you may know well that I shall fight none the worse for you if I must strive to win your consent."

"That is straightforward," he said, smiling as if he would seem content. "Let it be so. But it is only fair that before we close this bargain you should see the well-dowered fair lady of whom I speak."

"I will do so if this matter is unknown to her," I answered, "else would be trouble, perhaps, and discomfort. But it is of no use. I have eyes and heart but for that one. Do I know the lady already, perhaps?"

"I believe that you may do so," Alfred said, looking grieved, in a strange way, as if he were half minded to laugh at me for all his seeming vexation. "Odda says that you do, and so also says Etheldreda. Her name is Thora, daughter of Jarl Osmund, and she will have Wareham town and Poole in right of her marriage, as dower to her and to my sea captain."

So spoke the king quickly, and then he could make pretence no longer, but laughed joyously, putting his hands on my shoulders and shaking me a little, while he cried:

"Ay, Ranald; I did but play with you. True lover you are indeed, as I thought. If you are faithful to the king as to the maiden of your choice, both she and I are happy, and it is well."

Then I knew not how to thank him; but he said that Etheldreda and Odda, Heregar and the Lady Alswythe, and maybe Guthrum also, as Thora's guardian, were to be thanked as well.

"You have found many friends here in England already, Ranald my cousin," Alfred said. "Wait until you meet some gathering of them all at Wareham, presently perhaps, where Osmund and Thora are preparing for a wedding--and then make a great thanking if you will, and save words. But I wonder that I have never heard of this matter from you before, for we have been close comrades."

"You must have heard thereof today, my king," I answered; "and you were but beforehand with me. I could speak of such things now that peace has come. Yet I feared that you would be against my wedding a Danish lady."

"It was a natural thought," answered Alfred; "but Thora and Osmund are ours, surely. Perhaps I should have doubted were your mind set on any other. But I have no fears for you."

Then he pondered a little, and went on:

"You say that peace has come. So it has--for a time; and had we to do only with the force that is in England now, I think it would grow and strengthen. We cannot drive out the Danes, and there is room in England for both them and us, and in the days to come the difference of race will be forgotten--not in our time, Ranald, but hereafter, as long years go by. Some day one of my line, if God will, shall reign alone over a united England, stronger for the new blood that has come among us. But it is a great charge that I give to you, Ranald. What we have to fear are the new hosts that come from Denmark, and only a strong fleet can stay them from our shores. I can deal with those who are here, and these in time will help me against fresh comers to the land. There is that in English soil that makes every settler an Englishman in heart. But there is warfare before us yet, and the fleet must break the force of the storm, if it cannot altogether turn it aside."

Then his grave voice changed, and he laughed.

"Heavy things are these to speak in the ears of a bridegroom, but you know all I mean. Now go your ways, and seek Odda, who will rejoice to see you; for word comes from him that his master, Thord the viking, is saying hard things to him because the men do not come in readily to man the ships. At the summer's end I shall be in Winchester, and thence I will come to Wareham to see the fleet, and your wedding also. Go now, and all good go with you."

So Alfred the king set me forth in brotherly wise, speaking on the morrow to my men to bid them serve him and England well under me. And after that all came to pass as the king had planned, and at the summer's end there was a bright wedding for us in Wareham town, while in the wide haven rode at anchor the best fleet that England had ever seen.

So that is how I came to be called "King Alfred's Viking," and made this land my home. What this Wessex fleet of mine has done since those days has been written by others in better words than I can compass; and Harek, whom they call "King Alfred's Scald" nowadays, has made song of what he has seen at my side in English waters; and more he may have to make yet, for the North has not yet sent forth all her hosts. Only I will say this, that if we have not been altogether able to stay the coming of new Danish fleets to the long seaboard that must needs lie open to them here and there till our own fleets are greater, at least they know that the host may no longer come and go as they will, for Alfred's ships have to be reckoned with.

Now of ourselves I will add that Thora and I have many friends, but the best and closest are those whom we made in the days when Hubba came and fell under the shadow of the Quantock Hills, and they do not forget us.

Into our house sometimes come Heregar and Ethered, Denewulf the wise and humble, Odda, and many more, sure of welcome. Only the loved presence of Neot the holy is wanting, for he died in Cornwall in that year of the end of the troubles, and I think that in him I lost more than any save Alfred himself.

Osmund went back to East Anglia for a time, but there he grew wearied with the wrangling of the Danish chiefs as they shared out the new land between them; so he bides with us, finding all his pleasure in the life of farm and field, which is ever near to the heart of a Dane. With him goes old Thord, grumbling at the thralls in strange sea language, and yet well loved. Not until he was wounded sorely in a sea fight we had and won under the Isle of Wight would he leave the war deck; but even now he is the first on board when the ships come home, and he is the one who orders all for winter quarters or for sailing.

Now for long I would that I might look once more on Einar of the Orkneys, my kind foster father, who still bided there in peace, hearing of him now and then as some Norse ship, on her way to join Rolf's fleet in the new land of the Northmen beyond our narrow seas, put into our haven for repair, perhaps after the long voyage, or to see if King Alfred would hire her men for a cruise against the common foe--the Danes. And it was not until the news of his death came thus to me that the home longing for the old lands altogether left me; but since that day my thoughts have been, and will be, for England only. I have no thought or wish that I were sharer in Rolf's victories, nor have my comrades, Harek and Kolgrim and Thord; for we have with Alfred more than the viking could have given us.

I suppose that in days to come out of this long strife shall be wrought new strength and oneness for England, even as Alfred in his wisdom foresees; but as yet sword Helmbiter must be kept sharp, and the ships must be ever ready. But unless the wisdom of Alfred is forgotten, there will never again be wanting a ship captain of English race, as when I, a stranger, was called to the charge of the king's ships in Wessex. The old love of the sea is waking in the hearts of the sons of Hengist.

Therefore I am content, for here have I found the sweetest wife, and the noblest master, and the fairest land that man could wish. And the fear of the old gods is taken from me, and to me has come honour, and somewhat of the joy of victory in a good cause--the cause of freedom and of peace.

Now I write these things as springtime grows apace, and at any time--today, or tomorrow, or next day--into our hall may come Kolgrim my comrade, his scarred face bright with the light of coming battle, to say that Danish ships are once more on the gannet's path; and the sword of Sigurd will rattle in the golden scabbard, and a great English cheer will come from the haven, for King Alfred's ships are ready.

The End

In The Days of Giants by Abbie Farwell Brown

A Book of Norse Tales

The Beginning of Things

The oldest stories of every race of people tell about the Beginning of Things. But the various folk who first told them were so very different, the tales are so very old, and have changed so greatly in the telling from one generation to another, that there are almost as many accounts of the way in which the world began as there are nations upon the earth. So it is not strange that the people of the North have a legend of the Beginning quite different from that of the Southern, Eastern, and Western folk.

This book is made of the stories told by the Northern folk,—the people who live in the land of the midnight sun, where summer is green and pleasant, but winter is a terrible time of cold and gloom; where rocky mountains tower like huge giants, over whose heads the thunder rolls and crashes, and under whose feet are mines of precious metals. Therefore you will find the tales full of giants and dwarfs,—spirits of the cold mountains and dark caverns.

You will find the hero to be Thor, with his thunderbolt hammer, who dwells in the happy heaven of Asgard, where All-Father Odin is king, and where Balder the beautiful makes springtime with his smile. In the north countries, winter, cold, and frost are very real and terrible enemies; while spring, sunshine, and warmth are near and dear friends. So the story of the Beginning of Things is a story of cold and heat, of the wicked giants who loved the cold, and of the good Æsir, who basked in pleasant warmth.

In the very beginning of things, the stories say, there were two worlds, one of burning heat and one of icy cold. The cold world was in the north, and from it flowed Elivâgar, a river of poisonous water which hardened into ice and piled up into great mountains, filling the space which had no bottom. The other world in the south was on fire with bright flame, a place of heat most terrible. And in those days through all space there was nothing beside these two worlds of heat and cold.

But then began a fierce combat. Heat and cold met and strove to destroy each other, as they have tried to do ever since. Flaming sparks from the hot world fell upon the ice river which flowed from the place of cold. And though the bright sparks were quenched, in dying they wrought mischief, as they do to-day; for they melted the ice, which dripped and dripped, like tears from the suffering world of cold. And then, wonderful to say, these chilly drops became alive; became a huge, breathing mass, a Frost-Giant with a wicked heart of ice. And he was the ancestor of all the giants who came afterwards, a bad and cruel race.

At that time there was no earth nor sea nor heaven, nothing but the icy abyss without bottom, whence Ymir the giant had sprung. And there he lived, nourished by the milk of a cow which the heat had formed. Now the cow had nothing for her food but the snow and ice of Elivâgar, and that was cold victuals indeed! One day she was licking the icy rocks, which tasted salty to her, when Ymir noticed that the mass was taking a strange shape. The more the cow licked it, the plainer became the outline of the shape. And when evening came Ymir saw thrusting itself through the icy rock a head of hair. The next day the cow went on with her meal, and at night-time a man's head appeared above the rock. On the third day the cow licked away the ice until forth stepped a man, tall and powerful and handsome. This was no evil giant, for he was good; and, strangely, though he came from the ice his heart was warm. He was the ancestor of the kind Æsir; for All-Father Odin and his brothers Vili and Ve, the first of the gods, were his grandsons, and as soon as they were born they became the enemies of the race of giants.

Now after a few giant years,—ages and ages of time as we reckon it,—there was a great battle, for Odin and his brothers wished to destroy all the evil in the world and to leave only good. They attacked the wicked giant Ymir, first of all his race, and after hard fighting slew him. Ymir was so huge that when he died a mighty river of blood flowed from the wounds which Odin had given him; a stream so large that it flooded all space, and the frost-giants, his children and grandchildren, were drowned, except one who escaped with his wife in a chest. And but for the saving of these two, that would have been the end of the race of giants.

All-Father and his brothers now had work to do. Painfully they dragged the great bulk of Ymir into the bottomless space of ice, and from it they built the earth, the sea, and the heavens. Not an atom of his body went to waste. His blood made the great ocean, the rivers, lakes, and springs. His mighty bones became mountains. His teeth and broken bones made sand and pebbles. From his skull they fashioned the arching heaven, which they set up over the earth and sea. His brain became the heavy clouds. His hair sprouted into trees, grass, plants, and flowers. And last of all, the Æsir set his bristling eyebrows as a high fence around the earth, to keep the giants away from the race of men whom they had planned to create for this pleas-ant globe.

So the earth was made. And next the gods brought light for the heavens. They caught the sparks and cinders blown from the world of heat, and set them here and there, above and below, as sun and moon and stars. To each they gave its name and told what its duties were to be, and how it must perform them, day after day, and year after year, and century after century, till the ending of all things; so that the children of men might reckon time without mistake.

Sôl and Mâni, who drove the bright chariots of the sun and moon across the sky, were a fair sister and brother whose father named them Sun and Moon because they were so beautiful. So Odin gave them each a pair of swift, bright horses to drive, and set them in the sky forever. Once upon a time,—but that was many, many years later,—Mâni, the Man in the Moon, stole two children from the earth. Hiuki and Bil were going to a well to draw a pail of water. The little boy and girl carried a pole and a bucket across their shoulders, and looked so pretty that Mâni thrust down a long arm and snatched them up to his moon. And there they are to this day, as you can see on any moonlight night,—two little black shadows on the moon's bright face, the boy and the girl, with the bucket between them.

The gods also made Day and Night. Day was fair, bright, and beautiful, for he was of the warm-hearted Æsir race. But Night was dark and gloomy, because she was one of the cold giant-folk. Day and Night had each a chariot drawn by a swift horse, and each in turn drove about the world in a twenty-four hours' journey. Night rode first behind her dark horse, Hrîmfaxi, who scattered dew from his bit upon the sleeping earth. After her came Day with his beautiful horse, Glad, whose shining mane shot rays of light through the sky.

All these wonders the kind gods wrought that they might make a pleasant world for men to call their home. And now the gods, or Æsir as they were called, must choose a place for their own dwelling, for there were many of them, a glorious family. Outside of everything, beyond the great ocean which surrounded the world, was Jotunheim, the cold country where the giants lived. The green earth was made for men. The gods therefore decided to build their city above men in the heavens, where they could watch the doings of their favorites and protect them from the wicked giants. Asgard was to be their city, and from Asgard to Midgard, the home of men, stretched a wonderful bridge, a bridge of many colors. For it was the rainbow that we know and love. Up and down the rainbow bridge the Æsir could travel to the earth, and thus keep close to the doings of men.

Next, from the remnants of Ymir's body the gods made the race of little dwarfs, a wise folk and skillful, but in nature more like the giants than like the good Æsir; for they were spiteful and often wicked, and they loved the dark and the cold better than light and warmth. They lived deep down below the ground in caves and rocky dens, and it was their business to dig the precious metals and glittering gems that were hidden in the rocks, and to make wonderful things from the treasures of the under-world. Pouf! pouf! went their little bellows. Tink-tank! went their little hammers on their little anvils all day and all night. Sometimes they were friendly to the giants, and sometimes they did kindly deeds for the Æsir. But always after men came upon the earth they hated these new folk who eagerly sought for the gold and the jewels which the dwarfs kept hidden in the ground. The dwarfs lost no chance of doing evil to the race of men.

Now the gods were ready for the making of men. They longed to have a race of creatures whom they could love and protect and bless with all kinds of pleasures. So Odin, with his brothers Hœnir and Loki, crossed the rainbow bridge and came down to the earth. They were walking along the seashore when they found two trees, an ash and an elm. These would do as well as anything for their purpose. Odin took the two trees and warmly breathed upon them; and lo! they were alive, a man and a woman. Hœnir then gently touched their foreheads, and they became wise. Lastly Loki softly stroked their faces; their skin grew pink with ruddy color, and they received the gifts of speech, hearing, and sight. Ask and Embla were their names, and the ash and the elm became the father and mother of the whole human race whose dwelling was Midgard, under the eyes of the Æsir who had made them.

This is the story of the Beginning of Things.

How Odin Lost His Eye

In the beginning of things, before there was any world or sun, moon, and stars, there were the giants; for these were the oldest creatures that ever breathed. They lived in Jotunheim, the land of frost and darkness, and their hearts were evil. Next came the gods, the good Æsir, who made earth and sky and sea, and who dwelt in Asgard, above the heavens. Then were created the queer little dwarfs, who lived underground in the caverns of the mountains, working at their mines of metal and precious stones. Last of all, the gods made men to dwell in Midgard, the good world that we know, between which and the glorious home of the Æsir stretched Bifröst, the bridge of rainbows.

In those days, folk say, there was a mighty ash-tree named Yggdrasil, so vast that its branches shaded the whole earth and stretched up into heaven where the Æsir dwelt, while its roots sank far down below the lowest depth. In the branches of the big ash-tree lived a queer family of creatures. First, there was a great eagle, who was wiser than any bird that ever lived—except the two ravens, Thought and Memory, who sat upon Father Odin's shoulders and told him the secrets which they learned in their flight over the wide world. Near the great eagle perched a hawk, and four antlered deer browsed among the buds of Yggdrasil. At the foot of the tree coiled a huge serpent, who was always gnawing hungrily at its roots, with a whole colony of little snakes to keep him company,—so many that they could never be counted. The eagle at the top of the tree and the serpent at its foot were enemies, always saying hard things of each other. Between the two skipped up and down a little squirrel, a tale-bearer and a gossip, who repeated each unkind remark and, like the malicious neighbor that he was, kept their quarrel ever fresh and green.

In one place at the roots of Yggdrasil was a fair fountain called the Urdar-well, where the three Norn-maidens, who knew the past, present, and future, dwelt with their pets, the two white swans. This was magic water in the fountain, which the Norns sprinkled every day upon the giant tree to keep it green,—water so sacred that everything which entered it became white as the film of an eggshell. Close beside this sacred well the Æsir had their council hall, to which they galloped every morning over the rainbow bridge.

But Father Odin, the king of all the Æsir, knew of another fountain more wonderful still; the two ravens whom he sent forth to bring him news had told him. This also was below the roots of Yggdrasil, in the spot where the sky and ocean met. Here for centuries and centuries the giant Mimer had sat keeping guard over his hidden well, in the bottom of which lay such a treasure of wisdom as was to be found nowhere else in the world. Every morning Mimer dipped his glittering horn Giöll into the fountain and drew out a draught of the wondrous water, which he drank to make him wise. Every day he grew wiser and wiser; and as this had been going on ever since the beginning of things, you can scarcely imagine how wise Mimer was.

Now it did not seem right to Father Odin that a giant should have all this wisdom to himself; for the giants were the enemies of the Æsir, and the wisdom which they had been hoarding for ages before the gods were made was generally used for evil purposes. Moreover, Odin longed and longed to become the wisest being in the world. So he resolved to win a draught from Mimer's well, if in any way that could be done.

One night, when the sun had set behind the mountains of Midgard, Odin put on his broad-brimmed hat and his striped cloak, and taking his famous staff in his hand, trudged down the long bridge to where it ended by Mimer's secret grotto.

"Good-day, Mimer," said Odin, entering; "I have come for a drink from your well."

The giant was sitting with his knees drawn up to his chin, his long white beard falling over his folded arms, and his head nodding; for Mimer was very old, and he often fell asleep while watching over his precious spring. He woke with a frown at Odin's words. "You want a drink from my well, do you?" he growled. "Hey! I let no one drink from my well."

"Nevertheless, you must let me have a draught from your glittering horn," insisted Odin, "and I will pay you for it."

"Oho, you will pay me for it, will you?" echoed Mimer, eyeing his visitor keenly. For now that he was wide awake, his wisdom taught him that this was no ordinary stranger. "What will you pay for a drink from my well, and why do you wish it so much?"

"I can see with my eyes all that goes on in heaven and upon earth," said Odin, "but I cannot see into the depths of ocean. I lack the hidden wisdom of the deep,—the wit that lies at the bottom of your fountain. My ravens tell me many secrets; but I would know all. And as for payment, ask what you will, and I will pledge anything in return for the draught of wisdom."

Then Mimer's keen glance grew keener. "You are Odin, of the race of gods," he cried. "We giants are centuries older than you, and our wisdom which we have treasured during these ages, when we were the only creatures in all space, is a precious thing. If I grant you a draught from my well, you will become as one of us, a wise and dangerous enemy. It is a goodly price, Odin, which I shall demand for a boon so great."

Now Odin was growing impatient for the sparkling water. "Ask your price," he frowned. "I have promised that I will pay."

"What say you, then, to leaving one of those far-seeing eyes of yours at the bottom of my well?" asked Mimer, hoping that he would refuse the bargain. "This is the only payment I will take."

Odin hesitated. It was indeed a heavy price, and one that he could ill afford, for he was proud of his noble beauty. But he glanced at the magic fountain bubbling mysteriously in the shadow, and he knew that he must have the draught.

"Give me the glittering horn," he answered. "I pledge you my eye for a draught to the brim."

Very unwillingly Mimer filled the horn from the fountain of wisdom and handed it to Odin. "Drink, then," he said; "drink and grow wise. This hour is the beginning of trouble between your race and mine." And wise Mimer foretold the truth.

Odin thought merely of the wisdom which was to be his. He seized the horn eagerly, and emptied it without delay. From that moment he became wiser than any one else in the world except Mimer himself.

Now he had the price to pay, which was not so pleasant. When he went away from the grotto, he left at the bottom of the dark pool one of his fiery eyes, which twinkled and winked up through the magic depths like the reflection of a star. This is how Odin lost his eye, and why from that day he was careful to pull his gray hat low over his face when he wanted to pass unnoticed. For by this oddity folk could easily recognize the wise lord of Asgard.

In the bright morning, when the sun rose over the mountains of Midgard, old Mimer drank from his bubbly well a draught of the wise water that flowed over Odin's pledge. Doing so, from his underground grotto he saw all that befell in heaven and on earth. So that he also was wiser by the bargain. Mimer seemed to have secured rather the best of it; for he lost nothing that he could not spare, while Odin lost what no man can well part with,— one of the good windows wherethrough his heart looks out upon the world. But there was a sequel to these doings which made the balance swing down in Odin's favor.

Not long after this, the Æsir quarreled with the Vanir, wild enemies of theirs, and there was a terrible battle. But in the end the two sides made peace; and to prove that they meant never to quarrel again, they exchanged hostages. The Vanir gave to the Æsir old Niörd the rich, the lord of the sea and the ocean wind, with his two children, Frey and Freia. This was indeed a gracious gift; for Freia was the most beautiful maid in the world, and her twin brother was almost as fair. To the Vanir in return Father Odin gave his own brother Hœnir. And with Hœnir he sent Mimer the wise, whom he took from his lonely well.

Now the Vanir made Hœnir their chief, thinking that he must be very wise because he was the brother of great Odin, who had lately become famous for his wisdom. They did not know the secret of Mimer's well, how the hoary old giant was far more wise than any one who had not quaffed of the magic water. It is true that in the assemblies of the Vanir Hœnir gave excellent counsel. But this was because Mimer whispered in Hœnir's ear all the wisdom that he uttered. Witless Hœnir was quite helpless without his aid, and did not know what to do or say. Whenever Mimer was absent he would look nervous and frightened, and if folk questioned him he always answered:—

"Yes, ah yes! Now go and consult some one else."

Of course the Vanir soon grew very angry at such silly answers from their chief, and presently they began to suspect the truth. "Odin has deceived us," they said. "He has sent us his foolish brother with a witch to tell him what to say. Ha! We will show him that we understand the trick." So they cut off poor old Mimer's head and sent it to Odin as a present.

The tales do not say what Odin thought of the gift. Perhaps he was glad that now there was no one in the whole world who could be called so wise as himself. Perhaps he was sorry for the danger into which he had thrust a poor old giant who had never done him any wrong, except to be a giant of the race which the Æsir hated. Perhaps he was a little ashamed of the trick which he had played the Vanir. Odin's new wisdom showed him how to prepare Mimer's head with herbs and charms, so that it stood up by itself quite naturally and seemed not dead. Thenceforth Odin kept it near him, and learned from it many useful secrets which it had not forgotten.

So in the end Odin fared better than the unhappy Mimer, whose worst fault was that he knew more than most folk. That is a dangerous fault, as others have found; though it is not one for which many of us need fear being punished.

Kvasir's Blood

Once upon a time there lived a man named Kvasir, who was so wise that no one could ask him a question to which he did not know the answer, and who was so eloquent that his words dripped from his lips like notes of music from a lute. For Kvasir was the first poet who ever lived, the first of those wise makers of songs whom the Norse folk named skalds. This Kvasir received his precious gifts wonderfully; for he was made by the gods and the Vanir, those two mighty races, to celebrate the peace which was evermore to be between them.

Up and down the world Kvasir traveled, lending his wisdom to the use of men, his brothers; and wherever he went he brought smiles and joy and comfort, for with his wisdom he found the cause of all men's troubles, and with his songs he healed them. This is what the poets have been doing in all the ages ever since. Folk declare that every skald has a drop of Kvasir's blood in him. This is the tale which is told to show how it happened that Kvasir's blessed skill has never been lost to the world.

There were two wicked dwarfs named Fialar and Galar who envied Kvasir his power over the hearts of men, and who plotted to destroy him. So one day they invited him to dine, and while he was there, they begged him to come aside with them, for they had a very secret question to ask, which only he could answer. Kvasir never refused to turn his wisdom to another's help; so, nothing suspecting, he went with them to hear their trouble.

Thereupon this sly pair of wicked dwarfs led him into a lonely corner. Treacherously they slew Kvasir; and because their cunning taught them that his blood must be precious, they saved it in three huge kettles, and mixing it with honey, made thereof a magic drink. Truly, a magic drink it was; for whoever tasted of Kvasir's blood was straightway filled with Kvasir's spirit, so that his heart taught wisdom and his lips uttered the sweetest poesy. Thus the wicked dwarfs became possessed of a wonderful treasure.

When the gods missed the silver voice of Kvasir echoing up from the world below, they were alarmed, for Kvasir was very dear to them. They inquired what had become of him, and finally the wily dwarfs answered that the good poet had been drowned in his own wisdom. But Father Odin, who had tasted another wise draught from Mimer's well, knew that this was not the truth, and kept his watchful eye upon the dark doings of Fialar and Galar.

Not long after this the dwarfs committed another wicked deed. They invited the giant Gilling to row out to sea with them, and when they were a long distance from shore, the wicked fellows upset the boat and drowned the giant, who could not swim. They rowed back to land, and told the giant's wife how the "accident" had happened. Then there were giant shrieks and howls enough to deafen all the world, for the poor giantess was heartbroken, and her grief was a giant grief. Her sobs annoyed the cruel-hearted dwarfs. So Fialar, pretending to sympathize, offered to take her where she could look upon the spot where her dear husband had last been seen. As she passed through the gateway, the other dwarf, to whom his brother had made a sign, let a huge millstone fall upon her head. That was the ending of her, poor thing, and of her sorrow, which had so disturbed the little people, crooked in heart as in body.

But punishment was in store for them. Suttung, the huge son of Gilling, learned the story of his parents' death, and presently, in a dreadful rage, he came roaring to the home of the dwarfs. He seized one of them in each big fist, and wading far out to sea, set the wretched little fellows on a rock which at high tide would be covered with water.

"Stay there," he cried, "and drown as my father drowned!" The dwarfs screamed thereat for mercy so loudly that he had to listen before he went away.

"Only let us off, Suttung," they begged, "and you shall have the precious mead made from Kvasir's blood."

Now Suttung was very anxious to own this same mead, so at last he agreed to the bargain. He carried them back to land, and they gave him the kettles in which they had mixed the magic fluid. Suttung took them away to his cave in the mountains, and gave them in charge of his fair daughter

Gunnlöd. All day and all night she watched by the precious kettles, to see that no one came to steal or taste of the mead; for Suttung thought of it as his greatest treasure, and no wonder.

Father Odin had seen all these deeds from his seat above the heavens, and his eye had followed longingly the passage of the wondrous mead, for Odin longed to have a draught of it. Odin had wisdom, he had drained that draught from the bottom of Mimer's mystic fountain; but he lacked the skill of speech which comes of drinking Kvasir's blood. He wanted the mead for himself and for his children in Asgard, and it seemed a shame that this precious treasure should be wasted upon the wicked giants who were their enemies. So he resolved to try if it might not be won in some sly way.

One day he put on his favorite disguise as a wandering old man, and set out for Giant Land, where Suttung dwelt. By and by he came to a field where nine workmen were cutting hay. Now these were the servants of Baugi, the brother of Suttung, and this Odin knew. He walked up to the men and watched them working for a little while.

"Ho!" he exclaimed at last, "your scythes are dull. Shall I whet them for you?" The men were glad enough to accept his offer, so Odin took a whetstone from his pocket and sharpened all the scythes most wonderfully. Then the men wanted to buy the stone; each man would have it for his own, and they fell to quarreling over it. To make matters more exciting, Odin tossed the whetstone into their midst, saying:—

"Let him have it who catches it!" Then indeed there was trouble! The men fought with one another for the stone, slashing right and left with their sharp scythes until every one was killed. Odin hastened away, and went up to the house where Baugi lived. Presently home came Baugi, complaining loudly and bitterly because his quarrelsome servants had killed one another, so that there was not one left to do his work.

"What am I going to do?" he cried. "Here it is mowing time, and I have not a single man to help me in the field!"

Then Odin spoke up. "I will help you," he said. "I am a stout fellow, and I can do the work of nine men if I am paid the price I ask."

"What is the price which you ask?" queried Baugi eagerly, for he saw that this stranger was a mighty man, and he thought that perhaps he could do as he boasted.

"I ask that you get for me a drink of Suttung's mead," Odin answered.

Then Baugi eyed him sharply. "You are one of the gods," he said, "or you would not know about the precious mead. Therefore I know that you can do my work, the work of nine men. I cannot give you the mead. It is my brother's, and he is very jealous of it, for he wishes it all himself. But if you will work for me all the summer, when winter comes I will go with you to Suttung's home and try what I can do to get a draught for you."

So they made the bargain, and all summer Father Odin worked in the fields of Baugi, doing the work of nine men. When the winter came, he demanded his pay. So then they set out for Suttung's home, which was a cave deep down in the mountains, where it seems not hard to hide one's treasures. First Baugi went to his brother and told him of the agreement between him and the stranger, begging for a gift of the magic mead wherewith to pay the stout laborer who had done the work of nine. But Suttung refused to spare even a taste of the precious liquor.

"This laborer of yours is one of the gods, our enemies," he said. "Indeed, I will not give him of the precious mead. What are you thinking of, brother!" Then he talked to Baugi till the giant was ready to forget his promise to Odin, and to desire only the death of the stranger who had come forward to help him.

Baugi returned to Odin with the news that the mead was not to be had with Suttung's consent. "Then we must get it without his consent," declared Odin. "We must use our wits to steal it from under his nose. You must help me, Baugi, for you have promised."

Baugi agreed to this; but in his heart he meant to entrap Odin to his death. Odin now took from his pocket an auger such as one uses to bore holes. "Look, now," he said. "You shall bore a hole into the roof of Suttung's cave, and when the hole is large enough, I will crawl through and get the mead."

"Very well," nodded Baugi, and he began to bore into the mountain with all his might and main. At last he cried, "There, it is done; the mountain is pierced through!" But when Odin blew into the hole to see whether it did indeed go through into the cave, the dust made by the auger flew into his face. Thus he knew that Baugi was deceiving him, and thenceforth he was on his guard, which was fortunate.

"Try again," said Odin sternly. "Bore a little deeper, friend Baugi." So Baugi went at the work once more, and this time when he said the hole was finished, Odin found that his word was true, for the dust blew through the hole and disappeared in the cave. Now Odin was ready to try the plan which he had been forming.

Odin's wisdom taught him many tricks, and among them he knew the secret of changing his form into that of any creature he chose. He turned himself into a worm,—a long, slender, wiggly worm, just small enough to be able to enter the hole that Baugi had pierced. In a moment he had thrust his head into the opening, and was wriggling out of sight before Baugi had even guessed what he meant to do. Baugi jumped forward and made a stab at him with the pointed auger, but it was too late. The worm's striped tail quivered in out of sight, and Baugi's wicked attempt was spoiled.

When Odin had crept through the hole, he found himself in a dark, damp cavern, where at first he could see nothing. He changed himself back into his own noble form, and then he began to hunt about for the kettles of magic mead. Presently he came to a little chamber, carefully hidden in a secret corner of this secret grotto,—a chamber locked and barred and bolted on the inside, so that no one could enter by the door. Suttung had never thought of such a thing as that a stranger might enter by a hole in the roof!

At the back of this tiny room stood three kettles upon the floor; and beside them, with her head resting on her elbow, sat a beautiful maiden, sound asleep. It was Gunnlöd, Suttung's daughter, the guardian of the mead. Odin stepped up to her very softly, and bending over, kissed her gently upon the forehead. Gunnlöd awoke with a start, and at first she was horrified to find a stranger in the cave where it seemed impossible that a stranger could enter. But when she saw the beauty of Odin's face and the kind look of his eye, she was no longer afraid, but glad that he had come. For poor Gunnlöd often grew lonesome in this gloomy cellar-home, where Suttung kept her prisoner day and night to watch over the three kettles.

"Dear maiden," said Odin, "I have come a long, long distance to see you. Will you not bid me stay a little while?"

Gunnlöd looked at him kindly. "Who are you, and whence do you come so far to see me?" she asked.

"I am Odin, from Asgard. The way is long and I am thirsty. Shall I not taste the liquor which you have there?"

Gunnlöd hesitated. "My father bade me never let soul taste of the mead," she said "I am sorry for you, however, poor fellow. You look very tired and thirsty. You may have one little sip." Then Odin kissed her and thanked her, and tarried there with such pleasant words for the maiden that before he was ready to go she granted him what he asked,—three draughts, only three draughts of the mead.

Now Odin took up the first kettle to drink, and with one draught he drained the whole. He did the same by the next, and the next, till before she knew it, Gunnlöd found herself guarding three empty kettles. Odin had gained what he came for, and it was time for him to be gone before Suttung should come to seek him in the cave. He kissed fair Gunnlöd once again, with a sigh to think that he must treat her so unfairly. Then he changed himself into an eagle, and away he flew to carry the precious mead home to Asgard.

Meanwhile Baugi had told the giant Suttung how Odin the worm had pierced through into his treasure-cave; and when Suttung, who was watching, saw the great eagle fly forth, he guessed who this eagle must be. Suttung also put on an eagle's plumage, and a wonderful chase began. Whirr, whirr! The two enormous birds winged their way toward Asgard, Suttung close upon the other's flight. Over the mountains they flew, and the world was darkened as if by the passage of heavy storm-clouds, while the trees, blown by the breeze from their wings, swayed, and bent almost to the ground.

It was a close race; but Odin was the swifter of the two, and at last he had the mead safe in Asgard, where the gods were waiting with huge dishes to receive it from his mouth. Suttung was so close upon him, however, that he jostled Odin even as he was filling the last dish, and some of the mead was spilled about in every direction over the world. Men rushed from far and near to taste of these wasted drops of Kvasir's blood, and many had just enough to make them dizzy, but not enough to make them wise. These folk are the poor poets, the makers of bad verses, whom one finds to this day satisfied with their meagre, stolen portion, scattered drops of the sacred draught.

The mead that Odin had captured he gave to the gods, a wondrous gift; and they in turn cherished it as their most precious treasure. It was given into the special charge of old Bragi of the white beard, because his taste of the magic mead had made him wise and eloquent above all others. He was the sweetest singer of all the Æsir, and his speech was poetry. Sometimes Bragi gave a draught of Kvasir's blood to some favored mortal, and then he also became a great poet. He did not do this often,—only once or twice in the memory of an old man; for the precious mead must be made to last a long, long time, until the world be ready to drop to pieces, because this world without its poets would be too dreadful a place to imagine.

The Giant Builder

Ages and ages ago, when the world was first made, the gods decided to build a beautiful city high above the heavens, the most glorious and wonderful city that ever was known. Asgard was to be its name, and it was to stand on Ida Plain under the shade of Yggdrasil, the great tree whose roots were underneath the earth.

First of all they built a house with a silver roof, where there were seats for all the twelve chiefs. In the midst, and high above the rest, was the wonder-throne of Odin the All-Father, whence he could see everything that happened in the sky or on the earth or in the sea. Next they made a fair house for Queen Frigg and her lovely daughters. Then they built a smithy, with its great hammers, tongs, anvils, and bellows, where the gods could work at their favorite trade, the making of beautiful things out of gold; which they did so well that folk name that time the Golden Age. Afterwards, as they had more leisure, they built separate houses for all the Æsir, each more beautiful than the preceding, for of course they were continually growing more skillful. They saved Father Odin's palace until the last, for they meant this to be the largest and the most splendid of all.

Gladsheim, the home of joy, was the name of Odin's house, and it was built all of gold, set in the midst of a wood whereof the trees had leaves of ruddy gold,—like an autumn-gilded forest. For the safety of All-Father it was surrounded by a roaring river and by a high picket fence; and there was a great courtyard within.

The glory of Gladsheim was its wondrous hall, radiant with gold, the most lovely room that time has ever seen. Valhalla, the Hall of Heroes, was the name of it, and it was roofed with the mighty shields of warriors. The ceiling was made of interlacing spears, and there was a portal at the west end before which hung a great gray wolf, while over him a fierce eagle hovered. The hall was so huge that it had 540 gates, through each of which 800 men could march abreast. Indeed, there needed to be room, for this was the hall where every morning Odin received all the brave warriors who had died in battle on the earth below; and there were many heroes in those days.

This was the reward which the gods gave to courage. When a hero had gloriously lost his life, the Valkyries, the nine warrior daughters of Odin, brought his body up to Valhalla on their white horses that gallop the clouds. There they lived forever after in happiness, enjoying the things that they had most loved upon earth. Every morning they armed themselves and went out to fight with one another in the great courtyard. It was a wondrous game, wondrously played. No matter how often a hero was killed, he became alive again in time to return perfectly well to Valhalla, where he ate a delicious breakfast with the Æsir; while the beautiful Valkyries who had first brought him thither waited at table and poured the blessed mead, which only the immortal taste. A happy life it was for the heroes, and a happy life for all who dwelt in Asgard; for this was before trouble had come among the gods, following the mischief of Loki.

This is how the trouble began. From the beginning of time, the giants had been unfriendly to the Æsir, because the giants were older and huger and more wicked; besides, they were jealous because the good Æsir were fast gaining more wisdom and power than the giants had ever known. It was the Æsir who set the fair brother and sister, Sun and Moon, in the sky to give light to men; and it was they also who made the jeweled stars out of sparks from the place of fire. The giants hated the Æsir, and tried all in their power to injure them and the men of the earth below, whom the Æsir loved and cared for. The gods had already built a wall around Midgard, the world of men, to keep the giants out; built it of the bushy eyebrows of Ymir, the oldest and hugest of giants. Between Asgard and the giants flowed Ifing, the great river on which ice never formed, and which the gods crossed on the rainbow bridge. But this was not protection enough. Their beautiful new city needed a fortress.

So the word went forth in Asgard,—"We must build us a fortress against the giants; the hugest, strongest, finest fortress that ever was built."

Now one day, soon after they had announced this decision, there came a mighty man stalking up the rainbow bridge that led to Asgard city.

"Who goes there!" cried Heimdal the watchman, whose eyes were so keen that he could see for a hundred miles around, and whose ears were so sharp that he could hear the grass growing in the meadow and the wool on the backs of the sheep. "Who goes there! No one can enter Asgard if I say no."

"I am a builder," said the stranger, who was a huge fellow with sleeves rolled up to show the iron muscles of his arms. "I am a builder of strong towers, and I have heard that the folk of Asgard need one to help them raise a fair fortress in their city."

Heimdal looked at the stranger narrowly, for there was that about him which his sharp eyes did not like. But he made no answer, only blew on his golden horn, which was so loud that it sounded through all the world. At this signal all the Æsir came running to the rainbow bridge, from wherever they happened to be, to find out who was coming to Asgard. For it was Heimdal's duty ever to warn them of the approach of the unknown.

"This fellow says he is a builder," quoth Heimdal. "And he would fain build us a fortress in the city."

"Ay, that I would," nodded the stranger. "Look at my iron arm; look at my broad back; look at my shoulders. Am I not the workman you need?"

"Truly, he is a mighty figure," vowed Odin, looking at him approvingly. "How long will it take you alone to build our fortress? We can allow but one stranger at a time within our city, for safety's sake."

"In three half-years," replied the stranger, "I will undertake to build for you a castle so strong that not even the giants, should they swarm hither over Midgard,—not even they could enter without your leave."

"Aha!" cried Father Odin, well pleased at this offer. "And what reward do you ask, friend, for help so timely?"

The stranger hummed and hawed and pulled his long beard while he thought. Then he spoke suddenly, as if the idea had just come into his mind. "I will name my price, friends," he said; "a small price for so great a deed. I ask you to give me Freia for my wife, and those two sparkling jewels, the Sun and Moon."

At this demand the gods looked grave; for Freia was their dearest treasure. She was the most beautiful maid who ever lived, the light and life of heaven, and if she should leave Asgard, joy would go with her; while the Sun and Moon were the light and life of the Æsir's children, men, who lived in the little world below. But Loki the sly whispered that they would be safe enough if they made another condition on their part, so hard that the builder could not fulfill it. After thinking cautiously, he spoke for them all.

"Mighty man," quoth he, "we are willing to agree to your price—upon one condition. It is too long a time that you ask; we cannot wait three half-years for our castle; that is equal to three centuries when one is in a hurry. See that you finish the fort without help in one winter, one short winter, and you shall have fair Freia with the Sun and Moon. But if, on the first day of summer, one stone is wanting to the walls, or if any one has given you aid in the building, then your reward is lost, and you shall depart without payment." So spoke Loki, in the name of all the gods; but the plan was his own.

At first the stranger shook his head and frowned, saying that in so short a time no one unaided could complete the undertaking. At last he made another offer. "Let me have but my good horse to help me, and I will try," he urged. "Let me bring the useful Svadilföri with me to the task, and I will finish the work in one winter of short days, or lose my reward. Surely, you will not deny me this little help, from one four-footed friend."

Then again the Æsir consulted, and the wiser of them were doubtful whether it were best to accept the stranger's offer so strangely made. But again Loki urged them to accept. "Surely, there is no harm," he said. "Even with his old horse to help him, he cannot build the castle in the promised time. We shall gain a fortress without trouble and with never a price to pay."

Loki was so eager that, although the other Æsir did not like this crafty way of making bargains, they finally consented. Then in the presence of the heroes, with the Valkyries and Mimer's head for witnesses, the stranger and the Æsir gave solemn promise that the bargain should be kept.

On the first day of winter the strange builder began his work, and wondrous was the way he set about it. His strength seemed as the strength of a hundred men. As for his horse Svadilföri, he did more work by half than even the mighty builder. In the night he dragged the enormous rocks that were to be used in building the castle, rocks as big as mountains of the earth; while in the daytime the stranger piled them into place with his iron arms. The Æsir watched him with amazement; never was seen such strength in Asgard. Neither Týr the stout nor Thor the strong could match the power of the stranger. The gods began to look at one another uneasily. Who was this mighty one who had come among them, and what if after all he should win his reward? Freia trembled in her palace, and the Sun and Moon grew dim with fear.

Still the work went on, and the fort was piling higher and higher, by day and by night. There were but three days left before the end of winter, and already the building was so tall and so strong that it was safe from the attacks of any giant. The Æsir were delighted with their fine new castle; but their pride was dimmed by the fear that it must be paid for at all too costly a price. For only the gateway remained to be completed, and unless the stranger should fail to finish that in the next three days, they must give him Freia with the Sun and Moon.

The Æsir held a meeting upon Ida Plain, a meeting full of fear and anger. At last they realized what they had done; they had made a bargain with one of the giants, their enemies; and if he won the prize, it would mean sorrow and darkness in heaven and upon earth. "How did we happen to agree to so mad a bargain?" they asked one another. "Who suggested the wicked plan which bids fair to cost us all that we most cherish?" Then they remembered that it was Loki who had made the plan; it was he who had insisted that it be carried out and they blamed him for all the trouble.

"It is your counsels, Loki, that have brought this danger upon us," quoth Father Odin, frowning. "You chose the way of guile, which is not our way. It now remains for you to help us by guile, if you can. But if you cannot save for us Freia and the Sun and Moon, you shall die. This is my word." All the other Æsir agreed that this was just. Thor alone was away hunting evil demons at the other end of the world, so he did not know what was going on, and what dangers were threatening Asgard.

Loki was much frightened at the word of All-Father. "It was my fault," he cried, "but how was I to know that he was a giant? He had disguised himself so that he seemed but a strong man. And as for his horse,—it looks much like that of other folk. If it were not for the horse, he could not finish the work. Ha! I have a thought! The builder shall not finish the gate; the giant shall not receive his payment. I will cheat the fellow."

Now it was the last night of winter, and there remained but a few stones to put in place on the top of the wondrous gateway. The giant was sure of his prize, and chuckled to himself as he went out with his horse to drag the remaining stones; for he did not know that the Æsir had guessed at last who he was, and that Loki was plotting to outwit him. Hardly had he gone to work when out of the wood came running a pretty little mare, who neighed to Svadilföri as if inviting the tired horse to leave his work and come to the green fields for a holiday.

Svadilföri, you must remember, had been working hard all winter, with never a sight of four-footed creature of his kind, and he was very lonesome and tired of dragging stones. Giving a snort of disobedience, off he ran after this new friend towards the grassy meadows. Off went the giant after him, howling with rage, and running for dear life, as he saw not only his horse but his chance of success slipping out of reach. It was a mad chase, and all Asgard thundered with the noise of galloping hoofs and the giant's mighty tread. The mare who raced ahead was Loki in disguise, and he led Svadilföri far out of reach, to a hidden meadow that he knew; so that the giant howled and panted up and down all night long, without catching even a sight of his horse.

Now when the morning came the gateway was still unfinished, and night and winter had ended at the same hour. The giant's time was over, and he had forfeited his reward. The Æsir came flocking to the gateway, and how they laughed and triumphed when they found three stones wanting to complete the gate!

"You have failed, fellow," judged Father Odin sternly, "and no price shall we pay for work that is still undone. You have failed. Leave Asgard quickly; we have seen all we want of you and of your race."

Then the giant knew that he was discovered, and he was mad with rage. "It was a trick!" he bellowed, assuming his own proper form, which was huge as a mountain, and towered high beside the fortress that he had built. "It was a wicked trick. You shall pay for this in one way or another. I cannot tear down the castle which, ungrateful ones, I have built you, stronger than the strength of any giant. But I will demolish the rest of your shining city!" Indeed, he would have done so in his mighty rage; but at this moment Thor, whom Heimdal had called from the end of the earth by one blast of the golden horn, came rushing to the rescue, drawn in his chariot of goats. Thor jumped to the ground close beside the giant, and before that huge fellow knew what had happened, his head was rolling upon the ground at Father Odin's feet; for with one blow Thor had put an end to the giant's wickedness and had saved Asgard.

"This is the reward you deserve!" Thor cried. "Not Freia nor the Sun and Moon, but the death that I have in store for all the enemies of the Æsir."

In this extraordinary way the noble city of Asgard was made safe and complete by the addition of a fortress which no one, not even the giant who built it, could injure, it was so wonder-strong. But always at the top of the gate were lacking three great stones that no one was mighty enough to lift. This was a reminder to the Æsir that now they had the race of giants for their everlasting enemies. And though Loki's trick had saved them Freia, and for the world the Sun and Moon, it was the beginning of trouble in Asgard which lasted as long as Loki lived to make mischief with his guile.

The Magic Apples

It is not very amusing to be a king. Father Odin often grew tired of sitting all day long upon his golden throne in Valhalla above the heavens. He wearied of welcoming the new heroes whom the Valkyries brought him from wars upon the earth, and of watching the old heroes fight their daily deathless battles. He wearied of his wise ravens, and the constant gossip which they brought him from the four corners of the world; and he longed to escape from every one who knew him to some place where he could pass for a mere stranger, instead of the great king of the Æsir, the mightiest being in the whole universe, of whom every one was afraid.

Sometimes he longed so much that he could not bear it. Then—he would run away. He disguised himself as a tall old man, with white hair and a long gray beard. Around his shoulders he threw a huge blue cloak, that covered him from top to toe, and over his face he pulled a big slouch hat, to hide his eyes. For his eyes Odin could not change—no magician has ever learned how to do that. One was empty; he had given the eye to the giant Mimer in exchange for wisdom.

Usually Odin loved to go upon these wanderings alone; for an adventure is a double adventure when one meets it single-handed. It was a fine game for Odin to see how near he could come to danger without feeling the grip of its teeth. But sometimes, when he wanted company, he would whisper to his two brothers, Hœnir and red Loki. They three would creep out of the palace by the back way; and, with a finger on the lip to Heimdal, the watchman, would silently steal over the rainbow bridge which led from Asgard into the places of men and dwarfs and giants.

Wonderful adventures they had, these three, with Loki to help make things happen. Loki was a sly, mischievous fellow, full of his pranks and his capers, not always kindly ones. But he was clever, as well as malicious; and when he had pushed folk into trouble, he could often help them out again, as safe as ever. He could be the jolliest of companions when he chose, and Odin liked his merriment and his witty talk.

One day Loki did something which was no mere jest nor easily forgiven, for it brought all Asgard into danger. And after that Father Odin and his children thought twice before inviting Loki to join them in any journey or undertaking. This which I am about to tell was the first really wicked deed of which Loki was found guilty, though I am sure his red beard had dabbled in secret wrongs before.

One night the three high gods, Odin, Hœnir, and Loki, stole away from Asgard in search of adventure. Over mountains and deserts, great rivers and stony places, they wandered until they grew very hungry. But there was no food to be found—not even a berry or a nut.

Oh, how footsore and tired they were! And oh, how faint! The worst of it ever is that—as you must often have noticed—the heavier one's feet grow, the lighter and more hollow becomes one's stomach; which seems a strange thing, when you think of it. If only one's feet became as light as the rest of one feels, folk could fairly fly with hunger. Alas! this is not so.

The three Æsir drooped and drooped, and seemed on the point of starving, when they came to the edge of a valley. Here, looking down, they saw a herd of oxen feeding on the grass.

"Hola!" shouted Loki. "Behold our supper!" Going down into the valley, they caught and killed one of the oxen, and, building a great bonfire, hung up the meat to roast. Then the three sat around the fire and smacked their lips, waiting for the meat to cook. They waited for a long time.

"Surely, it is done now," said Loki, at last; and he took the meat from the fire. Strange to say, however, it was raw as ere the fire was lighted. What could it mean? Never before had meat required so long a time to roast. They made the fire brighter and re-hung the beef for a thorough basting, cooking it even longer than they had done at first. When again they came to carve the meat, they found it still uneatable. Then, indeed, they looked at one another in surprise.

"What can this mean?" cried Loki, with round eyes.

"There is some trick!" whispered Hœnir, looking around as if he expected to see a fairy or a witch meddling with the food.

"We must find out what this mystery betokens," said Odin thoughtfully. Just then there was a strange sound in the oak-tree under which they had built their fire.

"What is that?" Loki shouted, springing to his feet. They looked up into the tree, and far above in the branches, near the top, they spied an enormous eagle, who was staring down at them, and making a queer sound, as if he were laughing.

"Ho-ho!" croaked the eagle. "I know why your meat will not cook. It is all my doing, masters."

The three Æsir stared in surprise. Then Odin said sternly: "Who are you, Master Eagle? And what do you mean by those rude words?"

"Give me my share of the ox, and you shall see," rasped the eagle, in his harsh voice. "Give me my share, and you will find that your meat will cook as fast as you please."

Now the three on the ground were nearly famished. So, although it seemed very strange to be arguing with an eagle, they cried, as if in one voice: "Come down, then, and take your share." They thought that, being a mere bird, he would want but a small piece.

The eagle flapped down from the top of the tree. Dear me! What a mighty bird he was! Eight feet across the wings was the smallest measure, and his claws were as long and strong as ice-hooks. He fanned the air like a whirlwind as he flew down to perch beside the bonfire. Then in his beak and claws he seized a leg and both shoulders of the ox, and started to fly away.

"Hold, thief!" roared Loki angrily, when he saw how much the eagle was taking. "That is not your share; you are no lion, but you are taking the lion's share of our feast. Begone, Scarecrow, and leave the meat as you found it!" Thereat, seizing a pole, he struck at the eagle with all his might.

Then a strange thing happened. As the great bird flapped upward with his prey, giving a scream of malicious laughter, the pole which Loki still held stuck fast to the eagle's back, and Loki was unable to let go of the other end.

"Help, help!" he shouted to Odin and to Hœnir, as he felt himself lifted off his feet. But they could not help him. "Help, help!" he screamed, as the eagle flew with him, now high, now low, through brush and bog and briar, over treetops and the peaks of mountains. On and on they went, until Loki thought his arm would be pulled out, like a weed torn up by the roots. The eagle would not listen to his cries nor pause in his flight, until Loki was almost dead with pain and fatigue.

"Hark you, Loki," screamed the eagle, going a little more slowly; "no one can help you except me. You are bewitched, and you cannot pull away from this pole, nor loose the pole from me, until I choose. But if you will promise what I ask, you shall go free."

Then Loki groaned: "O eagle, only let me go, and tell me who you really are, and I will promise whatever you wish."

The eagle answered: "I am the giant Thiasse, the enemy of the Æsir. But you ought to love me, Loki, for you yourself married a giantess."

Loki moaned: "Oh, yes! I dearly love all my wife's family, great Thiasse. Tell me what you want of me?"

"I want this," quoth Thiasse gruffly. "I am growing old, and I want the apples which Idun keeps in her golden casket, to make me young again. You must get them for me."

Now these apples were the fruit of a magic tree, and were more beautiful to look at and more delicious to taste than any fruit that ever grew. The best thing about them was that whoever tasted one, be he ever so old, grew young and strong again. The apples belonged to a beautiful lady named Idun, who kept them in a golden casket. Every morning the Æsir came to her to be refreshed and made over by a bite of her precious fruit. That is why in Asgard no one ever waxed old or ugly. Even Father Odin, Hœnir, and Loki, the three travelers who had seen the very beginning of everything, when the world was made, were still sturdy and young. And so long as Idun kept her apples safe, the faces of the family who sat about the table of Valhalla would be rosy and fair like the faces of children.

"O friend giant!" cried Loki. "You know not what you ask! The apples are the most precious treasure of Asgard, and Idun keeps watch over them as if they were dearer to her than life itself. I never could steal them from her, Thiasse; for at her call all Asgard would rush to the rescue, and trouble would buzz about my ears like a hive of bees let loose."

"Then you must steal Idun herself, apples and all. For the apples I must have, and you have promised, Loki, to do my bidding."

Loki sniffed and thought, thought and sniffed again. Already his mischievous heart was planning how he might steal Idun away. He could hardly help laughing to think how angry the Æsir would be when they found their beauty-medicine gone forever. But he hoped that, when he had done this trick for Thiasse, now and then the giant would let him have a nibble of the magic apples; so that Loki himself would remain young long after the other Æsir were grown old and feeble. This thought suited Loki's malicious nature well.

"I think I can manage it for you, Thiasse," he said craftily. "In a week I promise to bring Idun and her apples to you. But you must not forget the great risk which I am running, nor that I am your relative by marriage. I may have a favor to ask in return, Thiasse."

Then the eagle gently dropped Loki from his claws. Falling on a soft bed of moss, Loki jumped up and ran back to his traveling companions, who were glad and surprised to see him again. They had feared that the eagle was carrying him away to feed his young eaglets in some far-off nest. Ah, you may be sure that Loki did not tell them who the eagle really was, nor confess the wicked promise which he had made about Idun and her apples.

After that the three went back to Asgard, for they had had adventure enough for one day.

The days flew by, and the time came when Loki must fulfill his promise to Thiasse. So one morning he strolled out into the meadow where Idun loved to roam among the flowers. There he found her, sitting by a tiny spring, and holding her precious casket of apples on her lap. She was combing her long golden hair, which fell from under a wreath of spring flowers, and she was very beautiful. Her green robe was embroidered with buds and blossoms of silk in many colors, and she wore a golden girdle about her waist. She smiled as Loki came, and tossed him a posy, saying: "Goodmorrow, red Loki. Have you come for a bite of my apples? I see a wrinkle over each of your eyes which I can smooth away."

"Nay, fair lady," answered Loki politely, "I have just nibbled of another apple, which I found this morning. Verily, I think it is sweeter and more magical than yours."

Idun was hurt and surprised.

"That cannot be, Loki," she cried. "There are no apples anywhere like mine. Where found you this fine fruit?" and she wrinkled up her little nose scornfully.

"Oho! I will not tell any one the place," chuckled Loki, "except that it is not far, in a little wood. There is a gnarled old apple-tree, and on its branches grow the most beautiful red-cheeked apples you ever saw. But you could never find it."

"I should like to see these apples, Loki, if only to prove how far less good they are than mine. Will you bring me some?"

"That I will not," said Loki teasingly. "Oh, no! I have my own magic apples now, and folk will be coming to me for help instead of to you."

Idun began to coax him, as he had guessed that she would: "Please, please, Loki, show me the place!"

At first he would not, for he was a sly fellow, and knew how to lead her on. At last, he pretended to yield.

"Well, then, because I love you, Idun, better than all the rest, I will show you the place, if you will come with me. But it must be a secret—no one must ever know."

All girls like secrets.

"Yes—yes!" cried Idun eagerly. "Let us steal away now, while no one is looking."

This was just what Loki hoped for.

"Bring your own apples," he said, "that we may compare them with mine. But I know mine are better."

"I know mine are the best in all the world," returned Idun, pouting. "I will bring them, to show you the difference."

Off they started together, she with the golden casket under her arm; and Loki chuckled wickedly as they went. He led her for some distance, further than she had ever strayed before, and at last she grew frightened.

"Where are you taking me, Loki?" she cried. "You said it was not far. I see no little wood, no old apple-tree."

"It is just beyond, just a little step beyond," he answered. So on they went. But that little step took them beyond the boundary of Asgard—just a little step beyond, into the space where the giants lurked and waited for mischief.

Then there was a rustling of wings, and whirr-rr-rr! Down came Thiasse in his eagle dress. Before Idun suspected what was happening, he fastened his claws into her girdle and flapped away with her, magic apples and all, to his palace in Jotunheim, the Land of Giants.

Loki stole back to Asgard, thinking that he was quite safe, and that no one would discover his villainy. At first Idun was not missed. But after a little the gods began to feel signs of age, and went for their usual bite of her apples. Then they found that she had disappeared, and a great terror fell upon them. Where had she gone? Suppose she should not come back!

The hours and days went by, and still she did not return. Their fright became almost a panic. Their hair began to turn gray, and their limbs grew stiff and gouty so that they hobbled down Asgard streets. Even Freia, the loveliest, was afraid to look in her mirror, and Balder the beautiful grew pale and haggard. The happy land of Asgard was like a garden over which a burning wind had blown,—all the flower-faces were faded and withered, and springtime was turned into yellow fall.

If Idun and her apples were not quickly found, the gods seemed likely to shrivel and blow away like autumn leaves. They held a council to inquire into the matter, endeavoring to learn who had seen Idun last, and whither she had gone. It turned out that one morning Heimdal had seen her strolling out of Asgard with Loki, and no one had seen her since. Then the gods understood; Loki was the last person who had been with her—this must be one of Loki's tricks. They were filled with anger. They seized and bound Loki and brought him before the council. They threatened him with torture and with death unless he should tell the truth. And Loki was so frightened that finally he confessed what he had done.

Then indeed there was horror in Asgard. Idun stolen away by a wicked giant! Idun and her apples lost, and Asgard growing older every minute! What was to be done? Big Thor seized Loki and threw him up in the air again and again, so that his heels touched first the moon and then the sea; you can still see the marks upon the moon's white face. "If you do not bring Idun back from the land of your wicked wife, you shall have worse than this!" he roared. "Go and bring her now."

"How can I do that?" asked Loki, trembling.

"That is for you to find," growled Thor. "Bring her you must. Go!"

Loki thought for a moment. Then he said:—

"I will bring her back if Freia will loan me her falcon dress. The giant dresses as an eagle. I, too, must guise me as a bird, or we cannot outwit him."

Then Freia hemmed and hawed. She did not wish to loan her feather dress, for it was very precious. But all the Æsir begged; and finally she consented.

It was a beautiful great dress of brown feathers and gray, and in it Freia loved to skim like a falcon among the clouds and stars. Loki put it on, and when he had done so he looked exactly like a great brown hawk. Only his bright black eyes remained the same, glancing here and there, so that they lost sight of nothing.

With a whirr of his wings Loki flew off to the north, across mountains and valleys and the great river Ifing, which lay between Asgard and Giant Land. And at last he came to the palace of Thiasse the giant.

It happened, fortunately, that Thiasse had gone fishing in the sea, and Idun was left alone, weeping and broken-hearted. Presently she heard a little tap on her window, and, looking up, she saw a great brown bird perching on the ledge. He was so big that Idun was frightened and gave a scream. But the bird nodded pleasantly and croaked: "Don't be afraid, Idun. I am a friend. I am Loki, come to set you free."

"Loki! Loki is no friend of mine. He brought me here," she sobbed. "I don't believe you came to save me."

"That is indeed why I am here," he replied, "and a dangerous business it is, if Thiasse should come back before we start for home."

"How will you get me out?" asked Idun doubtfully. "The door is locked, and the window is barred."

"I will change you into a nut," said he, "and carry you in my claws."

"What of the casket of apples?" queried Idun. "Can you carry that also?"

Then Loki laughed long and loudly.

"What welcome to Asgard do you think I should receive without the apples?" he cried. "Yes, we must take them, indeed."

Idun came to the window, and Loki, who was a skillful magician, turned her into a nut and took her in one claw, while in the other he seized the casket of apples. Then off he whirred out of the palace grounds and away toward Asgard's safety.

In a little while Thiasse returned home, and when he found Idun and her apples gone, there was a hubbub, you may be sure! However, he lost little time by smashing mountains and breaking trees in his giant rage; that fit was soon over. He put on his eagle plumage and started in pursuit of the falcon.

Now an eagle is bigger and stronger than any other bird, and usually in a long race he can beat even the swift hawk who has an hour's start. Presently Loki heard behind him the shrill scream of a giant eagle, and his heart turned sick. But he had crossed the great river, and already was in sight of Asgard. The aged Æsir were gathered on the rainbow bridge watching eagerly for Loki's return; and when they spied the falcon with the nut and the casket in his talons, they knew who it was. A great cheer went up, but it was hushed in a moment, for they saw the eagle close after the falcon; and they guessed that this must be the giant Thiasse, the stealer of Idun.

Then there was a great shouting of commands, and a rushing to and fro. All the gods, even Father Odin and his two wise ravens, were busy gathering chips into great heaps on the walls of Asgard. As soon as Loki, with his precious burden, had fluttered weakly over the wall, dropping to the ground beyond, the gods lighted the heaps of chips which they had piled, and soon there was a wall of fire, over which the eagle must fly. He was going too fast to stop. The flames roared and crackled, but Thiasse flew straight into them, with a scream of fear and rage. His feathers caught fire and burned, so that he could no longer fly, but fell headlong to the ground inside the walls. Then Thor, the thunder-lord, and Týr, the mighty war-king, fell upon him and slew him, so that he could never trouble the Æsir any more.

There was great rejoicing in Asgard that night, for Loki changed Idun again to a fair lady; whereupon she gave each of the eager gods a bite of her life-giving fruit, so that they grew young and happy once more, as if all these horrors had never happened.

Not one of them, however, forgot the evil part which Loki had played in these doings. They hid the memory, like a buried seed, deep in their hearts. Thenceforward the word of Loki and the honor of his name were poor coin in Asgard; which is no wonder.

Skadi's Choice

The giant Thiasse, whom Thor slew for the theft of Idun and the magic apples, had a daughter, Skadi, who was a very good sort of girl, as giantesses go. Most of them were evil-tempered, spiteful, and cruel creatures, who desired only to do harm to the gods and to all who were good. But Skadi was different. Stronger than the hatred of her race for the Æsir, stronger even than her wish to be revenged for her father's death, was her love for Balder the beautiful, the pride of all the gods. If she had not been a giantess, she might have hoped that he would love her also; but she knew that no one who lived in Asgard would ever think kindly of her race, which had caused so much trouble to Balder and his brothers. After her father was killed by the Æsir, however, Skadi had a wise idea.

Skadi put on her helm and corselet and set out for Asgard, meaning to ask a noble price to pay for the sorrow of Thiasse's death. The gods, who had all grown young and boyish once again, were sitting in Valhalla merrily enjoying a banquet in honor of Idun's safe return, when Skadi, clattering with steel, strode into their midst. Heimdal the watchman, astonished at the sight, had let this maiden warrior pass him upon the rainbow bridge. The Æsir set down their cups hastily, and the laughter died upon their lips; for though she looked handsome, Skadi was a terrible figure in her silver armor and with her spear as long as a ship's mast brandished in her giant hand.

The nine Valkyries, Odin's maiden warriors, hurried away to put on their own helmets and shields; for they would not have this other maiden, ten times as huge, see them meekly waiting at table, while they had battle-dresses as fine as hers to show the stranger.

"Who are you, maiden, and what seek you here?" asked Father Odin.

"I am Skadi, the daughter of Thiasse, whom your folk have slain," answered she, "and I come here for redress."

At these words the coward Loki, who had been at the killing of Thiasse, skulked low behind the table; but Thor, who had done the killing, straightened himself and clenched his fists tightly. He was not afraid of any giant, however fierce, and this maiden with her shield and spear only angered him.

"Well, Skadi," quoth Odin gravely, "your father was a thief, and died for his sins. He stole fair Idun and her magic apples, and for that crime he died, which was only just. Yet because our righteous deed has left you an orphan, Skadi, we will grant you a recompense, so you shall be at peace with us; for it is not fitting that the Æsir should quarrel with women. What is it you ask, O Skadi, as solace for the death of Thiasse?"

Skadi looked like an orphan who was well able to take care of herself; and this indeed her next words showed her to be. "I ask two things," she said, without a moment's hesitation: "I ask the husband whom I shall select from among you; and I ask that you shall make me laugh, for it is many days since grief has let me enjoy a smile."

At this strange request the Æsir looked astonished, and some of them seemed rather startled; for you can fancy that none of them wanted a giantess, however handsome, for his wife. They put their heads together and consulted long whether or not they should allow Skadi her two wishes.

"I will agree to make her laugh," grinned Loki; "but suppose she should choose me for her husband! I am married to one giantess already."

"No fear of that, Loki," said Thor; "you were too near being the cause of her father's death for her to love you overmuch. Nor do I think that she will choose me; so I am safe."

Loki chuckled and stole away to think up a means of making Skadi laugh.

Finally, the gods agreed that Skadi should choose one of them for her husband; but in order that all might have a fair chance of missing this honor which no one coveted, she was to choose in a curious way. All the Æsir were to stand in a row behind the curtain which was drawn across the end of the hall, so that only their feet were seen by Skadi; and by their feet alone Skadi was to select him who was to be her husband.

Now Skadi was very ready to agree to this, for she said to herself, "Surely, I shall know the feet of Balder, for they will be the most beautiful of any."

Amid nervous laughter at this new game, the Æsir ranged themselves in a row behind the purple curtain, with only their line of feet showing below the golden border. There were Father Odin, Thor the Thunderer, and Balder his brother; there was old Niörd the rich, with his fair son Frey; there were Týr the bold, Bragi the poet, blind Höd, and Vidar the silent; Vali and Ull the archers, Forseti the wise judge, and Heimdal the gold-toothed watchman. Loki alone, of all the Æsir, was not there; and Loki was the only one who did not shiver as Skadi walked up and down the hall looking at the row of feet.

Up and down, back and forth, went Skadi, looking carefully; and among all those sandaled feet there was one pair more white and fair and beautiful than the rest.

"Surely, these are Balder's feet!" she thought, while her heart thumped with eagerness under her silver corselet. "Oh, if I guess aright, dear Balder will be my husband!"

She paused confidently before the handsomest pair of feet, and, pointing to them with her spear, she cried, "I choose here! Few blemishes are to be found in Balder the beautiful."

A shout of laughter arose behind the curtain, and forth slunk—not young Balder, but old Niörd the rich, king of the ocean wind, the father of those fair twins, Frey and Freia. Skadi had chosen the handsome feet of old Niörd, and thenceforth he must be her husband.

Niörd was little pleased; but Skadi was heart-broken. Her face grew longer and sadder than before when he stepped up and took her hand sulkily, saying, "Well, I am to be your husband, then, and all my riches stored in Noatûn, the home of ships, are to be yours. You would have chosen Balder, and I wish that this luck had been his! However, it cannot be helped now."

"Nay," answered Skadi, frowning, "the bargain is not yet complete. No one of you has made me laugh. I am so sad now, that it will be a merry jest indeed which can wring laughter from my heavy heart." She sighed, looking at Balder. But Balder loved only Nanna in all the world.

Just then, out came Loki, riding on one of Thor's goat steeds; and the red-bearded fellow cut up such ridiculous capers with the gray-bearded goat that soon not only Skadi, but all the Æsir and Niörd himself were holding their sides with laughter.

"Fairly won, fairly won!" cried Skadi, wiping the tears from her eyes. "I am beaten. I shall not forget that it is Loki to whom I owe this last joke. Some day I shall be quits with you, red joker!" And this threat she carried out in the end, on the day of Loki's punishment.

Skadi was married to old Niörd, both unwilling; and they went to live among the mountains in Skadi's home, which had once been Thiasse's palace, where he had shut Idun in a prison cell. As you can imagine, Niörd and Skadi did not live happily ever after, like the good prince and princess in the story-book. For, in the first place, Skadi was a giantess; and there are few folk, I fancy, who could live happily with a giantess. In the second place, she did not love Niörd, nor did he love Skadi, and neither forgot that Skadi's choosing had been sorrow to them both. But the third reason was the most important of all; and this was because Skadi and Niörd could not agree upon the place which should be their home. For Niörd did not like the mountain palace of Skadi's people,—the place where roaring winds rushed down upon the sea and its ships. The sea with its ships was his friend, and he wanted to dwell in Noatûn, where he had greater wealth than any one else in the world,—where he could rule the fresh sea-wind and tame the wild ocean, granting the prayers of fisher-folk and the seafarers, who loved his name.

Finally, they agreed to dwell first in one place, then in the other, so that each might be happy in turn. For nine days they tarried in Thrymheim, and then they spent three in Noatûn. But even this arrangement could not bring peace. One day they had a terrible quarrel. It was just after they had come down from Skadi's mountain home for their three days in Niörd's sea palace, and he was so glad to be back that he cried,—

"Ah, how I hate your hills! How long the nine nights seemed, with the wolves howling until dawn among the dark mountains of Giant Land! What a discord compared to the songs of the swans who sail upon my dear, dear ocean!" Thus rudely he taunted his wife; but Skadi answered him with spirit.

"And I—I cannot sleep by your rolling sea-waves, where the birds are ever calling, calling, as they come from the woods on the shore. Each morning the sea-gull's scream wakes me at some unseemly hour. I will not stay here even for three nights! I will not stay!"

"And I will have no more of your windy mountain-tops," roared Niörd, beside himself with rage. "Go, if you wish! Go back to Thrymheim! I shall not follow you, be sure!"

So Skadi went back to her mountains alone, and dwelt in the empty house of Thiasse, her father. She became a mighty huntress, swift on the skees and ice-runners which she strapped to her feet. Day after day she skimmed over the snow-crusted mountains, bow in hand, to hunt the wild beasts which roamed there. "Skee-goddess," she was called; and never again did she come to Asgard halls. Quite alone in the cold country, she hunted hardily, keeping ever in her heart the image of Balder the beautiful, whom she loved, but whom she had lost forever by her unlucky choice.

The Dwarf's Gifts

Red Loki had been up to mischief again! Loki, who made quarrels and brought trouble wherever he went. He had a wicked heart, and he loved no one. He envied Father Odin his wisdom and his throne above the world. He envied Balder his beauty, and Týr his courage, and Thor his strength. He envied all the good Æsir who were happy; but he would not take the trouble to be good himself. So he was always unhappy, spiteful, and sour. And if anything went wrong in Asgard, the kingdom of the gods, one was almost sure to find Loki at the bottom of the trouble.

Now Thor, the strongest of all the gods, was very proud of his wife's beautiful hair, which fell in golden waves to her feet, and covered her like a veil. He loved it better than anything, except Sif herself. One day, while Thor was away from home, Loki stole into Thrudheim, the realm of clouds, and cut off all Sif's golden hair, till her head was as round and fuzzy as a yellow dandelion. Fancy how angry Thor was when he came rattling home that night in his thunder-chariot and found Sif so ugly to look at! He stamped up and down till the five hundred and forty floors of his cloud palace shook like an earthquake, and lightning flashed from his blue eyes. The people down in the world below cried: "Dear, dear! What a terrible thunderstorm! Thor must be very angry about something. Loki has been up to mischief, it is likely." You see, they also knew Loki and his tricks.

At last Thor calmed himself a little. "Sif, my love," he said, "you shall be beautiful again. Red Loki shall make you so, since his was the unmaking. The villain! He shall pay for this!"

Then, without more ado, off set Thor to find red Loki. He went in his thunder-chariot, drawn by two goats, and the clouds rumbled and the lightning flashed wherever he went; for Thor was the mighty god of thunder. At last he came upon the sly rascal, who was trying to hide. Big Thor seized him by the throat.

"You scoundrel!" he cried, "I will break every bone in your body if you do not put back Sif's beautiful hair upon her head."

"Ow—ow! You hurt me!" howled Loki. "Take off your big hand, Thor. What is done, is done. I cannot put back Sif's hair. You know that very well."

"Then you must get her another head of hair," growled Thor. "That you can do. You must find for her hair of real gold, and it must grow upon her head as if it were her own. Do this, or you shall die."

"Where shall I get this famous hair?" whined Loki, though he knew well enough.

"Get it of the black elves," said Thor; "they are cunning jewelers, and they are your friends. Go, Loki, and go quickly, for I long to see Sif as beautiful as ever."

Then Loki of the burning beard slunk away to the hills where, far under ground, the dwarfs have their furnaces and their workshops. Among great heaps of gold and silver and shining jewels, which they have dug up out of the earth, the little crooked men in brown blink and chatter and scold one another; for they are ugly fellows—the dwarfs. Tink-tank! tink-tank! go their little hammers all day long and all night long, while they make wonderful things such as no man has ever seen, though you shall hear about them.

They had no trouble to make a head of hair for Sif. It was for them a simple matter, indeed. The dwarfs work fast for such a customer as Loki, and in a little while the golden wires were beaten out, and drawn out, made smooth and soft and curly, and braided into a thick golden braid. But when Loki came away, he carried with him also two other treasures which the clever dwarfs had made. One was a golden spear, and the other was a ship.

Now these do not sound so very wonderful. But wait until you hear! The spear, which was named Gungnir, was bewitched, so that it made no difference if the person who held it was clumsy and careless. For it had this amazing quality, that no matter how badly it was aimed, or how unskillfully it was thrown, it was sure to go straight to the mark—which is a very obliging and convenient thing in one's weapon, as you will readily see.

And Skidbladnir—this was the harsh name of the ship—was even more wonderful. It could be taken to pieces and folded up so small that it would go into one's pocket. But when it was unfolded and put together, it would hold all the gods of Asgard for a sea-journey. Besides all this, when the sails were set, the ship was sure always to have a fair wind, which would make it skim along like a great bird, which was the best part of the charm, as any sailor will tell you.

Now Loki felt very proud of these three treasures, and left the hill cave stretching his neck and strutting like a great red turkey cock. Outside the gate, however, he met Brock, the black dwarf, who was the brother of Sindri, the best workman in all the underworld.

"Hello! what have you there?" asked Brock of the big head, pointing at the bundles which Loki was carrying.

"The three finest gifts in the world," boasted Loki, hugging his treasures tight.

"Pooh!" said Brock, "I don't believe it. Did my brother Sindri make them?"

"No," answered Loki; "they were made by the black elves, the sons of Ivaldi. And they are the most precious gifts that ever were seen."

"Pooh!" again puffed Brock, wagging his long beard crossly. "Nonsense! Whatever they be, my brother Sindri can make three other gifts more precious; that I know."

"Can he, though?" laughed Loki. "I will give him my head if he can."

"Done!" shouted the dwarf. "Let me see your famous gifts." So Loki showed him the three wonders: the gold hair for Sif, the spear, and the ship. But again the dwarf said: "Pooh! These are nothing. I will show you what the master-smith can do, and you shall lose your bragging red head, my Loki."

Now Loki began to be a little uneasy. He followed Brock back to the smithy in the mountain, where they found Sindri at his forge. Oh, yes! He could beat the poor gifts of which Loki was so proud. But he would not tell what his own three gifts were to be.

First Sindri took a pig's skin and laid it on the fire. Then he went away for a little time; but he set Brock at the bellows and bade him blow—blow—blow the fire until Sindri should return. Now when Sindri was gone, Loki also stole away; for, as usual, he was up to mischief. He had the power of changing his shape and of becoming any creature he chose, which was often very convenient. Thus he turned himself into a huge biting fly. Then he flew back into the smithy where Brock was blow—blow—blowing. Loki buzzed about the dwarf's head, and finally lighted on his hand and stung him, hoping to make him let go the bellows. But no! Brock only cried out, "Oh-ee!" and kept on blowing for dear life. Now soon back came Sindri to the forge and took the pigskin from the fire. Wonder of wonders! It had turned into a hog with golden bristles; a live hog that shone like the sun. Brock was not satisfied, however.

"Well! I don't think much of that," he grumbled.

"Wait a little," said Sindri mysteriously. "Wait and see." Then he went on to make the second gift.

This time he put a lump of gold into the fire. And when he went away, as before, he bade Brock stand at the bellows to blow—blow—blow without stopping. Again, as before, in buzzed Loki the gadfly as soon as the master-smith had gone out. This time he settled on Brock's swarthy neck, and stung him so sorely that the blood came and the dwarf roared till the mountain trembled. Still Brock did not let go the handle of the bellows, but blew and howled—blew and howled with pain till Sindri returned. And this time the dwarf took from the fire a fine gold ring, round as roundness.

"Um! I don't think so much of that," said Brock, again disappointed, for he had expected some wonderful jewel. But Sindri wagged his head wisely.

"Wait a little," he said. "We shall see what we shall see." He heaved a great lump of iron into the fire to make the third gift. But this time when he went away, leaving Brock at the bellows, he charged him to blow—blow—blow without a minute's rest, or everything would be spoiled. For this was to be the best gift of all.

Brock planted himself wide-legged at the forge and blew—blew—blew. But for the third time Loki, winged as a fly, came buzzing into the smithy. This time he fastened viciously below Brock's bushy eyebrow, and stung him so cruelly that the blood trickled down, a red river, into his eyes and the poor dwarf was blinded. With a howl Brock raised his hand to wipe away the blood, and of course in that minute the bellows stood still. Then Loki buzzed away with a sound that seemed like a mocking laugh. At the same moment in rushed Sindri, panting with fright, for he had heard that sound and guessed what it meant.

"What have you done?" he cried. "You have let the bellows rest! You have spoiled everything!"

"Only a little moment, but one little moment," pleaded Brock, in a panic. "It has done no harm, has it?"

Sindri leaned anxiously over the fire, and out of the flames he drew the third gift—an enormous hammer.

"Oh!" said Brock, much disappointed, "only an old iron hammer! I don't think anything of that. Look how short the handle is, too."

"That is your fault, brother," returned the smith crossly. "If you had not let the bellows stand still, the handle would have been long enough. Yet as it is—we shall see, we shall see. I think it will at least win for you red Loki's head. Take the three gifts, brother, such as they are, and bear them to Asgard. Let all the gods be judges between you and Loki, which gifts are best, his or yours. But stay—I may as well tell you the secrets of your three treasures, or you will not know how to make them work. Your toy that is not wound up is of no use at all." Which is very true, as we all know. Then he bent over and whispered in Brock's ear. And what he said pleased Brock so much that he jumped straight up into the air and capered like one of Thor's goats.

"What a clever brother you are, to be sure!" he cried.

At that moment Loki, who had ceased to be a gadfly, came in grinning, with his three gifts. "Well, are you ready?" he asked. Then he caught sight of the three gifts which Brock was putting into his sack.

"Ho! A pig, a ring, and a stub-handled hammer!" he shouted. "Is that all you have? Fine gifts, indeed! I was really growing uneasy, but now I see that my head is safe. Let us start for Asgard immediately, where I promise you that I with my three treasures shall be thrice more welcome than you with your stupid pig, your ugly ring, and your half-made hammer."

So together they climbed to Asgard, and there they found the Æsir sitting in the great judgment hall on Ida Plain. There was Father Odin on his high throne, with his two ravens at his head and his two wolves at his feet. There was Queen Frigg by his side; and about them were Balder the beautiful, Frey and Freia, the fair brother and sister; the mighty Thor, with Sif, his crop-haired wife, and all the rest of the great Æsir who lived in the upper world above the homes of men.

"Brother Æsir," said Loki, bowing politely, for he was a smooth rascal, "we have come each with three gifts, the dwarf and I; and you shall judge which be the most worthy of praise. But if I lose,—I, your brother,—I lose my head to this crooked little dwarf." So he spoke, hoping to put the Æsir on his side from the first. For his head was a very handsome one, and the dwarf was indeed an ill-looking fellow. The gods, however, nodded gravely, and bade the two show what their gifts might be.

Then Loki stepped forward to the foot of Odin's throne. And first he pulled from his great wallet the spear Gungnir, which could not miss aim. This he gave to Odin, the all-wise. And Odin was vastly pleased, as you may imagine, to find himself thenceforth an unequaled marksman. So he smiled upon Loki kindly and said: "Well done, brother."

Next Loki took out the promised hair for Sif, which he handed Thor with a grimace. Now when the golden locks were set upon her head, they grew there like real hair, long and soft and curling—but still real gold. So that Sif was more beautiful than ever before, and more precious, too. You can fancy how pleased Thor was with Loki's gift. He kissed lovely Sif before all the gods and goddesses, and vowed that he forgave Loki for the mischief which he had done in the first place, since he had so nobly made reparation.

Then Loki took out the third gift, all folded up like a paper boat; and it was the ship Skidbladnir,—I am sorry they did not give it a prettier name. This he presented to Frey the peaceful. And you can guess whether or not Frey's blue eyes laughed with pleasure at such a gift.

Now when Loki stepped back, all the Æsir clapped their hands and vowed that he had done wondrous well.

"You will have to show us fine things, you dwarf," quoth Father Odin, "to better the gifts of red Loki. Come, what have you in the sack you bear upon your shoulders?"

Then the crooked little Brock hobbled forward, bent almost double under the great load which he carried. "I have what I have," he said.

First, out he pulled the ring Draupnir, round as roundness and shining of gold. This the dwarf gave to Odin, and though it seemed but little, yet it was much. For every ninth night out of this ring, he said, would drop eight other rings of gold, as large and as fair. Then Odin clapped his hands and cried: "Oh, wondrous gift! I like it even better than the magic spear which Loki gave." And all the other Æsir agreed with him.

Then out of the sack came grunting Goldbristle, the hog, all of gold. Brock gave him to Frey, to match the magic ship of Loki. This Goldbristle was so marvelously forged that he could run more swiftly than any horse, on air or water. Moreover, he was a living lantern. For on the darkest night he bristled with light like a million-pointed star, so that one riding on his back would light the air and the sea like a firefly, wherever he went. This idea pleased Frey mightily, for he was the merriest of the gods, and he laughed aloud.

"'Tis a wondrous fine gift," he said. "I like old Goldbristle even better than the compressible boat. For on this lusty steed I can ride about the world when I am tending the crops and the cattle of men and scattering the rain upon them. Master dwarf, I give my vote to you." And all the other Æsir agreed with him.

Then out of the sack Brock drew the third gift. It was the short-handled hammer named Miölnir. And this was the gift which Sindri had made for Thor, the mightiest of the gods; and it was the best gift of all. For with it Thor could burst the hardest metal and shatter the thickest mountain, and nothing could withstand its power. But it never could hurt Thor himself; and no matter how far or how hard it was thrown, it would always fly back into Thor's own hand. Last of all, whenever he so wished, the great hammer would become so small that he could put it in his pocket, quite out of sight. But Brock was sorry that the handle was so short—all owing to his fault, because he had let the bellows rest for that one moment.

When Thor had this gift in his hand, he jumped up with a shout of joy. "'Tis a wondrous fine gift," he cried, "with short handle or with long. And I prize it even more than I prize the golden hair of Sif which Loki gave. For with it I shall fight our enemies, the Frost Giants and the mischievous Trolls and the other monsters—Loki's friends. And all the Æsir will be glad of my gift when they see what deeds I shall do therewith. Now, if I may have my say, I judge that the three gifts made by Sindri the dwarf are the most precious that may be. So Brock has gained the prize of Loki's red head,—a sorry recompense indeed for gifts so masterly." Then Thor sat down. And all the other Æsir shouted that he had spoken well, and that they agreed with him.

So Loki was like to lose his head. He offered to pay instead a huge price, if Brock would let him go. But Brock refused. "The red head of Loki for my gift," he insisted, and the gods nodded that it must be so, since he had earned his wish.

But when Loki saw that the count was all against him, his eyes grew crafty. "Well, take me, then—if you can!" he shouted. And off he shot like an arrow from a bow. For Loki had on magic shoes, with which he could run over sea or land or sky; and the dwarf could never catch him in the world. Then Brock was furious. He stood stamping and chattering, tearing his long beard with rage.

"I am cheated!" he cried. "I have won—but I have lost." Then he turned to Thor, who was playing with his hammer, bursting a mountain or two and splitting a tree here and there. "Mighty Thor," begged the dwarf, "catch me the fellow who has broken his word. I have given you the best gift,—your wonderful hammer. Catch me, then, the boasting red head which I have fairly bought."

Then Thor stopped his game and set out in pursuit of Loki, for he was ever on the side of fairness. No one, however fleet, can escape when Thor follows, for his is the swiftness of a lightning flash. So he soon brought Loki back to Ida Plain, and gave him up a prisoner to the dwarf.

"I have you now, boaster," said Brock fiercely, "and I will cut off your red head in the twinkling of an eye." But just as he was about to do as he said, Loki had another sly idea.

"Hold, sirrah dwarf," he said. "It is true that you have won my head, but not the neck, not an inch of the neck." And all the gods agreed that this was so. Then Brock was puzzled indeed, for how could he cut off Loki's head without an inch of the neck, too? But this he must not do, or he knew the just Æsir would punish him with death. So he was forced to be content with stopping Loki's boasting in another way. He would sew up the bragging lips.

He brought a stout, strong thread and an awl to bore the holes. And in a twinkling he had stitched up the lips of the sly one, firm and fast. So for a time, at least, he put an end to Loki's boasting and his taunts and his lies.

It is a pity that those mischief-making lips were not fastened up forever; for that would have saved much of the trouble and sorrow which came after. But at last, after a long time, Loki got his lips free, and they made great sorrow in Asgard for the gods and on earth for men, as you shall hear.

Now this is the end of the tale which tells of the dwarf's gifts, and especially of Thor's hammer, which was afterwards to be of such service to him and such bane to the enemies of the Æsir. And that also you shall hear before all is done.

Loki's Children

Red Loki, the wickedest of all the Æsir, had done something of which he was very much ashamed. He had married a giantess, the ugliest, fiercest, most dreadful giantess that ever lived; and of course he wanted no one to find out what he had done, for he knew that Father Odin would be indignant with him for having wedded one of the enemies of the Æsir, and that none of his brothers would be grateful to him for giving them a sister-in-law so hideous.

But at last All-Father found out the secret that Loki had been hiding for years. Worst of all, he found that Loki and the giantess had three ugly children hidden away in the dark places of the earth,—three children of whom Loki was even more ashamed than of their mother, though he loved them too. For two of them were the most terrible monsters which time had ever seen. Hela his daughter was the least ugly of the three, though one could scarcely call her attractive. She was half black and half white, which must have looked very strange; and she was not easily mistaken by any one who chanced to see her, you can well understand. She was fierce and grim to see, and the very sight of her caused terror and death to him who gazed upon her.

But the other two! One was an enormous wolf, with long fierce teeth and flashing red eyes. And the other was a scaly, slimy, horrible serpent, huger than any serpent that ever lived, and a hundred times more ferocious. Can you wonder that Loki was ashamed of such children as these? The wonder is, how he could find anything about them to love. But Loki's heart loved evil in secret, and it was the evil in these three children of his which made them so ugly.

Now when Odin discovered that three such monsters had been living in the world without his knowledge, he was both angry and anxious, for he knew that these children of mischievous Loki and his wicked giantess-wife were dangerous to the peace of Asgard. He consulted the Norns, the three wise maidens who lived beside the Urdar-well, and who could see into the future to tell what things were to happen in coming years. And they bade him beware of Loki's children; they told him that the three monsters would bring great sorrow upon Asgard, for the giantess their mother would teach them all her hatred of Odin's race, while they would have their father's sly wisdom to help them in all mischief. So Odin knew that his fears had warned him truly. Something must be done to prevent the dangers which threatened Asgard. Something must be done to keep the three out of mischief.

Father Odin sent for all the gods, and bade them go forth over the world, find the children of Loki in the secret places where they were hidden, and bring them to him. Then the Æsir mounted their horses and set out on their difficult errand. They scoured Asgard, Midgard the world of men, Utgard and Jotunheim where the giants lived. And at last they found the three horrible creatures hiding in their mother's cave. They dragged them forth and took them up to Asgard, before Odin's high throne.

Now All-Father had been considering what should be done with the three monsters, and when they came, his mind was made up. Hela, the daughter, was less evil than the other two, but her face was dark and gloomy, and she brought death to those who looked upon her. She must be prisoned out of sight in some far place, where her sad eyes could not look sorrow into men's lives and death into their hearts. So he sent her down, down into the dark, cold land of Niflheim, which lay below one root of the great tree Yggdrasil. Here she must live forever and ever. And, because she was not wholly bad, Odin made her queen of that land, and for her subjects she was to have all the folk who died upon the earth,—except the heroes who perished in battle; for these the Valkyries carried straight to Valhalla in Asgard. But all who died of sickness or of old age, all who met their deaths through accident or men's cruelty, were sent to Queen Hela, who gave them lodgings in her gloomy palace. Vast was her kingdom, huge as nine worlds, and it was surrounded by a high wall, so that no one who had once gone thither could ever return. And here thenceforth Loki's daughter reigned among the shadows, herself half shadow and half light, half good and half bad.

But the Midgard serpent was a more dangerous beast even than Death. Odin frowned when he looked upon this monster writhing before his throne. He seized the scaly length in his mighty arms and hurled it forth over the wall of Asgard. Down, down went the great serpent, twisting and twirling as he fell, while all the sky was black with the smoke from his nostrils, and the sound of his hissing made every creature tremble. Down, down he fell with a great splash into the deep ocean which surrounded the world. There he lay writhing and squirming, growing always larger and larger, until he was so huge that he stretched like a ring about the whole earth, with his tail in his mouth, and his wicked eyes glaring up through the water towards Asgard which he hated. Sometimes he heaved himself up, great body and all, trying to escape from the ocean which was his prison. At those times there were great waves in the sea, snow and stormy winds and rain upon the earth, and every one would be filled with fear lest he escape and bring horrors to pass. But he was never able to drag out his whole hideous length. For the evil in him had grown with his growth; and a weight of evil is the heaviest of all things to lift.

The third monster was the Fenris wolf, and this was the most dreadful of the three. He was so terrible that at first Father Odin decided not to let him out of his sight. He lived in Asgard then, among the Æsir. Only Týr the brave had courage enough to give him food. Day by day he grew huger and huger, fiercer and fiercer, and finally, when All-Father saw how mighty he had become, and how he bid fair to bring destruction upon all Asgard if he were allowed to prowl and growl about as he saw fit, Odin resolved to have the beast chained up. The Æsir then went to their smithies and forged a long, strong chain which they thought no living creature could break. They took it to the wolf to try its strength, and he, looking sidewise, chuckled to himself and let them do what they would with him. But as soon as he stretched himself, the chain burst into a thousand pieces, as if it were made of twine. Then the Æsir hurried away and made another chain, far, far stronger than the first.

"If you can break this, O Fenrir," they said, "you will be famous indeed."

Again the wolf blinked at his chain; again he chuckled and let them fasten him without a struggle, for he knew that his own strength had been increased since he broke the other; but as soon as the chain was fastened, he shook his great shoulders, kicked his mighty legs, and—snap!—the links of the chain went whirling far and wide, and once more the fierce beast was free.

Then the Æsir were alarmed for fear that they would never be able to make a chain mighty enough to hold the wolf, who was growing stronger every minute; but they sent Skirnir, Frey's trusty messenger, to the land of the dwarfs for help. "Make us a chain," was the message he bore from the Æsir,—"make us a chain stronger than any chain that was ever forged; for the Fenris wolf must be captured and bound, or all the world must pay the penalty."

The dwarfs were the finest workmen in the world, as the Æsir knew; for it was they who made Thor's hammer, and Odin's spear, and Balder's famous ship, besides many other wondrous things that you remember. So when Skirnir gave them the message, they set to work with their little hammers and anvils, and before long they had welded a wonderful chain, such as no man had ever before seen. Strange things went to the making of it,—the sound of a cat's footsteps, the roots of a mountain, a bear's sinews, a fish's breath, and other magic materials that only the dwarfs knew how to put together; and the result was a chain as soft and twistable as a silken cord, but stronger than an iron cable. With this chain Skirnir galloped back to Asgard, and with it the gods were sure of chaining Fenrir; but they meant to go about the business slyly, so that the wolf should not suspect the danger which was so near.

"Ho, Fenrir!" they cried. "Here is a new chain for you. Do you think you can snap this as easily as you did the last? We warn you that it is stronger than it looks." They handed it about from one to another, each trying to break the links, but in vain. The wolf watched them disdainfully.

"Pooh! There is little honor in breaking a thread so slender!" he said. "I know that I could snap it with one bite of my big teeth. But there may be some trick about it; I will not let it bind my feet,—not I."

"Oho!" cried the Æsir. "He is afraid! He fears that we shall bind him in cords that he cannot loose. But see how slender the chain is. Surely, if you could burst the chain of iron, O Fenrir, you could break this far more easily." Still the wolf shook his head, and refused to let them fasten him, suspecting some trick. "But even if you find that you cannot break our chain," they said, "you need not be afraid. We shall set you free again."

"Set me free!" growled the wolf. "Yes, you will set me free at the end of the world,—not before! I know your ways, O Æsir; and if you are able to bind me so fast that I cannot free myself, I shall wait long to have the chain made loose. But no one shall call me coward. If one of you will place his hand in my mouth and hold it there while the others bind me, I will let the chain be fastened."

The gods looked at one another, their mouths drooping. Who would do this thing and bear the fury of the angry wolf when he should find himself tricked and captured? Yet this was their only chance to bind the monster and protect Asgard from danger. At last bold Týr stepped forward, the bravest of all the Æsir. "Open your mouth, Fenrir," he cried, with a laugh. "I will pledge my hand to the trial."

Then the wolf yawned his great jaws, and Týr thrust in his good right hand, knowing full well that he was to lose it in the game. The Æsir stepped up with the dwarfs' magic chain, and Fenrir let them fasten it about his feet.

But when the bonds were drawn tight, he began to struggle; and the more he tugged, the tighter drew the chain, so that he soon saw himself to be entrapped. Then how he writhed and kicked, howled and growled, in his terrible rage! How the heavens trembled and the earth shook below! The Æsir set up a laugh to see him so helpless—all except Týr; for at the first sound of laughter the wolf shut his great mouth with a click, and poor brave Týr had lost the right hand which had done so many heroic deeds in battle, and which would never again wave sword before the warriors whom he loved and would help to win the victory. But great was the honor which he won that day, for without his generous deed the Fenris wolf could never have been captured.

And now the monster was safely secured by the strong chain which the dwarfs had made, and all his struggles to be free were in vain, for they only bound the silken rope all the tighter. The Æsir took one end of the chain and fastened it through a big rock which they planted far down in the earth, as far as they could drive it with a huge hammer of stone. Into the wolf's great mouth they thrust a sword crosswise, so that the hilt pierced his lower jaw while the point stuck through the upper one; and there in the heart of the world he lay howling and growling, but quite unable to move. Only the foam which dripped from his angry jaws trickled away and over the earth until it formed a mighty river; from his wicked mouth also came smoke and fire, and the sound of his horrible growls. And when men hear this and see this they run away as fast as they can, for they know that danger still lurks near where the Fenris wolf lies chained in the depths of the earth; and here he will lie until Ragnarök,—until the end of all things.

The Quest of the Hammer

One morning Thor the Thunderer awoke with a yawn, and stretching out his knotted arm, felt for his precious hammer, which he kept always under his pillow of clouds. But he started up with a roar of rage, so that all the palace trembled. The hammer was gone!

Now this was a very serious matter, for Thor was the protector of Asgard, and Miölnir, the magic hammer which the dwarf had made, was his mighty weapon, of which the enemies of the Æsir stood so much in dread that they dared not venture near. But if they should learn that Miölnir was gone, who could tell what danger might not threaten the palaces of heaven?

Thor darted his flashing eye into every corner of Cloud Land in search of the hammer. He called his fair wife, Sif of the golden hair, to aid in the search, and his two lovely daughters, Thrude and Lora. They hunted and they hunted; they turned Thrudheim upside down, and set the clouds to rolling wonderfully, as they peeped and pried behind and around and under each billowy mass. But Miölnir was not to be found. Certainly, some one had stolen it.

Thor's yellow beard quivered with rage, and his hair bristled on end like the golden rays of a star, while all his household trembled.

"It is Loki again!" he cried. "I am sure Loki is at the bottom of this mischief!" For since the time when Thor had captured Loki for the dwarf Brock and had given him over to have his bragging lips sewed up, Loki had looked at him with evil eyes; and Thor knew that the red rascal hated him most of all the gods.

But this time Thor was mistaken. It was not Loki who had stolen the hammer,—he was too great a coward for that. And though he meant, before the end, to be revenged upon Thor, he was waiting until a safe chance should come, when Thor himself might stumble into danger, and Loki need only to help the evil by a malicious word or two; and this chance came later, as you shall hear in another tale.

Meanwhile Loki was on his best behavior, trying to appear very kind and obliging; so when Thor came rumbling and roaring up to him, demanding, "What have you done with my hammer, you thief?" Loki looked surprised, but did not lose his temper nor answer rudely.

"Have you indeed missed your hammer, brother Thor?" he said, mumbling, for his mouth was still sore where Brock had sewed the stitches. "That is a pity; for if the giants hear of this, they will be coming to try their might against Asgard."

"Hush!" muttered Thor, grasping him by the shoulder with his iron fingers. "That is what I fear. But look you, Loki: I suspect your hand in the mischief. Come, confess."

Then Loki protested that he had nothing to do with so wicked a deed. "But," he added wheedlingly, "I think I can guess the thief; and because I love you, Thor, I will help you to find him."

"Humph!" growled Thor. "Much love you bear to me! However, you are a wise rascal, the nimblest wit of all the Æsir, and it is better to have you on my side than on the other, when giants are in the game. Tell me, then: who has robbed the Thunder-Lord of his bolt of power?"

Loki drew near and whispered in Thor's ear. "Look, how the storms rage and the winds howl in the world below! Some one is wielding your thunder-hammer all unskillfully. Can you not guess the thief? Who but Thrym, the mighty giant who has ever been your enemy and your imitator, and whose fingers have long itched to grasp the short handle of mighty Miölnir, that the world may name him Thunder-Lord instead of you. But look! What a tempest! The world will be shattered into fragments unless we soon get the hammer back."

Then Thor roared with rage. "I will seek this impudent Thrym!" he cried. "I will crush him into bits, and teach him to meddle with the weapon of the Æsir!"

"Softly, softly," said Loki, smiling maliciously. "He is a shrewd giant, and a mighty. Even you, great Thor, cannot go to him and pluck the hammer from his hand as one would slip the rattle from a baby's pink fist. Nay, you must use craft, Thor; and it is I who will teach you, if you will be patient."

Thor was a brave, blunt fellow, and he hated the ways of Loki, his lies and his deceit. He liked best the way of warriors,—the thundering charge, the flash of weapons, and the heavy blow; but without the hammer he could not fight the giants hand to hand. Loki's advice seemed wise, and he decided to leave the matter to the Red One.

Loki was now all eagerness, for he loved difficulties which would set his wit in play and bring other folk into danger. "Look, now," he said. "We must go to Freia and borrow her falcon dress. But you must ask; for she loves me so little that she would scarce listen to me."

So first they made their way to Folkvang, the house of maidens, where Freia dwelt, the loveliest of all in Asgard. She was fairer than fair, and sweeter than sweet, and the tears from her flower-eyes made the dew which blessed the earth-flowers night and morning. Of her Thor borrowed the magic dress of feathers in which Freia was wont to clothe herself and flit like a great beautiful bird all about the world. She was willing enough to lend it to Thor when he told her that by its aid he hoped to win back the hammer which he had lost; for she well knew the danger threatening herself and all the Æsir until Miölnir should be found.

"Now will I fetch the hammer for you," said Loki. So he put on the falcon plumage, and, spreading his brown wings, flapped away up, up, over the world, down, down, across the great ocean which lies beyond all things that men know. And he came to the dark country where there was no sunshine nor spring, but it was always dreary winter; where mountains were piled up like blocks of ice, and where great caverns yawned hungrily in blackness. And this was Jotunheim, the land of the Frost Giants.

And lo! when Loki came thereto he found Thrym the Giant King sitting outside his palace cave, playing with his dogs and horses. The dogs were as big as elephants, and the horses were as big as houses, but Thrym himself was as huge as a mountain; and Loki trembled, but he tried to seem brave.

"Good-day, Loki," said Thrym, with the terrible voice of which he was so proud, for he fancied it was as loud as Thor's. "How fares it, feathered one, with your little brothers, the Æsir, in Asgard halls? And how dare you venture alone in this guise to Giant Land?"

"It is an ill day in Asgard," sighed Loki, keeping his eye warily upon the giant, "and a stormy one in the world of men. I heard the winds howling and the storms rushing on the earth as I passed by. Some mighty one has stolen the hammer of our Thor. Is it you, Thrym, greatest of all giants,—greater than Thor himself?"

This the crafty one said to flatter Thrym, for Loki well knew the weakness of those who love to be thought greater than they are.

Then Thrym bridled and swelled with pride, and tried to put on the majesty and awe of noble Thor; but he only succeeded in becoming an ugly, puffy monster.

"Well, yes," he admitted. "I have the hammer that belonged to your little Thor; and now how much of a lord is he?"

"Alack!" sighed Loki again, "weak enough he is without his magic weapon. But you, O Thrym,—surely your mightiness needs no such aid. Give me the hammer, that Asgard may no longer be shaken by Thor's grief for his precious toy."

But Thrym was not so easily to be flattered into parting with his stolen treasure. He grinned a dreadful grin, several yards in width, which his teeth barred like jagged boulders across the entrance to a mountain cavern.

"Miölnir the hammer is mine," he said, "and I am Thunder-Lord, mightiest of the mighty. I have hidden it where Thor can never find it, twelve leagues below the sea-caves, where Queen Ran lives with her daughters, the white-capped Waves. But listen, Loki. Go tell the Æsir that I will give back Thor's hammer. I will give it back upon one condition,—that they send Freia the beautiful to be my wife."

"Freia the beautiful!" Loki had to stifle a laugh. Fancy the Æsir giving their fairest flower to such an ugly fellow as this! But he only said politely, "Ah, yes; you demand our Freia in exchange for the little hammer? It is a costly price, great Thrym. But I will be your friend in Asgard. If I have my way, you shall soon see the fairest bride in all the world knocking at your door. Farewell!"

So Loki whizzed back to Asgard on his falcon wings; and as he went he chuckled to think of the evils which were likely to happen because of his words with Thrym. First he gave the message to Thor,—not sparing of Thrym's insolence, to make Thor angry; and then he went to Freia with the word for her,—not sparing of Thrym's ugliness, to make her shudder. The spiteful fellow!

Now you can imagine the horror that was in Asgard as the Æsir listened to Loki's words. "My hammer!" roared Thor. "The villain confesses that he has stolen my hammer, and boasts that he is Thunder-Lord! Gr-r-r!"

"The ugly giant!" wailed Freia. "Must I be the bride of that hideous old monster, and live in his gloomy mountain prison all my life?"

"Yes; put on your bridal veil, sweet Freia," said Loki maliciously, "and come with me to Jotunheim. Hang your famous starry necklace about your neck, and don your bravest robe; for in eight days there will be a wedding, and Thor's hammer is to pay."

Then Freia fell to weeping. "I cannot go! I will not go!" she cried. "I will not leave the home of gladness and Father Odin's table to dwell in the land of horrors! Thor's hammer is mighty, but mightier the love of the kind Æsir for their little Freia! Good Odin, dear brother Frey, speak for me! You will not make me go?"

The Æsir looked at her and thought how lonely and bare would Asgard be without her loveliness; for she was fairer than fair, and sweeter than sweet.

"She shall not go!" shouted Frey, putting his arms about his sister's neck.

"No, she shall not go!" cried all the Æsir with one voice.

"But my hammer," insisted Thor. "I must have Miölnir back again."

"And my word to Thrym," said Loki, "that must be made good."

"You are too generous with your words," said Father Odin sternly, for he knew his brother well. "Your word is not a gem of great price, for you have made it cheap."

Then spoke Heimdal, the sleepless watchman who sits on guard at the entrance to the rainbow bridge which leads to Asgard; and Heimdal was the wisest of the Æsir, for he could see into the future, and knew how things would come to pass. Through his golden teeth he spoke, for his teeth were all of gold.

"I have a plan," he said. "Let us dress Thor himself like a bride in Freia's robes, and send him to Jotunheim to talk with Thrym and to win back his hammer."

But at this word Thor grew very angry. "What! dress me like a girl!" he roared. "I should never hear the last of it! The Æsir will mock me, and call me 'maiden'! The giants, and even the puny dwarfs, will have a lasting jest upon me! I will not go! I will fight! I will die, if need be! But dressed as a woman I will not go!"

But Loki answered him with sharp words, for this was a scheme after his own heart. "What, Thor!" he said. "Would you lose your hammer and keep Asgard in danger for so small a whim? Look, now: if you go not,

Thrym with his giants will come in a mighty army and drive us from As-gard; then he will indeed make Freia his bride, and moreover he will have you for his slave under the power of his hammer. How like you this picture, brother of the thunder? Nay, Heimdal's plan is a good one, and I myself will help to carry it out."

Still Thor hesitated; but Freia came and laid her white hand on his arm, and looked up into his scowling face pleadingly.

"To save me, Thor," she begged. And Thor said he would go.

Then there was great sport among the Æsir, while they dressed Thor like a beautiful maiden. Brunhilde and her sisters, the nine Valkyrie, daugh-ters of Odin, had the task in hand. How they laughed as they brushed and curled his yellow hair, and set upon it the wondrous headdress of silk and pearls! They let out seams, and they let down hems, and set on extra pieces, to make it larger, and so they hid his great limbs and knotted arms under Freia's fairest robe of scarlet; but beneath it all he would wear his shirt of mail and his belt of power that gave him double strength. Freia herself twisted about his neck her famous necklace of starry jewels, and Queen Frigg, his mother, hung at his girdle a jingling bunch of keys, such as was the custom for the bride to wear at Norse weddings. Last of all, that Thrym might not see Thor's fierce eyes and the yellow beard, that ill became a maiden, they threw over him a long veil of silver white which covered him to the feet. And there he stood, as stately and tall a bride as even a giant might wish to see; but on his hands he wore his iron gloves, and they ached for but one thing,—to grasp the handle of the stolen hammer.

"Ah, what a lovely maid it is!" chuckled Loki; "and how glad will Thrym be to see this Freia come! Bride Thor, I will go with you as your handmaiden, for I would fain see the fun."

"Come, then," said Thor sulkily, for he was ill pleased, and wore his maiden robes with no good grace. "It is fitting that you go; for I like not these lies and maskings, and I may spoil the mummery without you at my elbow."

There was loud laughter above the clouds when Thor, all veiled and dainty seeming, drove away from Asgard to his wedding, with maid Loki by his side. Thor cracked his whip and chirruped fiercely to his twin goats with golden hoofs, for he wanted to escape the sounds of mirth that echoed from the rainbow bridge, where all the Æsir stood watching. Loki, sitting with his hands meekly folded like a girl, chuckled as he glanced up at Thor's angry face; but he said nothing, for he knew it was not good to joke too far with Thor, even when Miölnir was hidden twelve leagues below the sea in Ran's kingdom.

So off they dashed to Jotunheim, where Thrym was waiting and long-ing for his beautiful bride. Thor's goats thundered along above the sea and land and people far below, who looked up wondering as the noise rolled overhead. "Hear how the thunder rumbles!" they said. "Thor is on a long journey to-night." And a long journey it was, as the tired goats found before they reached the end.

Thrym heard the sound of their approach, for his ear was eager. "Hola!" he cried. "Some one is coming from Asgard,—only one of Odin's children could make a din so fearful. Hasten, men, and see if they are bringing Freia to be my wife."

Then the lookout giant stepped down from the top of his mountain, and said that a chariot was bringing two maidens to the door.

"Run, giants, run!" shouted Thrym, in a fever at this news. "My bride is coming! Put silken cushions on the benches for a great banquet, and make the house beautiful for the fairest maid in all space! Bring in all my golden-horned cows and my coal-black oxen, that she may see how rich I am, and heap all my gold and jewels about to dazzle her sweet eyes! She shall find me richest of the rich; and when I have her,—fairest of the fair,—there will be no treasure that I lack,—not one!"

The chariot stopped at the gate, and out stepped the tall bride, hidden from head to foot, and her handmaiden muffled to the chin. "How afraid of catching cold they must be!" whispered the giant ladies, who were peering over one another's shoulders to catch a glimpse of the bride, just as the crowd outside the awning does at a wedding nowadays.

Thrym had sent six splendid servants to escort the maidens: these were the Metal Kings, who served him as lord of them all. There was the Gold King, all in cloth of gold, with fringes of yellow bullion, most glittering to see; and there was the Silver King, almost as gorgeous in a suit of spangled white; and side by side bowed the dark Kings of Iron and Lead, the one mighty in black, the other sullen in blue; and after them were the Copper King, gleaming ruddy and brave, and the Tin King, strutting in his trim-mings of gaudy tinsel which looked nearly as well as silver but were more economical. And this fine troop of lackey kings most politely led Thor and Loki into the palace, and gave them of the best, for they never suspected who these seeming maidens really were.

And when evening came there was a wonderful banquet to celebrate the wedding. On a golden throne sat Thrym, uglier than ever in his finery of purple and gold. Beside him was the bride, of whose face no one had yet caught even a glimpse; and at Thrym's other hand stood Loki, the waiting-maid, for he wanted to be near to mend the mistakes which Thor might make.

Now the dishes at the feast were served in a huge way, as befitted the table of giants: great beeves roasted whole, on platters as wide across as a ship's deck; plum-puddings as fat as feather-beds, with plums as big as footballs; and a wedding cake like a snow-capped haymow. The giants ate enormously. But to Thor, because they thought him a dainty maiden, they served small bits of everything on a tiny gold dish. Now Thor's long journey had made him very hungry, and through his veil he whispered to Loki, "I shall starve, Loki! I cannot fare on these nibbles. I must eat a goodly meal as I do at home." And forthwith he helped himself to such morsels as might satisfy his hunger for a little time. You should have seen the giants stare at the meal which the dainty bride devoured!

For first under the silver veil disappeared by pieces a whole roast ox. Then Thor made eight mouthfuls of eight pink salmon, a dish of which he was very fond. And next he looked about and reached for a platter of cakes and sweetmeats that was set aside at one end of the table for the lady guests, and the bride ate them all. You can fancy how the damsels drew down their mouths and looked at one another when they saw their dessert disappear; and they whispered about the table, "Alack! if our future mistress is to sup like this day by day, there will be poor cheer for the rest of us!" And to crown it all, Thor was thirsty, as well he might be; and one after another he raised to his lips and emptied three great barrels of mead, the foamy drink of the giants. Then indeed Thrym was amazed, for Thor's giant appetite had beaten that of the giants themselves.

"Never before saw I a bride so hungry," he cried, "and never before one half so thirsty!"

But Loki, the waiting-maid, whispered to him softly, "The truth is, great Thrym, that my dear mistress was almost starved. For eight days Freia has eaten nothing at all, so eager was she for Jotunheim."

Then Thrym was delighted, you may be sure. He forgave his hungry bride, and loved her with all his heart. He leaned forward to give her a kiss, raising a corner of her veil; but his hand dropped suddenly, and he started up in terror, for he had caught the angry flash of Thor's eye, which was glaring at him through the bridal veil. Thor was longing for his hammer.

"Why has Freia so sharp a look?" Thrym cried. "It pierces like lightning and burns like fire."

But again the sly waiting-maid whispered timidly, "Oh, Thrym, be not amazed! The truth is, my poor mistress's eyes are red with wakefulness and bright with longing. For eight nights Freia has not known a wink of sleep, so eager was she for Jotunheim."

Then again Thrym was doubly delighted, and he longed to call her his very own dear wife. "Bring in the wedding gift!" he cried. "Bring in Thor's hammer, Miölnir, and give it to Freia, as I promised; for when I have kept my word she will be mine,—all mine!"

Then Thor's big heart laughed under his woman's dress, and his fierce eyes swept eagerly down the hall to meet the servant who was bringing in the hammer on a velvet cushion. Thor's fingers could hardly wait to clutch the stubby handle which they knew so well; but he sat quite still on the throne beside ugly old Thrym, with his hands meekly folded and his head bowed like a bashful bride.

The giant servant drew nearer, nearer, puffing and blowing, strong though he was, beneath the mighty weight. He was about to lay it at Thor's feet (for he thought it so heavy that no maiden could lift it or hold it in her lap), when suddenly Thor's heart swelled, and he gave a most unmaidenly shout of rage and triumph. With one swoop he grasped the hammer in his iron fingers; with the other arm he tore off the veil that hid his terrible face, and trampled it under foot; then he turned to the frightened king, who cowered beside him on the throne.

"Thief!" he cried. "Freia sends you this as a wedding gift!" And he whirled the hammer about his head, then hurled it once, twice, thrice, as it rebounded to his hand; and in the first stroke, as of lightning, Thrym rolled dead from his throne; in the second stroke perished the whole giant household,—these ugly enemies of the Æsir; and in the third stroke the palace itself tumbled together and fell to the ground like a toppling play-house of blocks.

But Loki and Thor stood safely among the ruins, dressed in their tattered maiden robes, a quaint and curious sight; and Loki, full of mischief now as ever, burst out laughing.

"Oh, Thor! if you could see"—he began; but Thor held up his hammer and shook it gently as he said,—

"Look now, Loki: it was an excellent joke, and so far you have done well,—after your crafty fashion, which likes me not. But now I have my hammer again, and the joke is done. From you, nor from another, I brook no laughter at my expense. Henceforth we will have no mention of this masquerade, nor of these rags which now I throw away. Do you hear, red laugher?"

And Loki heard, with a look of hate, and stifled his laughter as best he could; for it is not good to laugh at him who holds the hammer.

Not once after that was there mention in Asgard of the time when Thor dressed him as a girl and won his bridal gift from Thrym the giant.

But Miölnir was safe once more in Asgard, and you and I know how it came there; so some one must have told. I wonder if red Loki whispered the tale to some outsider, after all? Perhaps it may be so, for now he knew how best to make Thor angry; and from that day when Thor forbade his laughing, Loki hated him with the mean little hatred of a mean little soul.

The Giantess Who Would Not

Of all the Æsir who sat in the twelve seats about Father Odin's wonder-throne none was so dear to the people of Midgard, the world of men, as Frey. For Frey, the twin brother of Freia the fair, was the god who sent sun-shine and rain upon the earth that men's crops might grow and ripen, and the fruits become sweet and mellow. He gave men cattle, and showed them how to till the fields; and it was he who spread peace and prosperity over the world. For he was lord of the Light-Elves, the spirits of the upper air, who were more beautiful than the sun. And these were his servants whom he sent to answer the prayers of the men who loved him. Frey was more beautiful, too, than any of the Æsir except young Balder. This was another reason why he was so beloved by all. But there came a time when Frey found some one who would not love him; and that was a new experience for him, a punish-ment for the only wrong he ever committed.

You remember that Father Odin had a wonderful throne in the silver-roofed house, a throne whence he could see everything that was happening in all the world? Well, no one was allowed to sit upon this throne except All-Father himself, for he would not have the others spying into affairs which only the King of Asgard was wise enough to understand. But one day, when Odin was away from home, Frey had such a longing to climb up where he might gaze upon all the world which he loved, that he could not resist the temptation. He stole up to the great throne when no one was look-ing, and mounting the steps, seated himself upon All-Father's wonder-seat.

Oh, marvelous, grand, and beautiful! He looked off into the heavens, and there he saw all the Æsir busy about their daily work. He looked above, into the shining realm of clear air. And there he saw his messengers, the pretty little Light-Elves, flying about upon their errands of help for men. Some were carrying seeds for the farmers to plant. Some were watering the fields with their little water-pots, making the summer showers. Some were pinching the cheeks of the apples to make them red, and others were reeling silk for the corn-tassels. Then Frey looked down upon the earth, where men were scurrying around like little ants, improving the blessings which his servants were sending, and often stopping their work to give thanks to their beloved Frey. And this made his kind heart glad.

Next he turned his gaze down into the depths of the blue ocean which flowed about Midgard like a great river. And down in the sea-caves he saw the mermaids playing, Queen Ran and her daughters the white-capped Waves, with their nets ready to catch the sailors who might be drowned at sea. And he saw King Œgir, among the whales and dolphins, with all the myriad wondrous creatures who lived in his watery empire. But Frey's father, old Niörd, lord of the ocean wind, would have been more interested than he in such a sight.

Last of all Frey bent his eyes upon the far, cold land of Jotunheim, beyond the ocean, where the giants lived; and as he did so, a beam of brightness dazzled him. He rubbed his eyes and looked again; and lo! the flash was from the bright arms of a beautiful maiden, who was passing from her father's hall to her own little bower. When she raised her arms to open the door, the air and water reflected their brightness so that the whole world was flooded with light, and one shaft shot straight into the heart of Frey, making him love her and long for her more than for anything he had ever seen. But because he knew that she must be a giant's daughter, how could he win her for his bride? Frey descended from Odin's throne very sadly, very hopelessly, and went home with a heavy heart which would let him neither eat nor sleep. This was the penalty which came for his disobedience in presuming to sit upon Odin's sacred throne.

For hours no one dared speak to Frey, he looked so gloomy and forbidding, quite unlike his own gay self. Niörd his father was greatly worried, and knew not what to do; at last he sent for Skirnir, who was Frey's favorite servant, and bade him find out what was the matter. Skirnir therefore went to his master, whom he found sitting all alone in his great hall, looking as if there were no more joy for him.

"What ails you, master?" asked Skirnir. "From the beginning of time when we were very young we two have lived together, and I have served you with loving care. You ought, then, to have confidence in me and tell me all your troubles."

"Ah, Skirnir, my faithful friend," sighed Frey, "how shall I tell you my sorrow? The sun shines every day, but no longer brings light to my sad heart. And all because I saw more than was good for me!"

So then he told Skirnir all the matter: how he had stolen into Odin's seat, and what he had seen from there; how he loved a giant's daughter whose arms were more bright than silver moonbeams.

"Oh, Skirnir, I love her very dearly," he cried; "but because our races are enemies she would never marry me, I know, even if her father would allow it. Therefore is it that I am so sad."

But Skirnir did not seem to think the case so hopeless. "Give me but your swift horse," he said, "which can bear me even through flames of fire and thick smoke; give me also your magic wand and your sword, which if he be brave who carries it, will smite by itself any giant who comes in its way,—and I will see what I can do for you."

Then Skirnir rode forth upon his dangerous errand; for a visit to Giant Land was ever a perilous undertaking, as you may well imagine. As Skirnir rode, he patted his good horse's neck and said to him, "Dark it is, friend, and we have to go over frosty mountains and among frosty people this night. Bear me well, good horse; for if you fail me the giants will catch us both, and neither of us will return to bring the news to our master Frey."

After a long night of hard riding over mountain and desolate snowfield, Skirnir came to that part of Jotunheim where the giant Gymir dwelt. This was the father of Gerd, the maiden whom Frey had seen and loved. But first he had to ride through a hedge of flame, which the horse passed bravely. Now when he came to the house of Gymir, he found a pack of fierce dogs chained about the door to keep strangers away.

"H'm!" thought Skirnir, "I like this little indeed. I must find out whether there be not some other entrance." So he looked around, and soon he saw a herdsman sitting on a little hill, tending his cattle. Skirnir rode up to him.

"Ho, friend," he cried. "Tell me, how am I to pass these growling curs so that I may speak with the young maiden who dwells in this house?"

"Are you mad, or are you a spirit who is not afraid of death!" exclaimed the herdsman. "Know you not that you can never enter there? That is Gymir's dwelling, and he lets no one speak with his fair and good daughter."

"If I choose to die, you need not weep for me," quoth Skirnir boldly. "But I do not think that I am yet to die. The Norn-maidens spun my fate centuries ago, and they only can tell what is to be." Now Skirnir's voice was loud and the hoof-beats of his horse were mighty. For this was one of the magic steeds of Asgard, used to bearing Frey himself on his broad back. And not without much noise had all these things been said and done. From her room in Gymir's mansion Gerd heard the stranger's voice, and to her waiting-maid she said, "What are these sounds that I hear? The earth is trembling and all the house shakes."

Then the servant ran to look out of the window, and in a minute she popped in her head, crying, "Here is a mighty stranger who has dismounted from his horse and leads him by the bridle to crop the grass."

Gerd was curious to see who this stranger might be; for her father kept her close and she saw few visitors.

"Bid him enter our hall," she said, "and give him a horn of bright mead to drink. I will see him, though I fear it is the slayer of my brother." For Gerd was the sister of Thiasse whom Thor slew.

So Skirnir came into the hall, and Gerd received him coldly. "Who are you?" she asked. "Which of the wise Æsir are you? For I know that only one of the mighty ones from Asgard would have the courage and the power to pass through the raging flames that surround my father's land."

"I come from Frey, O maiden," said Skirnir, "from Frey, whom all folk love. I come to beg that you also will love him and consent to be his wife. For Frey has seen your beauty, and you are very dear to him."

Gerd laughed carelessly. "I have heard of your fair Frey," she said, "and how he is more dear to all than sunshine and the sweet smell of flowers. But he is not dear to me. I do not wish the love of Frey, nor any of that race of giant-killers. Tell him that I will not be his bride."

"Stay, be not so hasty," urged Skirnir. "We have more words to exchange before I start for home. Look, I will give you eleven golden apples from Asgard's magic tree if you will go with me to Frey's dwelling."

Gerd would hear nothing of the golden apples. Then Skirnir promised her the golden ring, Draupnir, which the dwarfs had made for Odin, out of which every ninth night dropped eight other rings as large and bright. But neither would Gerd listen to word of this generous gift. "I have gold enough in my father's house," she said disdainfully. "With such trifles you cannot tempt me to marry your Frey."

Then Skirnir was very angry, and he began to storm and threaten. "I will strike you with the bright sword which I hold in my hand!" he cried. "It is Frey's magic sword, under which even that stout old giant your father must sink if he comes within its reach." But again Gerd laughed, though with less mirth in her laughter. "I will tame you with Frey's magic wand!" he threatened, "the wand with which he rules the Light-Elves, and changes folk into strange shapes. You shall vanish from the sight of men, and pass your life on the eagle's mount far above the sky, where you shall sit all day, too sad to eat. And when you come thence, after countless ages, you will be a hideous monster at which all creatures will stare in mockery and scorn."

These were dreadful words, and Gerd no longer laughed when she heard them. But she was obstinate. "I do not love Frey," she said, "and I will not be his bride."

Then Skirnir was angry indeed, and his fury blazed out in threats most horrible. "If you will not marry my dear master," he cried, "you shall be the most unhappy girl that ever lived. You shall cry all day long and never see joy again. You shall marry a hideous old three-headed giant, and from day to day you shall ever be in terror of some still more dreadful fate to come!"

Now Gerd began to tremble, for she saw that Frey's servant meant every word that he spoke. But she was not ready to yield. "Go back to the land of Elves," she taunted; "I will not be their Queen at any cost."

Now Skirnir grasped the magic wand, and waving it over her, spoke his last words of threat and anger. "The gods are angry with you, evil maiden!"

he cried. "Odin sees your obstinacy from his throne, and will punish you for your cruelty to kind Frey. Frey himself, instead of loving, will shun you when the gods arm themselves to destroy you and all your race. Listen, Giants, Dwarfs, Light-Elves, Men, and all friends of the Æsir! I forbid any one to have aught to do with this wicked girl,—only the old giant who shall carry her to his gloomy castle, barred and bolted and grated across. Misery, pain, and madness—this, Gerd, is the fate which I wave over you with my wand, unless speedily you repent and do my will."

Poor Gerd gasped and trembled under this dreadful doom. Her willfulness was quite broken, and now she sought only to make Skirnir unsay the words of horror. "Hold!" she cried; "be welcome, youth, in the name of your powerful master, Frey. I cannot afford to be enemy of such as he. Drink this icy cup of welcome filled with the giant's mead, and take with it my consent to be the bride of Frey. But alas! I never thought to be a friend to one of Asgard's race."

"You shall never repent, fair Gerd," said Skirnir gently. For now that he had won his will, he was all smiles and friendliness. "And when you see my dear master, you will be glad indeed that you did not insist upon wedding the old three-headed giant. For Frey is fair,—ay, as fair as are you yourself. And that is saying much, sweet lady."

So Gerd promised that in nine days she would come to be the bride of Frey. And the more she thought it over, the less unpleasant seemed the idea. So that before the time was passed, she was almost as eager as Frey for their happy meeting; not quite so eager, for you must remember that she had not yet seen him and knew not all his glory, while he knew what it was to long and long for what he had once seen.

Indeed, when Skirnir galloped back to Frey as fast as the good horse could take him, still Frey chided him for being slow. And when the faithful fellow told the good news of the bride who was to be his master's in nine short days, still Frey frowned and grumbled impatiently.

"How can I wait to see her?" he cried. "One day is long; two days are a century; nine days seem forever. Oh, Skirnir, could you not have done better than that for your dear master?"

But Skirnir forgave Frey for his impatience, for he knew that thenceforward his master would love all the better him who had done so nobly to win the beloved bride.

When Gerd married Frey and went with him to live in Elf Land, where he and she were king and queen, they were the happiest folk that the world ever saw. And Gerd was as grateful to Skirnir as Frey himself. For she could not help thinking of that dreadful old three-headed giant whom but for him she might have married, instead of her beautiful, kind Frey.

So you see that sometimes one is happier in the end if she is not allowed to have her own way.

Thor's Visit to the Giants

Nowadays, since their journey to get the stolen hammer, Thor and Loki were good friends, for Loki seemed to have turned over a new leaf and to be a very decent sort of fellow; but really he was the same sly rascal at heart, only biding his time for mischief. However, in this tale he behaves well enough.

It was a long time since Thor had slain any giants, and he was growing restless for an adventure. "Come, Loki," he said one day, "let us fare forth to Giant Land and see what news there is among the Big Folk."

Loki laughed, saying, "Let us go, Thor. I know I am safe with you;" which was a piece of flattery that happened to be true.

So they mounted the goat chariot as they had done so many times before and rumbled away out of Asgard. All day they rode; and when evening came they stopped at a little house on the edge of a forest, where lived a poor peasant with his wife, his son, and daughter.

"May we rest here for the night, friend?" asked Thor; and noting their poverty, he added, "We bring our own supper, and ask but a bed to sleep in." So the peasant was glad to have them stay. Then Thor, who knew what he was about, killed and cooked his two goats, and invited the family of peasants to sup with him and Loki; but when the meal was ended, he bade them carefully save all the bones and throw them into the goatskins which he had laid beside the hearth. Then Thor and Loki lay down to sleep.

In the morning, very early, before the rest were awake, Thor rose, and taking his hammer, Miölnir, went into the kitchen, where were the remains of his faithful goats. Now the magic hammer was skillful, not only to slay, but to restore, when Thor's hand wielded it. He touched with it the two heaps of skin and bones, and lo! up sprang the goats, alive and well, and as good as new. No, not quite as good as new. What was this? Thor roared with anger, for one of the goats was lame in one of his legs, and limped sorely. "Some one has meddled with the bones!" he cried. "Who has touched the bones that I bade be kept so carefully?"

Thialfi, the peasant's son, had broken one of the thigh-bones in order to get at the sweet marrow, and this Thor soon discovered by the lad's guilty face; then Thor was angry indeed. His knuckles grew white as he clenched the handle of Miölnir, ready to hurl it and destroy the whole unlucky house and family; but the peasant and the other three fell upon their knees, trembling with fear, and begged him to spare them. They offered him all that they owned,—they offered even to become his slaves,—if he would but spare their wretched lives.

They looked so miserable that Thor was sorry for them, and resolved at last to punish them only by taking away Thialfi, the son, and Röskva, the daughter, thenceforth to be his servants. And this was not so bad a bargain for Thor, for Thialfi was the swiftest of foot of any man in the whole world.

So he left the goats behind, and fared forth with his three attendants straight towards the east and Jotunheim. Thialfi carried Thor's wallet with their scanty store of food. They crossed the sea and came at last to a great forest, through which they tramped all day, until once more it was night; and now they must find a place in which all could sleep safely until morning. They wandered about here and there, looking for some sign of a dwelling, and at last they came to a big, queer-shaped house. Very queer indeed it was; for the door at one end was as broad as the house itself! They entered, and lay down to sleep; but at midnight Thor was wakened by a terrible noise. The ground shook under them like an earthquake, and the house trembled as if it would fall to pieces. Thor arose and called to his companions that there was danger about, and that they must be on guard. Groping in the dark, they found a long, narrow chamber on the right, where Loki and the two peasants hid trembling, while Thor guarded the doorway, hammer in hand. All night long the terrible noises continued, and Thor's attendants were frightened almost to death; but early in the morning Thor stole forth to find out what it all meant. And lo! close at hand in the forest lay an enormous giant, sound asleep and snoring loudly. Then Thor understood whence all their night's terror had proceeded, for the giant was so huge that his snoring shook even the trees of the forest, and made the mountains tremble. So much the better! Here at last was a giant for Thor to tackle. He buckled his belt of power more tightly to increase his strength, and laid hold of Miölnir to hurl it at the giant's forehead; but just at that moment the giant waked, rose slowly to his feet, and stood staring mildly at Thor. He did not seem a fierce giant, so Thor did not kill him at once. "Who are you?" asked Thor sturdily.

"I am the giant Skrymir, little fellow," answered the stranger, "and well I know who you are, Thor of Asgard. But what have you been doing with my glove?"

Then the giant stooped and picked up—what do you think?—the queer house in which Thor and his three companions had spent the night! Loki and the two others had run out of their chamber in affright when they felt it lifted; and their chamber was the thumb of the giant's glove. That was a giant indeed, and Thor felt sure that they must be well upon their way to Giant Land.

When Skrymir learned where they were going, he asked if he might not wend with them, and Thor said that he was willing. Now Skrymir untied his wallet and sat down under a tree to eat his breakfast, while Thor and his party chose another place, not far away, for their picnic. When all had finished, the giant said, "Let us put our provisions together in one bag, my friends, and I will carry it for you." This seemed fair enough, for Thor had so little food left that he was not afraid to risk losing it; so he agreed, and Skrymir tied all the provisions in his bag and strode on before them with enormous strides, so fast that even Thialfi could scarcely keep up with him.

The day passed, and late in the evening Skrymir halted under a great oak-tree, saying, "Let us rest here. I must have a nap, and you must have your dinner. Here is the wallet,—open it and help yourselves." Then he lay down on the moss, and was soon snoring lustily.

Thor tried to open the wallet, in vain; he could not loosen a single knot of the huge thongs that fastened it. He strained and tugged, growing angrier and redder after every useless attempt. This was too much; the giant was making him appear absurd before his servants. He seized his hammer, and bracing his feet with all his might, struck Skrymir a blow on his head. Skrymir stirred lazily, yawned, opened one eye, and asked whether a leaf had fallen on his forehead, and whether his companions had dined yet. Thor bit his lip with vexation, but he answered that they were ready for bed; so he and his three followers retired to rest under another oak.

But Thor did not sleep that night. He lay thinking how he had been put to shame, and how Loki had snickered at the sight of Thor's vain struggles with the giant's wallet, and he resolved that it should not happen again. At about midnight, once more he heard the giant's snore resounding like thunder through the forest. Thor arose, clenching Miölnir tight, and stole over to the tree where Skrymir slept; then with all his might he hurled the hammer and struck the giant on the crown of his head, so hard that the hammer sank deep into his skull. At this the giant awoke with a start, exclaiming, "What is that? Did an acorn fall on my head? What are you doing there, Thor?"

Thor stepped back quickly, answering that he had waked up, but that it was only midnight, so they might all sleep some hours longer. "If I can only give him one more blow before morning," he thought, "he will never see daylight again." So he lay watching until Skrymir had fallen asleep once more, which was near daybreak; then Thor arose as before, and going very softly to the giant's side, smote him on the temple so sore that the hammer sank into his skull up to the very handle. "Surely, he is killed now," thought Thor.

But Skrymir only raised himself on his elbow, stroked his chin, and said, "There are birds above me in the tree. Methinks that just now a feather fell upon my head. What, Thor! are you awake? I am afraid you slept but poorly this night. Come, now, it is high time to rise and make ready for the day. You are not far from our giant city,—Utgard we call it. Aha! I have heard you whispering together. You think that I am big; but you will see fellows taller still when you come to Utgard. And now I have a piece of advice to give you. Do not pride yourselves overmuch upon your importance. The followers of Utgard's king think little of such manikins as you, and will not bear any nonsense, I assure you. Be advised; return homeward before it is too late. If you will go on, however, your way lies there to the eastward. Yonder is my path, over the mountains to the north."

So saying, Skrymir hoisted his wallet upon his shoulders, and turning back upon the path that led into the forest, left them staring after him and hoping that they might never see his big bulk again.

Thor and his companions journeyed on until noon, when they saw in the distance a great city, on a lofty plain. As they came nearer, they found the buildings so high that the travelers had to bend back their necks in order to see the tops. "This must be Utgard, the giant city," said Thor. And Utgard indeed it was. At the entrance was a great barred gate, locked so that no one might enter. It was useless to try to force a passage in; even Thor's great strength could not move it on its hinges. But it was a giant gate, and the bars were made to keep out other giants, with no thought of folk so small as these who now were bent upon finding entrance by one way or another. It was not dignified, and noble Thor disliked the idea. Yet it was their only way; so one by one they squeezed and wriggled between the bars, until they stood in a row inside. In front of them was a wonderful great hall with the door wide open. Thor and the three entered, and found themselves in the midst of a company of giants, the very hugest of their kind. At the end of the hall sat the king upon an enormous throne. Thor, who had been in giant companies ere now, went straight up to the throne and greeted the king with civil words. But the giant merely glanced at him with a disagreeable smile, and said,—

"It is wearying to ask travelers about their journey. Such little fellows as you four can scarcely have had any adventures worth mentioning. Stay, now! Do I guess aright? Is this manikin Thor of Asgard, or no? Ah, no! I have heard of Thor's might. You cannot really be he, unless you are taller than you seem, and stronger too. Let us see what feats you and your companions can perform to amuse us. No one is allowed here who cannot excel others in some way or another. What can you do best?"

At this word, Loki, who had entered last, spoke up readily: "There is one thing that I can do,—I can eat faster than any man." For Loki was famished with hunger, and thought he saw a way to win a good meal.

Then the king answered, "Truly, that is a noble accomplishment of yours, if you can prove your words true. Let us make the test." So he called forth from among his men Logi,—whose name means "fire,"—and bade him match his powers with the stranger.

Now a trough full of meat was set upon the floor, with Loki at one end of it and the giant Logi at the other. Each began to gobble the meat as fast as he could, and it was not a pretty sight to see them. Midway in the trough they met, and at first it would seem as if neither had beaten the other. Loki had indeed done wondrous well in eating the meat from the bones so fast; but Logi, the giant, had in the same time eaten not only meat but bones also, and had swallowed his half of the trough into the bargain. Loki was vanquished at his own game, and retired looking much ashamed and disgusted.

The king then pointed at Thialfi, and asked what that young man could best do. Thialfi answered that of all men he was the swiftest runner, and that he was not afraid to race with any one whom the king might select.

"That is a goodly craft," said the king, smiling; "but you must be a swift runner indeed if you can win a race from my Hugi. Let us go to the racing-ground."

They followed him out to the plain where Hugi, whose name means "thought," was ready to race with young Thialfi. In the first run Hugi came in so far ahead that when he reached the goal he turned about and went back to meet Thialfi. "You must do better than that, Thialfi, if you hope to win," said the king, laughing, "though I must allow that no one ever before came here who could run so fast as you."

They ran a second race; and this time when Hugi reached the goal there was a long bow-shot between him and Thialfi.

"You are truly a good runner," exclaimed the king. "I doubt not that no man can race like you; but you cannot win from my giant lad, I think. The last time shall show." Then they ran for the third time, and Thialfi put forth all his strength, speeding like the wind; but all his skill was in vain. Hardly had he reached the middle of the course when he heard the shouts of the giants announcing that Hugi had won the goal. Thialfi, too, was beaten at his own game, and he withdrew, as Loki had done, shamefaced and sulky.

There remained now only Thor to redeem the honor of his party, for Röskva the maiden was useless here. Thor had watched the result of these trials with surprise and anger, though he knew it was no fault of Loki or of Thialfi that they had been worsted by the giants. And Thor was resolved to better even his own former great deeds. The king called to Thor, and asked him what he thought he could best do to prove himself as mighty as the stories told of him. Thor answered that he would undertake to drink more mead than any one of the king's men. At this proposal the king laughed aloud, as if it were a giant joke. He summoned his cup-bearer to fetch his horn of pun-ishment, out of which the giants were wont to drink in turn. And when they returned to the hall, the great vessel was brought to the king.

"When any one empties this horn at one draught, we call him a famous drinker," said the king. "Some of my men empty it in two trials; but no one is so poor a manikin that he cannot empty it in three. Take the horn, Thor, and see what you can do with it."

Now Thor was very thirsty, so he seized the horn eagerly. It did not seem to him so very large, for he had drunk from other mighty vessels ere now. But indeed, it was deep. He raised it to his lips and took a long pull, saying to himself, "There! I have emptied it already, I know." Yet when he set the horn down to see how well he had done, he found that he seemed scarcely to have drained a drop; the horn was brimming as before. The king chuckled.

"Well, you have drunk but little," he said. "I would never have believed that famous Thor would lower the horn so soon. But doubtless you will fin-ish all at a second draught."

Instead of answering, Thor raised the horn once more to his lips, re-solved to do better than before. But for some reason the tip of the horn seemed hard to raise, and when he set the vessel down again his heart sank, for he feared that he had drunk even less than at his first trial. Yet he had really done better, for now it was easy to carry the horn without spilling. The king smiled grimly. "How now, Thor!" he cried. "You have left too much for your third trial. I fear you will never be able to empty the little horn in three draughts, as the least of my men can do. Ho, ho! You will not be thought so great a hero here as the folk deem you in Asgard, if you can-not play some other game more skillfully than you do this one."

At this speech Thor grew very angry. He raised the horn to his mouth and drank lustily, as long as he was able. But when he looked into the horn, he found that some drops still remained. He had not been able to empty it in three draughts. Angrily he flung down the horn, and said that he would have no more of it.

"Ah, Master Thor," taunted the king, "it is now plain that you are not so mighty as we thought you. Are you inclined to try some other feats? For indeed, you are easily beaten at this one."

"I will try whatever you like," said Thor; "but your horn is a wondrous one, and among the Æsir such a draught as mine would be called far from little. Come, now,—what game do you next propose, O King?"

The king thought a moment, then answered carelessly, "There is a little game with which my youngsters amuse themselves, though it is so simple as to be almost childish. It is merely the exercise of lifting my cat from the ground. I should never have dared suggest such a feat as this to you, Thor of Asgard, had I not seen that great tasks are beyond your skill. It may be that you will find this hard enough." So he spoke, smiling slyly, and at that moment there came stalking into the hall a monstrous gray cat, with eyes of yellow fire.

"Ho! Is this the creature I am to lift?" queried Thor. And when they said that it was, he seized the cat around its gray, huge body and tugged with all his might to lift it from the floor. Then the wretched cat, lengthening and lengthening, arched its back like the span of a bridge; and though Thor tugged and heaved his best, he could manage to lift but one of its huge feet off the floor. The other three remained as firmly planted as iron pillars.

"Oho, oho!" laughed the king, delighted at this sight. "It is just as I thought it would be. Poor little Thor! My cat is too big for him."

"Little I may seem in this land of monsters," cried Thor wrathfully, "but now let him who dares come hither and try a hug with me."

"Nay, little Thor," said the king, seeking to make him yet more angry, "there is not one of my men who would wrestle with you. Why, they would call it child's play, my little fellow. But, for the joke of it, call in my old foster-mother, Elli. She has wrestled with and worsted many a man who seemed no weaker than you, O Thor. She shall try a fall with you."

Now in came the old crone, Elli, whose very name meant "age." She was wrinkled and gray, and her back was bent nearly double with the weight of the years which she carried, but she chuckled when she saw Thor standing with bared arm in the middle of the floor. "Come and be thrown, dearie," she cried in her cracked voice, grinning horribly.

"I will not wrestle with a woman!" exclaimed Thor, eyeing her with pity and disgust, for she was an ugly creature to behold. But the old woman taunted him to his face and the giants clapped their hands, howling that he was "afraid." So there was no way but that Thor must grapple with the hag.

The game began. Thor rushed at the old woman and gripped her tightly in his iron arms, thinking that as soon as she screamed with the pain of his mighty hug, he would give over. But the crone seemed not to mind it at all. Indeed, the more he crushed her old ribs together the firmer and stronger she stood. Now in her turn the witch attempted to trip up Thor's heels, and it was wonderful to see her power and agility. Thor soon began to totter, great Thor, in the hands of a poor old woman! He struggled hard, he braced himself, he turned and twisted. It was no use; the old woman's arms were as strong as knotted oak. In a few moments Thor sank upon one knee, and that was a sign that he was beaten. The king signaled for them to stop. "You need wrestle no more, Thor," he said, with a curl to his lip, "we see what sort of fellow you are. I thought that old Elli would have no difficulty in bringing to his knees him who could not lift my cat. But come, now, night is almost here. We will think no more of contests. You and your companions shall sup with us as welcome guests and bide here till the morrow."

Now as soon as the king had pleased himself in proving how small and weak were these strangers who had come to the giant city, he became very gracious and kind. But you can fancy whether or no Thor and the others had a good appetite for the banquet where all the giants ate so merrily. You can fancy whether or no they were happy when they went to bed after the day of defeats, and you can guess what sweet dreams they had.

The next morning at daybreak the four guests arose and made ready to steal back to Asgard without attracting any more attention. For this adventure alone of all those in which Thor had taken part had been a disgraceful failure. Silently and with bowed heads they were slipping away from the hall when the king himself came to them and begged them to stay.

"You shall not leave Utgard without breakfast," he said kindly, "nor would I have you depart feeling unfriendly to me."

Then he ordered a goodly breakfast for the travelers, with store of choicest dainties for them to eat and drink. When the four had broken fast, he escorted them to the city gate where they were to say farewell. But at the last moment he turned to Thor with a sly, strange smile and asked,—

"Tell me now truly, brother Thor; what think you of your visit to the giant city? Do you feel as mighty a fellow as you did before you entered our gates, or are you satisfied that there are folk even sturdier than yourself?"

At this question Thor flushed scarlet, and the lightning flashed angrily in his eye. Briefly enough he answered that he must confess to small pride in his last adventure, for that his visit to the king had been full of shame to the hero of Asgard. "My name will become a joke among your people," quoth he. "You will call me Thor the puny little fellow, which vexes me more than anything; for I have not been wont to blush at my name."

Then the king looked at him frankly, pleased with the humble manner of Thor's speech. "Nay," he said slowly, "hang not your head so shamedly, brave Thor. You have not done so ill as you think. Listen, I have somewhat to tell you, now that you are outside Utgard,—which, if I live, you shall never enter again. Indeed, you should not have entered at all had I guessed what noble strength was really yours,—strength which very nearly brought me and my whole city to destruction."

To these words Thor and his companions listened with open-mouthed astonishment. What could the king mean, they wondered? The giant continued:—

"By magic alone were you beaten, Thor. Of magic alone were my triumphs,—not real, but seeming to be so. Do you remember the giant Skrymir whom you found sleeping and snoring in the forest? That was I. I learned your errand and resolved to lower your pride. When you vainly strove to untie my wallet, you did not know that I had fastened it with invisible iron wire, in order that you might be baffled by the knots. Thrice you struck me with your hammer,—ah! what mighty blows were those! The least one would have killed me, had it fallen on my head as you deemed it did. In my hall is a rock with three square hollows in it, one of them deeper than the others. These are the dents of your wondrous hammer, my Thor. For, while you thought I slept, I slipped the rock under the hammer-strokes, and into this hard crust Miölnir bit. Ha, ha! It was a pretty jest."

Now Thor's brow was growing black at this tale of the giant's trickery, but at the same time he held up his head and seemed less ashamed of his weakness, knowing now that it had been no weakness, but lack of guile. He listened frowningly for the rest of the tale. The king went on:—

"When you came to my city, still it was magic that worsted your party at every turn. Loki was certainly the hungriest fellow I ever saw, and his deeds at the trencher were marvelous to behold. But the Logi who ate with him was Fire, and easily enough fire can consume your meat, bones, and wood itself. Thialfi, my boy, you are a runner swift as the wind. Never before saw I such a race as yours. But the Hugi who ran with you was Thought, my thought. And who can keep pace with the speed of winged thought? Next, Thor, it was your turn to show your might. Bravely indeed you strove. My heart is sick with envy of your strength and skill. But they availed you naught against my magic. When you drank from the long horn, thinking you had done so ill, in truth you had performed a miracle,—never thought I to behold the like. You guessed not that the end of the horn was out in the ocean, which no one might drain dry. Yet, mighty one, the draughts you swallowed have lowered the tide upon the shore. Henceforth at certain times the sea will ebb; and this is by great Thor's drinking. The cat also which you almost lifted,—it was no cat, but the great Midgard serpent himself who encircles the whole world. He had barely length enough for his head and tail to touch in a circle about the sea. But you raised him so high that he almost touched heaven. How terrified we were when we saw you heave one of his mighty feet from the ground! For who could tell what horror might happen had you raised him bodily. Ah, and your wrestling with old Elli! That was the most marvelous act of all. You had nearly overthrown Age itself; yet there has never lived one, nor will such ever be found, whom Elli, old age, will not cast to earth at last. So you were beaten, Thor, but by a mere trick. Ha, ha! How angry you looked,—I shall never forget! But now we must part, and I think you see that it will be best for both of us that we should not meet again. As I have done once, so can I always protect my city by magic spells. Yes, should you come again to visit us, even better prepared than now, yet you could never do us serious harm. Yet the wear and tear upon the nerves of both of us is something not lightly forgotten."

He ceased, smiling pleasantly, but with a threatening look in his eye. Thor's wrath had been slowly rising during this tedious, grim speech, and he could control it no longer.

"Cheat and trickster!" he cried, "your wiles shall avail you nothing now that I know your true self. You have put me to shame, now my hammer shall shame you beyond all reckoning!" and he raised Miölnir to smite the giant deathfully. But at that moment the king faded before his very eyes. And when he turned to look for the giant city that he might destroy it,—as he had so many giant dwellings,—there was in the place where it had been but a broad, fair plain, with no sign of any palace, wall, or gate. Utgard had vanished. The king had kept one trick of magic for the last.

Then Thor and his three companions wended their way back to Asgard. But they were slower than usual about answering questions concerning their last adventure, their wondrous visit to the giant city. Truth to tell, magic or no magic, Thor and Loki had showed but a poor figure that day. For the first time in all their meeting with Thor the giants had not come off any the worse for the encounter. Perhaps it was a lesson that he sorely needed. I am afraid that he was rather inclined to think well of himself. But then, he had reason, had he not?

Thor's Fishing

Once upon a time the Æsir went to take dinner with old Œgir, the king of the ocean. Down under the green waves they went to the coral palace where Œgir lived with his wife, Queen Ran, and his daughters, the Waves. But Œgir was not expecting so large a party to dinner, and he had not mead enough for them all to drink. "I must brew some more mead," he said to himself. But when he came to look for a kettle in which to make the brew, there was none in all the sea large enough for the purpose. At first Œgir did not know what to do; but at last he decided to consult the gods themselves, for he knew how wise and powerful his guests were, and he hoped that they might help him to a kettle.

Now when he told the Æsir his trouble they were much interested, for they were hungry and thirsty, and longed for some of Œgir's good mead. "Where can we find a kettle?" they said to one another. "Who has a kettle huge enough to hold mead for all the Æsir?"

Then Týr the brave turned to Thor with a grand idea. "My father, the giant Hymir, has such a kettle," he said. "I have seen it often in his great palace near Elivâgar, the river of ice. This famous kettle is a mile deep, and surely that is large enough to brew all the mead we may need."

"Surely, surely it is large enough," laughed Œgir. "But how are we to get the kettle, my distinguished guests? Who will go to Giant Land to fetch the kettle a mile deep?"

"That will I," said brave Thor. "I will go to Hymir's dwelling and bring thence the little kettle, if Týr will go with me to show me the way." So Thor and Týr set out together for the land of snow and ice, where the giant Hymir lived. They traveled long and they traveled fast, and finally they came to the huge house which had once been Týr's home, before he went to live with the good folk in Asgard.

Well Týr knew the way to enter, and it was not long before they found themselves in the hall of Hymir's dwelling, peering about for some sign of the kettle which they had come so far to seek; and sure enough, presently they discovered eight huge kettles hanging in a row from one of the beams in the ceiling. While the two were wondering which kettle might be the one they sought, there came in Týr's grandmother,—and a terrible grandmother she was. No wonder that Týr had run away from home when he was very little; for this dreadful creature was a giantess with nine hundred heads, each more ugly than the others, and her temper was as bad as were her looks. She began to roar and bellow; and no one knows what this evil old person would have done to her grandson and his friend had not there come into the hall at this moment another woman, fair and sweet, and glittering with golden ornaments. This was Týr's good mother, who loved him dearly, and who had mourned his absence during long years.

With a cry of joy she threw herself upon her son's neck, bidding him welcome forty times over. She welcomed Thor also when she found out who he was; but she sent away the wicked old grandmother, that she might not hear, for Thor's name was not dear to the race of giants, to so many of whom he had brought dole and death.

"Why have you come, dear son, after so many years?" she cried. "I know that some great undertaking calls you and this noble fellow to your father's hall. Danger and death wait here for such as you and he; and only some quest with glory for its reward could have brought you to such risks. Tell me your secret, Týr, and I will not betray it."

Then they told her how that they had come to carry away the giant kettle; and Týr's mother promised that she would help them all she could. But she warned them that it would be dangerous indeed, for that Hymir had been in a terrible temper for many days, and that the very sight of a stranger made him wild with rage. Hastily she gave them meat and drink, for they were nearly famished after their long journey; and then she looked around to see where she should hide them against Hymir's return, who was now away at the hunt.

"Aha!" she cried. "The very thing! You shall hide in the great kettle itself; and if you escape Hymir's terrible eye, it may hap that you will find a way to make off with your hiding-place, which is what you want." So the kind creature helped them to climb into the great kettle where it hung from one of the rafters in a row with seven others; but this one was the biggest and the strongest of them all.

Hardly had they snuggled down out of sight when Týr's mother began to tremble. "Hist!" she cried. "I hear him coming. Keep as still as ever you can, O Týr and Thor!" The floor also began to tremble, and the eight kettles to clatter against one another, as Hymir's giant footsteps approached the house. Outside they could hear the icebergs shaking with a sound like thunder; indeed, the whole earth quivered as if with fear when the terrible giant Hymir strode home from the hunt. He came into the hall puffing and blowing, and immediately the air of the room grew chilly; for his beard was hung with icicles and his face was frosted hard, while his breath was a winter wind,—a freezing blast.

"Ho! wife," he growled, "what news, what news? For I see by the footprints in the snow outside that you have had visitors to-day."

Then indeed the poor woman trembled; but she tried not to look frightened as she answered, "Yes, you have a guest, O Hymir!—a guest whom you have long wished to see. Your son Týr has returned to visit his father's hall."

"Humph!" growled Hymir, with a terrible frown. "Whom has he brought here with him, the rascal? There are prints of two persons' feet in the snow. Come, wife, tell me all; for I shall soon find out the truth, whether or no."

"He has brought a friend of his,—a dear friend, O Hymir!" faltered the mother. "Surely, our son's friends are welcome when he brings them to this our home, after so long an absence."

But Hymir howled with rage at the word "friend." "Where are they hidden?" he cried. "Friend, indeed! It is one of those bloody fellows from Asgard, I know,—one of those giant-killers whom my good mother taught me to hate with all my might. Let me get at him! Tell me instantly where he is hidden, or I will pull down the hall about your ears!"

Now when the wicked old giant spoke like this, his wife knew that he must be obeyed. Still she tried to put off the fateful moment of the discovery. "They are standing over there behind that pillar," she said. Instantly Hymir glared at the pillar towards which she pointed, and at his frosty glance—snick-snack!—the marble pillar cracked in two, and down crashed the great roof-beam which held the eight kettles. Smash! went the kettles; and there they lay shivered into little pieces at Hymir's feet,—all except one, the largest of them all, and that was the kettle in which Thor and Týr lay hidden, scarcely daring to breathe lest the giant should guess where they were. Týr's mother screamed when she saw the big kettle fall with the others: but when she found that this one, alone of them all, lay on its side unbroken, because it was so tough and strong, she held her breath to see what would happen next.

And what happened was this: out stepped Thor and Týr, and making low bows to Hymir, they stood side by side, smiling and looking as unconcerned as if they really enjoyed all this hubbub; and I dare say that they did indeed, being Týr the bold and Thor the thunderer, who had been in Giant Land many times ere this.

Hymir gave scarcely a glance at his son, but he eyed Thor with a frown of hatred and suspicion, for he knew that this was one of Father Odin's brave family, though he could not tell which one. However, he thought best to be civil, now that Thor was actually before him. So with gruff politeness he invited the two guests to supper.

Now Thor was a valiant fellow at the table as well as in war, as you remember; and at sight of the good things on the board his eyes sparkled. Three roast oxen there were upon the giant's table, and Thor fell to with a will and finished two of them himself! You should have seen the giant stare.

"Truly, friend, you have a goodly appetite," he said. "You have eaten all the meat that I have in my larder; and if you dine with us to-morrow, I must insist that you catch your own dinner of fish. I cannot undertake to provide food for such an appetite!"

Now this was not hospitable of Hymir, but Thor did not mind. "I like well to fish, good Hymir," he laughed; "and when you fare forth with your boat in the morning, I will go with you and see what I can find for my dinner at the bottom of the sea."

When the morning came, the giant made ready for the fishing, and Thor rose early to go with him.

"Ho, Hymir," exclaimed Thor, "have you bait enough for us both?"

Hymir answered gruffly, "You must dig your own bait when you go fishing with me. I have no time to waste on you, sirrah."

Then Thor looked about to see what he could use for bait; and presently he spied a herd of Hymir's oxen feeding in the meadow. "Aha! just the thing!" he cried; and seizing the hugest ox of all, he trotted down to the shore with it under his arm, as easily as you would carry a handful of clams for bait. When Hymir saw this, he was very angry. He pushed the boat off from shore and began to row away as fast as he could, so that Thor might not have a chance to come aboard. But Thor made one long step and planted himself snugly in the stern of the boat.

"No, no, brother Hymir," he said, laughing. "You invited me to go fishing, and a-fishing I will go; for I have my bait, and my hope is high that great luck I shall see this day." So he took an oar and rowed mightily in the stern, while Hymir the giant rowed mightily at the prow; and no one ever saw boat skip over the water so fast as this one did on the day when these two big fellows went fishing together.

Far and fast they rowed, until they came to a spot where Hymir cried, "Hold! Let us anchor here and fish; this is the place where I have best fortune."

"And what sort of little fish do you catch here, O Hymir?" asked Thor.

"Whales!" answered the giant proudly. "I fish for nothing smaller than whales."

"Pooh!" cried Thor. "Who would fish for such small fry! Whales, indeed; let us row out further, where we can find something really worth catching," and he began to pull even faster than before.

"Stop! stop!" roared the giant. "You do not know what you are doing. These are the haunts of the dreadful Midgard serpent, and it is not safe to fish in these waters."

"Oho! The Midgard serpent!" said Thor, delighted. "That is the very fish I am after. Let us drop in our lines here."

Thor baited his great hook with the whole head of the ox which he had brought, and cast his line, big round as a man's arm, over the side of the boat. Hymir also cast his line, for he did not wish Thor to think him a coward; but his hand trembled as he waited for a bite, and he glanced down into the blue depths with eyes rounded as big as dinner-plates through fear of the horrible creature who lived down below those waves.

"Look! You have a bite!" cried Thor, so suddenly that Hymir started and nearly tumbled out of the boat. Hand over hand he pulled in his line, and lo! he had caught two whales—two great flopping whales—on his one hook! That was a catch indeed.

Hymir smiled proudly, forgetting his fear as he said, "How is that, my friend? Let us see you beat this catch in your morning's fishing."

Lo, just at that moment Thor also had a bite—such a bite! The boat rocked to and fro, and seemed ready to capsize every minute. Then the waves began to roll high and to be lashed into foam for yards and yards about the boat, as if some huge creature were struggling hard below the water.

"I have him!" shouted Thor; "I have the old serpent, the brother of the Fenris wolf! Pull, pull, monster! But you shall not escape me now!"

Sure enough, the Midgard serpent had Thor's hook fixed in his jaw, and struggle as he might, there was no freeing himself from the line; for the harder he pulled the stronger grew Thor. In his Æsir-might Thor waxed so huge and so forceful that his legs went straight through the bottom of the boat and his feet stood on the bottom of the sea. With firm bottom as a brace for his strength, Thor pulled and pulled, and at last up came the head of the Midgard serpent, up to the side of the boat, where it thrust out of the water mountain high, dreadful to behold; his monstrous red eyes were rolling fiercely, his nostrils spouted fire, and from his terrible sharp teeth dripped poison, that sizzled as it fell into the sea. Angrily they glared at each other, Thor and the serpent, while the water streamed into the boat, and the giant turned pale with fear at the danger threatening him on all sides.

Thor seized his hammer, preparing to smite the creature's head; but even as he swung Miölnir high for the fatal blow, Hymir cut the fish-line with his knife, and down into the depths of ocean sank the Midgard serpent amid a whirlpool of eddies. But the hammer had sped from Thor's iron fingers. It crushed the serpent's head as he sank downward to his lair on the sandy bottom; it crushed, but did not kill him, thanks to the giant's treachery. Terrible was the disturbance it caused beneath the waves. It burst the rocks and made the caverns of the ocean shiver into bits. It wrecked the coral groves and tore loose the draperies of sea-weed. The fishes scurried about in every direction, and the sea-monsters wildly sought new places to hide themselves when they found their homes destroyed. The sea itself was stirred to its lowest depths, and the waves ran trembling into one another's arms. The earth, too, shrank and shivered. Hymir, cowering low in the boat, was glad of one thing, which was that the terrible Midgard serpent had vanished out of sight. And that was the last that was ever seen of him, though he still lived, wounded and sore from the shock of Thor's hammer.

Now it was time to return home. Silently and sulkily the giant swam back to land; Thor, bearing the boat upon his shoulders, filled with water and weighted as it was with the great whales which Hymir had caught, waded ashore, and brought his burden to the giant's hall. Here Hymir met him crossly enough, for he was ashamed of the whole morning's work, in which Thor had appeared so much more of a hero than he. Indeed, he was tired of even pretending hospitality towards this unwelcome guest, and was resolved to be rid of him; but first he would put Thor to shame.

"You are a strong fellow," he said, "good at the oar and at the fishing; most wondrously good at the hammer, by which I know that you are Thor. But there is one thing which you cannot do, I warrant,—you cannot break this little cup of mine, hard though you may try."

"That I shall see for myself," answered Thor; and he took the cup in his hand. Now this was a magic cup, and there was but one way of breaking it, but one thing hard enough to shatter its mightiness. Thor threw it with all his force against a stone of the flooring; but instead of breaking the cup, the stone itself was cracked into splinters. Then Thor grew angry, for the giant and all his servants were laughing as if this were the greatest joke ever played.

"Ho, ho! Try again, Thor!" cried Hymir, nearly bursting with delight; for he thought that now he should prove how much mightier he was than the visitor from Asgard. Thor clutched the cup more firmly and hurled it against one of the iron pillars of the hall; but like a rubber ball the magic cup merely bounded back straight into Hymir's hand. At this second failure the giants were full of merriment and danced about, making all manner of fun at the expense of Thor. You can fancy how well Thor the mighty enjoyed this! His brow grew black, and the glance of his eye was terrible. He knew there was some magic in the trick, but he knew not how to meet it. Just then he felt the soft touch of a woman's hand upon his arm, and the voice of Týr's mother whispered in his ear,—

"Cast the cup against Hymir's own forehead, which is the hardest substance in the world." No one except Thor heard the woman say these words, for all the giant folk were doubled up with mirth over their famous joke. But Thor dropped upon one knee, and seizing the cup fiercely, whirled it about his head, then dashed it with all his might straight at Hymir's forehead. Smash! Crash! What had happened? Thor looked eagerly to see. There stood the giant, looking surprised and a little dazed; but his forehead showed not even a scratch, while the strong cup was shivered into little pieces.

"Well done!" exclaimed Hymir hastily, when he had recovered a little from his surprise. But he was mortified at Thor's success, and set about to think up a new task to try his strength. "That was very well," he remarked patronizingly; "now you must perform a harder task. Let us see you carry the mead kettle out of the hall. Do that, my fine fellow, and I shall say you are strong indeed."

The mead kettle! The very thing Thor had come to get! He glanced at Týr; he shot a look at Týr's mother; and both of them caught the sparkle, which was very like a wink. To himself Thor muttered, "I must not fail in this! I must not, will not fail!"

"First let me try," cried Týr; for he wanted to give Thor time for a resting-spell. Twice Týr the mighty strained at the great kettle, but he could not so much as stir one leg of it from the floor where it rested. He tugged and heaved in vain, growing red in the face, till his mother begged him to give over, for it was quite useless.

Then Thor stepped forth upon the floor. He grasped the rim of the kettle, and stamped his feet through the stone of the flooring as he braced himself to lift. One, two, three! Thor straightened himself, and up swung the giant kettle to his head, while the iron handle clattered about his feet. It was a mighty burden, and Thor staggered as he started for the door; but Týr was close beside him, and they had covered long leagues of ground on their way home before the astonished giants had recovered sufficiently to follow them. When Thor and Týr looked back, however, they saw a vast crowd of horrible giants, some of them with a hundred heads, swarming out of the caverns in Hymir's land, howling and prowling upon their track.

"You must stop them, Thor, or they will never let us get away with their precious kettle,—they take such long strides!" cried Týr. So Thor set down the kettle, and from his pocket drew out Miölnir, his wondrous hammer. Terribly it flashed in the air as he swung it over his head; then forth it flew towards Jotunheim; and before it returned to Thor's hand it had crushed all the heads of those many-headed giants, Hymir's ugly mother and Hymir himself among them. The only one who escaped was the good and beautiful mother of Týr. And you may be sure she lived happily ever after in the palace which Hymir and his wicked old mother had formerly made so wretched a home for her.

Now Týr and Thor had the giant kettle which they had gone so far and had met so many dangers to obtain. They took it to Œgir's sea-palace, where the banquet was still going on, and where the Æsir were still waiting patiently for their mead; for time does not go so fast below the quiet waves as on shore. Now that King Œgir had the great kettle, he could brew all the mead they needed. So every one thanked Týr and congratulated Thor upon the success of their adventure.

"I was sure that Thor would bring the kettle," said fair Sif, smiling upon her brave husband.

"What Thor sets out to do, that he always accomplishes," said Father Odin gravely. And that was praise enough for any one.

Thor's Duel

In the days that are past a wonderful race of horses pastured in the meadows of heaven, steeds more beautiful and more swift than any which the world knows to-day. There was Hrîmfaxi, the black, sleek horse who drew the chariot of Night across the sky and scattered the dew from his foaming bit. There was Glad, behind whose flying heels sped the swift chariot of Day. His mane was yellow with gold, and from it beamed light which made the whole world bright. Then there were the two shining horses of the sun, Arvakur the watchful, and Alsvith the rapid; and the nine fierce battle-chargers of the nine Valkyries, who bore the bodies of fallen heroes from the field of fight to the blessedness of Valhalla. Each of the gods had his own glorious steed, with such pretty names as Gold-mane and Silver-top, Light-foot and Precious-stone; these galloped with their masters over clouds and through the blue air, blowing flame from their nostrils and glinting sparks from their fiery eyes. The Æsir would have been poor indeed without their faithful mounts, and few would be the stories to tell in which these noble creatures do not bear at least a part.

But best of all the horses of heaven was Sleipnir, the eight-legged steed of Father Odin, who because he was so well supplied with sturdy feet could gallop faster over land and sea than any horse which ever lived. Sleipnir was snow-white and beautiful to see, and Odin was very fond and proud of him, you may be sure. He loved to ride forth upon his good horse's back to meet whatever adventure might be upon the way, and sometimes they had wild times together.

One day Odin galloped off from Asgard upon Sleipnir straight towards Jotunheim and the Land of Giants, for it was long since All-Father had been to the cold country, and he wished to see how its mountains and ice-rivers looked. Now as he galloped along a wild road, he met a huge giant standing beside his giant steed.

"Who goes there?" cried the giant gruffly, blocking the way so that Odin could not pass. "You with the golden helmet, who are you, who ride so famously through air and water? For I have been watching you from this mountain-top. Truly, that is a fine horse which you bestride."

"There is no finer horse in all the world," boasted Odin. "Have you not heard of Sleipnir, the pride of Asgard? I will match him against any of your big, clumsy giant horses."

"Ho!" roared the giant angrily, "an excellent horse he is, your little Sleipnir. But I warrant he is no match for my Gullfaxi here. Come, let us try a race; and at its end I shall pay you for your insult to our horses of Jotunheim."

So saying, the giant, whose ugly name was Hrungnir, sprang upon his horse and spurred straight at Odin in the narrow way. Odin turned and galloped back towards Asgard with all his might; for not only must he prove his horse's speed, but he must save himself and Sleipnir from the anger of the giant, who was one of the fiercest and wickedest of all his fierce and wicked race.

How the eight slender legs of Sleipnir twinkled through the blue sky! How his nostrils quivered and shot forth fire and smoke! Like a flash of lightning he darted across the sky, and the giant horse rumbled and thumped along close behind like the thunder following the flash.

"Hi, hi!" yelled the giant. "After them, Gullfaxi! And when we have overtaken the two, we will crush their bones between us!"

"Speed, speed, my Sleipnir!" shouted Odin. "Speed, good horse, or you will never again feed in the dewy pastures of Asgard with the other horses. Speed, speed, and bring us safe within the gates!"

Well Sleipnir understood what his master said, and well he knew the way. Already the rainbow bridge was in sight, with Heimdal the watchman prepared to let them in. His sharp eyes had spied them afar, and had recognized the flash of Sleipnir's white body and of Odin's golden helmet. Gallop and thud! The twelve hoofs were upon the bridge, the giant horse close behind the other. At last Hrungnir knew where he was, and into what danger he was rushing. He pulled at the reins and tried to stop his great beast. But Gullfaxi was tearing along at too terrible a speed. He could not stop. Heimdal threw open the gates of Asgard, and in galloped Sleipnir with his precious burden, safe. Close upon them bolted in Gullfaxi, bearing his giant master, puffing and purple in the face from hard riding and anger. Cling-clang! Heimdal had shut and barred the gates, and there was the giant prisoned in the castle of his enemies.

Now the Æsir were courteous folk, unlike the giants, and they were not anxious to take advantage of a single enemy thus thrown into their power. They invited him to enter Valhalla with them, to rest and sup before the long journey of his return. Thor was not present, so they filled for the giant the great cups which Thor was wont to drain, for they were nearest to the giant size. But you remember that Thor was famous for his power to drink deep. Hrungnir's head was not so steady; Thor's draught was too much for him. He soon lost his wits, of which he had but few; and a witless giant is a most dreadful creature. He raged like a madman, and threatened to pick up Valhalla like a toy house and carry it home with him to Jotunheim. He said he would pull Asgard to pieces and slay all the gods except Freia the fair and Sif, the golden-haired wife of Thor, whom he would carry off like little dolls for his toy house.

The Æsir knew not what to do, for Thor and his hammer were not there to protect them, and Asgard seemed in danger with this enemy within its very walls. Hrungnir called for more and more mead, which Freia alone dared to bring and set before him. And the more he drank the fiercer he became. At last the Æsir could bear no longer his insults and his violence. Besides, they feared that there would be no more mead left for their banquets if this unwelcome visitor should keep Freia pouring out for him Thor's mighty goblets. They bade Heimdal blow his horn and summon Thor; and this Heimdal did in a trice.

Now rumbling and thundering in his chariot of goats came Thor. He dashed into the hall, hammer in hand, and stared in amazement at the unwieldy guest whom he found there.

"A giant feasting in Asgard hall!" he roared. "This is a sight which I never saw before. Who gave the insolent fellow leave to sit in my place? And why does fair Freia wait upon him as if he were some noble guest at a feast of the high gods? I will slay him at once!" and he raised the hammer to keep his word.

Thor's coming had sobered the giant somewhat, for he knew that this was no enemy to be trifled with. He looked at Thor sulkily and said: "I am Odin's guest. He invited me to this banquet, and therefore I am under his protection."

"You shall be sorry that you accepted the invitation," cried Thor, balancing his hammer and looking very fierce; for Sif had sobbed in his ear how the giant had threatened to carry her away.

Hrungnir now rose to his feet and faced Thor boldly, for the sound of Thor's gruff voice had restored his scattered wits. "I am here alone and without weapons," he said. "You would do ill to slay me now. It would be little like the noble Thor, of whom we hear tales, to do such a thing. The world will count you braver if you let me go and meet me later in single combat, when we shall both be fairly armed."

Thor dropped the hammer to his side. "Your words are true," he said, for he was a just and honorable fellow.

"I was foolish to leave my shield and stone club at home," went on the giant. "If I had my arms with me, we would fight at this moment. But I name you a coward if you slay me now, an unarmed enemy."

"Your words are just," quoth Thor again. "I have never before been challenged by any foe. I will meet you, Hrungnir, at your Stone City, midway between heaven and earth. And there we will fight a duel to see which of us is the better fellow."

Hrungnir departed for Stone City in Jotunheim; and great was the excitement of the other giants when they heard of the duel which one of their number was to fight with Thor, the deadliest enemy of their race.

"We must be sure that Hrungnir wins the victory!" they cried. "It will never do to have Asgard victorious in the first duel that we have fought with her champion. We will make a second hero to aid Hrungnir."

All the giants set to work with a will. They brought great buckets of moist clay, and heaping them up into a huge mound, moulded the mass with their giant hands as a sculptor does his image, until they had made a man of clay, an immense dummy, nine miles high and three miles wide. "Now we must make him live; we must put a heart into him!" they cried. But they could find no heart big enough until they thought of taking that of a mare, and that fitted nicely. A mare's heart is the most cowardly one that beats.

Hrungnir's heart was a three-cornered piece of hard stone. His head also was of stone, and likewise the great shield which he held before him when he stood outside of Stone City waiting for Thor to come to the duel. Over his shoulder he carried his club, and that also was of stone, the kind from which whetstones are made, hard and terrible. By his side stood the huge clay man, Möckuralfi, and they were a dreadful sight to see, these two vast bodies whom Thor must encounter.

But at the very first sight of Thor, who came thundering to the place with swift Thialfi his servant, the timid mare's heart in the man of clay throbbed with fear; he trembled so that his knees knocked together, and his nine miles of height rocked unsteadily.

Thialfi ran up to Hrungnir and began to mock him, saying, "You are careless, giant. I fear you do not know what a mighty enemy has come to fight you. You hold your shield in front of you; but that will serve you nothing. Thor has seen this. He has only to go down into the earth and he can attack you conveniently from beneath your very feet."

At this terrifying news Hrungnir hastened to throw his shield upon the ground and to stand upon it, so that he might be safe from Thor's under-stroke. He grasped his heavy club with both hands and waited. He had not long to wait. There came a blinding flash of lightning and a peal of crashing thunder. Thor had cast his hammer into space. Hrungnir raised his club with both hands and hurled it against the hammer which he saw flying towards him. The two mighty weapons met in the air with an earsplitting shock. Hard as was the stone of the giant's club, it was like glass against the power of Miölnir. The club was dashed into pieces; some fragments fell upon the earth; and these, they say, are the rocks from which whetstones are made unto this day. They are so hard that men use them to sharpen knives and ax-es and scythes. One splinter of the hard stone struck Thor himself in the forehead, with so fierce a blow that he fell forward upon the ground, and Thialfi feared that he was killed. But Miölnir, not even stopped in its course by meeting the giant's club, sped straight to Hrungnir and crushed his stony skull, so that he fell forward over Thor, and his foot lay on the fallen hero's neck. And that was the end of the giant whose head and heart were of stone.

Meanwhile Thialfi the swift had fought with the man of clay, and had found little trouble in toppling him to earth. For the mare's cowardly heart in his great body gave him little strength to meet Thor's faithful servant; and the trembling limbs of Möckuralfi soon yielded to Thialfi's hearty blows. He fell like an unsteady tower of blocks, and his brittle bulk shivered into a thousand fragments.

Thialfi ran to his master and tried to raise him. The giant's great foot still rested upon his neck, and all Thialfi's strength could not move it away. Swift as the wind he ran for the other Æsir, and when they heard that great Thor, their champion, had fallen and seemed like one dead, they came rushing to the spot in horror and confusion. Together they all attempted to raise Hrungnir's foot from Thor's neck that they might see whether their hero lived or no. But all their efforts were in vain. The foot was not to be lifted by Æsir-might.

At this moment a second hero appeared upon the scene. It was Magni, the son of Thor himself; Magni, who was but three days old, yet already in his babyhood he was almost as big as a giant and had nearly the strength of his father. This wonderful youngster came running to the place where his father lay surrounded by a group of sad-faced and despairing gods. When Magni saw what the matter was, he seized Hrungnir's enormous foot in both his hands, heaved his broad young shoulders, and in a moment Thor's neck was free of the weight which was crushing it.

Best of all, it proved that Thor was not dead, only stunned by the blow of the giant's club and by his fall. He stirred, sat up painfully, and looked around him at the group of eager friends. "Who lifted the weight from my neck?" he asked.

"It was I, father," answered Magni modestly. Thor clasped him in his arms and hugged him tight, beaming with pride and gratitude.

"Truly, you are a fine child!" he cried; "one to make glad your father's heart. Now as a reward for your first great deed you shall have a gift from me. The swift horse of Hrungnir shall be yours,—that same Gullfaxi who was the beginning of all this trouble. You shall ride Gullfaxi; only a giant steed is strong enough to bear the weight of such an infant prodigy as you, my Magni."

Now this word did not wholly please Father Odin, for he thought that a horse so excellent ought to belong to him. He took Thor aside and argued that but for him there would have been no duel, no horse to win. Thor answered simply,—

"True, Father Odin, you began this trouble. But I have fought your battle, destroyed your enemy, and suffered great pain for you. Surely, I have won the horse fairly and may give it to whom I choose. My son, who has saved me, deserves a horse as good as any. Yet, as you have proved, even Gullfaxi is scarce a match for your Sleipnir. Verily, Father Odin, you should be content with the best." Odin said no more.

Now Thor went home to his cloud-palace in Thrudvang. And there he was healed of all his hurts except that which the splinter of stone had made in his forehead. For the stone was imbedded so fast that it could not be taken out, and Thor suffered sorely therefor. Sif, his yellow-haired wife, was in despair, knowing not what to do. At last she bethought her of the wise woman, Groa, who had skill in all manner of herbs and witch charms. Sif sent for Groa, who lived all alone and sad because her husband Örvandil had disappeared, she knew not whither. Groa came to Thor and, standing beside his bed while he slept, sang strange songs and gently waved her hands over him. Immediately the stone in his forehead began to loosen, and Thor opened his eyes.

"The stone is loosening, the stone is coming out!" he cried. "How can I reward you, gentle dame? Prithee, what is your name?"

"My name is Groa," answered the woman, weeping, "wife of Örvandil who is lost."

"Now, then, I can reward you, kind Groa!" cried Thor, "for I can bring you tidings of your husband. I met him in the cold country, in Jotunheim, the Land of Giants, which you know I sometimes visit for a bit of good hunting. It was by Elivâgar's icy river that I met Örvandil, and there was no way for him to cross. So I put him in an iron basket and myself bore him over the flood. Br-r-r! But that is a cold land! His feet stuck out through the meshes of the basket, and when we reached the other side one of his toes was frozen stiff. So I broke it off and tossed it up into the sky that it might become a star. To prove that what I relate is true, Groa, there is the new star shining over us at this very moment. Look! From this day it shall be known to men as Örvandil's Toe. Do not you weep any longer. After all, the loss of a toe is a little thing; and I promise that your husband shall soon return to you, safe and sound, but for that small token of his wanderings in the land where visitors are not welcome."

At these joyful tidings poor Groa was so overcome that she fainted. And that put an end to the charm which she was weaving to loosen the stone from Thor's forehead. The stone was not yet wholly free, and thenceforth it was in vain to attempt its removal; Thor must always wear the splinter in his forehead. Groa could never forgive herself for the carelessness which had thus made her skill vain to help one to whom she had reason to be so grateful.

Now because of the bit of whetstone in Thor's forehead, folk of olden times were very careful how they used a whetstone; and especially they knew that they must not throw or drop one on the floor. For when they did so, the splinter in Thor's forehead was jarred, and the good Asa suffered great pain.

In the Giant's House

Although Thor had slain Thiasse the giant builder, Thrym the thief, Hrungnir, and Hymir, and had rid the world of whole families of wicked giants, there remained many others in Jotunheim to do their evil deeds and to plot mischief against both gods and men; and of these Geirröd was the fiercest and the wickedest. He and his two ugly daughters—Gialp of the red eyes, and Greip of the black teeth—lived in a large palace among the mountains, where Geirröd had his treasures of iron and copper, silver and gold; for, since the death of Thrym, Geirröd was the Lord of the Mines, and all the riches that came out of the earth-caverns belonged to him.

Thrym had been Geirröd's friend, and the tale of Thrym's death through the might of Thor and his hammer had made Geirröd very sad and angry. "If I could but catch Thor, now, without his weapons," he said to his daughters, "what a lesson I would give him! How I would punish him for his deeds against us giants!"

"Oh, what would you do, father?" cried Gialp, twinkling her cruel red eyes, and working her claw fingers as if she would like to fasten them in Thor's golden beard.

"Oh, what would you do, father?" cried Greip, smacking her lips and grinding her black teeth as if she would like a bite out of Thor's stout arm.

"Do to him!" growled Geirröd fiercely. "Do to him! Gr-r-r! I would chew him all up! I would break his bones into little bits! I would smash him into jelly!"

"Oh, good, good! Do it, father, and then give him to us to play with," cried Gialp and Greip, dancing up and down till the hills trembled and all the frightened sheep ran home to their folds thinking that there must be an earthquake; for Gialp was as tall as a pine-tree and many times as thick, while Greip, her little sister, was as large around as a haystack and high as a flagstaff. They both hoped some day to be as huge as their father, whose legs were so long that he could step across the river valleys from one hilltop to another, just as we human folk cross a brook on stepping-stones; and his arms were so stout that he could lift a yoke of oxen in each fist, as if they were red-painted toys.

Geirröd shook his head at his two playful daughters and sighed. "We must catch Master Thor first, my girls, before we do these fine things to him. We must catch him without his mighty hammer, that never fails him, and without his belt, that doubles his strength whenever he puts it on, or even I cannot chew and break and smash him as he deserves; for with these his weapons he is the mightiest creature in the whole world, and I would rather meddle with thunder and lightning than with him. Let us wait, children."

Then Gialp and Greip pouted and sulked like two great babies who cannot have the new plaything which they want; and very ugly they were to see, with tears as big as oranges rolling down their cheeks.

Sooner than they expected they came very near to having their heart's desire fulfilled. And if it had happened as they wished, and if Asgard had lost its goodliest hero, its strongest defense, that would have been red Loki's fault, all Loki's evil planning; for you are now to hear of the wickedest thing that up to this time Loki had ever done. As you know, it was Loki who was Thor's bitterest enemy; and for many months he had been awaiting the chance to repay the Thunder Lord for the dole which Thor had brought upon him at the time of the dwarf's gifts to Asgard.

This is how it came about: Loki had long remembered the fun of skimming as a great bird in Freia's falcon feathers. He had longed to borrow the wings once again and to fly away over the round world to see what he could see; for he thought that so he could learn many secrets which he was not meant to know, and plan wonderful mischief without being found out. But Freia would not again loan her feather dress to Loki. She owed him a grudge for naming her as Thrym's bride; and besides, she remembered his treatment of Idun, and she did not trust his oily tongue and fine promises. So Loki saw no way but to borrow the feathers without leave; and this he did one day when Freia was gone to ride in her chariot drawn by white cats. Loki put on the feather dress, as he had done twice before,—once when he went to Jotunheim to bring back stolen Idun and her magic apples, once when he went to find out about Thor's hammer.

Away he flew from Asgard as birdlike as you please, chuckling to himself with wicked thoughts. It did not make any particular difference to him where he went. It was such fun to flap and fly, skim and wheel, looking and feeling for all the world like a big brown falcon. He swooped low, thinking, "I wonder what Freia would say to see me now! Whee-e-e! How angry she would be!" Just then he spied the high wall of a palace on the mountains.

"Oho!" said Loki. "I never saw that place before. It may be a giant's dwelling. I think this must be Jotunheim, from the bigness of things. I must just peep to see." Loki was the most inquisitive of creatures, as wily minded folk are apt to be.

Loki the falcon alighted and hopped to the wall, then giving a flap of his wings he flew up and up to the window ledge, where he perched and peered into the hall. And there within he saw the giant Geirröd with his daughters eating their dinner. They looked so ugly and so greedy, as they sat there gobbling their food in giant mouthfuls, that Loki on the window-sill could not help snickering to himself. Now at that sound Geirröd looked up and saw the big brown bird peeping in at the window.

"Heigha!" cried the giant to one of his servants. "Go you and fetch me the big brown bird up yonder in the window."

Then the servant ran to the wall and tried to climb up to get at Loki; but the window was so high that he could not reach. He jumped and slipped, scrambled and slipped, again and again, while Loki sat just above his clutching fingers, and chuckled so that he nearly fell from his perch. "Te-he! te-he!" chattered Loki in the falcon tongue. It was such fun to see the fellow grow black in the face with trying to reach him that Loki thought he would wait until the giant's fingers almost touched him, before flying away.

But Loki waited too long. At last, with a quick spring, the giant gained a hold upon the window ledge, and Loki was within reach. When Loki flapped his wings to fly, he found that his feet were tangled in the vine that grew upon the wall. He struggled and twisted with all his might,—but in vain. There he was, caught fast. Then the servant grasped him by the legs, and so brought him to Geirröd, where he sat at table. Now Loki in his feather dress looked exactly like a falcon—except for his eyes. There was no hiding the wise and crafty look of Loki's eyes. As soon as Geirröd looked at him, he suspected that this was no ordinary bird.

"You are no falcon, you!" he cried. "You are spying about my palace in disguise. Speak, and tell me who you are." Loki was afraid to tell, because he knew the giants were angry with him for his part in Thrym's death,— small though his part had really been in that great deed. So he kept his beak closed tight, and refused to speak. The giant stormed and raged and threatened to kill him; but still Loki was silent.

Then Geirröd locked the falcon up in a chest for three long months without food or water, to see how that would suit his bird-ship. You can imagine how hungry and thirsty Loki was at the end of that time,—ready to tell anything he knew, and more also, for the sake of a crumb of bread and a drop of water.

So then Geirröd called through the keyhole, "Well, Sir Falcon, now will you tell me who you are?" And this time Loki piped feebly, "I am Loki of Asgard; give me something to eat!"

"Oho!" quoth the giant fiercely. "You are that Loki who went with Thor to kill my brother Thrym! Oho! Well, you shall die for that, my feathered friend!"

"No, no!" screamed Loki. "Thor is no friend of mine. I love the giants far better! One of them is my wife!"—which was indeed true, as were few of Loki's words.

"Then if Thor is no friend of yours, to save your life will you bring him into my power?" asked Geirröd.

Loki's eyes gleamed wickedly among the feathers. Here all at once was his chance to be free, and to have his revenge upon Thor, his worst enemy. "Ay, that I will!" he cried eagerly. "I will bring Thor into your power."

So Geirröd made him give a solemn promise to do that wrong; and upon this he loosed Loki from the chest and gave him food. Then they formed the wicked plan together, while Gialp and Greip, the giant's ugly daughters, listened and smacked their lips.

Loki was to persuade Thor to come with him to Geirrödsgard. More; he must come without his mighty hammer, and without the iron gloves of power, and without the belt of strength; for so only could the giant have Thor at his mercy.

After their wicked plans were made, Loki bade a friendly farewell to Geirröd and his daughters and flew back to Asgard as quickly as he could. You may be sure he had a sound scolding from Freia for stealing her feather dress and for keeping it so long. But he told such a pitiful story of being kept prisoner by a cruel giant, and he looked in truth so pale and thin from his long fast, that the gods were fain to pity him and to believe his story, in spite of the many times that he had deceived them. Indeed, most of his tale was true, but he told only half of the truth; for he spoke no word of his promise to the giant. This he kept hidden in his breast.

Now, one day not long after this, Loki invited Thor to go on a journey with him to visit a new friend who, he said, was anxious to know the Thunder Lord. Loki was so pleasant in his manner and seemed so frank in his speech that Thor, whose heart was simple and unsuspicious, never dreamed of any wrong, not even when Loki added,—"And by the bye, my Thor, you must leave behind your hammer, your belt, and your gloves; for it would show little courtesy to wear such weapons in the home of a new friend."

Thor carelessly agreed; for he was pleased with the idea of a new adventure, and with the thought of making a new friend. Besides, on their last journey together, Loki had behaved so well that Thor believed him to have changed his evil ways and to have become his friend. So together they set off in Thor's goat chariot, without weapons of any kind except those which Loki secretly carried. Loki chuckled as they rattled over the clouds, and if Thor had seen the look in his eyes, he would have turned the chariot back to Asgard and to safety, where he had left gentle Sif his wife. But Thor did not notice, and so they rumbled on.

Soon they came to the gate of Giant Land. Thor thought this strange, for he knew they were like to find few friends of his dwelling among the Big Folk. For the first time he began to suspect Loki of some treacherous scheme. However, he said nothing, and pretended to be as gay and careless as before. But he thought of a plan to find out the truth.

Close by the entrance was the cave of Grid, a good giantess, who alone of all her race was a friend of Thor and of the folk in Asgard.

"I will alight here for a moment, Loki," said Thor carelessly. "I long for a draught of water. Hold you the goats tightly by the reins until I return."

So he went into the cave and got his draught of water. But while he was drinking, he questioned good mother Grid to some purpose.

"Who is this friend Geirröd whom I go to see?" he asked her.

"Geirröd your friend! You go to see Geirröd!" she exclaimed. "He is the wickedest giant of us all, and no friend to you. Why do you go, dear Thor?"

"H'm!" muttered Thor. "Red Loki's mischief again!" He told her of the visit that Loki had proposed, and how he had left at home the belt, the gloves, and the hammer which made him stronger than any giant. Then Grid was frightened.

"Go not, go not, Thor!" she begged. "Geirröd will kill you, and those ugly girls, Gialp and Greip, will have the pleasure of crunching your bones. Oh, I know them well, the hussies!"

But Thor declared that he would go, whether or no. "I have promised Loki that I will go," he said, "and go I will; for I always keep my word."

"Then you shall have three little gifts of me," quoth she. "Here is my belt of power—for I also have one like your own." And she buckled about his waist a great belt, at whose touch he felt his strength redoubled. "This is my iron glove," she said, as she put one on his mighty hand, "and with it, as with your own, you can handle lightning and touch unharmed the hottest of red-hot metal. And here, last of all," she added, "is Gridarvöll, my good staff, which you may find useful. Take them, all three; and may Sif see you safe at home again by their aid."

Thor thanked her and went out once more to join Loki, who never suspected what had happened in the cave. For the belt and the glove were hidden under Thor's cloak. And as for the staff, it was quite ordinary looking, as if Thor might have picked it up anywhere along the road.

On they journeyed until they came to the river Vimer, the greatest of all rivers, which roared and tossed in a terrible way between them and the shore which they wanted to reach. It seemed impossible to cross. But Thor drew his belt a little tighter, and planting Grid's staff firmly on the bottom, stepped out into the stream. Loki clung behind to his cloak, frightened out of his wits. But Thor waded on bravely, his strength doubled by Grid's belt, and his steps supported by her magic staff. Higher and higher the waves washed over his knees, his waist, his shoulders, as if they were fierce to drown him. And Thor said,—

"Ho there, river Vimer! Do not grow any larger, I pray. It is of no use. The more you crowd upon me, the mightier I grow with my belt and my staff!"

But lo! as he nearly reached the other side, Thor spied some one hiding close down by the bank of the river. It was Gialp of the red eyes, the big elder daughter of Geirröd. She was splashing the water upon Thor, making the great waves that rolled up and threatened to drown him.

"Oho!" cried he. "So it is you who are making the river rise, big little girl. We must see to that;" and seizing a huge boulder, he hurled it at her. It hit her with a thud, for Thor's aim never missed. Giving a scream as loud as a steam-whistle, Gialp limped home as best she could to tell her father, and to prepare a warm reception for the stranger who bore Loki at his back.

When Thor had pulled himself out of the river by some bushes, he soon came to the palace which Loki had first sighted in his falcon dress. And there he found everything most courteously made ready for him. He and Loki were received like dear old friends, with shouts of rejoicing and ringing of bells. Geirröd himself came out to meet them, and would have embraced his new friend Thor; but the Thunder Lord merely seized him by the hand and gave him so hearty a squeeze with the iron glove that the giant howled with pain. Yet he could say nothing, for Thor looked pleased and gentle. And Geirröd said to himself, "Ho, ho, my fine little Thor! I will soon pay you for that handshake, and for many things beside."

All this time Gialp and Greip did not appear, and Loki also had taken himself away, to be out of danger when the hour of Thor's death should come. For he feared that dreadful things might happen before Thor died; and he did not want to be remembered by the big fist of the companion whom he had betrayed. Loki, having kept his promise to the giant, was even now far on the road back to Asgard, where he meant with a sad face to tell the gods that Thor had been slain by a horrible giant; but never to tell them how.

So Thor was all alone when the servants led him to the chamber which Geirröd had made ready for his dear friend. It was a wonderfully fine chamber, to be sure; but the strange thing about it was that among the furnishings there was but one chair, a giant chair, with a drapery all about the legs. Now Thor was very weary with his long journey, and he sat down in the chair to rest. Then, wonderful to tell!—if elevators had been invented in those days, he might have thought he was in one. For instantly the seat of the chair shot up towards the roof, and against this he was in danger of being crushed as Geirröd had longed to see him. But quick as a flash Thor raised the staff which good old Grid had given him, and pushed it against the rafters with all his might to stop his upward journey. It was a tremendous push that he gave. Something cracked; something crashed; the chair fell to the ground as Thor leaped off the seat, and there were two terrible screams.

Then Thor found—what do you think? Why, that Gialp and Greip, the giant's daughters, had hidden under the seat of the chair, and had lifted it up on their backs to crush Thor against the roof! But instead of that, it was Thor who had broken their backs, so that they lay dead upon the floor like limp rag dolls.

Now this little exercise had only given Thor an excellent appetite for supper. So that when word came bidding him to the banquet, he was very glad.

"First," said big Geirröd, grinning horribly, for he did not know what had happened to his daughters,—"first we will see some games, friend Thor."

Then Thor came into the hall, where fires were burning in great chimney places along the walls. "It is here that we play our little games," cried Geirröd. And on the moment, seizing a pair of tongs, he snatched a red-hot wedge of iron from one of the fires and hurled it straight at Thor's head. But Thor was quicker than he. Swift as a flash he caught the flying spark in his iron glove, and calling forth all the might of Grid's belt, he cast the wedge back at the giant. Geirröd dodged behind an iron pillar, but it was in vain. Thor's might was such as no iron could meet. Like a bolt of lightning the wedge passed through the pillar, through Geirröd himself, through the thick wall of the palace, and buried itself deep in the ground, where it lodges to this day, unless some one has dug it up to sell for old iron.

So perished Geirröd and his children, one of the wickedest families of giants that ever lived in Jotunheim. And so Thor escaped from the snares of Loki, who had never done deed worse than this.

When Thor returned home to Asgard, where from Loki's lying tale he found all the gods mourning him as dead, you can fancy what a joyful reception he had. But for Loki, the false-hearted, false-tongued traitor to them all, there was only hatred. He no longer had any friends among the good folk. The wicked giants and the monsters of Utgard were now his only friends, for he had grown to be like them, and even these did not trust him overmuch.

Balder and the Mistletoe

Loki had given up trying to revenge himself upon Thor. The Thunder Lord seemed proof against his tricks. And indeed nowadays Loki hated him no more than he did the other gods. He hated some because they always frowned at him; he hated others because they only laughed and jeered. Some he hated for their distrust and some for their fear. But he hated them all because they were happy and good and mighty, while he was wretched, bad, and of little might. Yet it was all his own fault that this was so. He might have been an equal with the best of them, if he had not chosen to set himself against everything that was good. He had made them all his enemies, and the more he did to injure them, the more he hated them,—which is always the way with evil-doers. Loki longed to see them all unhappy. He slunk about in Asgard with a glum face and wrinkled forehead. He dared not meet the eyes of any one, lest they should read his heart. For he was plotting evil, the greatest of evils, which should bring sorrow to all his enemies at once and turn Asgard into a land of mourning. The Æsir did not guess the whole truth, yet they felt the bitterness of the thoughts which Loki bore; and whenever in the dark he passed unseen, the gods shuddered as if a breath of evil had blown upon them, and even the flowers drooped before his steps.

Now at this time Balder the beautiful had a strange dream. He dreamed that a cloud came before the sun, and all Asgard was dark. He waited for the cloud to drift away, and for the sun to smile again. But no; the sun was gone forever, he thought; and Balder awoke feeling very sad. The next night Balder had another dream. This time he dreamed that it was still dark as before; the flowers were withered and the gods were growing old; even Idun's magic apples could not make them young again. And all were weeping and wringing their hands as though some dreadful thing had happened. Balder awoke feeling strangely frightened, yet he said no word to Nanna his wife, for he did not want to trouble her.

When it came night again Balder slept and dreamed a third dream, a still more terrible one than the other two had been. He thought that in the dark, lonely world there was nothing but a sad voice, which cried, "The sun is gone! The spring is gone! Joy is gone! For Balder the beautiful is dead, dead, dead!"

This time Balder awoke with a cry, and Nanna asked him what was the matter. So he had to tell her of his dream, and he was sadly frightened; for in those days dreams were often sent to folk as messages, and what the gods dreamed usually came true. Nanna ran sobbing to Queen Frigg, who was

Balder's mother, and told her all the dreadful dream, asking what could be done to prevent it from coming true.

Now Balder was Queen Frigg's dearest son. Thor was older and stronger, and more famous for his great deeds; but Frigg loved far better gold-haired Balder. And indeed he was the best-beloved of all the Æsir; for he was gentle, fair, and wise, and wherever he went folk grew happy and light-hearted at the very sight of him, just as we do when we first catch a glimpse of spring peeping over the hilltop into Winterland. So when Frigg heard of Balder's woeful dream, she was frightened almost out of her wits.

"He must not die! He shall not die!" she cried. "He is so dear to all the world, how could there be anything which would hurt him?"

And then a wonderful thought came to Frigg. "I will travel over the world and make all things promise not to injure my boy," she said. "Nothing shall pass my notice. I will get the word of everything."

So first she went to the gods themselves, gathered on Ida Plain for their morning exercise; and telling them of Balder's dream, she begged them to give the promise. Oh, what a shout arose when they heard her words!

"Hurt Balder!—our Balder! Not for the world, we promise! The dream is wrong,—there is nothing so cruel as to wish harm to Balder the beautiful!" they cried. But deep in their hearts they felt a secret fear which would linger until they should hear that all things had given their promise. What if harm were indeed to come to Balder! The thought was too dreadful.

Then Frigg went to see all the beasts who live in field or forest or rocky den. Willingly they gave their promise never to harm hair of gentle Balder. "For he is ever kind to us," they said, "and we love him as if he were one of ourselves. Not with claws or teeth or hoofs or horns will any beast hurt Balder."

Next Frigg spoke to the birds and fishes, reptiles and insects. And all—even the venomous serpents—cried that Balder was their friend, and that they would never do aught to hurt his dear body. "Not with beak or talon, bite or sting or poison fang, will one of us hurt Balder," they promised.

After doing this, the anxious mother traveled over the whole round world, step by step; and from all the things that are she got the same ready promise never to harm Balder the beautiful. All the trees and plants promised; all the stones and metals; earth, air, fire, and water; sun, snow, wind, and rain, and all diseases that men know,—each gave to Frigg the word of promise which she wanted. So at last, footsore and weary, she came back to Asgard with the joyful news that Balder must be safe, for that there was nothing in the world but had promised to be his harmless friend.

Then there was rejoicing in Asgard, as if the gods had won one of their great victories over the giants. The noble Æsir and the heroes who had died in battle upon the earth, and who had come to Valhalla to live happily ever after, gathered on Ida Plain to celebrate the love of all nature for Balder.

There they invented a famous game, which was to prove how safe he was from the bite of death. They stationed Balder in the midst of them, his face glowing like the sun with the bright light which ever shone from him. And as he stood there all unarmed and smiling, by turns they tried all sorts of weapons against him; they made as if to beat him with sticks, they stoned him with stones, they shot at him with arrows and hurled mighty spears straight at his heart.

It was a merry game, and a shout of laughter went up as each stone fell harmless at Balder's feet, each stick broke before it touched his shoulders, each arrow overshot his head, and each spear turned aside. For neither stone nor wood nor flinty arrow-point nor barb of iron would break the promise which each had given. Balder was safe with them, just as if he were be-witched. He remained unhurt among the missiles which whizzed about his head, and which piled up in a great heap around the charmed spot whereon he stood.

Now among the crowd that watched these games with such enthusiasm, there was one face that did not smile, one voice that did not rasp itself hoarse with cheering. Loki saw how every one and every thing loved Bald-er, and he was jealous. He was the only creature in all the world that hated Balder and wished for his death. Yet Balder had never done harm to him. But the wicked plan that Loki had been cherishing was almost ripe, and in this poison fruit was the seed of the greatest sorrow that Asgard had ever known.

While the others were enjoying their game of love, Loki stole away un-perceived from Ida Plain, and with a wig of gray hair, a long gown, and a staff, disguised himself as an old woman. Then he hobbled down Asgard streets till he came to the palace of Queen Frigg, the mother of Balder.

"Good-day, my lady," quoth the old woman, in a cracked voice. "What is that noisy crowd doing yonder in the green meadow? I am so deafened by their shouts that I can hardly hear myself think."

"Who are you, good mother, that you have not heard?" said Queen Frigg in surprise. "They are shooting at my son Balder. They are proving the word which all things have given me,—the promise not to injure my dear son. And that promise will be kept."

The old crone pretended to be full of wonder. "So, now!" she cried. "Do you mean to say that every single thing in the whole world has prom-ised not to hurt your son? I can scarce believe it; though, to be sure, he is as fine a fellow as I ever saw." Of course this flattery pleased Frigg.

"You say true, mother," she answered proudly, "he is a noble son. Yes, everything has promised,—that is, everything except one tiny little plant that is not worth mentioning."

The old woman's eyes twinkled wickedly. "And what is that foolish little plant, my dear?" she asked coaxingly.

"It is the mistletoe that grows in the meadow west of Valhalla. It was too young to promise, and too harmless to bother with," answered Frigg carelessly.

After this her questioner hobbled painfully away. But as soon as she was out of sight from the Queen's palace, she picked up the skirts of her gown and ran as fast as she could to the meadow west of Valhalla. And there sure enough, as Frigg had said, was a tiny sprig of mistletoe growing on a gnarled oak-tree. The false Loki took out a knife which she carried in some hidden pocket and cut off the mistletoe very carefully. Then she trimmed and shaped it so that it was like a little green arrow, pointed at one end, but very slender.

"Ho, ho!" chuckled the old woman. "So you are the only thing in all the world that is too young to make a promise, my little mistletoe. Well, young as you are, you must go on an errand for me to-day. And maybe you shall bear a message of my love to Balder the beautiful."

Then she hobbled back to Ida Plain, where the merry game was still going on around Balder. Loki quietly passed unnoticed through the crowd, and came close to the elbow of a big dark fellow who was standing lonely outside the circle of weapon-throwers. He seemed sad and forgotten, and he hung his head in a pitiful way. It was Höd, the blind brother of Balder.

The old woman touched his arm. "Why do you not join the game with the others?" she asked, in her cracked voice. "Are you the only one to do your brother no honor? Surely, you are big and strong enough to toss a spear with the best of them yonder."

Höd touched his sightless eyes madly. "I am blind," he said. "Strength I have, greater than belongs to most of the Æsir. But I cannot see to aim a weapon. Besides, I have no spear to test upon him. Yet how gladly would I do honor to dear Balder!" and he sighed deeply.

"It were a pity if I could not find you at least a little stick to throw," said Loki sympathetically. "I am only a poor old woman, and of course I have no weapon. But ah,—here is a green twig which you can use as an arrow, and I will guide your arm, poor fellow."

Höd's dark face lighted up, for he was eager to take his turn in the game. So he thanked her, and grasped eagerly the little arrow which she put into his hand. Loki held him by the arm, and together they stepped into the circle which surrounded Balder. And when it was Höd's turn to throw his weapon, the old woman stood at his elbow and guided his big arm as it hurled the twig of mistletoe towards where Balder stood.

Oh, the sad thing that befell! Straight through the air flew the little arrow, straight as magic and Loki's arm could direct it. Straight to Balder's heart it sped, piercing through jerkin and shirt and all, to give its bitter message of "Loki's love," as he had said. With a cry Balder fell forward on the grass. And that was the end of sunshine and spring and joy in Asgard, for the dream had come true, and Balder the beautiful was dead.

When the Æsir saw what had happened, there was a great shout of fear and horror, and they rushed upon Höd, who had thrown the fatal arrow.

"What is it? What have I done?" asked the poor blind brother, trembling at the tumult which had followed his shot.

"You have slain Balder!" cried the Æsir. "Wretched Höd, how could you do it?"

"It was the old woman—the evil old woman, who stood at my elbow and gave me a little twig to throw," gasped Höd. "She must be a witch."

Then the Æsir scattered over Ida Plain to look for the old woman who had done the evil deed; but she had mysteriously disappeared.

"It must be Loki," said wise Heimdal. "It is Loki's last and vilest trick."

"Oh, my Balder, my beautiful Balder!" wailed Queen Frigg, throwing herself on the body of her son. "If I had only made the mistletoe give me the promise, you would have been saved. It was I who told Loki of the mistletoe,—so it is I who have killed you. Oh, my son, my son!"

But Father Odin was speechless with grief. His sorrow was greater than that of all the others, for he best understood the dreadful misfortune which had befallen Asgard. Already a cloud had come before the sun, so that it would never be bright day again. Already the flowers had begun to fade and the birds had ceased to sing. And already the Æsir had begun to grow old and joyless,—all because the little mistletoe had been too young to give a promise to Queen Frigg.

"Balder the beautiful is dead!" the cry went echoing through all the world, and everything that was sorrowed at the sound of the Æsir's weeping.

Balder's brothers lifted up his beautiful body upon their great war shields and bore him on their shoulders down to the seashore. For, as was the custom in those days, they were going to send him to Hela, the Queen of Death, with all the things he best had loved in Asgard. And these were,—after Nanna his wife,—his beautiful horse, and his ship Hringhorni. So that they would place Balder's body upon the ship with his horse beside him, and set fire to this wonderful funeral pile. For by fire was the quickest passage to Hela's kingdom.

But when they reached the shore, they found that all the strength of all the Æsir was unable to move Hringhorni, Balder's ship, into the water. For it was the largest ship in the world, and it was stranded far up the beach.

"Even the giants bore no ill-will to Balder," said Father Odin. "I heard the thunder of their grief but now shaking the hills. Let us for this once bury our hatred of that race and send to Jotunheim for help to move the ship."

So they sent a messenger to the giantess Hyrrockin, the hugest of all the Frost People. She was weeping for Balder when the message came.

"I will go, for Balder's sake," she said. Soon she came riding fast upon a giant wolf, with a serpent for the bridle; and mighty she was, with the strength of forty Æsir. She dismounted from her wolf-steed, and tossed the wriggling reins to one of the men-heroes who had followed Balder and the Æsir from Valhalla. But he could not hold the beast, and it took four heroes to keep him quiet, which they could only do by throwing him upon the ground and sitting upon him in a row. And this mortified them greatly.

Then Hyrrockin the giantess strode up to the great ship and seized it by the prow. Easily she gave a little pull and presto! it leaped forward on its rollers with such force that sparks flew from the flint stones underneath and the whole earth trembled. The boat shot into the waves and out toward open sea so swiftly that the Æsir were likely to have lost it entirely, had not Hyrrockin waded out up to her waist and caught it by the stern just in time.

Thor was angry at her clumsiness, and raised his hammer to punish her. But the other Æsir held his arm.

"She cannot help being so strong," they whispered. "She meant to do well. She did not realize how hard she was pulling. This is no time for anger, brother Thor." So Thor spared her life, as indeed he ought, for her kindness.

Then Balder's body was borne out to the ship and laid upon a pile of beautiful silks, and furs, and cloth-of-gold, and woven sunbeams which the dwarfs had wrought. So that his funeral pyre was more grand than anything which had ever been seen. But when Nanna, Balder's gentle wife, saw them ready to kindle the flames under this gorgeous bed, she could bear her grief no longer. Her loving heart broke, and they laid her beside him, that they might comfort each other on their journey to Hela. Thor touched the pile gently with his hammer that makes the lightning, and the flames burst forth, lighting up the faces of Balder and Nanna with a glory. Then they cast upon the fire Balder's war-horse, to serve his master in the dark country to which he was about to go. The horse was decked with a harness all of gold, with jewels studding the bridle and headstall. Last of all Odin laid upon the pyre his gift to Balder, Draupnir, the precious ring of gold which the dwarf had made, from which every ninth night there dropped eight other rings as large and brightly golden.

"Take this with you, dear son, to Hela's palace," said Odin. "And do not forget the friends you leave behind in the now lonely halls of Asgard."

Then Hyrrockin pushed the great boat out to sea, with its bonfire of precious things. And on the beach stood all the Æsir watching it out of sight, all the Æsir and many besides. For there came to Balder's funeral great crowds of little dwarfs and multitudes of huge frost giants, all mourning for Balder the beautiful. For this one time they were all friends together, forgetting their quarrels of so many centuries. All of them loved Balder, and were united to do him honor.

The great ship moved slowly out to sea, sending up a red fire to color all the heavens. At last it slid below the horizon softly, as you have often seen the sun set upon the water, leaving a brightness behind to lighten the dark world for a little while.

This indeed was the sunset for Asgard. The darkness of sorrow came in earnest after the passing of Balder the beautiful.

But the punishment of Loki was a terrible thing. And that came soon and sore.

The Punishment of Loki

After the death of Balder the world grew so dreary that no one had any heart left for work or play. The Æsir sat about moping and miserable. They were growing old,—there was no doubt about that. There was no longer any gladness in Valhalla, where the Valkyries waited on table and poured the foaming mead. There was no longer any mirth on Ida Plain, when every morning the bravest of earth-heroes fought their battles over again. Odin no longer had any pleasure in the daily news brought by his wise ravens, Thought and Memory, nor did Freia enjoy her falcon dress. Frey forgot to sail in his ship Skidbladnir, and even Thor had almost wearied of his hammer, except as he hoped that it would help him to catch Loki. For the one thought of all of them now was to find and punish Loki.

Yet they waited; for Queen Frigg had sent a messenger to Queen Hela to find if they might not even yet win Balder back from the kingdom of death.

Odin shook his head. "Queen Hela is Loki's daughter," he said, "and she will not let Balder return." But Frigg was hopeful; she had employed a trusty messenger, whose silver tongue had won many hearts against their will.

It was Hermod, Balder's brother, who galloped down the steep road to Hela's kingdom, on Sleipnir, the eight-legged horse of Father Odin. For nine nights and nine days he rode, through valleys dark and chill, until he came to the bridge which is paved with gold. And here the maiden Modgard told him that Balder had passed that way, and showed him the path northward to Hela's city. So he rode, down and down, until he came to the high wall which surrounded the grim palace where Hela reigned. Hermod dismounted and tightened the saddle-girths of gray Sleipnir, whose eight legs were as frisky as ever, despite the long journey. And when he had mounted once more, the wonderful horse leaped with him over the wall, twenty feet at least!

Then Hermod rode straight into the palace of Hela, straight up to the throne where she sat surrounded by gray shadows and spirit people. She was a dreadful creature to see, was this daughter of Loki,—half white like other folk, but half black, which was not sunburn, for there was no sunshine in this dark and dismal land. Yet she was not so bad as she looked; for even Hela felt kindly towards Balder, whom her father had slain, and was sorry that the world had lost so dear a friend. So when Hermod begged of her to let his brother return with him to Asgard, she said very gently,—

"Freely would I let him go, brave Hermod, if I might. But a queen can-not always do as she likes, even in her own kingdom. His life must be bought; the price must be paid in tears. If everything upon earth will weep for Balder's death, then may he return, bringing light and happiness to the upper world. Should one creature fail to weep, Balder must remain with me."

Then Hermod was glad, for he felt sure that this price was easily paid. He thanked Hela, and made ready to depart with the hopeful message. Be-fore he went away he saw and spoke with Balder himself, who sat with Nanna upon a throne of honor, talking of the good times that used to be. And Balder gave him the ring Draupnir to give back to Father Odin, as a remembrance from his dear son; while Nanna sent to mother Frigg her silver veil with other rich presents. It was hard for Hermod to part with Balder once again, and Balder also wept to see him go. But Hermod was in duty bound to bear the message back to Asgard as swiftly as might be.

Now when the Æsir heard from Hermod this news, they sent messen-gers forth over the whole world to bid every creature weep for Balder's death. Heimdal galloped off upon Goldtop and Frey upon Goldbristle, his famous hog; Thor rumbled away in his goat chariot, and Freia drove her team of cats,—all spreading the message in one direction and another. There really seemed little need for them to do this, for already there was mourning in every land and clime. Even the sky was weeping, and the flower eyes were filled with dewy tears.

So it seemed likely that Balder would be ransomed after all, and the Æsir began to hope more strongly. For they had not found one creature who refused to weep. Even the giants of Jotunheim were sorry to lose the gentle fellow who had never done them any harm, and freely added their giant tears to the salt rivers that were coursing over all the world into the sea, making it still more salt.

It was not until the messengers had nearly reached home, joyful in the surety that Balder was safe, that they found an ugly old giantess named Thökt hidden in a black cavern among the mountains.

"Weep, mother, weep for Balder!" they cried. "Balder the beautiful is dead, but your tears will buy him back to life. Weep, mother, weep!"

But the sulky old woman refused to weep.

"Balder is nothing to me," she said. "I care not whether he lives or dies. Let him bide with Hela—he is out of mischief there. I weep dry tears for Balder's death."

So all the work of the messengers was in vain, because of this one obstinate old woman. So all the tears of the sorrowing world were shed in vain. Because there were lacking two salty drops from the eyes of Thökt, they could not buy back Balder from the prison of death.

When the messengers returned and told Odin their sad news, he was wrathful.

"Do you not guess who the old woman was?" he cried. "It was Loki— Loki himself, disguised as a giantess. He has tricked us once more, and for a second time has slain Balder for us; for it is now too late,—Balder can never return to us after this. But it shall be the last of Loki's mischief. It is now time that we put an end to his deeds of shame."

"Come, my brothers!" shouted Thor, flourishing his hammer. "We have wept and mourned long enough. It is now time to punish. Let us hasten back to Thökt's cave, and seize Loki as quickly as may be."

So they hurried back into the mountains where they had left the giantess who would not weep. But when they came to the place, the cave was empty. Loki was too sharp a fellow to sit still and wait for punishment to overtake him. He knew very well that the Æsir would soon discover who Thökt really was. And he had taken himself off to a safer place, to escape the questions which a whole world of not too gentle folk were anxious to ask him.

The one desire of the Æsir was now to seize and punish Loki. So when they were unable to find him as easily as they expected, they were wroth indeed. Why had he left the cave? Whither had he gone? In what new disguise even now was he lurking, perhaps close by?

The truth was that when Loki found himself at war with the whole world which he had injured, he fled away into the mountains, where he had built a strong castle of rocks. This castle had four doors, one looking into the north, one to the south, one to the east, and one to the west; so that Loki could keep watch in all directions and see any enemy who might approach. Besides this, he had for his protection the many disguises which he knew so well how to don. Near the castle was a river and a waterfall, and it was Loki's favorite game to change himself into a spotted pink salmon and splash about in the pool below the fall.

"Ho, ho! Let them try to catch me here, if they can!" he would chuckle to himself. And indeed, it seemed as if he were safe enough.

One day Loki was sitting before the fire in his castle twisting together threads of flax and yarn into a great fish-net which was his own invention. For no one had ever before thought of catching fish with a net. Loki was a clever fellow; and with all his faults, for this one thing at least the fishermen of to-day ought to be grateful to him. As Loki sat busily knotting the meshes of the net, he happened to glance out of the south door,—and there were the Æsir coming in a body up the hill towards his castle.

Now this is what had happened: from his lookout throne in Asgard, Odin's keen sight had spied Loki's retreat. This throne, you remember, was in the house with a silver roof which Odin had built in the very beginning of time; and whenever he wanted to see what was going on in the remotest corner of Asgard, or to spy into some secret place beyond the sight of gods or men, he would mount this magic throne, whence his eye could pierce thick mountains and sound the deepest sea. So it was that the Æsir had found out Loki's castle, well-hidden though it was among the furthest mountains of the world. They had come to catch him, and there was nothing left for him but to run.

Loki jumped up and threw his half-mended net into the fire, for he did not want the Æsir to discover his invention; then he ran down to the river and leaped in with a great splash. When he was well under water, he changed himself into a salmon, and flickered away to bask in his shady pool and think how safe he was.

By this time the Æsir had entered his castle and were poking among the ashes which they found smouldering on the hearth.

"What is this?" asked Thor, holding up a piece of knotted flax which was not quite burned. "The knave has been making something with little cords."

"Let me see it," said Heimdal, the wisest of the Æsir,—he who once upon a time had suggested Thor's clever disguise for winning back his hammer from the giant Thrym. He took now the little scrap of fish-net and studied it carefully, picking out all the knots and twists of it.

"It is a net," said Heimdal at last. "He has been making a net, and—pfaugh!—it smells of fish. The fellow must have used it to trap fish for his dinner, though I never before heard of such a device."

"I saw a big splash in the river just as we came up," said Thor the keen-eyed,—"a very big splash indeed. It seemed too large for any fish."

"It was Loki," declared Heimdal. "He must have been here but a moment since, for this fire has just gone out, and the net is still smouldering. That shows he did not wish us to find this new-fangled idea of his. Why was that? Let me think. Aha! I have it. Loki has changed himself into a fish, and did not wish us to discover the means of catching him."

"Oho!" cried the Æsir regretfully. "If only we had another net!"

"We can make one," said wise Heimdal. "I know how it is done, for I have studied out this little sample. Let us make a net to catch the slyest of all fish."

"Let us make a net for Loki," echoed the Æsir. And they all sat down cross-legged on the floor to have a lesson in net-weaving from Heimdal. He found hemp cord in a cupboard, and soon they had contrived a goodly net, big enough to catch several Lokis, if they should have good fisherman's luck.

They dragged the net to the river and cast it in. Thor, being the strongest, held one end of the net, and all the rest drew the other end up and down the stream. They were clumsy and awkward, for they had never used a net before, and did not know how to make the best of it. But presently Thor exclaimed, "Ha! I felt some live thing touch the meshes!"

"So did we!" cried the others. "It must be Loki!" And Loki it was, sure enough; for the Æsir had happened upon the very pool where the great salmon lay basking so peacefully. But when he felt the net touch him, he darted away and hid in a cleft between two rocks. So that, although they dragged the net to and fro again and again, they could not catch Loki in its meshes; for the net was so light that it floated over his head.

"We must weight the net," said Heimdal wisely; "then nothing can pass beneath it." So they tied heavy stones all along the under edge, and again they cast the net, a little below the waterfall. Now Loki had seized the chance to swim further down the stream. But ugh! suddenly he tasted salt water. He was being swept out to sea! That would never do, for he could not live an hour in the sea. So he swam back and leaped straight over the net up into the waterfall, hoping that no one had noticed him. But Thor's sharp eyes had spied the flash of pink and silver, and Thor came running to the place.

"He is here!" he shouted. "Cast in the net above the fall! We have him now!"

When Loki saw the net cast again, so that there was no choice for him but to be swept back over the falls and out to sea, or to leap the net once more still further up the river, he hesitated. He saw Thor in the middle of the stream wading towards him; but behind him was sure death. So he set his teeth and once more he leaped the net. There was a huge splash, a scuffle, a scramble, and the water was churned into froth all about Thor's feet. He was struggling with the mighty fish. He caught him once, but the salmon slipped through his fingers. He caught him again, and this time Thor gripped hard. The salmon almost escaped, but Thor's big fingers kept hold of the end of his tail, and he flapped and flopped in vain. It was the grip of Thor's iron glove; and that is why to this day the salmon has so pointed a tail. The next time you see a salmon you must notice this, and remember that he may be a great-great-great-grand-descendant of Loki.

So Loki was captured and changed back into his own shape, sullen and fierce. But he had no word of sorrow for his evil deeds; nor did he ask for mercy, for he knew that it would be in vain. He kept silent while the Æsir led him all the weary way back to Asgard.

Now the whole world was noisy with the triumph of his capture. As the procession passed along it was joined by all the creatures who had mourned for Balder,—all the creatures who longed to see Loki punished. There were the men of Midgard, the place of human folk, shouting, "Kill him! kill him!" at the top of their lungs; there were armies of little mountain dwarfs in their brown peaked caps, who hobbled along, prodding Loki with their picks; there were beasts growling and showing their teeth as if they longed to tear Loki in pieces; there were birds who tried to peck his eyes, insects who came in clouds to sting him, and serpents that sprang up hissing at his feet to poison him with their deadly bite.

But to all these Thor said, "Do not kill the fellow. We are keeping him for a worse punishment than you can give." So the creatures merely followed and jostled Loki into Asgard, shouting, screaming, howling, growling, barking, roaring, spitting, squeaking, hissing, croaking, and buzzing, according to their different ways of showing hatred and horror.

The Æsir met on Ida Plain to decide what should be done with Loki. There were Idun whom he had cheated, and Sif whose hair he had cut off. There were Freia whose falcon dress he had stolen and Thor whom he had tried to kill. There were Höd whom he had made a murderer; Frigg and Odin whose son he had slain. There was not one of them whom Loki had not injured in some way; and besides, there was the whole world into which he had brought sorrow and darkness; for the sake of all these Loki must be punished. But it was hard to think of any doom heavy enough for him. At last, however, they agreed upon a punishment which they thought suited to so wicked a wretch.

The long procession formed again and escorted Loki down, down into a damp cavern underground. Here sunlight never came, but the cave was full of ugly toads, snakes, and insects that love the dark. These were Loki's evil thoughts, who were to live with him henceforth and torment him always. In this prison chamber side by side they placed three sharp stones, not far apart, to make an uneasy bed. And these were for Loki's three worst deeds, against Thor and Höd and Balder. Upon these rocks they bound Loki with stout thongs of leather. But as soon as the cords were fastened they turned into iron bands, so that no one, though he had the strength of a hundred giants, could loosen them. For these were Loki's evil passions, and the more he strained against them, the more they cut into him and wounded him until he howled with pain.

Over his head Skadi, whose father he had helped to slay, hung a venomous, wriggling serpent, from whose mouth dropped poison into Loki's face, which burned and stung him like fire. And this was the deceit which all his life Loki had spoken to draw folk into trouble and danger. At last it had turned about to torture him, as deceit always will do to him who utters it. Yet from this one torment Loki had some relief; for alone of all the world Sigyn, his wife, was faithful and forgiving. She stood by the head of the painful bed upon which the Red One was stretched, and held a bowl to catch the poison which dropped from the serpent's jaws, so that some of it did not reach Loki's face. But as often as the bowl became full, Sigyn had to go out and empty it; and then the bitter drops fell and burned till Loki made the cavern ring with his cries.

So this was Loki's punishment, and bad enough it was,—but not too bad for such a monster. Under the caverns he lies there still, struggling to be free. And when his great strength shakes the hills so that the whole ground trembles, men call it an earthquake. Sometimes they even see his poisonous breath blowing from the top of a mountain-chimney, and amid it the red flame of wickedness which burns in Loki's heart. Then all cry, "The volcano, the volcano!" and run away as fast as they can. For Loki, poisoned though he is, is still dangerous and full of mischief, and it is not good to venture near him in his torment.

But there for his sins he must bide and suffer, suffer and bide, until the end of all sorrow and suffering and sin shall come, with Ragnarök, the ending of the world.

True and Untrue by George Webbe Dasent

Once on a time there were two brothers; one was called True, and the other Untrue. True was always upright and good towards all, but Untrue was bad and full of lies, so that no one could believe what he said. Their mother was a widow, and hadn't much to live on; so when her sons had grown up, she was forced to send them away, that they might earn their bread in the world. Each got a little scrip with some food in it, and then they went their way.

Now, when they had walked till evening, they sat down on a windfall in the wood, and took out their scraps, for they were hungry after walking the whole day, and thought a morsel of food would be sweet enough.

'If you're of my mind', said Untrue, 'I think we had better eat out of your scrip, so long as there is anything in it, and after that we can take to mine.'

Yes! True was well pleased with this, so they fell to eating, but Untrue got all the best bits, and stuffed himself with them, while True got only the burnt crusts and scraps.

Next morning they broke their fast off True's food, and they dined off it too, and then there was nothing left in his scrip. So when they had walked till late at night, and were ready to eats again, True wanted to eat out of his brother's scrip, but Untrue said 'No', the food was his, and he had only enough for himself.

'Nay! but you know you ate out of my scrip so long as there was anything in it', said True.

'All very fine, I daresay', answered Untrue; 'but if you are such a fool as to let others eat up your food before your face, you must make the best of it; for now all you have to do is to sit here and starve.'

'Very well!' said True, 'you're Untrue by name and untrue by nature; so you have been, and so you will be all your life long.'

Now when Untrue heard this, he flew into a rage, and rushed at his brother, and plucked out both his eyes. 'Now, try if you can see whether folk are untrue or not, you blind buzzard!' and so saying, he ran away and left him.

Poor True! there he went walking along and feeling his way through the thick wood. Blind and alone, he scarce knew which way to turn, when all at once he caught hold of the trunk of a great bushy lime- tree, so he thought he would climb up into it, and sit there till the night was over for fear of the wild beasts.

'When the birds begin to sing', he said to himself, 'then I shall know it is day, and I can try to grope my way farther on.' So he climbed up into the lime-tree. After he had sat there a little time, he heard how some one came and began to make a stir and clatter under the tree, and soon after others came; and when they began to greet one another, he found out it was Bruin the bear, and Greylegs the wolf, and Slyboots the fox, and Longears the hare who had come to keep St. John's eve under the tree. So they began to eat and drink, and be merry; and when they had done eating, they fell to gossipping together. At last the Fox said:

'Shan't we, each of us, tell a little story while we sit here?' Well! the others had nothing against that. It would be good fun, they said, and the Bear began; for you may fancy he was king of the company.

'The king of England', said Bruin, 'has such bad eyesight, he can scarce see a yard before him; but if he only came to this lime-tree in the morning, while the dew is still on the leaves, and took and rubbed his eyes with the dew, he would get back his sight as good as ever.'

'Very true!' said Greylegs. 'The king of England has a deaf and dumb daughter too; but if he only knew what I know, he would soon cure her. Last year she went to the communion. She let a crumb of the bread fall out of her mouth, and a great toad came and swallowed it down; but if they only dug up the chancel floor, they would find the toad sitting right under the altar rails, with the bread still sticking in his throat. If they were to cut the toad open and take and give the bread to the princess, she would be like other folk again as to her speech and hearing.'

'That's all very well', said the Fox; 'but if the king of England knew what I know, he would not be so badly off for water in his palace; for under the great stone, in his palace-yard, is a spring of the clearest water one could wish for, if he only knew to dig for it there.'

'Ah!' said the Hare in a small voice; 'the king of England has the finest orchard in the whole land, but it does not bear so much as a crab, for there lies a heavy gold chain in three turns round the orchard. If he got that dug up, there would not be a garden like it for bearing in all his kingdom.'

'Very true, I dare say', said the Fox; 'but now it's getting very late, and we may as well go home.'

So they all went away together.

After they were gone, True fell asleep as he sat up in the tree; but when the birds began to sing at dawn, he woke up, and took the dew from the leaves, and rubbed his eyes with it, and so got his sight back as good as it was before Untrue plucked his eyes out.

Then he went straight to the king of England's palace, and begged for work, and got it on the spot. So one day the king came out into the palace-yard, and when he had walked about a bit, he wanted to drink out of his pump; for you must know the day was hot, and the king very thirsty; but when they poured him out a glass, it was so muddy, and nasty, and foul, that the king got quite vexed.

'I don't think there's ever a man in my whole kingdom who has such bad water in his yard as I, and yet I bring it in pipes from far, over hill and dale', cried out the king. 'Like enough, your Majesty', said True; 'but if you would let me have some men to help me to dig up this great stone which lies here in the middle of your yard, you would soon see good water, and plenty of it.'

Well! the king was willing enough; and they had scarcely got the stone well out, and dug under it a while, before a jet of water sprang out high up into the air, as clear and full as if it came out of a conduit, and clearer water was not to be found in all England.

A little while after the king was out in his palace-yard again, and there came a great hawk flying after his chicken, and all the king's men began to clap their hands and bawl out, 'There he flies!' 'There he flies!' The king caught up his gun and tried to shoot the hawk, but he couldn't see so far, so he fell into great grief.

'Would to Heaven', he said, 'there was any one who could tell me a cure for my eyes; for I think I shall soon go quite blind!'

'I can tell you one soon enough', said True; and then he told the king what he had done to cure his own eyes, and the king set off that very afternoon to the lime-tree, as you may fancy, and his eyes were quite cured as soon as he rubbed them with the dew which was on the leaves in the morning. From that time forth there was no one whom the king held so dear as True, and he had to be with him wherever he went, both at home and abroad.

So one day, as they were walking together in the orchard, the king said, 'I can't tell how it is that I can't! there isn't a, man in England who spends so much on his orchard as I, and yet I can't get one of the trees to bear so much as a crab.'

'Well! well!' said True; 'if I may have what lies three times twisted round your orchard, and men to dig it up, your orchard will bear well enough.'

Yes! the king was quite willing, so True got men and began to dig, and at last he dug up the whole gold chain. Now True was a rich man; far richer indeed than the king himself, but still the king was well pleased, for his orchard bore so that the boughs of the trees hung down to the ground, and such sweet apples and pears nobody had ever tasted.

Another day too the king and True were walking about, and talking together, when the princess passed them, and the king was quite downcast when he saw her.

'Isn't it a pity, now, that so lovely a princess as mine should want speech and hearing', he said to True.

'Ay, but there is a cure for that', said True.

When the king heard that, he was so glad that he promised him the princess to wife, and half his kingdom into the bargain, if he could get her right again. So True took a few men, and went into the church, and dug up the toad which sat under the altar-rails. Then he cut open the toad, and took out the bread and gave it to the king's daughter; and from that hour she got back her speech, and could talk like other people.

Now True was to have the princess, and they got ready for the bridal feast, and such a feast had never been seen before; it was the talk of the whole land. Just as they were in the midst of dancing the bridal-dance in came a beggar lad, and begged for a morsel of food, and he was so ragged and wretched that every one crossed themselves when they looked at him; but True knew him at once, and saw that it was Untrue, his brother.

'Do you know me again?' said True.

'Oh! where should such a one as I ever have seen so great a lord', said Untrue.

'Still you have seen me before', said True. 'It was I whose eyes you plucked out a year ago this very day. Untrue by name, and untrue by nature; so I said before, and so I say now; but you are still my brother, and so you shall have some food. After that, you may go to the lime-tree where I sat last year; if you hear anything that can do you good, you will be lucky.'

So Untrue did not wait to be told twice. 'If True has got so much good by sitting in the lime-tree, that in one year he has come to be king over half England, what good may not I get', he thought. So he set off and climbed up into the lime-tree. He had not sat there long, before all the beasts came as before, and ate and drank, and kept St. John's eve under the tree. When they had left off eating, the Fox wished that they should begin to tell stories, and Untrue got ready to listen with all his might, till his ears were almost fit to fall off. But Bruin the bear was surly, and growled and said:

'Some one has been chattering about what we said last year, and so now we will hold our tongues about what we know'; and with that the beasts bade one another 'Good-night', and parted, and Untrue was just as wise as he was before, and the reason was, that his name was Untrue, and his nature untrue too.

Little Annie the Goose-girl by Peter Christen Asbjørnsen

Once on a time there was a King who had so many geese he was forced to have a lassie to tend them and watch them; her name was Annie, and so they called her 'Annie the Goose-girl'. Now you must know there was a King's son from England who went out to woo; and as he came along Ann sat herself down in his way.

'Sitting all alone there, you little Annie?' said the King's son.

'Yes', said little Annie, 'here I sit and put stitch to stitch and patch on patch. I'm waiting to-day for the King's son from England.'

'Him you mustn't look to have', said the Prince.

'Nay, but if I'm to have him', said little Annie, 'have him I shall, after all.'

And now limners were sent out into all lands and realms to take the likenesses of the fairest Princesses, and the Prince was to chose between them. So he thought so much of one of them, that he set out to seek her, and wanted to wed her, and he was glad and happy when he got her for his sweetheart.

But now I must tell you this Prince had a stone with him which he laid by his bedside, and that stone knew everything, and when the Princess came little Annie told her, if so be she'd had a sweetheart before, or didn't feel herself quite free from anything which she didn't wish the Prince to know, she'd better not step on that stone which lay by the bedside.

'If you do, it will tell him all about you', said little Annie.

So when the Princess heard that she was dreadfully downcast, and she fell upon the thought to ask Annie if she would get into bed that night in her stead and lie down by the Prince's side; and then when he was sound asleep, Annie should get out and the Princess should get in, and so when he woke up in the morning he would find the right bride by his side.

So they did that, and when Annie the goose-girl came and stepped upon the stone the Prince asked:

'Who is this that steps into my bed?'

'A maid pure and bright', said the stone, and so they lay down to sleep; but when the night wore on the Princess came and lay down in Annie's stead.

But next morning, when they were to get up, the Prince asked the stone again:

'Who is this that steps out of my bed?'

'One that has had three bairns', said the stone. When the Prince heard that he wouldn't have her, you may know very well; and so he packed her off home again, and took another sweetheart.

But as he went to see her, little Annie went and sat down in his way again.

'Sitting all alone there, little Annie, the goose-girl', said the Prince.

'Yes, here I sit, and put stitch to stitch, and patch on patch; for I'm waiting to-day for the king's son from England', said Annie.

'Oh! you mustn't look to have him', said the king's son.

'Nay, but if I'm to have him, have him I shall, after all'; that was what Annie thought.

Well, it was the same story over again with the Prince; only this time, when his bride got up in the morning, the stone said she'd had six bairns.

So the Prince wouldn't have her either, but sent her about her business; but still he thought he'd try once more if he couldn't find one who was pure and spotless; and he sought far and wide in many lands, till at last he found one he thought he might trust. But when he went to see her, little Annie the goose-girl had put herself in his way again.

'Sitting all alone there, you little Annie, the goose-girl', said the Prince.

'Yes, here I sit, and put stitch to stitch, and patch on patch; for I'm waiting to-day for the king's son from England', said Annie.

'Him you mustn't look to have', said the Prince.

'Nay, but if I'm to have him, have him I shall, after all', said little Annie.

So when the Princess came, little Annie the goose-girl told her the same as she had told the other two, if she'd had any sweetheart before, or if there was anything else she didn't wish the Prince to know, she mustn't tread on the stone that the Prince had put at his bedside; for, said she:

'It tells him everything.'

The Princess got very red and downcast when she heard that, for she was just as naughty as the others, and asked Annie if she would go in her stead and lie down with the Prince that night; and when he was sound asleep, she would come and take her place, and then he would have the right bride by his side when it was light next morning.

Yes! they did that. And when little Annie the goose-girl came and stepped upon the stone, the Prince asked:

'Who is this that steps into my bed.'

'A maid pure and bright', said the stone; and so they lay down to rest.

Farther on in the night the Prince put a ring on Annie's finger, and it fitted so tight she couldn't get it off again; for the Prince saw well enough there was something wrong, and so he wished to have a mark by which he might know the right woman again.

Well, when the Prince had gone off to sleep, the Princess came and drove Annie away to the pigsty, and lay down in her place. Next morning, when they were to get up, the Prince asked:

'Who is this that steps out of my bed?'

'One that's had nine bairns', said the stone.

When the Prince heard that he drove her away at once, for he was in an awful rage; and then he asked the stone how it all was with these Princesses who had stepped on it, for he couldn't understand it at all, he said.

So the stone told him how they had cheated him, and sent little Annie the goose-girl to him in their stead.

But as the Prince wished to have no mistake about it, he went down to her where she sat tending her geese, for he wanted to see if she had the ring too, and he thought, 'if she has it, 'twere best to take her at once for my queen'.

So when he got down he saw in a moment that she had tied a bit of rag round one of her fingers, and so he asked her why it was tied up.

'Oh! I've cut myself so badly', said little Annie the goose-girl.

So he must and would see the finger, but Annie wouldn't take the rag off. Then he caught hold of the finger; but Annie, she tried to pull it from him, and so between them the rag came off, and then he knew his ring.

So he took her up to the palace, and gave her much fine clothes and attire, and after that they held their wedding feast; and so little Annie the goose-girl came to have the king of England's son for her husband after all, just because it was written that she should have him.

CPSIA information can be obtained
at www.ICGtesting.com
Printed in the USA
LVOW04s0311300816

502341LV00030B/1117/P